FOOD LOVERS' SERIES

FOOD LOVERS'
GUIDE TO
BOSTON

The Best Restaurants, Markets & Local Culinary Offerings

1st Edition

Patricia Harris & David Lyon

gpp

Guilford, Connecticut

Copyright © 2012 Morris Book Publishing, LLC

Editor: Amy Lyons
Project Editor: Julie Marsh
Layout Artist: Mary Ballachino
Text Design: Sheryl Kober
Illustrations by Jill Butler with additional art by Carleen Moira Powell and MaryAnn Dubé
Maps: Trailhead Graphics Inc. © Morris Book Publishing, LLC

ISBN 978-0-7627-7941-3

Printed in the United States of America
10 9 8 7 6 5 4 3 2 1

All the information in this guidebook is subject to change. We recommend that you call ahead
to obtain current information before traveling.

Contents

Introduction:
Boston—Not Your Grandmother's Baked Beans, 1

How to Use This Book, 5

Getting Around, 8

Keeping Up with Food News, 9

Street Eats, 11

North End, Charlestown, East Boston & Chelsea, 15

Foodie Faves, 17

Landmarks, 35

Specialty Stores, Markets & Producers, 36

Farmers' Markets, 47

Beacon Hill, Downtown & the Waterfront, 49

Foodie Faves, 51

Landmarks, 76

Specialty Stores, Markets & Producers, 78

Farmers' Markets, 88

Back Bay & the Fenway, 91

    Foodie Faves, 92

    Specialty Stores, Markets & Producers, 118

Chinatown, South End & Roxbury, 123

    Foodie Faves, 125

    Landmarks, 151

    Specialty Stores, Markets & Producers, 151

    Farmers' Markets, 165

Jamaica Plain, 167

    Foodie Faves, 168

    Landmarks, 179

    Specialty Stores, Markets & Producers, 180

    Farmers' Markets, 185

South Boston & Dorchester, 187

    Foodie Faves, 188

    Landmarks, 196

    Specialty Stores, Markets & Producers, 197

    Farmers' Markets, 202

Allston, Brighton & Brookline, 205

> Foodie Faves, 206

> Specialty Stores, Markets & Producers, 219

Cambridge, 231

> Foodie Faves, 232

> Specialty Stores, Markets & Producers, 283

> Farmers' Markets, 305

Arlington & Somerville, 307

> Foodie Faves, 309

> Landmarks, 325

> Specialty Stores, Markets & Producers, 326

> Farmers' Markets, 338

Belmont, Lexington & Concord, 339

> Foodie Faves, 341

> Specialty Stores, Markets & Producers, 346

> Farmers' Markets, 359

Newton, Wellesley, Waltham & Watertown, 361

    Foodie Faves, 362

    Specialty Stores, Markets & Producers, 372

    Farmers' Markets, 385

Bars, Pubs & Lounges, 386

Culinary Instruction, 410

Food Festivals & Events, 416

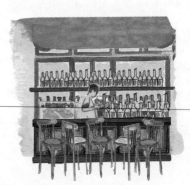

Recipes, 423

Caramelized Shallot and Goat Cheese Pizza with Savory Chocolate Crust (Chef and Instructor Heather Wish of Create a Cook), 425

Insalata di Pasta Arrabbiata (Michele Topor of Boston Food Tours), 427

Al's Favorite Quick Tomato Sauce (Albert Capone of Capone Foods), 428

Red Lentil Soup (Mercimek Corbasi) (Chef Sezar Yavuz of Cafe de Boston), 430

Green Bean and Summer Squash Ratatouille with Couscous (Harvest Co-op Market), 431

Uncle John's Lobster Thermidor (John Hook of James Hook + Co.), 432

Beer-Braised Lamb Shoulder (Chef de Cuisine Nuno Alves of Tavolo), 433

Grilled Beef with Asian Sesame Dressing (The Meat House), 435

Chocolate Croissant Bread Pudding (Executive Pastry Chef Jed Hackney of Langham Boston), 437

Nanny Sheila's Carrot Cake (Pastry Chef Clare Garland of Ashmont Grill), 439

Molten Spiced Taza Chocolate Cake (Taza Chocolate), 441

Appendices, 442

    Appendix A: For Further Reading, 443

    Appendix B: Dishes, Specialties & Specialty Food, 445

Index, 455

About the Authors

Patricia Harris and David Lyon buy their meat from their neighborhood Portuguese butcher, their fruits and vegetables from local farmers, and their pasta from a little shop in Union Square. They met over ratatouille made from fresh garden vegetables, courted over fudge-topped brownies, and are still cooking, traveling, and writing about it for their *Hungry Travelers* food and travel blog (hungrytravelers.com). They are coauthors of Globe Pequot Press's *The Meaning of Food, Food Lovers' Guide to Massachusetts, Food Lovers' Guide to Montreal, Food Lovers' Guide to Vermont & New Hampshire,* and the forthcoming *Food Lovers' Guide to Rhode Island.* They have written about Vermont cheese, Belgian beer, Tahitian *poisson cru,* New Hampshire hot dogs, Neapolitan pizza, Maine lobster, and Spanish elvers for such publications as the *Boston Globe,* the *Robb Report,* and *Cooking Light.* Based in Cambridge, they were happy to stay home for this book, which celebrates the flavors of Boston and its wonderful food culture.

This book is dedicated to hungry travelers everywhere.

Acknowledgments

We would like to acknowledge the skills, hospitality, and generosity of everyone in the Boston-area food trades. We are especially thankful to the cooks and chefs who shared their recipes for this volume, and to Naomi King for testing those recipes and offering sage advice on adjusting them for home cooks. We are also grateful to Chris Lyons and Chris Haynes, who kept us from some terrible oversights and helped speed our on-the-ground research. We offer a memorial salute to the late Laura Strom for conceiving the Food Lovers' series, and thank Amy Lyons for letting us take such an active role in the much-expanded series. We also want to thank editors Lynn Zelem and Julie Marsh for shepherding this manuscript to publication.

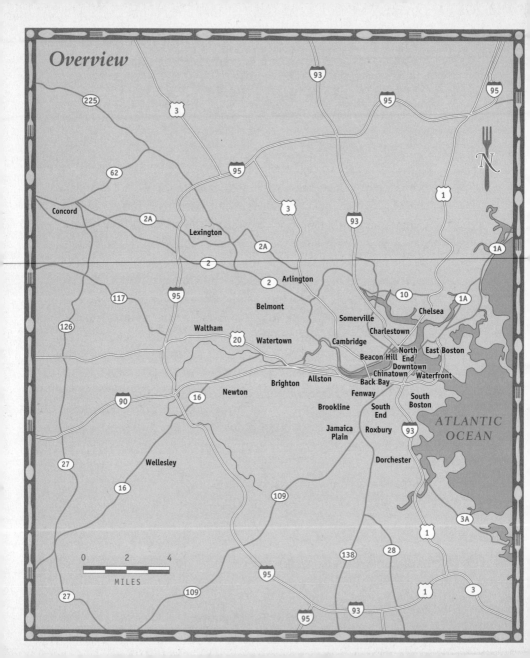

Introduction: Boston—Not Your Grandmother's Baked Beans

Needless to say, we had a lot of great meals while researching this book. One stands out, though, for what it says about eating in Boston. We were dining in a Senegalese restaurant but couldn't quite place the accent of our waiter. It turned out that he was from Poland, and soon he was telling us his favorite markets for borscht and blintzes in the Polish Triangle, where South Boston and Dorchester meet. His enthusiasm grew by the moment, as he then ticked off his favorite places in Chinatown to have bubble tea with his Chinese girlfriend. For anyone with curiosity and an adventurous spirit, Boston is a great place to eat.

Our city's reputation as "the home of the bean and the cod" only scratches the surface of Boston gastronomy. Mind you, there's nothing wrong with either dish. A great roast cod is a succulent plate of fish at its best, and a pot of slightly crusty baked beans, long-simmered with good molasses and a hunk of salt pork, puts over-salted, over-sugared boiled beans in a can to shame. We consider it a badge of honor that you can find delicious roast cod and tasty baked beans in the trendiest bistro as well as in restaurants that first opened their doors nearly 200 years ago.

Boston has been an immigrant gateway to the American continent ever since a couple of boatloads of English Puritans landed here in 1630 looking for good soil and fresh water. Fortunately, the English were followed by other tribes from all across the globe, and every immigrant seems to arrive with a packet of seeds from the garden back home and a passel of recipes from her mother and grandmother.

Although it sometimes seems that Guinness flows down the streets of Boston, especially on St. Patrick's Day, Boston's ethnic makeup is not entirely Irish and we do not live on corned beef, boiled cabbage, and green beer. In the historic North End, it's almost impossible to walk down Hanover Street without stopping for cannoli at one of the Italian bakeries, or for coffee and grappa at one of the Italian caffès. If you are struck with a sudden craving for *lamejun* or any of a dozen variations of baklava, you need only patronize the shops that serve Watertown's Armenian community. Spanish speakers from Cuba and the Dominican Republic account for the island fare found in Jamaica Plain (a lively debate rages over who makes the best Cubano sandwich), while the large Indian and Pakistani community in Waltham supports supermarkets with entire aisles devoted to lentils and dal. An older generation of Chinese immigrants brought Cantonese food to Chinatown, while a newer generation of Southeast Asian immigrants has opened *pho* restaurants all over Chinatown and Dorchester. It's no surprise that more than four dozen cuisines are represented in this book, many of them by mom-and-pop establishments where the proprietors serve cultural pride with every plate.

One of the reasons Boston food is so good is that we have terrific local ingredients. Only one farm remains within city limits, but dozens stand on the outskirts. Come summer, it seems as if a farmers' market pops up on every square and plaza. As you gently squeeze tomatoes and inhale the heady aroma of a bunch of basil, you could easily be rubbing shoulders with some of the city's top chefs—or the cooks for small ethnic restaurants. Everyone wants the freshest produce from the local fields. Locavore dining is a given in Boston.

The same holds true with seafood. The "cod" part of "the bean and the cod" refers to the incredible fishery that first made Boston wealthy. We sit on the ocean, and while Boston isn't quite the fishing port it once was, the busy harbors of Gloucester and New Bedford are but an hour away by truck. The catch could wind up starring with pasta at a North End Italian place, taking center stage in a seafood stew at a Salvadoran eatery in East Boston, or showing up as a whole fish baked in salt at a Chinatown restaurant. Dusted with black truffle, a modest local fish like hake becomes royalty in a fine dining establishment. One net, many cuisines.

Boston can boast a dozen or so fine dining restaurants that are at the cutting edge of American cuisine today, and the city has spawned its fair share of celebrity chefs as well as young Turks who compete on the various TV cooking shows. Food culture is pervasive, reaching all the way down to modest eateries that are little more than sub shops, taverns, or roadhouses with gastronomic ambitions.

But that's nothing new. Bostonians, it seems, have always taken food seriously, going back at least to the founding of the Boston Cooking School in 1879. Nearly a century later, Cambridge's great Julia Child launched a revolution in American gastronomy with *Mastering the Art of French Cooking* (1961) and her first broadcasts of *The French Chef* from Boston's own WGBH in 1963. Julia did much more than cook, of course. She loved to dine at local restaurants and, we hope, would have approved of this volume as a modest field guide. We raise a glass to her memory and wish all who use this book, "Bon appétit!"

How to Use This Book

We agonized over where to draw a line around Boston. The city proper is actually quite small and has a population of about 618,000. The metropolitan area, as defined by the US Census, stretches much wider and has 4.5 million people. *Food Lovers' Boston* lies somewhere between the two. In the final analysis, we included the heavily populated contiguous communities and a few of the commuter suburbs inside Route 128.

The book is divided into eleven geographic regions—seven of them within the city of Boston itself. Some adjacent neighborhoods were treated as a single area, and once we leave Boston and Cambridge, several towns and cities are covered in a single chapter. The limitations of space—and in some cases, our own ignorance—mean that some worthy restaurants, shops, or growers may have been overlooked. As a general rule, we have not included national chain restaurants or stores unless they have a powerfully local character. We caution our readers not to become too wed to geographic distinctions. For example, some wonderful ethnic shops we had expected to find in Watertown were across the street—placing them in Belmont. Whenever possible, we have identified establishments by their neighborhoods.

Given the increasing interest in cocktails, craft beers, and artisanal spirits, we have given bars, pubs, and lounges their own chapter. Many drinking establishments have solid bar food, and a few even offer bar food with aspirations. The converse is also true: Many restaurants have superb cocktail programs, but places where food is more important than drink are found in their respective neighborhood chapters. Another area of burgeoning interest—culinary instruction—has been broken out into an independent chapter as well.

Listings in the geographic chapters are broken down into a few easy-to-use categories:

Foodie Faves

These are principally restaurants and more casual eateries that represent some of the best dining in the region. Each is identified by type of cuisine.

Landmarks

This designation identifies a few places that are iconic and that may have even helped define the neighborhood where they are located.

Specialty Stores, Markets & Producers

This section of each chapter is devoted to places where you can get all the wonderful ingredients to prepare a great meal or a picnic and the shops where you can purchase the kitchen hardware to turn provender into repast. The category also includes pastry shops, bakeries, coffee roasters, and breweries. Confectioners, butchers, and cheesemongers also share this category.

Farmstands

Since the Boston area is so urban, the few farmstands that exist are substantial stores that operate year-round and sell honey, jam, pickles, breads, and maybe even meats in addition to fresh fruits and vegetables. These are listed under the Specialty Stores, Markets & Producers sections.

Farmers' Markets

Small family farms near Boston have found that selling direct to consumers at city farmers' markets can mean enough extra profit to stay in business. We welcome the arrival of the markets every year—it's like seeing old friends after a long winter. Farmers selling at the markets often feel they must offer something special, something you cannot get from the local grocery store. That may be an heirloom fruit or vegetable, an unusual ethnic varietal, or the assurance that the food you buy is free of chemicals.

Price Code

Each restaurant carries a price code to give you a rough approximation of what you will spend. We chose to base the code on dinner entree prices. As a general rule, double the figure to estimate the cost of a three-course meal with a glass of wine. The codes only represent the majority of dinner entrees; most restaurants will have a few dishes that are less expensive and a few that are more expensive. The cost of lunch is almost always lower.

$	under $15
$$	$15 to $25
$$$	$25 to $40
$$$$	more than $40 or prix fixe

Getting Around

We did the bulk of the research for this book on foot. That might surprise even Bostonians, who often don't realize how small the city really is. Let us clarify: We took the subway—the T, in local parlance—to a neighborhood and *then* we walked. And we met some of the nicest people we've ever encountered, once again putting the lie to the old canard about rude and distant Bostonians. We've indicated the appropriate T stop for every entry in the book that is within easy walking distance.

So we suggest that you take the T for the central Boston chapters, Brookline, Cambridge, Somerville, and most of Newton. For some parts of Newton, Lexington, and Concord, use the commuter rail. For the rest, alas, you'll have to drive, or fall back on the less convenient MBTA buses. It's worth plugging your starting point and desired destination into the MBTA Trip Planner to see if the results are worth leaving the car at home. Here's the URL: mbta.com/rider_tools/trip_planner.

Keeping Up with Food News

Not surprisingly, the lively Boston food scene has attracted a lot of bloggers and other opinion mongers who are only too happy to put in their two cents' worth. Here are some information sources that may have an opinionated point of view but speak with authority.

Boston Globe

Restaurant reviews and "cheap eats" reviews of casual spots are published in the Wednesday G section. About a year of these reviews are archived on the free *Globe* website Boston.com. Many years of reviews are archived on the *Globe*'s pay site, BostonGlobe.com.

Dishing

This free column by *Boston Globe* staff appears on the Boston.com website (boston.com/lifestyle/food/dishing). Many of the posts are devoted to recipes and cooking news. Many others are behind-the-scenes notebook pieces by some of the reviewers. Restaurant news also appears frequently on Dishing.

Boston Phoenix

The free entertainment weekly boasts the restaurant reviewer with the longest track record in Boston and greatest historical perspective. Reviews of more casual eateries are written by another reviewer who, behind his look-Ma-no-hands writing style, is actually perceptive and thoughtful. Restaurant news in the *Phoenix* is limited mostly to openings and closings. Past reviews can be found online at thephoenix.com/boston/food/restaurantreviews.

Boston Herald

While the *Herald* gave up on serious restaurant reviewing when Mat Schaffer retired, the paper and its website cover the local food scene closely, noting openings and closings and changes of personnel and often writing feature pieces on folks in the food trades. Most useful for paper readers is the Fast Food column. Online, the *Fork Lifts* blog (www.bostonherald.com/blogs/lifestyle/fork_lift/) features posts by staff and by such luminaries as Roger Berkowitz of Legal Sea Foods and Chef Lydia Shire.

Grub Street

The coverage of Boston restaurant openings and closings and chef changes on Grub Street (boston.grubstreet.com) can be surprisingly good for a publication whose heart (and server) is in New York.

BostonChefs.com

Almost all the news of interest about the Boston restaurant scene appears first on BostonChefs.com. Track all the events, find out about soft openings, and see where the jobs are. (When a place is advertising for a head chef, you might want to eat elsewhere.)

Edible Boston Magazine

Chances are that it won't be news by the time this quarterly publishes, but feature coverage of restaurants, growers, and producers tends to be insightful and even thought provoking, on occasion. Magazine is given away free at foodie locations and can be found online at ediblecommunities.com/boston.

Boston Magazine

Boston's city lifestyle magazine may be best known for bestowing Best of Boston awards, but it also features good, if sometimes pompous, restaurant criticism. For lively, contemporary dish on the dining scene by talented younger writers, see *Boston*'s dining blog, *Chowder,* at blogs.bostonmagazine.com/chowder.

Street Eats

You have to hand it to the bureaucrats in Boston and surrounding communities. Once the clamor began for more food trucks, they snipped through much of the red tape pronto. The argument went something like, "Why should Financial District office workers miss out on good food that the kids at MIT can get?"

Boston's food truck scene began, in fact, with falafel and burrito trucks parked in front of MIT on Massachusetts Avenue in Cambridge, and itinerant sandwich trucks that popped around town to construction sites, their shiny quilted steel sides gleaming in the sunshine. Then Clover Food Truck began selling gourmet veggie fare in front of MIT in 2008 and the race was on. Trucks continue to proliferate in Boston, and some have even competed in TV food truck reality shows. Most, though, are too busy to seek that 15 minutes of pop culture fame.

Like the blooming magnolia trees on Commonwealth Avenue, the arrival of food trucks has become a sign of spring in the city. As a general rule, food trucks congregate in Boston on the Rose Fitzgerald Kennedy Greenway, near City Hall, at the Park Street T station, and at the SoWA Open Market on Harrison Avenue on weekends. You'll also find them in Cambridge in front of MIT and at the Science Center just outside Harvard Yard. In Brookline, look for them near Boston University on Commonwealth Avenue and St. Mary's Street, near Cleveland Circle on Beacon Street, and on Washington Square on Beacon Street. Since the trucks are often on the move, they can be tracked best via Twitter. Here are some of the most popular:

Bon Me Truck, @bonme. Rice bowls, noodle salads, and Vietnamese *banh mi* sandwiches are the main fare, but don't miss the tea-cured deviled eggs.

Boston Speed Dog, @Americas hotdog. Billed as "paradise in a parking lot," the half-pound Pearl hot dogs are marinated in apple cider and brown sugar. Proclaimed America's best by the *Wall Street Journal*.

Clover Food Truck, @cloverfoodtruck. Biodiesel-powered fleet of three trucks serves veggie sandwiches, salads, and amazing fries with deep-fried fresh rosemary. For stationary locations, see p. 243.

Grilled Cheese Nation, @GCNBoston. Local farm produce goes into the tomato soup and salads, but the grilled cheese sandwiches are the main attraction.

Grillo's Pickles, @grillospickles. The garlicky half-sour spears are tangy and crisp, and pickled carrots and green tomatoes are revelations.

Kickass Cupcakes, @kickasscupcakes. Same great cakes, same great icings as the Somerville store (see p. 332).

Lobsta Love, @LobstaLoveTruck. Lobster rolls are the main deal, including the classic on a hot dog roll or an Asian fusion version with ponzu, sesame oil, and fresh basil. Excellent clam chowder and lobster bisque.

Silk Road BBQ, @silkroadbbq. Central Asian (read Mongolian) barbecue with jerk chicken, pork tenderloin, and leg of lamb skewers as well as goat and chicken stews, white bean chili, and pulled pork sandwiches.

Staff Meal, @staffmealtruck. Budget foodie fare is based on the kind of meals prepared for a restaurant's kitchen staff. Often still out on the streets at 2 a.m. when bars close.

North End, Charlestown, East Boston & Chelsea

The North End is the centerpiece of this chapter. It's an easy enough place to find—just follow the red stripe of the Freedom Trail embedded in the sidewalk. It leads into Boston's oldest neighborhood to highlight Paul Revere's House, Old North Church, Copp's Hill Burying Ground, and other icons of Boston's Revolutionary War history. You can be forgiven for thinking, however, that it delineates the fast track to some of Boston's best dining. Although the North End was settled in 1630 and was the city's African-American neighborhood in the years after the Civil War, it became solidly Italian by 1900. The residents are more mixed today, but the restaurant scene has a uniformly Italian accent, from the old-fashioned *caffès* to gleaming Modernist rooms serving cutting-edge Italian cuisine. The red line of the Freedom Trail continues to Charlestown to the

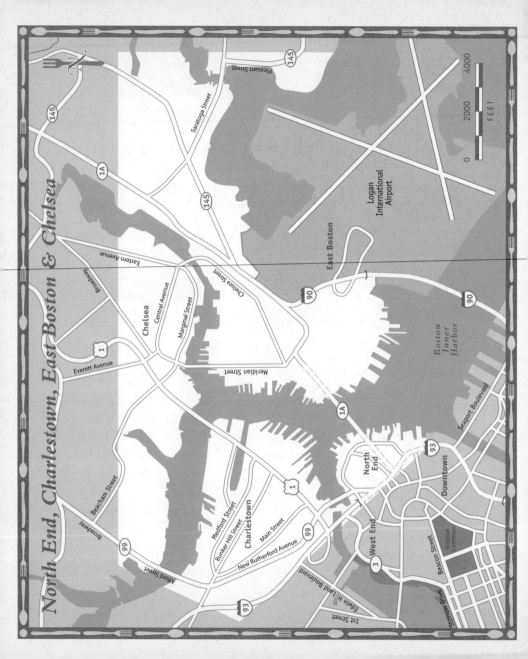

North End, Charlestown, East Boston & Chelsea

USS *Constitution* (Old Ironsides) and the Bunker Hill Monument. Sandwiched between them is the circa 1780 public house named for one of the heroes of the Battle of Bunker Hill, Joseph Warren. Musket-toting rebels are long gone, but it's still serving drink and victuals to hungry visitors. Recently gentrified, Charlestown has a passel of good spots to eat and drink. The Freedom Trail ends here, but the chapter continues by leapfrogging over the harbor to East Boston and over the Mystic River to Chelsea, both communities whose recent gastronomic enrichment owes much to Spanish-speaking new Bostonians.

Foodie Faves

Angela's Cafe, 131 Lexington St., East Boston, Boston, MA 02128; (617) 567-4972; angelascaferestaurant.com; Mexican; $$; T: Airport. Bostonians tend to think of Mexican food as a monolithic cuisine composed primarily of fish tacos, burritos, *mole poblano,* and the occasional tamale. Angela Atenco Lopez thinks otherwise, but then she comes from Puebla, the region that gave birth to the chocolate- and spice-tinged *mole poblano*. The small restaurant that she runs with her family in a residential hillside of East Boston ought to be an antidote to all that Boston bar food masquerading as Mexican. Angela's serves authentic Pueblan home cooking, from *flautas* (crisp corn tortillas filled with lettuce, avocado, Mexican cheese, and cubes of potato) to warming bowls of *sopa Azteca* (chicken and tomato broth with strips of crisp tortillas) to the famous *mole poblano* and the less famous but equally deserving *pepian verde*. She serves the green *pepian verde* (made with sesame and pumpkin seeds, tomatillos, and jalapeño peppers) on a choice of chicken breast or sliced pork loin. That's not to say that the staff won't make tacos (the taco *el pastor* is filled with roasted pork in an adobo sauce with diced fresh pineapple) or even burritos, but the real prizes are those plates using the delicious Puebla sauces.

Antico Forno, 93 Salem St., North End, Boston, MA 02113; (617) 723-6733; anticofornoboston.com; Italian; $$; T: Haymarket. One of the first restaurants in the North End to rely primarily on a wood-fired brick oven, Antico Forno has been a neighborhood favorite since 1996. From the stuffed eggplant on the antipasti menu to the baked pastas of the *primi* to the oven-roasted chicken and the wood-grilled swordfish of the *secondi,* there's no escaping the kiss of smoke and fire. Since the restaurant starts serving dinner in the late afternoon, many folks in the North End pop in for an early supper of a glass of house wine with one of the ample pizzas. Our favorite features homemade sausage and mozzarella, broccoli rabe, and cherry tomatoes.

Artù Rosticceria & Trattoria, 6 Prince St., North End, Boston, MA 02113; (617) 742-4336; artuboston.com; Italian; $$; T: Haymarket. Artù's roasted meats set it apart from other North End eateries and the best—and least expensive—way to try them is

to order a panini sandwich at lunch-time. Choices from the rotisserie include chicken with tomato and basil; beef with lettuce, tomato, and cheese; and either leg of lamb or pork with marinated egg-plant. That eggplant is also part of a delicious vegetable antipasto plate that makes a perfect accompaniment to the sandwiches or to a side dish of homemade meatballs with tomato sauce. A more traditional trattoria menu prevails at dinner, with pastas such as linguine with squid and mussels in tomato sauce and meat dishes including sweet Italian sausage with peppers and potatoes and veal stuffed with prosciutto, provolone, and mushrooms.

Bricco, 241 Hanover St., North End, Boston, MA 02113; (617) 248-6800; depasqualeventures.com; Italian; $$$; T: Haymarket. Bricco is a social scene worthy of an Italian film, especially in the summer when the windows are thrown open and the party nearly spills onto the sidewalk. One of the higher-end restaurants operated by Frank De Pasquale, Bricco shows its owner's penchant for uncovering the best specialty ingredients. Let everyone else serve prosciutto *de Parma* on their antipasti menus—Bricco has the more delicate and nuanced prosciutto *de Daniele*. Pastas at Bricco are truly something special, from the ravioli made around the corner at **DePasquale's Homemade Pasta Shoppe** (see p. 38) to the "Big Night" *timpano,* which is a drum-shaped pasta filled with meatballs and a slow-braised meat ragù. Oven-finished meat and fish dishes (grilled bone-in swordfish, oven-braised sea bass, veal osso bucco with saffron risotto) tend to be large, but there's no harm in ordering a pasta each and splitting a *secondi*. Wood-fired pizzas are available at the bar after 11 p.m.

Carmen, 33 North Square, North End, Boston, MA 02113; (617) 742-6421; carmenboston.com; Italian; $$$; T: Haymarket. If Carmen had been in this spot in the 18th century, we bet that Paul Revere would have slipped out of his house down the street to visit this little *enoteca* for a glass of Montepulciano and a plate of roasted rack of pork with acorn squash. Carmen is snug, cozy, and dark, all of which translate as romantic. Chef-Owner Jeff Malloy assembles a seasonal menu that draws extensively on regional farms and fishermen, so his Italian always has a New England accent. The restaurant is a favorite for neighborhood denizens who sneak in early and order mostly off the pasta menu.

Daily Catch, 323 Hanover St., North End, Boston, MA 02113; (617) 523-8567; thedailycatch.com; Seafood/Italian; $; T: Haymarket. The Daily Catch opened in 1973 and we swear it has had a line out the door every night since, partly because the food is so good and partly because it is no-nonsense cheap. Locals call the place the Calamari Cafe, as it was the first place in the North End to popularize squid for the tourists. On any given night the menu might feature fried calamari, calamari meatballs, calamari salad, and calamari with pasta and sauce. Most of the other proteins are shellfish—clams, mussels, scallops, and shrimp—though monkfish, haddock, scrod, and lobster put in frequent appearances. The menu is scrawled daily on a chalkboard, and you may be seated with strangers. Beer and wine are available. Cash only.

D'Amelio's Off the Boat, 26–28 Porter St., East Boston, Boston, MA 02128; (617) 561-8800; offtheboatseafood.com; Seafood; $$; T: Maverick. Practically in the shadow of the Sumner Tunnel toll-booths, D'Amelio's is hiding in plain sight. Once you're inside, it's a different world where the D'Amelio family kitchen reigns. Sure, you could order the standard fried seafood dinners, but the house specialties are bona fide Italian. For example, the Fusilli Marchi features house-made pasta in a butter sauce tossed with lobster, crab, and shrimp. The restaurant uses New Zealand green mussels in its mussel dishes (closer in taste and texture to those found in the Adriatic Sea) and serves them over pasta with a choice of red tomato sauce or simple garlic and olive oil. The garlic-and-oil sauce figures prominently in many of the house specials because it goes so well with seafood. A variant of the fusilli with seafood features shrimp, scallops, lobster, and broccoli rabe with the garlic oil.

Dough, 20 Maverick St., East Boston, Boston, MA 02128; (617) 567-8787; doughpizza.com; Pizza; $; T: Maverick. Michael Sanchez has been in the restaurant business since forever; partner Kevin Curley came to the kitchen via gene-sequencing for a biotech company. Their sandwich and pizza shop across from an artists' studio building has carved out a name for itself as much through the sandwiches as through the pizzas. People drive from literally miles around to get their Cajun chicken cheesesteak sandwich, which slathers peppers and onions on several pieces of Cajun-spiced chicken that have been toasted black on the grill under a weight. Equally famous is the Vermonter sandwich, an oven-baked monster of smoked turkey, smoked Gouda cheese, smoked bacon, fresh apple, red onion, and sun-dried tomato mayonnaise on multigrain bread. Because it has so many ingredients and the whole thing must be baked in the oven, it takes about 10 minutes to prepare. (It's worth the wait.) Pizzas get high marks from Eastie artists. One of the more unusual is also one of the best. The Hawaiian starts with a base of olive oil and garlic on the dough, followed by a sprinkling of grated coconut, diced pineapple, prosciutto, and mozzarella. The coconut gets toasted in the oven, giving the whole pie a nuttier, less sweet taste.

Figs, 67 Main St., Charlestown, Boston, MA 02129; (617) 242-2229; toddenglish.com; Italian; $$; T: Community College. Holding down the spot where the Todd English saga began, this Charlestown branch of Figs showcases what English does best—delicious thin-crust free-form pizzas and simple baked pastas. One of the founding dishes was the fig and prosciutto pizza and it remains a favorite: a crisp rosemary-flecked crust, fig and balsamic jam, prosciutto, and crumbles of Gorgonzola cheese. The mountain of food in the chicken Parmesan (crisp chicken cutlet, heap of baked rigatoni, smothering quantities of mozzarella cheese) ensures that you'll have plenty to reheat for tomorrow's lunch. There's another branch on Charles Street (see p. 56).

Fusion Foods, 11 Everett Ave., Chelsea, MA 02150; (857) 776-7575; fusion-foods.net; Vietnamese/Thai; $. Melissa Vo calls her restaurant Fusion Foods, but in fact she makes and sells authentic Southeast Asian dishes. Yes, she does serve *pho,* but her fresh vegetable dishes set her menu apart from the plethora of Vietnamese soup shops in the city. Her spring rolls, for example, are made to order. Don't miss the tilapia version, which contains seared fish, some thin noodles, mint and *hojiso* (a Vietnamese herb also known as *shiso*), chopped cucumber, bean sprouts, and sautéed scallions all wrapped in sticky rice paper and served with garlic-lime *nuoc mam* for dipping. For a nice contrast, we also love her spicy turkey "turnovers" of flaky pastry filled with spiced ground turkey and long slivers of carrot and onion. Vo offers the extensive menu for takeout, but if you've come all the way to Chelsea to taste the food, you might as well eat in her lovely second-floor dining room. A number of vegan dishes are available, along with wonderful hot and cold herbal and fruit drinks. Cash only.

Galleria Umberto, 289 Hanover St., North End, Boston, MA 02113; (617) 227-5709; Italian; $; T: Haymarket. Everyone from construction crews working in the area to well-dressed women on a nostalgia trip back to the old neighborhood starts lining up before noon at this lunch-only North End hole in the wall. But standing in line will give you plenty of time to consult with the regulars who will help you decide between a spinach, cheese, or sausage calzone or an *arancini* (rice ball) filled with ground meat, peas, and tomato sauce. Many diners, by the way, throw in a slice of pizza for good measure. You can get your food to go or settle in at one of the small Formica tables.

Giacomo's, 355 Hanover St., North End, Boston, MA 02113; (617) 523-9026; Italian; $–$$; T: Haymarket. This North End casual dining stalwart is frill-free: no parking, no reservations, no credit cards, and certainly no pretensions. The food is extremely straightforward: chicken or veal with tomato sauce and pasta; all forms of shellfish on linguine with a choice of pesto, *fra diavolo,* red, or house cream sauce; and some dishes that combine fish and pasta, chicken and pasta, or (for the vegetarian in the group) eggplant and pasta or pumpkin and pasta. None of the main dishes will break the bank, and the house wine is comparably cheap. Lines stretch down the block on most nights, and while the food doesn't pretend to be fancy, it's tasty and filling, and the room is loud and fun. Cash only.

KO Pub and Pies, 256 Marginal St., Building 16, East Boston, Boston, MA 02128; (617) 418-5234; www.kocateringandpies.com; Australian; $; T: Maverick. Sam Jackson of **KO Catering and Pies** (see p. 190) in South Boston jumped at the chance in early 2012 to open a second location at the East Boston shipyard. Jackson built a loyal following in Southie based on his Australian meat pies and is offering a somewhat expanded menu of Aussie treats (and beer) in this second venue, which, as he notes, has Harpoon Brewery in its sightlines.

La Famiglia Giorgio, 112 Salem St., North End, Boston, MA 02113; (617) 367-6711; lafamigliagiorgio.com; Italian; $–$$; T: Haymarket. Once you get past the heavy-handed Olive Garden/ Godfather atmospherics in the decor and the background music, La Famiglia Giorgio is pretty much what it claims to be—a Roman-style family restaurant that serves gigantic portions of pasta dishes. The pick-a-pasta then pick-a-sauce routine appeals to a lot of diners, though it's a far cry from what you'd encounter in Italy. But the Giorgio folks are not sticklers for authenticity—they would rather have a lot of happy diners. It is perhaps one of the best restaurants in the North End for families with small children in tow, because you can order a few entrees and ask for extra plates. There will almost cer-tainly be enough to go around— and probably enough to take home.

Lucca, 226 Hanover St., North End, Boston, MA 02113; (617) 742-9200; luccaboston.com; Italian; $$$; T: Haymarket. The North End was crying out for alternatives to pasta houses when Lucca opened several years ago serving a fish- and meat-centric northern Italian menu. That's not to say there aren't pasta dishes on the menu, but they are not the typical first-course plates. You might find rabbit ravioli with sautéed baby vegetables and a red wine demi-glace, for example, or homemade linguine tossed with cockles, Manila clams, pancetta, and baby tomatoes. Appetizer courses tend toward oven dishes, like the rustic duck tart with caramelized onions, goat cheese, and spinach, or a lasagna of layered potatoes, wild mushrooms, spinach, and balsamic glaze. If your heart is set on "red gravy," look elsewhere.

Mamma Maria, 3 North Square, North End, Boston, MA 02113; (617) 523-0077; mammamaria.com; Italian; $$$; T: Haymarket. Seemingly a world apart from the bustle of Hanover Street, Mamma Maria is a warren of five small dining rooms in an old brick townhouse steps from the Paul Revere House. It is frequently cited as one of Boston's most romantic dining spots, partly for the low lighting and partly for the intimacy of the dining spaces. The kitchen follows the spirit of modern Italian cooking by crafting top New England seafood and garden vegetables into beautiful plates of food with bold, bright flavors. For example, the rabbit pappardelle features slowly braised Vermont rabbit with homemade pasta and crispy pancetta, and the halibut is line-caught off the local coast and seared with Oregon morels. What more could you ask?

Marco, 253 Hanover St., 2nd floor, North End, Boston, MA 02113; (617) 742-1276; marcoboston.com; Italian; $$$; T: Haymarket. It's worth climbing the stairs to this unassuming second-story restaurant with bare brick walls, simple tables, and a working fireplace for extra winter coziness. It's run by Marc Orfaly, also chef-owner of **Pigalle** (see p. 107). Marco is Orfaly's homage to the neighborhood Roman trattoria where families pop in for dishes like homemade gnocchi with sage brown butter, or risotto Milanese as a counterpoint to osso bucco. Marco features a large selection of cured meats, including capocollo and prosciutto, as well as Orfaly's own house-made sausages. His lasagna uses eggplant in place of pasta with the tomato sauce and three cheeses (ricotta, mozzarella, Parmigiana) and never seems to go off the menu. For a treat, try the grilled Florentine steak with arugula and lemon.

Mare Oyster Bar, 135 Richmond St., North End, Boston, MA 02113; (617) 723-MARE; marenatural.com; Italian/Seafood; $$$; T: Haymarket. With broad plate-glass windows and big mirrors on the wall, Mare (pronounced the Italian way as MAH-ray) has a bit of the look of a modernist aquarium, but perhaps that's appropriate for a restaurant dedicated to tip-top seafood. In slow seasons there are just a half-dozen oysters from East Coast farms; when business picks up, another half-dozen oysters from the West Coast or Europe join the mix at the shucking station. But oysters are just the beginning at Mare, where Greg Jordan presides over a kitchen that turns out two of the region's great lobster rolls: hot with herbed butter and scallions, or cold with lemon mayonnaise made in-house. Both are served on a fresh brioche bun baked at sister restaurant **Bricco** (see p. 19). Truffle-crusted grilled tuna—always served rare—is another striking treat, as is Jordan's Italian seafood soup of a half lobster, scallops, mussels, cockles, and clams in a light tomato broth.

Maurizio's, 364 Hanover St., North End, Boston, MA 02113; (617) 367-1123; mauriziosboston.com; Italian; $$; T: Haymarket. Maurizio Loddo was one of the neighborhood's first chefs to break away from Italian-American cooking. He and his wife, Linda, opened Maurizio's in 1993 to serve the light, seafood-oriented cuisine of Sardinia, and they've never looked back. In fact, if you're lucky enough to land one of the tables in view of the tiny kitchen, you'll notice he barely ever looks up—he's so busy dancing around the small space with a couple of assistants. This is a place to taste some truly distinctive regional Italian dishes, like the antipasto of *mazzamurru*, a Sardinian peasant bowl of toasted bread, chicken broth, and tomato sauce topped with a poached egg and tangy grated sheep's milk cheese and then baked. The fish dishes, however, are where the kitchen really shines. Loddo always manages to get some of the best fish available. His Sardinian-style sole is not to be missed. You might not think of red wine with fish, but Loddo always carries a couple of ruby-red Sardinian reds based on the Monica grape (which typically has pleasant, bright cherry flavors followed by hints of soft chocolate) that pairs very well with assertive fish.

Navy Yard Bistro, 6th St. at 1st Ave., Charlestown, Boston, MA 02129; (617) 242-0036; navyyardbistro.com; New American; $$; T: Community College/North Station. Situated among the Boston Navy Yard condominium development, this smart little bar and dining room is the picture of a modern American neighborhood bistro. The food is straightforward and tasty—grilled hanger steak with fries, ginger-sake glazed salmon, pan-roasted duck breast with polenta and a tart cherry glaze. Sunday and Monday nights are "neighborhood nights," featuring even less expensive homey meat loaf or veal Marsala and specials on wines. Like the food, the wines are mostly New World.

Neptune Oyster, 63 Salem St., North End, Boston, MA 02113; (617) 742-3474; neptuneoyster.com; Seafood; $$$; T: Haymarket. With just 18 seats at the raw bar in the front and 26 more seats along a banquette, Neptune has decided that good things come in small packages. That includes the menu, which is mostly about which kinds of oysters are ready for shucking. Actually, there are a few nicely chosen entrees (mostly fish) that change with the fishing season. Oven-roasted Atlantic striped bass is usually available, as is bronzini, its Mediterranean cousin. The other chief focus besides the bivalves is the wines. The standard list features more than 80 bottles averaging around $40, while the shorter "Pearls" list has some of the pricier alternatives. Both favor Italy over other regions.

Paolo's Trattoria, 251 Main St., Charlestown, Boston, MA 02129; (617) 242-7229; paolosboston.com; Italian; $$; T: Community College. Since it never gets any publicity, few people outside the neighborhood even know that this romantic family-owned trattoria is even here. But many neighbors consider Paolo's wood-fired pizzas some of the best in the city. Ask for your pizza extra crisp, and note that the 16-inch size is only marginally more expensive than the 12-inch. The *melanzana* (eggplant) is a favorite, as it features both ricotta and mozzarella cheese. The house special (the Paolo's), topped with kalamata olives and sopresatta, betrays the family's Greek heritage. Most diners not having pizza opt for one of the pastas or the scallops risotto, which is a saffron risotto topped with scallops seared in a cast-iron pan. The restaurant also offers free delivery within Charlestown.

Pollo Campero, 115 Park St., Chelsea, MA 02150; (617) 884-0070; and 188 Border St., East Boston, Boston, MA 02128; (617) 568-9500; T: Maverick; Guatemalan; $; global.campero.com. The Central American populations of Chelsea and East Boston welcomed this Guatemalan fast food chain with open arms, and given the quality of the food and the fair prices, it's easy to see why. A family of up to eight can feast on a whole grilled or fried chicken with side dishes for under $20. We're partial to the chicken empanadas. There are three variations: spicy chicken has green tomatillo salsa, Monterey Jack cheese, and chopped cilantro; citrus-marinated chicken comes with grilled onions, tamarind sauce, and shredded Monterey Jack; or the vegetarian version has black beans and cheese with chopped tomatoes and jalapeño peppers. You can also get chicken tacos. Side dishes include yucca or plantain fries (with a mayo-ketchup dipping sauce) or black beans and rice. Save room for caramel flan or tres leches cake for dessert.

Pomodoro, 319 Hanover St., North End, Boston, MA 02113; (617) 367-4348; Italian; $; T: Haymarket. Widely considered one of the best date restaurants in Boston—partly because it's so reasonably priced, partly because it is adorably cute—Pomodoro also has terrific food. The first hint comes when the server brings the excellent bread, olive oil, and a small bowl of olives. Some diners are disappointed that the pasta dishes are roughly the same price as the meat and fish dishes, but stick to the nightly specials for the best flavors and best deals. If nothing else appeals, fall back on the roasted cod served with a pomodoro sauce, capers, kalamata olives, and a small mound of linguine. Cash only.

Prezza, 24 Fleet St., North End, Boston, MA 02113; (617) 227-1577; prezza.com; Italian; $$$; T: Haymarket. The restaurant is named for the hometown of Chef-Owner Anthony Caturano's grand-mother, but the elegantly composed dishes are not exactly Nonna's cooking. The pasta is all made in-house, as are the soft pillows of gnocchi. Caturano likes to cook with wood, so many of the main dishes come from the grill, including swordfish served with saffron rice, lobster broth, and mussels. Meat eaters get their fill with oven-roasted meatballs, sausage, and ribs served with creamy polenta

and roasted tomato. Once a week Prezza offers a bargain-priced plate of tagliatelle and meatballs to eat at the bar, with a similarly good deal on wine.

Rabia's, 73 Salem St., North End, Boston, MA 02113; (617) 227-6637; rabias.com; Italian/Seafood; $$$; T: Haymarket. With so many high-end oyster bars springing up, it's hard to beat Rabia's as a family-oriented, reasonably priced restaurant for seafood with an Italian accent. Actually, one of our favorite dishes isn't fish at all. It's the ravioli filled with Red Delicious apple and fig and served in a Gorgonzola cream sauce with aged pecorino Romano cheese. This is also one of the few North End restaurants serving charcoal-grilled baby octopus, which comes with an addictive pesto aioli.

Regina Pizza, 11½ Thacher St., North End, Boston, MA 02113; (617) 227-0765; reginapizza.com; Pizza; $–$$; T: Haymarket. The vertical neon sign beckons on tiny Thacher Street—probably the only way most newcomers will ever find the North End's original pizza shop, established in 1926. Day or night, there will probably be a line of people waiting to get into the tiny establishment. We have never, ever scored one of the wooden booths here, but seats at the bar are just dandy. The pizza style is closer to Neapolitan than American, relying on a yeasty dough and light, slightly spicy sauce. Minimal toppings will keep the crust crisp on the bottom and chewy instead of soggy on top.

Santarpio's Pizza, 111 Chelsea St., East Boston, Boston, MA 02128; (617) 567-9871; santarpiospizza.com; Pizza; $; T: Maverick. It's worth crossing the harbor in the Callahan Tunnel to get to Santarpio's, which was founded in 1903. Hard-core fans generally order the cheese and garlic pizza with extra garlic and place a second order for the homemade sausages or the lamb skewers. Like Charlestown, East Boston bred many a pro boxer, and Santarpio's used to be the place where the fight crowd would hang and drink. But the smoky fight-bar atmosphere of years gone by has been cleaned up and brightened, and the faded signed posters have been taken down. The pizza, however, remains unchanged. Be prepared for a long line on weekends, especially Sunday afternoons and evenings. Cash only.

Tangierino, 73–83 Main St., Charlestown, Boston, MA 02129; (617) 242-6009; tangierino.com; Moroccan; $$$; T: Community College. Chef-Owner Samad Naamad is Moroccan and has invested this restaurant and the downstairs hookah and cigar lounge (called Koullshi) with Arabian Nights trappings (including belly dancers). But the place is not all for show. While not purely Moroccan, the food is North African in style and flavor. The grilled lamb, for example, is seasoned with zaatar. One version comes with eggplant, figs, and

apricots; another is accompanied by an almond couscous, dates, and prunes. Several tagines are offered, including both the classic chicken with preserved lemon and a more Americanized version with salmon, olives, and roasted chickpeas.

If there's anything to disappoint, it's the lack of Moroccan chopped vegetable salads.

Taranta, 210 Hanover St., North End, Boston, MA 02113; (617) 720-0052; tarantarist.com; Italian/Peruvian; $$$; T: Haymarket. Born in Peru, Chef-Owner Jose Duarte grew up in an Italian immigrant community in Venezuela, so his marriage of Peruvian flavors with southern Italian cuisine comes naturally. To get an idea of how well the two go together, try his *orechiette con salsicchia*, cooked with South American *aji* peppers, Abruzzi sausage, broccoli rabe, and cherry tomatoes. He also makes gnocchi with cassava root (yucca) and serves them with a spicy green lamb ragù and shaved Parmigiana cheese. Pasta portions tend to be restrained, while the more expensive meat and fish dishes are often huge. The brined double-cut pork chop coated with a glaze of sugarcane and rocoto pepper is enough for two, especially because it is accompanied by a sauté of Peruvian giant corn, caramelized onions, and spinach.

Topacio Restaurant, 120 Meridian St., East Boston, Boston, MA 02128; (617) 567-9523; topaciorestaurant.com; Salvadoran/ Seafood; $; T: Maverick. Many of the customers at this principally Spanish-speaking restaurant order the roasted chicken or the *plato* *montañero* (grilled steak, fried eggs, beans, rice, and tortillas), but the real house specialty is the seafood feast called *sopa de mariscos,* or shellfish soup. Think of it as a Central American take on bouillabaisse, filled with bits and pieces of New England finfish, clams, shrimp, and lobster. The fried fish dinner (with rice, salad, and tortillas) could be flounder, cod, pollock, or even tilapia, depending on which is most readily available.

Landmarks

Warren Tavern, 2 Pleasant St., Charlestown, Boston, MA 02129; (617) 241-8142; warrentavern.com; Traditional American; $–$$; T: Community College. Dating roughly from 1780 and thus probably the oldest building still standing in Charlestown (the British burned down the rest), the Warren Tavern has a pleasant, old-fashioned feel. Many customers dine on burgers, even at dinnertime, and it's not a bad idea. The themed Paul Revere burger, FYI, comes with Swiss cheese and sautéed mushrooms. Best among the entrees are the Polish mac and cheese (with kielbasa) and the grilled meat loaf with mashed potatoes and mushroom gravy. The bar does channel the founding fathers with a choice of 16 mostly local beers on draft.

A. Bova & Sons Modern Bakery, 134 Salem St., North End, Boston, MA 02113; (617) 523-5601; bovabakeryboston.com; Bakery; T: Haymarket. Family-owned since 1932, Bova is a North End institution. Open 24 hours, it's also the answer to a midnight craving for a flaky *sfogliatelle* or a creamy cannoli. Many a clubgoer makes a late-night or early morning stop for a slice of pizza or an overstuffed sandwich on a *spucadella* roll. But perhaps early risers have it best, since they can tote home a loaf of bread still hot from the oven for a simple, but satisfying, breakfast.

Caffè Dello Sport, 308 Hanover St., North End, Boston, MA 02113; (617) 523-5063; caffèdellosport.us; Coffee Shop; T: Haymarket. You might see a television tuned to a European soccer match in any number of North End establishments, but if you want to enjoy a game in the company of hard-core and knowledgeable fans, Dello Sport is the place to be. In fact, the upcoming soccer schedule is posted on the door and club memorabilia is on sale inside. Fans don't go hungry while rooting for their favorite teams. Dello Sport's panini choices include the Zambrotta with Genoa salami, provolone, grilled eggplant, and hot peppers, or the Perotta with artichokes, Gorgonzola, tomatoes, and basil. Imported beers include Peroni and Moretti from Italy.

Caffè Paradiso, 255 Hanover St., North End, Boston, MA 02113; (617) 742-1768; caffèparadiso.com; Coffee Shop; T: Haymarket. No one will think the less of you if you settle in at a small marble-topped table and order a simple espresso. But other options abound at Paradiso and making choices is half the fun. The menu, in fact, offers 14 varieties of international coffees including the Italian with espresso, hazelnut, and Hennessy, or the Greek, which adds ouzo and Metaxa to that espresso. Of the 15 martinis, the signature Paradiso-tini is made with Absolut vodka, Campari, limoncello, and orange juice. If you decide to stick with that espresso after all, you might want a scoop of gelato to go with it. Paradiso serves 12 flavors, but there's no choice here. Stick with the Zuppa Inglese, the house creation of strawberries, rum, and panettone (a fruitcake-like bread). You've got to love a cafe that can turn bread into ice cream.

Caffè Vittoria, 290–296 Hanover St., North End, Boston, MA 02113; (617) 227-7606; vittoriacaffè.com; Coffee Shop; T: Haymarket. This caffè has been part of the scene in the North End since 1929, and every old-timer has a tale to tell about a semifamous criminal or a visiting opera singer. We take them all with a grain of salt. The two separate entrances to the caffè used to define the smoking and (much smaller) nonsmoking sections; since Massachusetts banned smoking in food and drink establishments, the stairway between the two rooms leads upstairs to Stanza dei Sigari, a cigar bar. The pastries and espresso taste better in the clear air downstairs.

The Cheese Shop, 20 Fleet St., North End, Boston, MA 02113; (617) 973-9500; Cheesemonger; T: Haymarket. It was a sad day for cheese fans when the previous owner of this shop went to a federal medical center to serve a six-year bit for extortion, gaming, and bribery. But under new owners, there is again a source for fresh ricotta, fresh mozzarella, and all the wonderful aged imported Parmigiana Reggiano, pecorino Romano, and Asiago necessary to truly eat Italian. They even carry cold cuts and make good sandwiches at lunchtime.

V. Cirace & Son Inc., 173 North St., North End, Boston, MA 02109; (617) 227-3193; vcirace.com; Wine, Beer & Spirits; T: Haymarket. Founded in 1906 and now operated by the third generation of the Cirace family, this shop does a lot of its own importing. That translates into some fabulous deals on northern Italian wines, especially Barbera and Barbaresco, as well as one of the largest selections of grappas and aqua vitae we have ever encountered on this side of the Atlantic or even in Italy. The family also owns the Herbe di Amalfi brand of herb- and flower-infused liqueurs, and even has its own brand of limoncello.

DePasquale's Homemade Pasta Shoppe, 66A Cross St., North End, Boston, MA 02113; homemade-pasta.com; Specialty Shop; T: Haymarket. At her flour-covered workbench in front of a big picture window, Zoya Kogan turns out about 50 types of pasta, some of which are featured on the menu at **Bricco** restaurant (see p. 19).

She's not the only one who's busy. Cheesemaker Joseph Locilento makes fresh mozzarella almost every day and "sometimes twice a day," he says, "especially in the summer when we have fresh tomatoes." Locilento also dries some of the mozzarella for three or four days. "It's great for pizzas and baked pastas," he says. Locilento is also happy to advise on the best sauce for squid ink and tomato pappardelle or for braised short rib and escarole ravioli. To round out a meal, the shop also carries a variety of cold cuts and cheeses, including a pecorino forte with a red pepper rind made in New York. Locilento recommends serving it with the shop's truffle honey or fig and cocoa spread.

GiGi Gelateria, 272 Hanover St., North End, Boston, MA 02113; depasqualeventures.com; Ice Cream/Yogurt; T: Haymarket. GiGi offers a veritable rainbow of fruit gelatos (melon, passion fruit, green apple, grapefruit, tangerine, watermelon, lemon, strawberry, peach . . .) and the pure flavors are incredibly refreshing on a hot summer day. But those who like a little more oomph in their gelato will also find pistachio, hazelnut, tiramisu, mint chocolate, and Gianduia Torino, a mixture of vanilla, hazelnuts, and chocolate chips.

Katz Bagel Bakery, 139 Park St., Chelsea, MA 02150; (617) 884-9738; katzbagels.com; Bakery. Family-owned and -operated since 1938, Katz recalls the days when Chelsea had a large central European Jewish population. Most folks have moved on from the old neighborhood, but this terrific little bagel shop remains.

Traditionalists can still get plain, poppy seed, sesame, pumpernickel, and a half-dozen other varieties, but Katz achieved a certain culinary notoriety for inventing the pizza bagel in the early 1970s. So instead of picking up some lox or cream cheese for a schmear, you can take home the pizza bagels and bake for 10 minutes. It's a happy mixed marriage.

Maria's Pastry Shop, 46 Cross St., North End, Boston, MA 02113; (617) 523-1196; mariaspastry.com; Bakery; T: Haymarket. You can follow the change of the seasons by checking out the specialties in this storefront bakery: *pignolata* (frosted fried dough) for Ash Wednesday; marzipan lambs and ricotta pies with rice for Easter; "Bones of the Dead" cookies for All Souls Day in November; fruit-filled pies for Thanksgiving; and panettone and mustaccioli spice cookies for Christmas. Of course, on any day you can enjoy a fresh-filled cannoli, a slice of rum cake, or an almond or anise biscotti.

Mike's Pastry, 300 Hanover St., North End, Boston, MA 02113; (617) 742-3050; mikespastry.com; Bakery; T: Haymarket. Sometimes it seems that every other person on the sidewalk is carrying a blue and white box from Mike's Pastry. The North End's largest and most famous bakery meets the demand with no fewer than 17 flavors of cannoli (including pistachio, espresso, strawberry, and pecan caramel) and a range of cupcakes, cookies, brownies, and cakes. Macaroon flavors include almond, raspberry, apricot, green cherry, and red nut. If you are lucky, you might be able to grab one of the small tables and enjoy your treat in the shop rather than at home.

Modern Pastry, 257 Hanover St., North End, Boston, MA 02113; (617) 523-3783; modernpastry.com; Bakery; T: Haymarket. You'll find a full array of cakes, cookies, cannoli, biscotti, and breads made from Old World recipes at this North End stalwart that has been in the same family for three generations. But locals line up for the shop's *torrone,* often made by octogenarian Giovanni Picariello. He combines sugar, honey, nuts, and egg whites into a nougat-like treat. It's available in a variety of flavors, including peanut butter, chocolate, caramel, and espresso, as well as the family's secret-recipe vanilla *torrone* with roasted almonds.

Monica's Mercato, 130 Salem St., North End, Boston, MA 02113; (617) 742-4101; monicasboston.com; Grocery; T: Haymarket. This small storefront is a popular place at lunchtime for meatball or grilled chicken subs and equally busy in the early evening for its heat-and-eat prepared meals, including stuffed peppers or tomatoes, baked stuffed eggplant, meatballs, tomato sauce, and a variety of homemade pastas. Monica's also has a good selection of meats and cheeses. A couple of the more unusual items in the deli case are a *sopressata* (cured dry salami) handmade in New York and a delicious black truffle pecorino cheese from Sardinia.

Mangia! Mangia!

One whiff of garlic and olive oil wafting from restaurant doors in the North End tells you that the district is among the best-established Italian communities in the country. To find out where the locals buy their goods, sign up for the North End Market Tour, a half day of walking and tasting with Italian food expert Michele Topor. She's on a first-name basis with all the shopowners, who will almost certainly offer you samples of prosciutto and salami, mozzarella and ricotta, biscotti and amaretti, and bread hot from the oven. The three-hour tours are offered Wednesday, Friday, and Saturday. Reservations are essential. See Topor's recipe for **Insalata di Pasta Arrabbiata** on p. 427.

Michele Topor's Boston Food Tours, (617) 523-6032; bostonfoodtours.com. Tickets must be purchased in advance from Zerve: zerve.com/MicheleTopor/BCMT.

North End Fish—Mercato del Mare, 99 Salem St., North End, Boston, MA 02113; (857) 362-7477; northendfish.com; Fishmonger; T: Haymarket. The two owners of this boutique fish store quit their corporate gigs to sell fish in the North End, and they've transformed a semi-subterranean storefront on Salem Street into a bright show-case of both the local catch and select imports. Prices are good, cooking recommendations are spot-on, and Chef Bo is always slaving away in the front window rolling, assembling, and cutting some of the prettiest sushi we've ever seen. He'll even roll with brown rice on request. The shop validates parking at the Parcel 7 garage (next to Haymarket), letting you park up to 3 hours for just $1.

J. Pace & Son, 42 Cross St., North End, Boston, MA 02113; (617) 227-9673; jpaceandson.com; Grocery/Sandwich Shop; T: Haymarket. Pace has always been one of the North End's best sources for dried pasta in about a zillion shapes and from a dozen or more Italian and American manufacturers. It's the ideal spot to find tiny soup pasta as well as monster shells for stuffing and baking. At midday, though, Pace turns into a sandwich and pasta shop, offering a range of cold-cut and hot subs as well as plates of pasta, roasted meats, and eggplant or chicken Parm to go or to eat at the tables now occupying half the space.

A. Parziale's Bakery, 80 Prince St., North End, Boston, MA 02113; (617) 523-6368; parzialebakery .com; Bakery; T: Haymarket. A little off the beaten path, it's worth stopping in to pay homage to the shop that claims to have introduced pizza to Boston. The bakery was founded in 1907 by Joe and Anna Parziale and is now run by the third generation of their family. After you've sampled a slice, you can pick up a loaf of raisin walnut bread, beautiful knotted rolls, or an apple or raspberry turnover. Parziale's also sells its pizza dough if you want to make your own pie.

Polcari's Coffee, 105 Salem St., North End, Boston, MA 02113; (617) 227-0786; polcariscoffee.com; Grocery; T: Haymarket. "We've been here since 1932," says Nicky LaBonte as he points out the big coffee bins that are even older than the store. "Back then we sold only black, brown, and mixed coffees." Today Polcari's offers about 50 types of coffee, along with 25 teas, more than 100 herbs and spices, and a variety of nuts and pastas. Founder Anthony Polcari's house blend of dark and light roast coffee beans remains the sentimental choice, but the smoky dark Italian roast is the most popular. Beans are still weighed on the same scale that has been used since Polcari set up shop. Polcari's no longer roasts on premises, but they will grind beans for you—getting the perfect espresso grind that's almost impossible to replicate on home equipment. "The cash register is fairly new," says LaBonte. "It's only about 60 years old."

Salem True Value Hardware Store, 89 Salem St., North End, Boston, MA 02113; (617) 523-4759; Housewares; T: Haymarket. This well-stocked hardware store demonstrates its allegiance to its neighborhood by stocking just about any hand or electric kitchen appliance you could possibly need to whip up an Italian meal. Just turn left when you enter the door and you'll find pasta machines, pasta drying racks, gnocchi boards, ravioli stamps, pizza stones, food mills, table-mounted cheese graters, and fruit and vegetable strainers. That's not to mention the espresso makers, pitchers for frothing milk, espresso and cappuccino cups, cannoli forms, and pizelle bakers. And if the thought of a wonderful meal inspires you to redecorate, you can pick up a can of paint for your dining room while you're at it.

Salumeria Italiana, 151 Richmond St., North End, Boston, MA 02109; (617) 523-8743; salumeriaitaliana.com; Grocery; T: Haymarket. "That'll be $10," jokes one of the counter men after he lifts the bell jar off some white truffles to let us take a sniff. Such seasonal treats are a big part of the business at this gourmet shop where many North End chefs shop. But even when truffles aren't in season, SI has all manner of imported sausages as well as the key grating cheeses (Grana Padano, Parmigiana Reggiano, pecorino Romano, Asiago, Montasio . . .), imported canned tomatoes, pastas, and even packets of salt-packed capers. It's a good place to pick up speck, the wonderful smoked ham from the Alto-Adige region of Italy on the border with Austria.

Sulmona Meat Market, 32 A Parmenter St., North End, Boston, MA 02113; (617) 742-2791; Butcher; T: Haymarket. Buying meat at Sulmona is nothing like getting plastic-wrapped meat at the super-market. Very little if any meat is displayed in this shop because everything is cut to order, trimmed down from whole carcasses. You discuss your needs with one of the butchers and he makes recom-mendations. This may require hauling out primal and subprimal cuts to show you what he's proposing to cut. When you've decided, it will be cut, trimmed, and tied to order—even boned if you like. Alternatively, you can also walk in and ask for a pound of chuck and have it ground on the spot. Most meat is USDA prime (not a grade you'll see in supermarkets), and Sulmona either carries or can get virtually any meat, including obscure wild game. Cash only.

Wine Bottega, 341 Hanover St., North End, Boston, MA 02113; (617) 227-6607; thewinebottega.com; Wine, Beer & Spirits; T: Haymarket. This shop has its work cut out for it to compete with **V. Cirace** (see p. 38), but in truth they are complementary. Wine Bottega is tiny and quirky, choosing to carry a lot of extremely well-made wines from small producers all over the world. We appreciate that they not only carry Manzanilla sherries, but also have a selection that goes beyond La Gitana. The staff is deeply knowledgeable (unlike another place where a staff member, when asked what the store's specialty was, answered "wine") and can talk intelligently about whether a given producer makes traditional wine for the region or has embraced modern techniques. They seem to know the backstory on every bottle. Free weekly tastings are held in the cellar.

Zume's Coffee House, 223 Main St., Charlestown, Boston, MA 02129; (617) 242-0038; Coffee Shop; T: Community College. With pastries from the **Danish Pastry House** (see p. 374), hot breakfast food, and cool sandwiches like the cranberry chicken walnut salad with sliced cucumber and red leaf lettuce, this laid-back room is a perfect spot to hang out. The espresso is top-notch, the Wi-Fi signal is strong, and all the chairs, couches, and ottomans are overstuffed leather.

Farmers' Markets

Charlestown Farmers' Market, Thompson Square at Main and Austin Streets, Charlestown. Wed from 2 to 7 p.m., July through late Oct.

Chelsea Farmers' Market, Chelsea Square, Chelsea. Sat from 10 a.m. to 2 p.m., July through Oct.

East Boston Farmers' Market, Central Square, East Boston. Thurs from 3 to 7 p.m., early July through late Oct.

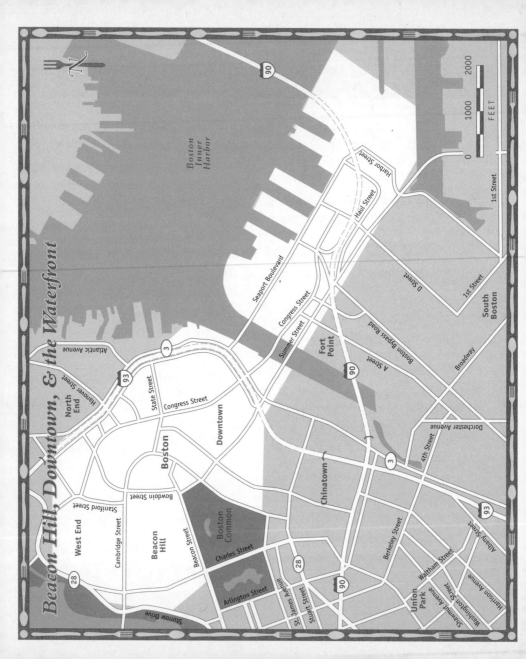

Beacon Hill, Downtown, & the Waterfront

N

Boston Inner Harbor

FEET
0   1000   2000

North End

Hanover Street

Atlantic Avenue

90

3

93

State Street

Congress Street

Boston
Downtown

Staniford Street
Bowdoin Street

Cambridge Street

West End

28

Beacon Street

Beacon Hill

Charles Street

Boston Common

Storrow Drive

Arlington Street

St. James Avenue

Stuart Street

28

90

Chinatown

Berkeley Street

Waltham Street

Union Park

Shawmut Avenue
Washington Street
Harrison Avenue

Albany Street

93

3

Dorchester Avenue

4th Street

Broadway

South Boston

1st Street

1st Street

D Street

A Street

Boston Bypass Road

90

Fort Point

Summer Street

Congress Street

Seaport Boulevard

Haul Street

Harbor Street

Beacon Hill, Downtown & the Waterfront

This chapter spans Boston from one of its oldest areas to one of its newest. Beacon Hill took shape at the end of the 18th century and became the home of Boston's codfish aristocracy, the monied class lampooned by Oliver Wendell Holmes as Boston Brahmins. Despite the presence of the statehouse, Beacon Hill remains intensely residential, filled with restaurateurs and purveyors who cater to the carriage trade. Yet steps across ancient Boston Common, modern mercantile Boston begins. The series of parallel streets that connect the Common to Washington Street have seen an influx of bars and restaurants, leading to a designation as the Ladder District. Just downhill the towers of the Financial District rise with competing visions of greatness in steel and glass. In their shadows sit dozens of terrific lunch spots, the merchants (especially of fine wine and premium spirits) who cater to the inhabitants of corner offices, and a handful of exquisite restaurants suitable for celebrating a successful merger.

Boston's most famous tourist magnet is just across State Street from the money managers: Faneuil Hall Marketplace and Quincy Market. This historic market district (the docks used to come up to its edge) sports some of the oldest eateries in Boston—indeed, some of the oldest in the US. This part of the city used to be cordoned off from the harbor by a raised expressway that has since been buried underground. In its place is a cordon of parkland known as the Rose Kennedy Greenway. It provides the transition from bustling city to bustling waterfront and an arena for many food trucks.

The rim of Boston Harbor was ripe for development following the opening of the New England Aquarium in 1969, and the stretch from Long Wharf to Rowes Wharf evolved over the next 20 years. After the removal of the elevated Central Artery, developers looked across the Fort Point Channel to an otherwise industrial neighborhood pioneered by artists who had colonized old wool warehouse buildings in the 1980s. Since the beginning of the 21st century, development has accelerated so fast that no consensus has developed on the name for the new waterfront. Some call it Fort Point, others the South Boston Waterfront, and still others the Seaport District. City planners point to all kinds of evidence that the neighborhood has come together, but for us the tipping point comes when lots of good food becomes available. The neighborhood is suddenly replete with places where workers can buy breakfast and lunch and where they can kick back with a drink after work—or linger for a great dinner. The future is now.

Barking Crab, 88 Sleeper St., Waterfront, Boston, MA 02210; (617) 426-2722; barkingcrab.com; Seafood; $$; T: Courthouse (Silver Line). Nowhere in Boston will you get closer to the shoreline fish shack experience than at the Barking Crab, perched on the edge of Fort Point Channel. In fact, if you have a boat in Boston Harbor, you can tie up at the floating dock and walk up the ramp to dinner. Prices vary widely through the year with availability, but you can always count on local clams, oysters, mussels, and stuffed quahogs. It's unfortunate but true that many tourists gravitate to the formerly frozen Alaskan crab legs over the smaller and sweeter local Atlantic crabs, but BC tries to have them both, along with plenty of lobster. In the summer, when the local fishery gets into high gear, we like eating at the picnic tables in the open air, ordering the grilled catch of the day and a bucket of longnecks. It may not be Cape Cod, but it's a good facsimile.

Beacon Hill Bistro, 25 Charles St., Beacon Hill, Boston, MA 02114; (617) 723-1133; beaconhillhotel.com/bistro; French; $$$; T: Charles Street. Integrated with a small boutique hotel (Beacon Hill Hotel, naturally), this bistro is no mere hotel restaurant despite serving three meals per day. Breakfast service is aimed mainly at hotel guests, and the lunch menu is replete with American favorites, like a grilled sirloin burger or a chicken club sandwich. At night, though, the kitchen swaps baseball hat for beret with dishes like roasted cod with a potato-apple mille-feuille, roasted monkfish with hen-of-the-woods mushrooms and steamed mussels, or cassoulet with confit duck leg and pork sausage. House-made charcuterie and fresh oysters are available nightly as starters.

Bin 26 Enoteca, 26 Charles St., Beacon Hill, Boston, MA 02114; (617) 723-5939; bin26.com; Italian; $$$; T: Charles Street. The high-tech wine system at this charmingly modern and surprisingly casual Beacon Hill restaurant means that you can get about 70 of Bin 26's 300 wines by the glass, making it a terrific place to learn about wine. Selections are skewed to Italian but cover the globe. Many diners/drinkers prefer to order small plates of antipasti while tasting several wines. Appetizer plates range from mozzarella wrapped in smoky speck on grilled eggplant to hot foie gras with pureed white beans, green beans, and potato salad. Pasta courses are reasonable and imaginative. The cocoa tagliatelle with porcini mushroom ragù, for example, is seasoned with nepitella, a fresh Italian herb that tastes like a cross between mint and oregano. The kitchen does a wonderful interpretation of the signature fish stew of Livorno, *cacciucco,* using hake from the Gulf of Maine. If you're craving a Barolo to drink, ask for the Friuli-style wild boar goulash with polenta.

BiNA Osteria, 581 Washington St., Ladder District, Boston, MA 02111; (617) 956-0888; binaboston.com; Italian; $$$; T: Chinatown/Downtown Crossing/Boylston. With Chef Will Foden at the helm, BiNA has found its niche with fresh market-driven, contemporary Italian food served at the edge of Chinatown. The first-course pastas are particularly strong. One of our favorites is a dish of chestnut-flour pasta rolled thin and cut randomly into "rags," or *stracci,* then served with a mushroom ragù and a truffled sheep's milk cheese. Foden also does a terrific Puglian dish of pasta tossed with clams, sea urchins, hot peppers, and roasted tomatoes. The *secondi,* or meat and fish dishes, are similarly simple, whether they're braised pork cheeks with polenta, or a grilled whole fish wrapped in escarole and accompanied by grilled lemon. The lunch menu is very similar to the dinner menu, but with smaller portions and lower prices.

Blue, Inc., 131 Broad St., Downtown, Boston, MA 02110; (617) 737-1777; blueincboston.com; New American; $$–$$$; T: Aquarium. This Greenway/Financial District upstart is named for the color of Chef Jason Santos's hair. Santos is a mad scientist who loves to play with the tools of so-called molecular gastronomy, delighting in serving a liquid nitrogen salsa that smolders on the plate or an orange gel that turns into noodles when it hits hot broth. Probably the best way to ease into the cuisine is to drink at the bar and order from the "bucket list" that includes treats like rosemary and sea salt kettle corn, pretzel roll pizza, fresh cinnamon donuts, a liquid nitrogen milkshake, or truffle and Gouda tater tots.

Think of the food as the kind of bistro fare you'd expect in the

staff kitchen at Cirque du Soleil. So the braised Berkshire pork belly comes with crunchy barbecue grits and a poached pear and Gorgonzola salad. The signature duck confit is glazed with honey and hoisin sauce and served with a dish composed of sticky rice, mango, cashews, and coconut milk.

Bond Restaurant/Lounge, Langham Boston Hotel, 250 Franklin St., Downtown, Boston, MA 02110; (617) 956-8765; bondboston .com; New American; $$; T: State. Bond has to be the most staggeringly beautiful casual dining room in Boston, and it has a dress code to match: "Dress to impress." Lodged in the handsome Renaissance revival former Federal Reserve building, Bond caters to the Financial District money managers, stock traders, and arbitrage hawks—and to the guests of the luxury hotel. Lunch is the busier meal, featuring the likes of a bowl of clam chowder with a small Maine lobster roll, or a maple and chile grilled chicken BLT. Bond serves a lovely London-style afternoon tea (a very civilized way to do business), complete with scones and Devonshire cream; sandwiches of English cucumber, farmer's cheese, and dill; and a large selection of hot or iced teas. The dinner plates are more surprising, including poutine with duck gravy, fried calamari, and potato and cheese pierogi—some of the most upscale bar food in Boston. Dinner dissolves into cocktails, and more cocktails. See Executive

Pastry Chef Jed Hackney's recipe for **Chocolate Croissant Bread Pudding,** p. 437.

Cafe de Boston, 75 Federal St., Downtown, Boston, MA 02110; (617) 482-1006; cafedeboston.com; Mediterranean; $; T: State. "We have 20 cooks who make everything fresh every day. Nothing comes from a can," says Ashley Gauvin, Cafe de Boston's catering manager. That's a tall order for this buffet-style breakfast and lunch spot that focuses on healthy Mediterranean dishes. Daily soups might include minted red lentil or chicken lemon, while the cold meze bar might offer artichoke salad, zucchini fritters, and spinach pie. Daily hot entrees could range from chicken stuffed with feta and spinach to stuffed peppers with ground beef, Turkish-style kebabs, or an all-American hamburger. After such a healthy lunch, there's no reason not to indulge in some Italian gelato, a mini cream puff, or a piece of baklava flown in from Turkey. See Chef Sezar Yavuz's recipe for **Mercimek Corbasi (Red Lentil Soup)** on p. 430.

Daily Catch, 2 Northern Ave., Waterfront, Boston, MA 02210; (617) 772-4400; thedailycatch.com; Seafood/Italian; $$; T: Courthouse (Silver Line). The **North End Daily Catch** (see p. 20) has been a dining fixture since 1973. This 21st-century branch in the Moakley Courthouse right on the Harborwalk brings the simple menu of Sicilian seafood and pasta to one of the freshest outdoor spots in

Sampling the Sweet Side of the City

You can hop aboard an Old Town Trolley for a tour of Boston's historic sites any time, but the **Boston Chocolate Tour** is offered only on Saturday from January through April. Guides touch on the city's culinary history as the trolleys travel between chocolate tasting spots. Highlights include Boston cream pie at the Omni Parker House Hotel, where it was invented, and the lavish **Chocolate Bar,** an all-you-can-eat buffet of chocolate desserts, at the Langham Boston Hotel. For information, contact (617) 269-7010; trolleytours .com. The Chocolate Bar is located in the hotel's Cafe Fleuri on Saturday from September through June. For information, contact (617) 451-1900, ext. 7125; boston.langhamhotels .com/restaurants/chocolate-bar.htm.

the city. Even if it's raining, the outdoor tables sit safely under the building's overhang so you can watch boats in the harbor and admire the Financial District architecture while chowing down on calamari and linguine or a plate of monkfish Marsala. There's indoor dining as well, should the weather seem unwelcoming.

Figs, 42 Charles St., Beacon Hill, Boston, MA 02114; (617) 742-3447; toddenglish.com; Italian; $$; T: Charles Street. Among the pizzas available at this Beacon Hill outpost of the Charlestown original (p. 22) is Isabelle's, named for Chef Todd English's daughter.

It features country ham, aged provolone cheese, fresh asparagus, and sweet onions. If you're curious about more of Isabelle's food preferences, check out the cupcake shop, **Isabelle's Curly Cakes** (see p. 85), across the street.

The Hungry I, 71½ Charles St., Beacon Hill, Boston, MA 02114; (617) 227-3524; hungryiboston.com; French; $$$; T: Charles Street. Peter Ballarin, the executive chef and owner of this "garden"-level restaurant, is a great believer in tradition. For more than a quarter century, the Hungry I has been serving unapologetic old-school fine French food in an intimate, dare we say, romantic setting that glows golden from candlelight. Ballarin's most popular dish—on the menu since the early days—is a black-pepper venison. Thin slices are peppered and sautéed, flambéed with a splash of cognac, and finished with red wine and sour cream. Hardly a main dish ever appears naked, that is, without a classic sauce. The three-course Sunday brunch is a very popular option for diners who find romance in the daylight as well.

Kingston Station, 25 Kingston St., Downtown, Boston, MA 02111; (617) 482-6282; kingstonstation.com; New American; $$; T: Downtown Crossing. Something of a sleeper, this outstanding little bar with a smart, reasonably priced bistro menu is tucked down a side street off Downtown Crossing. It's only a few minutes' stroll from the Opera House, which makes Kingston Station a good spot for pre-performance dining. The bar's cocktails hark back to the era when a drink was supposed to relax your neck muscles and pique your appetite. The Partly Cloudy accomplishes both with Brugal *añejo* rum, ginger beer, and fresh ginger. It goes well with the truffle fries appetizer (fries, truffle oil, gruyère cheese), which should prepare you for a plate of cider-braised pork belly with polenta, roasted duck with potato and mushrooms, or seared scallops with potato gnocchi. Kingston Station also serves excellent soup and sandwich combos at lunch along with **George Howell Coffee** (see p. 377) and MEM Tea, in case you're skipping wine in favor of a productive afternoon.

Kinsale Irish Pub & Restaurant, 2 Center Plaza, Downtown, Boston, MA 02108; (617) 742-5577; classicirish.com/kinsale-home .php; Irish; $–$$; T: Government Center. This favorite lunchtime haunt of Government Center workers was designed and built in Ireland, then shipped over and assembled here—which explains what an old-fashioned Irish pub is doing in a modernist office building. Sandwiches, soups, and salads are the lunchtime mainstays, including a selection of burgers that runs the gamut from beef to salmon. Evening main dishes veer toward hearty pub fare, like a classic Irish stout beef stew, bangers and mash with onion gravy, beef stroganoff, and crumb-crusted baked haddock. Brunch dishes on the weekends include a full Irish breakfast, several variants of eggs Benedict, and a slew of omelets.

KO Prime, 90 Tremont St., Downtown, Boston, MA 02108; (617) 772-0202; koprimeboston.com; Steak House; $$$–$$$$; T: Park Street. When Ken Oringer, the man behind **Clio** (p. 97) and **Toro** (p. 149), tackles steak, you do not get your grandpa's steak house. This glamorous dining room in the Nine Zero Hotel remains true to tradition by fairly oozing prestige and power, but the menu is full of invention and imagination. The appetizer menu, for example, offers escargot as a fricassee with tiny carrots, mushrooms, and salsify. The beef tartare is Kobe beef accompanied by roasted jalapeño aioli and a deep-fried duck egg in place of the conventional raw chicken's egg. Oringer and company grow the salad greens on the restaurant's rooftop, and get most of the other veggies (in season) from small farms near Boston. The whole panoply of steaks is available, including a massive porterhouse for two, but so is a more reasonable Kobe burger with foie gras, crisply fried skate, and even a seafood bouillabaisse with Moroccan-style lamb sausage. Some of the steakhouse classics survive intact (how do you improve on oysters Rockefeller?), while others are brilliantly reinvented, like the corned beef tongue hash with a poached duck egg.

Lala Rokh, 97 Mount Vernon St., Beacon Hill, Boston, MA 02108; (617) 720-5511; lalarokh.com; Persian; $$; T: Charles Street. Persian cuisine is one of the world's oldest and, many chefs argue, most influential. You can get a good introduction to the subtle and elegant flavors at Lala Rokh, where owners Azita-Bina Seibel and Babak Bina share the homestyle Persian cooking they learned from their mother. You might begin with *ash,* a thick soup flavored with spinach, beans, tomatoes, dried plums, and the juice of unripened grapes. One of the most popular main courses is Baghla Pollo, a lamb shank braised in tomato sauce and served with a mixture of rice, dill, and fava beans. The exotic food and setting make Lala Rokh a good choice for a romantic evening.

Legal Harborside, 270 Northern Ave., Waterfront, Boston, MA 02210; (617) 477-2900; legalseafoods.com; Seafood; $–$$$$; T: World Trade Center (Silver Line). The new flagship complex of the Legal Sea Foods group returns to its roots with an old-fashioned fish market, an oyster bar, and a casual restaurant with the option of takeout on the first floor; a fine dining venue on the second level; and a rocking bar with seafood bar bites on the top level. Each overlooks Boston Harbor. The fine dining includes unusual dishes like sautéed abalone served with lemon risotto and brussels sprouts seasoned with *guanciale.* Caviar service is available, and even the seared foie gras starter is served with an unexpected chocolate brioche, cherries, and candied ginger.

Legal Sea Foods Long Wharf, 255 State St., Waterfront, Boston, MA 02109; (617) 742-5300; legalseafoods.com; Seafood; $$–$$$; T: Aquarium. Somewhat incongruously situated steps from the New

England Aquarium, this branch of the chain specializes in serving what we think of as Legal's greatest hits menu: baked scrod, crab cakes, wood-grilled mahimahi, a fisherman's platter of fried seafood, and a sautéed Atlantic salmon fillet. Because it's in the heart of the tourist district, this location also serves gallons and gallons of Legal's clam chowder and does a bang-up lunch business in lobster rolls, crab rolls, and tuna burgers.

Legal Test Kitchen, 225 Northern Ave., Waterfront, Boston, MA 02210; (617) 330-7430; ltkbarandkitchen.com; Seafood; $$; T: World Trade Center (Silver Line). Right across Northern Avenue from **Legal Harborside** (see p. 60), LTK makes up for the diminished view with a sassier room and a menu that strikes the midpoint between the fried food of Harborside's Level 1 and the white-tablecloth dining of Level 2. Minimalists can simply pick a fish (usually scallops, scrod, rainbow trout, shrimp, Atlantic salmon, mahimahi, or tuna), a preparation (grilled or baked), and some sauces and sides. The more adventurous can opt for LTK's dishes of the moment, which can range from mixed shellfish with a saffron tomato broth on pasta to truffled lobster mac and cheese. LTK also features fish dishes from around the world in a changing rotation.

Mantra, 52 Temple Place, Ladder District, Boston, MA 02111; (617) 542-8111; mantrarestaurant.com; Indian; $$$; T: Park Street. When this pioneer of the Ladder District first opened, all anyone could talk about was the over-the-top decor (including a chain-mail curtain to divide the room and crushed ice in the urinals). That was too bad, because the French-Indian fusion food is really interesting. The novelty of the design has worn off, but the fusion food is still a big attraction in the evening, when such specials as spice-marinated halibut with turmeric and red chile oil or sesame-crusted pork tenderloin with grilled beets are on the menu. If you're curious about the look and want to visit on a budget, go for the daily all-you-can-eat fusion-free Indian lunch buffet.

Menton, 354 Congress St., Waterfront, Boston, MA 02210; (617) 737-0099; mentonboston.com; New American; $$$$; T: South Station. It's hard to find enough superlatives to describe Barbara Lynch's fine dining operation on Fort Point Channel named for a French Riviera town on the Italian border halfway between Nice and Sanremo. The menu formats are limited to a four-course prix fixe or a seven course tasting menu, with or without wine pairings, and the attention to tiny details justifies the prices. Lynch was named a Relais & Châteaux Grand Chef in 2012, the only woman in North America with the title, and when you start deconstructing the dishes, it's easy to see why. For example, she has always been a fan of langoustines and serves them wrapped in *kataifi* (like shredded phyllo dough) with fresh local Greek yogurt from **Sophia's Greek**

Pantry (see p. 354), honey, and a homemade French-Indian curry powder. Her foie gras terrine is served with chewy, partially dehydrated segments of grapefruit and pomelo with warm brioche and a pine-nut brittle. Texture and balance are important in every dish, but that doesn't stop her from presenting bold plates like roast lamb with olives and black garlic. This is luxury dining at its best in Boston.

Meritage, Boston Harbor Hotel, 70 Rowes Wharf, Waterfront, Boston, MA 02110; (617) 439-3995; meritagetherestaurant.com; New American; $$$; T: Aquarium/South Station. It is almost as if the **Boston Wine Festival** (see p. 416) continues all year long at Chef Daniel Bruce's fine dining restaurant in the Boston Harbor Hotel. Named for the term applied to Bordeaux-style blends of American wines, Meritage divides its menu by wine styles rather than courses in the meal. If you're drinking a spicy red (a Nebbiolo de Langhe, or a Gigondas), for example, Bruce offers blackberry and five-spice-rubbed duck with fennel and leek ravioli, or cocoa-rubbed ostrich fillet over baby brussels sprouts. With a light white (Pinot Grigio or Sancerre), he might suggest pan-seared cod with tiny clams and chorizo, or pan-fried soft-shell crab with a salsa of tomato and asparagus. Every plate is available in small or full-size portions, and since many of the wines are available by the glass, it's possible to mix and match a complex feast.

Mooo . . . , 15 Beacon St., Beacon Hill, Boston, MA 02108; (617) 670-2515; mooorestaurant.com; Steak House/New American; $$$;

T: Park Street. As the house restaurant for the luxe XV Beacon Hotel, Mooo . . . serves all meals every day and brunch on the weekends. It is a surprisingly charming lunch spot with a classy yet affordable menu of burgers, grilled sandwiches, a lobster roll, and even a small steak with truffled fries. Of course, getting in can be hard. If you're seated in the bar area, ask for a table farthest from the Mooo . . . entrance to avoid the draft. At dinnertime the menu lowers the pitch of its voice to become Executive Chef Jamie Mammano's upscale modernization of the classic steak house. Since Mammano loves small plates, there's no shortage of great appetizers, whether your preference runs to sushi-grade tuna tartare; broiled oysters with spinach, bacon, and hollandaise; or simply baby beets with Vermont goat cheese. Steaks, of course, are the main event, and each one comes with something of a pedigree (grass- and grain-fed all-natural sirloin from Painted Hills Farm in Minnesota, or for four times the price, sirloin of Australian Kobe beef). In marvelously recherché style, the steaks are all served with roasted garlic and bone marrow butter.

No Name Restaurant, 15½ Fish Pier, Waterfront, Boston, MA 02210; (617) 423-2705; nonamerestaurant.com; Seafood; $–$$; T: World Trade Center (Silver Line). Boston's first "hidden secret" restaurant (and listed as such in every guidebook), No Name used to be where folks in the fish trade ate lunch and remains a reliable spot for fried and broiled fish and steamed shellfish. We've always been partial to the fish chowder, which is what fishermen used to call "trim" chowder—full of all the pieces too good to waste that had been trimmed off bigger fish. The chowder varies with the catch, but that's half the fun of a real fish restaurant—it's as seasonal as a vegetable garden.

No. 9 Park, 9 Park St., Beacon Hill, Boston, MA 02108; (617) 742-9991; no9park.com; French/Italian; $$$$; T: Park Street. This first restaurant by Barbara Lynch has evolved over the years from a classy spot where high rollers and lawmakers ate lunch to an elegant dinner-only fine dining restaurant in the shadow of the statehouse. The dining room menu is available as a three-course prix fixe or a la carte, or diners have the option of a seven-course chef's tasting menu. This food is simpler and less baroque than Lynch's dishes at **Menton** (p. 62). Flavors are clean and bold—bacon-wrapped monkfish served with Himalayan red rice, sweet potato, and black trumpet mushrooms, for example. And she's not above injecting a little Boston humor into a dish. Seared foie gras is served with quince, Boston brown bread, and molasses—a historically appropriate combo for the Beacon Hill Brahmins whose ancestors engaged in the Triangle Trade (in this case, the trading of African slaves for Caribbean molasses, then rum from the molasses to buy more slaves).

Paramount, 44 Charles St., Beacon Hill, Boston, MA 02114 (617) 720-1152; paramountboston.com; Casual American; $-$$; T: Charles Street. This casual eatery has been feeding the rich and poor of Beacon Hill since 1937. Breakfast service is often a cheerful madhouse, as everyone lines up to order eggs, pancakes, waffles, and all their permutations. Steam rises and the smell of hot bacon permeates the air. (Order first, *then* sit—that's the house rule.) The jostling scene is repeated at lunch, except that everyone is ordering sandwiches, salads, and burgers—especially burgers. Those patties (beef, turkey, black bean, or salmon) stay on the evening menu, where they're joined by steak-frites, tacos (tuna, steak, or chicken), pasta Bolognese, and the all-American grill favorite, steak tips in barbecue sauce with mashed potatoes. The big difference in the evening is that the tables are set with nice linens, and waitstaff materialize to take orders and serve the food. Oddly, prices rise only a little. Unlike many diner-style eateries, the Paramount has wine and beer.

Petit Robert Central, 101 Arch St., Downtown, Boston, MA 02110; (617) 737-1777; petitrobertcentral.com; French; $$; T: Downtown Crossing. HGTV's Taniya Nayak did the interior design here, and she managed to re-create a Parisian brasserie in the heart of Downtown Crossing. Jacky Robert did the food, and he's made PR Central a bigger version of his other PR locations (see pp. 106, 144, and 213) without sacrificing the value and flavor of the food. The bar area here is big, and it fills up after work with wine-sippers. The tables and booths, however, can be quite intimate, in case you'd like to conduct a romantic tête-à-tête over plates of beef short rib Bourguignon, cassoulet, or hake fillet with baby clams, mussels, scallops, and shrimp. Bistro pricing ensures that Petit Robert Central is an excellent spot for pursuing romance without finance.

Pierrot Bistrot Français, 272 Cambridge St., Beacon Hill, Boston, MA 02114; (617) 725-8855; pierrotbistrot.com; French; $$; T: Charles Street. We confess to being suckers for a classic French bistro menu—even in a restaurant with clowns (Pierrot) on the walls. French-born Chef-Owner Pierre Sosnitsky at one time ran the dining room of Maison Robert (Boston's preeminent French restaurant for 30 years), so the dishes on the menu are authentic, from the house pâté to the onion soup gratinée to the *brandade de morue* (salt cod *brandade*). As with all restaurants that have long menus and small kitchens, the best meals are the daily specials, since they're put together from scratch. Pierrot is an utterly charming place to enjoy a croque monsieur or madame—or an endive salad with smoked duck—for lunch.

Radius, 8 High St., Downtown, Boston, MA 02110; (617) 426-1234; radiusrestaurant.com; New American; $$$–$$$; T: South Station. Decorated in the silvery color palette used by Rolls-Royce and Bentley for their automobiles, Radius radiates confidence, ease, and wealth. Billions of dollars are under management in nearby buildings, and the men and women who manage those funds often eat here, whether they're having a lobster BLT for lunch, a

Radius Manhattan (rye, Carpano Punt e Mes sweet vermouth, and a Luxardo Maraschino cherry) after work, or the 5-course tasting menu for dinner. Chef-Owner Michael Schlow is almost shockingly down to earth, so the food is playful and fun (including an interesting version of Peking duck) and the atmosphere is light. Despite the heavy-hitting clientele, one of the most popular spots in the house is the raised communal table where diners interact with one another. At the same time, you can have a more private table and expect the perfect and knowledgeable service that goes with dining in a restaurant consistently rated among the top 50 in the US.

Rowes Wharf Sea Grille, Boston Harbor Hotel, 70 Rowes Wharf, Waterfront, Boston, MA 02110; (617) 856-7744; roweswharfsea grille.com; Seafood; $$$; T: Aquarium/South Station. Chef Daniel Bruce, who also oversees **Meritage** (see p. 63), demonstrates why he keeps winning awards as hotel chef of the year. This bright contemporary restaurant looking out onto Boston Harbor serves imaginative fish dishes that are beautifully presented. Tuna tartare, for example, is tossed with white soy sauce and served with an electric-green mound of avocado puree and a toupée of microgreens. Caramelized jumbo sea scallops come with white and green asparagus and a cream of sweet corn. Pescaphobes eat well, too: Chicken, lamb, beef, and vegetarian options are always available. In nice weather you can dine outside on the water. As an especially nice perk, the hotel screens outdoor movies on select summer evenings.

Saus, 33 Union St., Downtown, Boston, MA 02108; (617) 248-8835; eatfrites.com; Belgian; $; T: Haymarket. The Lowlands are well represented by this snazzy casual spot that specializes in Belgian frites, or fries, to be eaten with dipping sauces that range from ketchup and white truffle oil to peanut butter, soy sauce, and chile paste. One of the best sandwiches to accompany those fries is a *frikandel,* a sausage-shaped mix of ground meat that is a popular Dutch street food. You can also order a beer-braised chicken breast sandwich or a vegetarian croquette served in pita bread. Wash it all down with a craft beer and save room for a Belgian waffle for dessert.

75 Chestnut, 75 Chestnut St., Beacon Hill, Boston, MA 02108; (617) 227-2175; 75chestnut.com; Traditional American; $$; T: Charles Street. Dining at 75 Chestnut is the next best thing to being invited to dinner in the Beacon Hill home of a really terrific cook. The room epitomizes gracious comfort and the food—shrimp cocktail, classic Caesar salad, beef stew, crab cakes—while not the most inventive, is nonetheless deeply satisfying. From September through June, 75 Chestnut also serves a popular Sunday brunch where you can count on traditional eggs Benedict. The restaurant also offers a number of specials during the week, such as Sunday Suppers and Sweet Tooth Tuesdays.

Silvertone, 69 Bromfield St., Downtown, Boston, MA 02108; (617) 338-7887; silvertonedowntown.com; Casual American; $–$$; T: Park Street. This subterranean gastropub takes its style cues from images of a Bakelite tube table radio sold by Sears & Roebuck in the early 1950s. The whole ebullient postwar Streamline style pops up at every turn, and while the prices aren't exactly on a par with the Eisenhower years, they're among the lowest in the city for food this good. American comfort food is big—you could get a grilled cheese sandwich and spicy tomato soup from late morning until late night, and mac and cheese is available with several optional toppings: peas, honey chile chicken, crispy bacon, or grilled steak. Meat loaf and mashed potatoes are served with (wait for it) . . . vegetable of the day. The lemon-thyme oven-roasted half chicken is a perennial favorite. After 4 p.m. the menu expands to include some larger, more ambitious main dishes, including a steak au poivre.

Sportello, 348 Congress St., Waterfront, Boston, MA 02210; (617) 737-1234; sportelloboston.com; Italian; $$–$$$; T: South Station. Tucked into the same building with Barbara Lynch's **Drink** (see p. 392) and **Menton** (see p. 62), Sportello is her vision of a 21st-century diner serving trattoria-inspired dishes and offering great take-out lunches from the bakery counter. In fact, the place is jammed on weekdays with local coders and artists loading up on the bargain set-price "lunchbox" of sandwich, drink, and chips. There are counter stools where you sit to eat luncheon plates, but it's hard to escape the jostle of the take-out crowd. The sit-down spots are better for dinner, when Lynch offers simple rustic fare like polenta with a choice of porcini, eggplant, or wild boar ragù; hand-rolled *strozzapreti* ("priest-choker") pasta with braised rabbit; or simple *bucatini* with pecorino Romano, Parmagiana-Reggiano, and black pepper (the Roman dish known as *bucatini cacio e pepe*).

Sultan's Kitchen, 116 State St., Downtown, Boston, MA 02109; (617) 570-9009; sultans-kitchen.com; Turkish; $; T: Aquarium. Chef-Owner Özcan Ozan's hummus, tabbouleh, and baba ghanoush are legendary among downtown office workers. They're all included on the meze *tabagi,* a platter that also adds stuffed grape leaves, feta cheese, and black olives. Ozan has several kinds of kebabs, but the most popular are the kofta kebabs of spiced ground lamb shaped into link sausages. For a special treat, order the *patlican iman bavildi*: a small baked eggplant stuffed with sautéed onion, garlic, tomatoes, and parsley. It's served cold with mixed greens and feta cheese.

Teatro, 177 Tremont St., Downtown, Boston, MA 02111; (617) 778-6841; teatroboston.com; Italian; $$; T: Boylston. One of the great spots for dinner before or after a Theater District show, Teatro produces contemporary revivals of Italian culinary classics. Four pizzas are available along with seven dishes using pasta made in-house. Pastas and the two risottos, by the way, are all available in appetizer or main dish portions. We're partial to the shells (*conchiglie*) with Maine lobster and Vermont butter, and the wild mushroom and truffle oil risotto. Probably the most interesting part of the menu is the antipasti, which range from simple but inspired truffled deviled eggs to a small hot dish of grilled octopus, sopressata sausage, and crispy potatoes. We're happy grazing on antipasti and drinking by the carafe from the excellent wine list.

Tia's on the Waterfront, 200 Atlantic Ave., Waterfront, Boston, MA 02110; (617) 227-0828; tiaswaterfront.com; Casual American/Seafood; $–$$$; T: Aquarium. Located on the Christopher Columbus Park side of Long Wharf, Tia's is a seasonal outdoor waterfront cafe and bar where you can enjoy anything from a burger or some steamed mussels to a charcoal-grilled swordfish steak or a baked stuffed lobster. It is perhaps the ideal place to nurse a bucket of steamed clams and successive bottles of Anheuser-Busch beers while reading a beach novel and enjoying the sunshine. Tia's also offers a kiddie menu for children 12 and younger—with a $4 surcharge if an adult wants the same thing. Open Apr through Oct.

Times Irish Pub & Restaurant, 112 Broad St., Downtown, Boston, MA 02110; (617) 357-8463; timesirishpub.com; Casual American/Irish; $; T: Aquarium. Billing itself as a "post-*Riverdance*" Irish pub, the Times has one of the most enviable outdoor spaces in the city, having waited out decades of construction and destruction for its porch on the Rose Kennedy Greenway. In typically Irish fashion, the Times has a good selection of Irish beers and whiskeys, and believes that people drink more if you feed them good food. Thus the menu is replete with burger variations, thick sandwiches like two variants of the Reuben, and comforting pub-grub main dishes like fish and chips, beef stew, chicken potpie, broiled scrod, and bangers and mash.

Toscano Restaurant, 47 Charles St., Beacon Hill, Boston, MA 02108; (617) 723-4090; toscanoboston.com; Italian; $$$; T: Charles Street. With dark woodwork and stained walnut floors, rich leather banquettes, and exposed stone and brick walls, Toscano is the perfect visual synthesis of Tuscan countryside and Beacon Hill propriety. Chef Andrew D'Alessandro has the touch to make it work, crafting delicious and tender potato gnocchi that he serves with the classic four-cheese sauce, braising his own Florentine-style duck, and grilling a double-thick bone-in pork chop to perfection. That same big oven also turns out terrific pizzas, including one topped with smoky Tyrolean speck, tomato, fresh mozzarella, and arugula. Wines are served by the bottle or the *quartino,* a sensible Italian pour of 250 ml, or one-third of a bottle.

Trade, 540 Atlantic Ave., Waterfront, Boston, MA 02210; (617) 451-1234; trade-boston.com; New American; $$–$$$; T: South Station. Located near the Federal Reserve Building and South Station, it's no wonder that this big, airy brasserie does such a land-rush business at lunchtime. The food is eclectic, bold, and well conceived and the place is so well run that you can squeeze in for a

real lunch (say, Arctic char with saffron quinoa or a flatbread topped with mushrooms, figs, Gorgonzola, sage pesto, and walnuts) and still get back to the office on time. Trade also flourishes in the evening as destination dining. (It must be a destination. The closest condos are across Fort Point Channel.) The restaurant is the brainchild of Jody Adams, but she keeps to her kitchen at **Rialto** (see p. 271) in Cambridge, and her former Sous-Chef Andrew Hebert leads the kitchen here. The site used to be Griffith Wharf, famous for the Boston Tea Party, and the "Trade" concept plays with the idea that spices and foodstuffs come from all over the world. Ironically, while the flavors represent global thinking, most of the ingredients are local. They're pulled together in Adams's signature style of a protein paired with a strongly flavored complement—seared chicken with burnt orange, dates, pistachios, and quinoa, for example, or grilled lobster with pickled artichoke aioli. Nobody will be throwing these taste treats into the harbor.

Umbria Prime, 295 Franklin St., Downtown, Boston, MA 02110; (617) 338-1000; umbriaprime.com; Steak House; $$$–$$$$; T: Aquarium. This Financial District location is precisely the right spot for a luxury-priced steak house serving dry-aged prime Angus beef. Chef Gianni Caruso augments that perfect meat with superb Umbrian pasta dishes (pappardelle with braised wild boar ragù, for example) and bold fish plates (swordfish grilled on the bone, grilled 2-pound lobsters). Most of the same dishes are available at lunchtime—all the better to seal a deal and go home early.

Wagamama, 1 Faneuil Hall, Quincy Market Building, Downtown, Boston, MA 02109; (617) 742-9242; wagamama.us; Asian; $; T: Haymarket. Modeled on Japanese ramen bars, this London-based chain has been hugely successful in feeding lots of people very quickly with hearty and healthy food—not a bad trick. Everything is cooked to order, resulting in staggered delivery times, and customers are encouraged to share. The nifty thing about Wagamama for families is that most kids like noodles, and adults can indulge in slightly more challenging fare like chicken teriyaki, which comes garnished with mixed leaves and red pickles.

Woodward at Ames, 1 Court St., Downtown, Boston, MA 02108; (617) 979-8201; woodwardatames.com; New American; $$$; T: State. Designed as a modern tavern for grown-ups, Woodward has a dining room (upstairs) and a drinking room (downstairs). Actually, both spaces have dining tables and a bar, but the raucous ground-level scene can interfere with enjoying the food, so head up to enjoy Mark Goldberg's contemporary American bistro food. He does serve the ubiquitous "brick chicken" but at least it comes with quinoa, potato, confit tomatoes, and parsley. But he also serves braised lamb breast (the fatty cut that includes the spare ribs) with greens and roasted squash. Even the small plates are interesting and just a little different from what you find elsewhere downtown. Why not begin a meal with roasted bone marrow with *fines herbes*, lemon, and pickled shallots? Or a plate of steak tartare with pickled beets and a fried quail egg?

Chart House, 60 Long Wharf, Waterfront, Boston, MA 02110; (617) 227-1576; chart-house.com; Traditional American; $$$; T: Aquarium. Ensconced in a 1760 structure on Long Wharf, the Chart House is redolent of old Boston in its shipping heyday. The food is not quite 18th century, but it is solidly 20th century, with coconut crunchy shrimp and macadamia-nut crusted mahimahi. The "New Wave Surf and Turf" consists of braised short ribs and a choice of scallops in ginger soy sauce or grilled citrus salmon. Despite the iconic location, the best dishes on the menu are prime rib and grilled steaks. Ask about the AARP discount if you're eligible.

Durgin-Park, 340 Faneuil Hall Marketplace, Downtown, Boston, MA 02109; (617) 227-2038; durgin-park.com; Traditional American; $–$$; T: Haymarket. Boston's quintessential Yankee dining room was famously established "before you were born," in the 1820s to feed the workers at Quincy Market (see below). With its red-and-white checked tablecloths and long communal tables, it's still the place to go for lively conversation and such time-honored food standbys as roast prime rib, Yankee pot roast, baked scrod, Boston baked beans, and baked Indian pudding. Diners are sometimes disappointed that the waitresses, while brisk and efficient, seem to lack the legendary surliness. "I've been here 20 years," Laura Seluta told us when we last visited, "and we have our moments."

Locke-Ober, 3 Winter Place, Downtown, Boston, MA 02108; (617) 542-1340; lockeober.com; Traditional American; $$$$; T: Park Street/Downtown Crossing. Founded in the late 19th century, Locke-Ober was for many years the most prestigious gourmet restaurant in Boston—the place where Boston Brahmins dined with their money managers. Absolutely redolent of old Boston, Locke-Ober can feel like a museum, with its Victorian decor and menu standards like the JFK Lobster Stew, broiled scrod, and calf's liver with sautéed onions and bacon. Meals are pricey, but Locke-Ober is one of a kind.

Quincy Market, Faneuil Hall Marketplace, Downtown, Boston, MA 02108; faneuilhallmarketplace.com; Eclectic; $–$$; T: Haymarket. To get an idea of the importance of food in the lives of early Bostonians, you need look no further than Quincy Market. The elegant granite structure was built in the Greek revival style with huge columns at each end and a massive dome on top. Completed in 1836, it served as the city's central market for meat, fish, produce, and dairy products. Today it is the literal centerpiece of Faneuil Hall Marketplace, which opened in 1976 and inspired similar "festival marketplaces" around the country. True to its roots, 535-foot-long Quincy Market is now packed with food vendors, and claims to be the largest food hall in New England. We can't vouch for the claim, but we can certainly attest to the wide variety of foods available, from New England standards such as lobster rolls, clam chowder, and stuffed quahogs to international specialties that those early Bostonians never even dreamed of: Thai spring rolls, Greek spanakopita, Indian lamb vindaloo, Mexican enchiladas, Japanese chicken teriyaki, and more. There's also Italian gelato, lots of ice cream, and other sweets.

Union Oyster House, 41 Union St., Downtown, Boston, MA 02108; (617) 227-2750; unionoysterhouse.com; Traditional American/ Seafood; $$$; T: Haymarket. Claiming to be America's oldest restaurant (established in 1826), Union Oyster House can claim many famous customers, from Daniel Webster (who drank brandy and water with his daily plates of raw oysters) to John F. Kennedy, who used to read the Sunday papers in a booth on the second floor. The best seats in the house, however, are on the horseshoe oyster bar at the entrance. The oysters come from many different spots, and you can spend a happy afternoon trying them all. Tourists are always impressed by the heaping servings of the seafood plates.

Specialty Stores, Markets & Producers

Al's State Street Cafe, 112 State St., Downtown, Boston, MA 02109; (617) 720-5555; alscafes.com; Sandwich Shop; T: Aquarium. At lunchtime the sidewalks are crowded with people carrying bags from this popular sub shop and you can easily pick out the

light eaters (with the 10-inch-long bag)
from those with hearty enough appetites
to devour a 16-inch sub. In either case,
choices range from steak and peppers or
chicken salad to eggplant Parmesan or the Italian's Italian with
mortadella, Genoa salami, sweet capicola, and provolone cheese. A
10-inch sub with soda and chips is a particularly good deal.

Barrington Coffee, 346 Congress St., Waterfront, Boston, MA
02210; (857) 277-1914; barringtoncoffee.com; Coffee Shop; T:
South Station. We got hooked on Barrington Coffee when it started
out in the early 1990s in Great Barrington, Massachusetts. Gregg
Charbonneau and Barth Anderson are coffee fanatics who buy from
small farms and cooperatives around the world and customize their
roasting to bring out the best qualities in each green coffee crop.
Their coffee shop at Fort Point Channel brews espresso drinks and
serves a few pastries to go with them. Best yet, it sells a limited
selection of the company's vacuum-packed roasted beans.

Beacon Hill Chocolates, 91 Charles St., Beacon Hill, Boston,
MA 02114; (617) 725-1900; beaconhillchocolates.com; Chocolatier;
T: Charles Street. Owner and chocolate lover Paula Barth has
assembled a carefully curated selection of artisan chocolates from
greater Boston and around the world—all of which can be tucked
into unique gift boxes featuring vintage Boston scenes. Barth also
created the shop's signature Caramel Sushi, a swirl of marshmallow
and caramel dipped in milk or dark chocolate. Other unusual treats

include the sticky bun of cinnamon ganache with caramel and candied pecans, or another ganache flavored with olive oil and sea salt and covered with dark chocolate. Purists can stick with the BHC, a luscious chunk of single-origin dark chocolate.

Beacon Hill Wine & Spirits, 63 Charles St., Beacon Hill, Boston, MA 02114; (617) 742-8571; beaconhillwine.com; Wine, Beer & Spirits; T: Charles Street. Peruse the shelves of this venerable wine merchant and you'd think it was still the 19th century and Bostonians were still drinking little except claret and port. Those categories, in fact, are the strengths of Beacon Hill Wine & Spirits, and the recherché concentration makes for some delightful finds in the secondary lines of some Bordeaux producers. We almost expect the current owners to discover dusty bottles of Madeira in the cellar.

BiNA Alimentari, 571 Washington St., Ladder District, Boston, MA 02111; (617) 357-0888; binaboston.com; Grocery; T: Chinatown/Downtown Crossing/Boylston. Talk about culture shock. In just a couple of blocks you can visit the bustling Chinese **C-Mart Supermarket** (see p. 153) and then enter this small, European-style gourmet shop, with its carefully selected lines of pastas, mustards, oils, vinegars, honeys, and even wines. Alimentari has an excellent cheese case and even makes its own gelato. Take-out sandwiches (tuna salad with cranberries, raw onion, and tomato, for example) and salads (mixed greens with goat cheese, walnuts, and grapes) are popular with nearby office workers.

Boston Wine Exchange, 181 Devonshire St., Downtown, Boston, MA 02110; (617) 422-0100; bostonwineexchange.com; Wine, Beer & Spirits; T: State. Offering eco-friendly delivery through Metro Pedal Power, this broad-ranging shop is a pleasure to browse, thanks to the open wooden racks with clear displays. The focus is on mid-tier table wines, largely in the $15–$30 range, from all over the world. (Premium Burgundies, Barolos, Tuscans, Bordeaux, and California cabs are secured in locking shelves.) The shop uses a nitrogen system to offer free sips of eight wines, with the selection changing weekly. The current selections are always listed on the website. There are also organized tastings a couple of evenings per week. BWX, as the owners style the shop, also has an impressive selection of craft beers.

Brix Wine Shop, 105 Broad St., Downtown, Boston, MA 02110; (617) 542-2749; brixwineshop.com; Wine, Beer & Spirits; T: Aquarium. This second of the Brix shops operated by Klaudia Mally and Carrie Wroblewski is less focused on the small-producer, value wines of the South End location (see p. 152) and more oriented to stocking some of the hairy-chested wines that appeal to the Financial District clientele, like higher-end big reds from Bordeaux, Burgundy, and Napa, not to mention the Super Tuscans. You'll also find the ingredients essential for artisanal cocktails, including Crème Yvette violet petal liqueur and the popular St. Germain elderflower liqueur.

Cafe Vanille, 70 Charles St., Beacon Hill, Boston, MA 02114; (617) 523-9200; cafevanilleboston.com; Bakery Cafe; T: Charles Street. In France, many families enjoy a *buche de Noel,* or Yule log, every Sunday during the month of December. Chefs Philipe Odier and Bruno Biagianti, born and trained in Paris, carry on the tradition by creating beautifully decorated chocolate logs (as well as one other rotating flavor) during the holidays. The rest of the year you can enjoy napoleons, éclairs, fruit tarts, buttery croissants and brioche, quiches, and freshly baked baguettes and multigrain loaves. A slice of quiche or veggie torte makes a great lunch, as does a sandwich of salmon, cream cheese, and cucumber on a baguette, or egg salad, bacon, lettuce, and tomato on a croissant.

Federal Wine, 29 State St., Downtown, Boston, MA 02109; (617) 367-8605; federalwine.com; Wine, Beer & Spirits; T: State. From the small size of the shop you'd never guess that Federal has long been one of Boston's most important wine merchants. The staff does an astute job of stocking the street-level room with wines ready to drink that evening—suitable for everything from a casual supper to a fine dinner with friends. But to tap into the store's riches, head down the narrow staircase into the cellar, where racks display samples of Federal's uncommon fine wines, including some collectibles. Probably the best way to keep up with the treasures that pass through Federal is to subscribe to the store's newsletter and attend its Wednesday tastings.

Flour Bakery + Cafe, 12 Farnsworth St., Waterfront, Boston, MA 02210; flourbakery.com; Bakery Cafe; T: South Station. In addition to all the sandwiches and baked goods also available in the South End (p. 153) and Cambridge (p. 253) shops, Flour's waterfront outpost is the site of classes for those who hope to learn how to make their own sticky buns, chocolate Oreo cookies, or Pop-Tarts.

Fóumami Asian Sandwich Bar, 225 Franklin St., Downtown, Boston, MA 02110; (617) 426-8858; foumami.com; Sandwich Shop; T: State. *Shao bing,* a traditional Chinese bread that is soft and chewy on the inside, but crisp and flaky on the outside, forms the basis for the sandwiches at this sleek breakfast and lunch spot in the Financial District. The bread itself hails from the Shandong province, but the sandwich fillings draw inspiration from throughout the Far East. The grilled rib eye steak with a soy garlic marinade, for example, leans toward Korea, while a chicken sandwich with cabbage and tomatoes is flavored with sweet and tangy Japanese *katsu* sauce. The salada, with apples, potatoes, raisins, and cabbage is

LUNCH IN THE SUNSHINE

Office workers in the Financial District and Waterfront are well served by take-out lunch spots. But if you're just visiting the area and don't have a desk to return to, here are a couple of our favorite places for a picnic. For great views of Fort Point Channel and the Financial District skyscrapers, grab one of the picnic tables on the **Harborwalk** right in front of the Boston Children's Museum, at 308 Congress St. If you'd rather enjoy a shady spot on a bench or prefer to lounge on the grass, try **Norman B. Leventhal Park** (aka Post Office Square Park), which is bounded by Milk, Franklin, Pearl, and Congress Streets. A favorite with office workers, it even has free Wi-Fi and a small cafe for lunchtime sandwiches, soups, and salads. (Sip Cafe, Zero Post Office Square, Downtown, Boston, MA 02109; 617-338-3080; sipboston.com; Bakery Cafe; T: State.)

popular throughout Asia. Soups, such as wonton or string bean noodle, and salads, including a wasabi Caesar, are also available, along with delicious iced tea drinks.

Haymarket International Food, 88 Blackstone St., Downtown, Boston, MA 02109; (617) 918-9988; Butcher; T: Haymarket. While this operation does have a small cafe selling east African Halal food, the main attraction is the Halal butcher shop in the back. It is not a store for the squeamish, as the butchers work in the open to break down entire carcasses, but if you're looking for the best (and most humanely treated) goat and lamb, this is a perfect source.

Isabelle's Curly Cakes, 81 Charles St., Beacon Hill, Boston, MA 02114; (617) 720-2260; izzyscurlycakes.com; Bakery Cafe; T: Charles Street. The most popular cupcake at this joint venture between star chef Todd English and his daughter Isabelle is the red velvet, a classic cocoa cake topped with cream cheese frosting, then dipped in melted white chocolate. Or you can select that same red velvet cake filled with mint chocolate pastry cream and topped with minted cream cheese frosting and chopped peppermint candies. For simple elegance, stick to the vanilla butter cake with vanilla buttercream frosting and white chocolate shavings.

James Hook + Co., 15–17 Northern Ave., Waterfront, Boston, MA 02210; (617) 423-5501; jameshooklobster.com; Fishmonger; T: South Station. In business since 1925, the Hook family ships more than 50,000 pounds of lobster a day to wholesalers, restaurants, and individuals around the country. But it's much more satisfying to shop in the no-nonsense retail market that manages to hold its own even as skyscrapers rise around it. So beloved is James Hook that when the original building burned down in May 2008, it was rebuilt and reopened in September. You can enjoy a lobster roll on the spot and pick up some live lobsters to take home along with such prepared fish classics as clam chowder, lobster bisque, lobster pie, lobster newburg, and lobster mac and cheese. To make things easy in the kitchen, Hook also offers frying clams, minced clams, and shucked oysters. For the recipe for **Uncle John's Lobster Thermidor,** see p. 432.

Linens on the Hill, 52 Charles St., Beacon Hill, Boston, MA 02114; (617) 227-1255; linensonthehill.com; Housewares; T: Charles Street. You can add a French accent to your dining room with richly patterned French jacquard napkins and tablecloths and Sabre tableware with jewel-toned acrylic handles. Displays in this small but elegant shop might also give you some decorating ideas.

Panificio Bistro & Bakery, 144 Charles St., Beacon Hill, Boston, MA 02114; (617) 227-4340; panificioboston.com; Bakery Cafe; T: Charles Street. Panificio is such an inviting hangout that we imagine Beacon Hill neighbors never want to leave. In fact, they could easily spend the day enjoying french toast on apple-cinnamon raisin bread for breakfast, a sandwich of chicken salad with grapes and almonds on country bread for lunch, and a plate of vegetable gnocchi with house-made marinara sauce for dinner. Panificio uses local produce and ingredients whenever possible and bakes a range of breads as well as giant cream puffs, pistachio muffins, apple crisp tarts, carrot cake cupcakes, and other luscious treats. Brunch is served Saturday and Sunday.

Savenor's Market, 160 Charles St., Beacon Hill, Boston, MA 02114; (617) 723-6328; savenorsmarket.com; Grocery; T: Charles Street. Like the Cambridge original (see p. 299), this branch of Savenor's specializes in cuts of meat not usually found in traditional markets. In addition to exotics (elk, bison, alligator, kangaroo, ostrich, and yak), the shop also carries extensive lines of top restaurant-quality beef, poultry, and pork. This branch also has a broad selection of good produce and even some groceries, making it a single stop for preparing a gourmet meal.

Sorelle Bakery & Cafe, 282 Congress St., Waterfront, Boston, MA 02210; (617) 426-5475; sorellecafe.com; Bakery Cafe; T: South Station. There's a healthy competition for the take-out lunch business along the waterfront, and Sorelle holds its own by offering a number of unusual sandwich variations, such as the tuna aioli with roasted red peppers and arugula or the roasted salmon with avocado, tomato, greens, red onion, and béarnaise sauce. Breakfast sandwiches are equally inventive. We can think of few things better than a Nutella and banana panini or a grilled PBJ to start the day on a soothing note.

Thinking Cup, 165 Tremont St., Downtown, Boston, MA 02111; (617) 482-5555; thinkingcup.com; Bakery Cafe; T: Park Street/ Boylston. The local alternative to coffee mega chains on Boston Common, Thinking Cup is a great place for a fresh pastry, a wrap sandwich, and a cup of joe. The coffee comes from the Brooklyn, New York, roasting facility of Portland, Oregon–based Stumptown Coffee, which is the darling of the New York media. It doesn't quite match up to some of the more local roasters, like **Barrington Coffee** (see p. 79) or the Terroir Select coffees of **George Howell Coffee Company** (see p. 377), but it's a very good cup and the store fills a definite niche in what is otherwise a coffee desert.

Yankee Lobster Fish Market, 300 Northern Ave., Waterfront, Boston, MA 02210; (617) 345-9799; yankeelobstercompany.com; Fishmonger; T: Silver Line Way (SL1). There are plenty of new glam restaurants, many of them serving fish, along Northern Avenue, but for sheer value in casual seafood, you have to keep walking to get to this Boston Harbor fixture of more than half a century. Principally a year-round wholesaler of fish and lobster, Yankee also runs a small cafe focused on all the favorites of the New England shore, from fried clams to stuffed quahogs to steamed lobster.

Farmers' Markets

At this writing, plans are under way for a year-round public market in Boston along the lines of Philadelphia's Reading Terminal Market or Seattle's Pike Place Market. When it does finally open, it will probably be on or near the site of the city's long-running outdoor produce market, Haymarket. Fruit and vegetable vendors gather here on Friday and Saturday roughly dawn to dusk to sell inexpensive produce. Vendors set up tables along Blackstone Street between North and Hanover Streets in front of the Halal butcher shops on the back side of Faneuil Hall Marketplace. Most of the goods are approaching the end of their holding periods, so must be used quickly before they spoil. Incredible bargains are available if you're willing to take a whole flat of strawberries, a basket of peaches, or a case of broccoli. Best bargains (and poorest selection) are available late Saturday afternoon.

Boston/South Station/Dewey Square Farmers' Market, Dewey Square at South Station, Boston. Tues and Thurs from 11:30 a.m. to 6:30 p.m., late May through late Nov.

Boston/South Station/Dewey Square Winter Farmers' Market, Dewey Square at South Station, Boston. Tues and Thurs from 11:30 a.m. to 2:30 p.m., late Nov to late Dec.

City Hall Plaza Farmers' Market, City Hall Plaza, Government Center, Boston. Mon and Wed from 11 a.m. to 6 p.m., late May to late Nov (closes 5 p.m. in Nov).

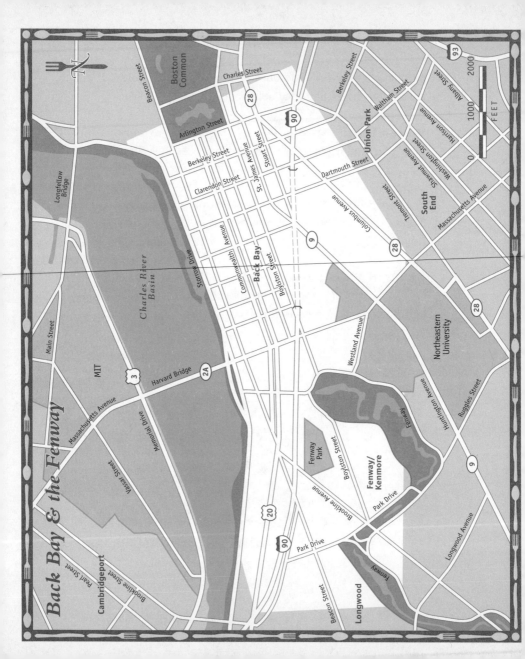

Back Bay & the Fenway

Back Bay has been one of Boston's toniest addresses ever since the late 19th century, when the city started to fill the Charles River marshes and developers began erecting Victorian brownstones along its measured grid of streets. For a century and a half, Back Bay held sway with the fanciest shops, the best restaurants, and the most beautiful architecture. Flanked by Trinity Church, Boston Public Library, and the reflective Hancock skyscraper, Copley Square embodied Boston's self-image of brilliance, artistry, and daring. Although all the new construction and most of the new restaurant openings have shifted to the waterfront, Back Bay remains a place where Bostonians and conventioneers alike go to play, drink, and dine. The adjacent Fenway neighborhood has some equally elegant buildings, but two institutions call the shots: Boston University, which has largely devoured Kenmore Square, and the Boston Red Sox, whose presence has made the area around legendary Fenway

Park a year-round entertainment district. The Fenway is full of bars, nightclubs, and modestly priced restaurants that appeal to baseball fans and BU students alike, but the area also contains some elegant restaurants, grown-up bars, and great little places to kick back and slurp oysters or nibble on sushi.

Foodie Faves

Audubon Circle, 838 Beacon St., Fenway, Boston, MA 02215; (617) 421-1910; auduboncircle.us; New American; $–$$; T: St. Mary's Street/Blandford Street. So well disguised from the street that passersby mistake it for a bike shop, this casual neighborhood restaurant and bar is easygoing and friendly with a menu to match. Student country is all around, so the menu leans toward inexpensive pressed sandwiches, burgers, and salads. The culinary high points, though, are the appetizers—which include excellent pot stickers and New England crab cakes—and the slightly more expensive entrees, such as pan-seared Atlantic salmon with spaetzle and brussels sprouts. The wine menu is quirky and predominantly southern hemisphere. Cocktails lean toward the sweet and the very sweet.

Basho Japanese Brasserie, 1338 Boylston St., Back Bay, Boston, MA 02215; (617) 262-1338; bashosushi.com; Japanese; $$–$$$; T: Kenmore. Sister restaurant to **Douzo** (see p. 98), this visually arresting eatery has a lot of small plates in the style of Japanese

izakaya: sushi, sashimi, and tempura by the piece as well as the less common *robata-yaki*, or skewers grilled over charcoal. Spicy duck with mushroom exemplifies the meat skewers, but some of the best are all-vegetable, like tiny Japanese eggplant with a light barbecue sauce. The themed sushi rolls are excellent—the Fenway has all the green stuff on the outside—and several are sprinkled with flying fish roe for a nice, crunchy finish. It's a stylish place for light, healthy eating. Too bad you can't find parking nearby when the Sox are in town.

Bistro du Midi, 272 Boylston St., Back Bay, Boston, MA 02116; (617) 426-7878; bistrodumidi.com; French; $$$; T: Arlington. As utterly bourgeois as a French banker holding the door of his Peugeot for his mistress, this bistro across from the Public Garden is our first choice for a sidewalk lunch on a croque monsieur, a *burger-frites*, or ratatouille Provençale. Dinner is a bigger affair, perhaps best taken indoors and upstairs to start with crispy pork belly and some of that sweet ratatouille before moving on to a classic bouillabaisse or a simple Provençal beef *daube*. Bistro du Midi also keeps a wonderful range of East Coast oysters on hand as starters or even as a snack in the afternoon with a glass of Muscadet.

Brasserie Jo, Colonnade Hotel, 120 Huntington Ave., Back Bay, Boston, MA 02116; (617) 425-3240; brasseriejo.com; French; $$; T: Prudential. Even in warm weather, we usually forgo the sidewalk tables for a seat inside, where the dark wood, white tablecloths, and tile floors so perfectly re-create the ambience of a French bras-serie. Wherever you sit, you'll be served by waitstaff wearing black vests and white aprons and delivering plates of pork tenderloin with prunes, coq au vin, steak-frites, or mussels *marinière*. As in France, Brasserie Jo offers good value *plats du jour* (choucroute Alsacienne on Monday, for example, or Moroccan braised lamb shank on Saturday) at dinner and equally reasonable "Express" soup and salad lunches.

Bristol Lounge, Four Seasons Hotel, 200 Boylston St., Back Bay, Boston, MA 02116; (617) 351-2037; fourseasons.com/boston; New American; $$$; T: Arlington. With floor-to-ceiling windows facing the Public Garden, an enormous fireplace, and overstuffed sofas, the Bristol Lounge introduced Bostonians to a standard of relaxed, effortless elegance that they quickly embraced. All meals are served here (including a Sunday buffet breakfast and a Saturday night dessert buffet), and the tab can be pricey if you opt for the grilled prime New York strip steak or the broiled 1½-pound lobster. But you will not be disappointed if you order the Bristol burger with aged Vermont cheddar, house-made pickles, and truffle french fries. It is a Boston classic. For afternoon tea, see p. 117.

Cafeteria, 279a Newbury St., Back Bay, Boston, MA 02115; (617) 536-2233; cafeteriaboston.com; Casual American; $–$$; T: Hynes. Updated casual food and a big outdoor patio make Cafeteria equally appealing to ladies toting bags from Diane von Furstenberg and

BURIED IN THE BOOKS

Even the most assiduous scholar needs sustenance, and a hard day of turning paper pages on real books can give you quite an appetite. The old "shush" and no eating rules of the Boston Public Library get a reprieve in its hidden dining spots. The **Map Room Cafe** (in the old map room, of course) has coffee and pastry in the morning, and soup, salads, and sandwiches at lunchtime. For a more elegant setting with table service and views of the BPL courtyard, opt for the adjacent **Courtyard Restaurant.** Luncheon favorites include the Courtyard Cobb salad and a plate called the "New England Soup & Sandwich": a lobster roll and a cup of clam chowder. The Courtyard also serves afternoon tea (see p. 117).

Map Room Cafe and Courtyard Restaurant, Boston Public Library, 700 Boylston St., Back Bay, Boston, MA 02116; (617) 385-5660; thecateredaffair.com; Casual American/New American; $–$$; T: Copley.

kids showing off their latest purchase from the Converse store. The kitchen relies on organic grass-fed beef and lamb, free-range chicken, fresh fish, and organic, local produce to turn out such classics as a big Caesar salad, meat loaf sandwich with bacon, or roasted chicken with tater tots and butternut squash. *Plats du jour,* such as Saturday's chicken potpie, are a good deal. Desserts, including carrot cake with cream cheese frosting or a brownie sundae, are satisfyingly retro.

Church, 69 Kilmarnock St., Fenway, Boston, MA 02215; (617) 236-7600; churchofboston.com; New American; $$; T: Fenway. Church believes that seasonal comfort food and a steady diet of rock and roll will save your soul. The menu is a significant upgrade from bar food, but retains the casual spontaneity of good pub grub. So, yes, you can order beer-battered haddock with salt-and-vinegar fries (aka fish and chips), but you can also get Georges Bank scallops with spring vegetable risotto or roast lamb with a lemon-caper caponata, or slow-roasted organic chicken with dumplings. The beer and wine lists are carefully curated and cocktails are . . . very rock and roll. Speaking of which, the club portion is next door to the dining room and the bands start doing sound checks around 9 p.m.

Citizen Public House and Oyster Bar, 1310 Boylston St., Fenway, Boston, MA 02215; (617) 450-9000; citizenpub.com; Casual American/New American; $$; T: Kenmore/Fenway. Chef Brian Reyelt would have been at home in 19th-century New Orleans, where both beer and oysters came in barrels and patrons indulged without restraint. But it's a new day, and he rises to the challenge of advanced gastropub cuisine. There are oysters—lots of oysters—on the half shell or done as oysters Rockefeller or oysters casino. Reyelt even serves an oyster BLT among the bar snacks. But his entrees speak directly to our hungers: braised pork cheek, pan-roasted day-boat hake from Chatham, a fresh tuna burger with pickled ginger. You have to love a menu when it talks dirty like that.

Clio, 370 Commonwealth Ave., Back Bay, Boston, MA 02215; (617) 536-7200; cliorestaurant.com; French/New American; $$$$; T: Hynes. When Ken Oringer opened Clio in 1997, it was a rather formal French restaurant designed to upgrade the dining scene at the recently overhauled Eliot Hotel. To say it worked is an understatement. Clio earned Oringer the James Beard Best Chef Northeast award, an appearance on *Iron Chef,* and a bevy of investors delighted to back some of his other ventures (**Coppa** on p. 131, **Toro** on p. 149, and **La Verdad** on p. 103). Clio remains Oringer's platform for invention, from his signature tomato-water nonalcoholic "martini" that captures the essence of tomato flavor, to escargot cooked with butter, ginger, and lemongrass and paired with stewed oxtail with chocolate and cocoa nibs. Clio can become precious, no doubt, but it is one of a handful of Boston establishments offering all the subtleties of food and service one expects from a world-class restaurant.

Deuxave, 371 Commonwealth Ave., Back Bay, Boston, MA 02115; (617) 517-5915; deuxave.com; New American/French; $$$; T: Hynes. Chef Christopher Coombs first made his name in Boston cooking elevated comfort food at **dbar** (see p. 189), but Deuxave (pronounced doo-ahv, to emphasize that it's sort of French and at the intersection of Massachusetts and Commonwealth Avenues) lets him spread his fine dining wings. Certain French classics are menu perennials, like the 9-Hour French Onion Soup, with a beef bone marrow crouton and a cap of melted Comté, or the duck liver pâté made in-house. Duck is big on the menu, ranging from confit leg and the pâté among the apps to duck breast with French lentils and a prune gastrique. Hold off salting your food without tasting first. A lot of the dishes rely on salt to make the vegetables melt just so and the meats brown.

Douzo, 131 Dartmouth St., Back Bay, Boston, MA 02116; (617) 859-8886; douzosushi.com; Japanese; $$–$$$; T: Back Bay Station. This modern Japanese restaurant and lounge at the entrance to Back Bay Station not only serves beautiful plates of sushi, sashimi, and special rolls—it packages them to go in little bento boxes so commuters can grab dinner on the way home. Slick and shiny and even a little post-industrial in its look, Douzo aims less for Japanese authenticity than delicious plates and stylish surroundings. Sushi and sashimi are predictably excellent, but Douzo also offers some innovative dishes like tuna tempura rolled with seaweed around a scallion. If you're drinking sake, the *omakase* special is a good dinner choice, since here it is less a round of sashimi tastes than a sampler of the house special sushi rolls.

Eastern Standard, 528 Commonwealth Ave., Fenway, Boston, MA 02215; (617) 532-9100; easternstandardboston.com; New American; $$; T: Kenmore. Located in the Hotel Commonwealth, Eastern Standard harks back to a (probably fictional) golden age of American restaurants when chefs crafted the same menu all the time, drawing from the unwritten playbook of great standard dishes. This is the Eastern Standard, which is to say, metro America by way of Paris. The dishes are indeed standards, but the kitchen adds surprising little touches, like the chestnut puree with the roast chicken or the lamb sausage with the baked rigatoni. Daily specials rotate and repeat each week with an inexpensive homey dish like pork cutlet smothered in mushrooms on Monday and a pricier lobster gnocchi with Meyer lemon brown butter on Friday. You can get sandwiches and salads for dinner, if you like. Be sure to start with a cocktail from the bar. Jackson Cannon oversees the mixology—both here and at **Hawthorne** (see p. 395) in the same building.

El Pelón Taqueria, 92 Peterborough St., Fenway, Boston, MA 02215; (617) 262-9090; elpelon.com; Mexican; $; T: Fenway/ Kenmore. It's worth seeking out El Pelón in this out-of-the-way spot if you're a fan of big, overstuffed burritos in the northern Mexican style. The braised pork (*carnitas*) enchiladas are even better. Most customers order chicken, pork, steak, or veggie plates, which come with heaping sides of rice, beans, and salad.

Elephant Walk, 900 Beacon St., Fenway, Boston, MA 02215; (617) 247-1500; elephantwalk.com; Cambodian/French; $$; T: St. Mary's Street. Elephant Walk's blend of French and Cambodian dishes works just as well at brunch as it does for lunch or dinner. Morning diners can select crepes or omelets or opt instead for Cambodian chicken soup or soba noodle salad. For other locations in Cambridge and Waltham, see p. 250 and p. 367.

Erbaluce, 69 Church St., Back Bay, Boston, MA 02116; (617) 426-6969; erbaluce-boston.com; Italian; $$$; T: Arlington. Chef-Owner Chuck Draghi is so brilliant that you wonder why he isn't nationally famous. It's probably because he spends all his time in the kitchen, leaving occasionally to, say, cook at the James Beard House in New York. Draghi changes the menu at Erbaluce every night—sometimes a little, sometimes a lot—so you can't count on any given dish reappearing until its ingredients are at their peak. Draghi's source of inspiration is Piemonte, that region of northern Italy that gives us Barolo, lardo, wonderful hand-twisted pastas, and, of course, white truffles. Wild boar dishes are very popular in Piemonte, and when Draghi offers one, snap it up. We hesitate to say this, since it depends on how many courses you gobble up, but Draghi's cooking is so light (most dishes are made without added fats) that you'll float as you walk away. Your wallet, however, will still be full of cash. The wine list is laser-focused on great Italian choices at fair prices.

Finale Desserterie & Bakery, One Columbus Ave., Back Bay, Boston, MA 02116; (617) 423-3184; finaledesserts.com; Bakery Cafe; $; T: Arlington. It's a bit of a walk between Finale and the Theater District, but we think that it's worth it, whether you want to stop in for a light dinner (such as a crab and corn pizza) before a show or for a nice dessert after. Or for both. A dessert sampler plate lets you select mini versions of some of Finale's most popular concoctions, including crème brûlée, lemon roulade, and apple cranberry tart. For the Cambridge location, see p. 252.

Grill 23, 161 Berkeley St., Back Bay, Boston, MA 02117; (617) 542-2255; grill23.com; Steak House; $$$$; T: Arlington. Located in the historic Salada Tea building, Grill 23 opened in 1983 and has outlasted every other steak house in Back Bay. When a place does local oysters on the half shell, steak tartare, classic Caesar salad with shaved Grana Padano, and a monster 100-day rib eye this well, who needs competition? Actually, Grill 23 has an alter ego with such dishes as vegetable-of-the-day vegetarian risotto, a locally famous meat loaf, and the catch of the day, always prepared whichever way that fish tastes best. Eat downstairs to be seen, or ask for an upstairs table for a discreet meal of love or business.

Island Creek Oyster Bar, 500 Commonwealth Ave., Fenway, Boston, MA 02215; (617) 532-5300; islandcreekoysterbar.com; Seafood; $–$$; T: Kenmore. Island Creek happens to be a Duxbury farmer of stupendous oysters, and this oyster bar is an attempt to bridge the gap between producer and consumer. Besides the fantastic oysters (including some farmed elsewhere), you can expect plates of scallops from New Bedford, local fluke and flounder, steamed littlenecks, and maybe even roast halibut. Burger, steak, and chicken breast are available for the member of the dinner party

FOOD ARTS

All those lovely post-Impressionist paintings at the Museum of Fine Arts Boston are the perfect preparation for dining at **Bravo,** the museum's top dining venue. Think of the restaurant scenes of late 19th-century Paris, or the colorful landscapes filled with oh-so-civilized folk. Bravo evokes that spirit, with its roasted beet salad with arugula, delicate crab cakes, and silken lobster bisque. It is an upper-class experience, and priced accordingly.

At the nearby Isabella Stewart Gardner Museum, **Cafe G** occupies a glassed-in corner of the new Renzo Piano building, and offers more of a cafe experience, with light dishes, like an onion and gruyère quiche, polenta with creamy mushrooms and ricotta made on-site, or a plate of pan-roasted Cape Cod oysters with brioche.

Bravo, Museum of Fine Arts, 465 Huntington Ave., Fenway, Boston, MA 02116; (617) 369-3474; mfa.org; New American; $$$; T: MFA.

Cafe G, Isabella Stewart Gardner Museum, 280 The Fenway, Boston, MA 02116; (617) 566-1088; gardnermuseum .org; New American; $–$$; T: MFA.

who doesn't like fish. The wines, though, are mostly premier whites and rosés designed to pair with shellfish and finfish.

Jasper White's Summer Shack, 50 Dalton St., Back Bay, Boston, MA 02115; (617) 867-9955; summershackrestaurant.com; Seafood;

$$; T: Hynes. Summer Shack opens for lunch during baseball season so that fans who don't want to eat a frank at **Fenway** (see p. 109) can enjoy a cup of clam chowder, corn bread–fried oyster taco, or crab cakes with sweet potato fries. For the original Cambridge location, see p. 260.

L'Espalier, 774 Boylston St., Back Bay, Boston, MA 02199; (617) 262-3023; lespalier.com; French/New American; $$$$; T: Copley. When the Mandarin Oriental opened a luxury hotel in Boston, the company convinced Frank McClelland to move L'Espalier from its town house digs into the modern hotel. The move gave L'Espalier a much larger (and exposed) kitchen, more seating, and the option of offering lunch as well as dinner. The restaurant team, led by McClelland in the kitchen and Louis Risoli in the dining room, is always in pursuit of perfection, and some of the most inspired (and complex) dishes we've tasted in the US have been at L'Espalier. If you're not ready to commit to a multi-course prix fixe or tasting menu, you can also opt for "bites" in the Salon. These range from servings of caviar, oysters, or farmstead cheeses, to small plates that hint at the brilliance of the dining room menus: roasted foie gras with cèpes and a black trumpet mushroom cake, perhaps, or slow-cooked gray sole with Moroccan orange peel puree, pickled fennel, and olive oil. Desserts by Pastry Chef Jiho Kim are similarly complex little masterpieces. For afternoon tea, see p. 116.

La Verdad Taqueria, 1 Lansdowne St., Fenway, Boston, MA 02215; (617) 421-9595; laverdadtaqueria.com; Mexican; $; T:

Kenmore. Ken Oringer might make exquisitely complex French and New American food at **Clio** (see p. 97), but the man also loves gutsy Mexican fare, which is what La Verdad serves in spades. He knows his way around the various moles and salsas and the regional cuisines of Mexico, and La Verdad draws liberally on all the different street food traditions. Mole negro is reserved for the lamb enchilada, which also contains sweet potato and swiss chard and is topped with a wild sprinkle of chopped hazelnuts. Looking for a big meal? Order the *carne asade*—grilled hanger steak over tortillas, salsa verde, and grated Oaxacan cheese, served with a pair of eggs fried sunny side up. It's the perfect hangover preventive if you've been slurping down the addictive tequila drinks.

La Voile Boston Brasserie, 261 Newbury St., Back Bay, Boston, MA 02116; (617) 587-4200; lavoileboston.net; French; $$$; T: Hynes/Copley. Truly a French import, La Voile was brought over from Cannes in late 2007—lock, stock, zinc bar, and even some staff. That gives La Voile ("The Sail") a stronger French pedigree than most Boston restaurants, and the menu does not disappoint, offering three preparations of foie gras, a truly Provençal version of fish soup, and some form of western Atlantic fish (often snapper) pan-seared and served with a fricassee of baby artichokes and an arugula and black olive tapenade. A three-course bargain menu is also offered nightly. Service is impeccable and professional.

Legal Sea Foods, 26 Park Plaza, Back Bay, Boston, MA 02116; (617) 426-4444; legalseafoods.com; Seafood; $$–$$$; T: Arlington. Though it lacks the waterside location of **Legal Harborside** (see p. 60) and **Legal Sea Foods Long Wharf** (see p. 60), the fish is equally fresh and this Legal has a huge wine cellar and 40-page wine menu. You'll be sure to find the perfect bottle to complement your baked stuffed shrimp or wood-grilled mahimahi.

Met Back Bay, 279 Dartmouth St., Back Bay, Boston, MA 02116; (617) 267-0451; metbackbay.com; Casual American/ Traditional American; $$–$$$; T: Copley. One of the great places to grab a burger or salad for lunch, Met dresses up with finer linens and glassware at night, when you might order a good steak and salad, or a baked whole fish served with potato poached in olive oil. We're surprised that the restaurant charges for its bread basket (buttermilk biscuits and grilled garlic bread). Arrive early if you want patio seating for the weekend brunch.

Mistral, 223 Columbus Ave., Back Bay, Boston, MA 02116; (617) 867-9300; mistralbistro.com; French; $$$; T: Back Bay Station. The first of Chef-Owner Jamie Mammano's restaurants, Mistral shows the chef's preference for unfussy classic country cooking in a relaxed atmosphere. That's not to say the dishes lack finesse—far from it. He is likely to plate a whole roasted fish with a spicy ginger-lime broth to bring out the sweetness of the flesh, for example, or use a tart, fresh goat cheese in his polenta as a counterpoint to the unctuous lamb osso bucco. Mistral even offers thin-crust grilled pizzas, and a wine list slanted to Burgundy and North American Pinot Noir.

Parish Cafe, 361 Boylston St., Back Bay, Boston, MA 02116; (617) 247-4777; parishcafe.com; Casual American; $; T: Arlington. More than a dozen local chefs have contributed a signature sandwich to the Parish menu, so you can dine on a slow-roasted pork butt sandwich with lime and green curry tartar sauce created by Michael Leviton of **Lumière** (see p. 370) or a lobster roll with bacon and tomato confit dreamed up by Barbara Lynch of **B&G Oyster** (see p. 127). But there's also plenty on the menu to showcase the creativity of the cafe's own chef, Sean Simmons, including his chipotle meat loaf sandwich with bacon, lettuce, tomatoes, and chipotle aioli.

Petit Robert Bistro, 468 Commonwealth Ave., Fenway, Boston, MA 02215; (617) 375-0699; petitrobertbistro.com; French; $$; T: Kenmore. Boston University students have all the luck. We wish our college neighborhood had had such a terrific little French bistro serving perfect date food at perfect student date prices. This was the first of Jacky Robert's bistro network, and with its subterranean location down tricky narrow steps, it remains the one that feels most like a find. Settle in for coq au vin or steak-frites with a carafe of wine and soulful glances. For other locations, see pp. 66, 144, and 213.

Pigalle, 7 Charles Street South, Back Bay, Boston, MA 02116; (617) 423-4944; pigalleboston.com; French; $$$; T: Arlington/Boylston.

Pigalle looks like a perfect period piece—enough to make your heart ache with nostalgia for the years right after World War II captured in the photos of Willy Ronis and the songs of Edith Piaf. The food, fortunately, is a fully contemporary reimagining of classic French bistro plates. Chef-Owner Marc Orfaly offers tilapia fillet crusted with sea urchin roe, for example, while presenting a cassoulet that would do a French country housewife proud: braised lamb shank, duck leg confit, and his own garlic sausage. The casual yet elegant setting makes the restaurant perfectly suited for dining before or after a performance elsewhere in the Theater District.

Poe's Kitchen at the Rattlesnake, 384 Boylston St., Back Bay, Boston, MA 02116; (617) 859-7772; rattlesnakebar.com; Southwestern; $–$$; T: Arlington. What happens when a fine dining chef goes into business with a Southwestern-themed tequila bar? You get entrees like mac and cheese with local Taza chocolate, applewood-smoked bacon, and smoked Fresno chile peppers. You also get ancho- and lime-marinated scallop tacos, a BLT built on rosemary olive bread, and a jalapeño fried chicken sandwich. Chef Brian Poe cooked in the Southwest before coming to Boston. An inveterate traveler and fan of Latin cuisines, he expresses his inner chef with the weekly specials titled "Poe Unleashed."

Post 390, 406 Stuart St., Back Bay, Boston, MA 02116; (617) 399-0015; post390restaurant.com; New American; $$$; T: Copley. On first impression, Post 390 looks like a watering hole for advertising men, with its rattle of ice cubes in old-fashioned glasses and unrelieved dark wood. That's the tavern. The dining rooms, however, are dotted with intimate tables, each enveloped in its own spot lighting, and the menu offers some very good grilled meat and fish. Ownership is the same as **Grill 23** (see p. 101). Chef Eric Brennan's straightforward style plays up the quality of his ingredients, whether it's the lobster off a boat in Scituate, day-boat cod from Fish Pier, or Brandt Farm beef (same as at Grill 23) for the skirt steak. At lunch don't miss the great elongated flatbreads, including a classic Margherita with snipped basil, and a merguez lamb sausage with feta cheese.

Salty Pig, 130 Dartmouth St., Back Bay, Boston, MA 02116; (617) 536-6200; thesaltypig.com; Casual American/New American; $; T: Back Bay Station. This restaurant builds its entire menu around pork charcuterie—hams, sausages, pâtés, porchetta, pig tails . . . Even the skillet of wood-grilled clams comes with roasted peppers and bacon, and the ragù for the orrechiette pasta is made by cooking down pig trotters (utterly unctuous, by the way). The same menu holds from late morning until very early morning, and during nice weather, you'll have to eat lunch early to reliably snag one of the outdoor tables across from the entrance to Back Bay Station.

Take Me Out to the Ballgame

According to the National Hot Dog and Sausage Council, fans consume more than 20 million hot dogs in Major League ballparks each season. And about 1.5 million of those franks are eaten at Fenway Park. The **Fenway frank,** manufactured by Kayem Foods in Chelsea, is a fairly lean but meaty dog with hints of garlic and smoke. While other ballparks may top their dogs with mango slaw or mini potato pierogies or wrap them in tortillas, Fenway preserves the tradition of good brown mustard, relish, and a squishy bun. The hot dogs are also available in some grocery stores.

Sel de la Terre, 774 Boylston St., Back Bay, Boston, MA 02109; (617) 266-8600; www.seldelaterre.com; French; $$$; T: Hynes. Dishes at Sel de la Terre represent the best of country French cooking, although Chef-Owner Frank McClelland and his assistants are just as wed to locally sourced meat, fish, and produce as they are at **L'Espalier** (see p. 103) next door. Sel de la Terre is a popular spot for business folk to grab the "express lunch" (pan-seared hake, grilled pork chop) or sit down to a moderately priced Provençal dinner that could range from potato gnocchi with pesto and fresh vegetables to skillet-roasted rack of lamb, the house version of bouillabaisse, or almond-crusted trout with lemon risotto.

Sonsie, 327 Newbury St., Back Bay, Boston, MA 02115; (617) 351-2500; sonsieboston.com; French/New American; $$-$$$; T: Hynes. Open from 7 a.m. to 1 a.m. every day, Sonsie is the ultimate neighborhood bistro for Back Bay—the place where you come for morning espresso and croissants that you enjoy in a nice leather chair in the lounge, and then return in the evening for drinks and Chef Bill Poirier's goat cheese ravioli or grilled trout with crab falafel at a sidewalk table for dinner. Sonsie is the opposite of a moveable feast—it is the still feast in the midst of the fast-paced world of upper Newbury Street. Open since 1983, it has become a Back Bay institution.

Sorellina, One Huntington Ave., Back Bay, Boston, MA 02116; (617) 412-4600; sorellinaboston.com; Italian; $$$; T: Copley. The Italian "little sister" of Chef Jamie Mammano's **Mistral** (see p. 105), Sorellina is Italian the way Gucci is Italian. It's a Lamborghini, not a Fiat. The room sits on the point of a triangular building and though it is surrounded by hulking structures, the big glass windows and high ceilings give the restaurant an open and airy feel. Mammano gets most of his fish and as much of his produce as possible from local suppliers—even matching local oysters with a rose petal–Prosecco granita and local baby beets with a Vermont chèvre. Pastas here are large, bold plates with specialty ingredients—exotic mushrooms and truffle butter, for example. Meat and fish plates are similarly bold and are well matched by voluptuous northern Italian and Napa wines.

Stephanie's on Newbury, 190 Newbury St., Back Bay, Boston, MA 02116; (617) 236-0990; stephaniesonnewbury.com; New American; $$$; T: Copley. An institution in mid–Back Bay since 1994, Stephanie's shines in the summer when diners vie for the sidewalk tables to eat her signature fruit salad for lunch and look glamorous. Dinner entrees break down between the comfort food classics (a giant burger, an open-faced turkey sandwich, meat loaf stuffed with cheddar cheese) and American bistro fare like thyme-braised bone-in short rib with a white bean ragù or pan-seared salmon with maple-roasted butternut squash. If you want the full Stephanie's experience, order the "tower" of buttermilk-breaded onion rings, which comes with spicy mayo for dipping.

Sweet Cheeks, 1381 Boylston St., Fenway, Boston, MA 02215; (617) 266-1300; sweetcheeksq.com; Barbecue; $–$$; T: Fenway. For starters, Bostonians think Tiffani Faison was robbed on *Top Chef*. The gal can cook with sass and class, though Sweet Cheeks is all about the sass—specifically about barbecue as practiced in her native Texas. Walk into this Fenway restaurant and you'll see piles and piles of split hardwood logs. Like a classic Texas BBQ joint, the menu offers trays. Pick a meat (pulled chicken, pulled pork, turkey leg, ribs, short rib, brisket), a hot scoop (black-eyed peas, mac and cheese, collards), and a cold scoop (potato salad, coleslaw, carrot and raisin salad). Then add some hush puppies, and maybe a bucket of biscuits. That should hold you until the next meal. Everything on the menu is available to go.

Tasty Burger, 1301 Boylston St., Fenway, Boston, MA 02215; (617) 425-4444; tastyburger.com; Casual American; $; T: Fenway. Tasty Burger has excellent beef burgers at a good price, more than 30 craft and not-so-craft beers in cans, and citrus freeze slushies, and it stays open until 2 a.m. Best of all, it's close to Fenway Park. That makes this burger joint in a former gas station pretty close to burger nirvana. There's even a burger of the day. If you're lucky, it might be the 1950s Housewife, which is topped with Lipton's French onion dip, bacon bits, and fried onions. The sommelier suggests pairing with a Pabst Blue Ribbon 16-ounce tall boy. On a sunny day, eat outside on the picnic tables. During a rain delay, there are indoor tables, too.

Tico, 222 Berkeley St., Back Bay, Boston, MA 02116; (617) 351-0400; ticoboston.com; New American; $$–$$$; T: Arlington. Michael Schlow's small-plates restaurant for pairing with tequila is one of the more unusual in Boston, but it works surprisingly well. For one thing, good tequila is a smoky, shape-shifting beast that can be aggressive or sultry, depending on your mood and what it's paired with. Thus, Schlow's braised pork with white beans, smoked bacon, kale, and cumin (a full-size plate, for the record) is great with the agave liquor, but so is his lobster croquette with a yellow aji pepper sauce. You could spend a small fortune here eating pricey little plates—or get out for a song with a terrific hamburger and a margarita. The place is always jumping.

Towne Stove and Spirits, 900 Boylston St., Back Bay, Boston, MA 02199; (617) 247-0400; towneboston.com; New American; $$$; T: Hynes. It's amazing to think that a restaurant with nearly 400 seats can have a line waiting for a table, but that's Towne on the weekend—or whenever there's a conference at the Hynes Convention Center. It's a brilliant collaboration between entertainment magnate Patrick Lyons (who learned to pack them in during his years as a rock impresario) and near-legend chefs Lydia Shire and Jasper White. Beyond all the hoopla (and there's plenty—it's prime celebrity-spotting turf), the best reason to visit Towne is to eat well. Lobster is very much evident—from lobster popovers among the apps; to lobster pizza with swiss chard, pine nuts, and Parmesan; to wood-grilled lobster tails with drawn butter and charred lemon. Shire's way with offal shows up mostly in the charcuterie plate. Don't miss the Duck Crisp, served in the spring with a brown butter maple tart, huckleberries, and parsnips that overwintered in the New England soil. Big and celebratory, Towne is also all about the tastes of Boston.

Trattoria Toscana, 130 Jersey St., Fenway, Boston, MA 02215; (617) 247-9508; Italian; $$; T: Kenmore. Possibly the closest thing to a romantic little Lady-and-the-Tramp Italian restaurant as you'll find in Boston, TT is a family-run Tuscan trattoria with a menu so limited that you can't go wrong. Pasta fans are treated to pappardelle tossed with a ragù of wild boar and vegetables cooked down with Chianti. If there is a pasta with red sauce, order it and prepare for a revelation, since TT doesn't bother with red sauce except when it can be made from fresh tomatoes. The gnocchi, served with Gorgonzola and hazelnuts, are pillowy soft and creamy. Most meats are done in the oven, though the single salmon dish is boldly grilled and drizzled with olive oil.

Troquet, 140 Boylston St., Back Bay, Boston, MA 02116; (617) 695-9463; troquetboston.com; French; $$$; T: Boylston. Troquet is one of those terrific restaurants that people either love or hate. It is very French and rather formal, so if you stumble in badly dressed expecting to grab an app and a dessert, you'll be accommodated at the bar. Come in for a full meal with wines and you'll feel like

the place is full of old friends. Fussy eaters should be forewarned that the house specialties are the duo of foie gras and roast suckling pig. Vegans need not apply. On the other hand, Troquet has a super list of wines by the glass available in 2-ounce and 4-ounce pours and the menu suggests what dishes to pair with the wines. (Yes, they encourage you to pick the wines first . . .) The food tends to be small portions, which is the real reason French women don't get fat. That gives you license to eat the excellent bread spread with the best butter you have ever tasted, flown in from Normandy. Tourists and theatergoers often dine at the downstairs tables or the bar. The best views and nicer tables, though, are upstairs, where large windows provide a glorious view of Boston Common.

Uni Sashimi Bar, 370 Commonwealth Ave., Back Bay, Boston, MA 02215; (617) 536-7200; unisashimi bar.com; Japanese; $–$$; T: Hynes. Located in the lobby outside **Clio** (see p. 97), Uni was created by Ken Oringer as a simple sashimi bar serving beautiful cuts of local fish as well as specialty fish flown in from Tokyo's Tsukiji market. You can get a bargain-priced taste of Oringer's culinary genius by popping in for a bowl of umami ramen and a cocktail. In fact, on weekends you can get late-night ramen from 11 p.m. to closing.

Via Matta, 79 Park Plaza, Back Bay, Boston, MA 02116; (617) 422-0008; viamattarestaurant.com; Italian; $$; T: Arlington. Michael Schlow's "crazy way" is a breezy northern Italian caffè–cum–American bar–cum–trattoria. In warm weather the patio scene could have been transported from any of the spots ringing the main squares in Bologna, Turin, or Genova. The food hails from there as well, but with Schlow's own touch. For example, he takes the basic cheese and pepper sauce (*cacio e pepe*) and adds leaves from brussels sprouts. His stewed pork loin with lentils comes with a puddle of pear puree. Pan-seared monkfish is accompanied by eggplant

TEA FOR TWO

The very proper Ritz-Carlton began serving afternoon tea when the hotel opened in Back Bay in 1927, and the tradition continues in the same building, now the **Taj Boston.** These days the formal French room, with its big mirrors and sparkling chandeliers, is the setting for tea, which is served Friday through Sunday, and accompanied by a harpist. You can opt for pastries and petits fours along with your tea of choice or add sandwiches and canapes. To cultivate the next generation, the Taj also offers a children's tea with a peanut butter and jelly sandwich, chocolate chip cookie, chocolate-dipped strawberry, and hot chocolate. Taj Boston, 15 Arlington St., Back Bay, Boston, MA 02116; (617) 536-5700; tajhotels.com; T: Arlington.

The afternoon tea tradition thrives in Back Bay. **L'Espalier** restaurant, one of the city's best (see p. 103), serves afternoon tea on Saturday and Sunday and the sweets and savories highlight the imagination and finesse of the kitchen. The petits fours and pastries option might feature Earl Grey chocolate trifle and lemon chamomile and cherry crimsonberry scones. The more elaborate tea adds sandwiches such as a lobster profiterole and, of course, English cucumber with herbs, cream cheese, and candied lemon. L'Espalier,

caponata. The all-Italian wine list is a veritable necklace: all gems or pearls.

Wagamama, 800 Boylston St. #117, Back Bay, Boston, MA 02199; (617) 778-2344; wagamama.us; Asian; $; T: Hynes. **This Prudential**

774 Boylston St., Back Bay, Boston, MA 02199; (617) 262-3023; lespalier.com; T: Copley.

During winter everyone taking tea at the **Bristol Lounge** at the Four Seasons Hotel on Saturday or Sunday covets a table by the fireplace. Tea choices all include scones, breads, sandwiches, and pastries, along with strawberry jam, lemon curd, and Devonshire cream to make the delicious scones an even more decadent treat. You can also opt to add a glass of Kir Royale to accompany your pot of tea. Bristol Lounge, Four Seasons Hotel, 200 Boylston St., Back Bay, Boston, MA 02116; (617) 351-2037; T: Arlington.

With the exception of the children's tea, expect to pay between $30 and $40 per person for the options above. For a less expensive tea in an equally lovely setting, check out the Wednesday through Friday tea at the **Courtyard Restaurant at the Boston Public Library** (see p. 95). Assorted sandwiches, scones, and tarts to accompany tea are less than $25. Courtyard Restaurant, Boston Public Library, 700 Boylston St., Back Bay, Boston, MA 02116; (617) 859-2251; T: Copley.

Center branch of Wagamama follows the same model as the Quincy Market and Cambridge outlets (see p. 75 and p. 280). With Japanese ramen bars in its DNA, Wagamama quickly and efficiently serves noodle dishes and other easily prepared fare, like teriyaki and tempura.

Specialty Stores, Markets & Producers

Bacco's Wine & Cheese, 31 St. James Ave., Back Bay, Boston, MA 02116; (617) 574-1751; baccoswineandcheese.com; Wine, Beer & Spirits; T: Arlington. Bacco's is a find for wine lovers. While the selection is small compared to that of most wine shops, it is full of surprises, counterintuitive choices, and good buys. Owner Bob Bacco uses a "wine guy" rating system, labeling wines as "value," "best buy," and "favorite." It's idiosyncratic, but breaks out of the *Spectator/Advocate* straitjacket. The cheeses are similarly limited but extraordinary, and the charcuterie is just enough to make sure you have a great spread. Bacco happily assembles picnic boxes, though you'll have to be circumspect about drinking wine in public in Boston.

Berry Line, 1377 Boylston St., Fenway, Boston, MA 02215; (617) 236-0082; berryline.com; Ice Cream/Yogurt; T: Fenway. The last time we visited Berry Line, the yogurt flavors of the week were peanut butter and lychee, along with, of course, the unadulterated original. The flavors are so unique that staff gladly hand out small samples. For Cambridge locations, see p. 284.

Blue State Coffee, 957 Commonwealth Ave., Fenway, Boston, MA 02215; (617) 254-0929; bluestatecoffee.com; Coffee Shop; T: Packard's Corner. Simply put, Blue State offers good coffee with a conscience. All the beans are fair-traded, organic, and shade-grown, and the company principals travel to the source to meet the farmers. A cut of the profits is channeled to nonprofits in New Haven, Connecticut, Providence, Rhode Island, and Boston, where the five stores are located. Roasts range from light to dark, and beans are roasted frequently and ground just before brewing to ensure an optimally fresh cup.

Boston Olive Oil Co., 262 Newbury St., Back Bay, Boston, MA 02116; (857) 277-0007; bostonoliveoilcompany.com; Specialty Shop; T: Copley/Hynes. It was a slippery slope from appreciating good Mediterranean food to opening an olive oil specialty shop, but Patrick and Gail Vadaro have become Boston's biggest advocates for the spectrum of tastes offered by single-variety olive oils from around the world. Their stock shifts seasonally between northern and southern hemispheres to bring customers the freshest, most recently pressed oil. Their favorite? A peppery oil pressed from the Frantoia olive.

DeLuca's Market, 239 Newbury St., Back Bay, Boston, MA 02115; (617) 262-5990; delucasmarket.com; Grocery; T: Copley. This Back Bay gourmet shop sells its own line of jellies, jams, hot sauces, mustards, and pickled fruits and vegetables, along with flavored honeys, canned marzipan, agave nectar, and other specialty items. But you can also pick up a deli sandwich and a small container of potato salad or an assortment of cheeses and salamis for a quick picnic meal. For a fancy dinner at home, opt for the sautéed fresh salmon and steamed asparagus, or stuffed pork roast and cheese-topped twice-baked potatoes.

Hotel Chocolat, 141A Newbury St., Back Bay, Boston, MA 02116; (617) 391-0513; hotelchocolat.com; Chocolatier; T: Copley. When you enter this elegant chocolate shop, a staff member will greet you with a tray and invite you to select a sample. He or she might also tell you that the best way to taste chocolate is to let the first bite melt in your mouth. This is truly chocolate to savor, made by a British-based company that starts with beans from its own estate in Saint Lucia (and a few others) and follows the philosophy of "less sugar, more cocoa." The simple bars of 66 percent dark chocolate best convey the intense flavor, but you can also select white chocolate raspberry truffles or dark chocolate with almonds and pistachios. By the way, Hotel Chocolat chose the Boston area for its debut into the US market.

Japonaise Bakery & Cafe, 1032 Commonwealth Ave., Fenway, Boston, MA 02215; (617) 738-7200; japonaisebakery.com; Bakery Cafe; T: Packard's Corner. In warm weather the outside patio is the perfect place for an espresso or fruit shake with one of Japonaise's luscious pastries. For the original shop, see p. 225.

KitchenWares by Blackstones, 215 Newbury St., Back Bay, Boston, MA 02116; (857) 366-4237; kitchenwaresboston.com; Housewares; T: Copley. Good knives are the backbone of the kitchen and this shop takes them seriously, offering 10 brands along with a sharpening service. You can protect your new—or newly sharpened—knives with clever edge guards available in the gadget section. Other helpful gadgets include rubber rings to slip onto rolling pins to gauge the thickness of dough and long-handled juicers that promise to extract 20 percent more juice. KitchenWares has a good selection of small appliances; elegant kitchen scales; stone, stainless steel, and ceramic mortar and pestles; and a full range of barware.

Mike & Patty's, 12 Church St., Back Bay, Boston, MA 02116; (617) 423-3447; mikeandpattys.com; Sandwich Shop; T: Arlington/ Tufts Medical Center. The galley kitchen at this breakfast and lunch spot is smaller than many apartment kitchens but the chef-owners manage to turn out an amazing amount of amazingly good food. Once you've sampled their breakfast sandwich of fried egg, avocado, cheddar, and red onion, you won't be able to wait to return for a turkey and avocado BLT for lunch. Mike and Patty use only organic, cage-free eggs and make their own chorizo. They also enthusiastically embrace all-American hot dogs, serving them with chili, cheese, barbecue sauce, sauerkraut, and a variety of other enhancements.

Shaw's, 53 Huntington Ave., Back Bay, Boston, MA 02199; (617) 262-4688; shaws.com; Grocery; T: Copley. It's easy to find this Back Bay supermarket—just look for the Duck Tours amphibious vehicles on the street out front. With its large Shop the World Food Hall, Shaw's has an unusually broad selection of deli sandwiches, packaged sushi, soups, salads, and hot dishes for a quick and relatively inexpensive meal on the go. There are even a few tables in the mezzanine level wine department.

Simon Pearce, 103 Newbury St., Back Bay, Boston, MA 02116; (617) 450-8388; simonpearce.com; Housewares; T: Arlington/Copley. The handblown glass and handmade and glazed pottery from the Vermont studios of Irish-born Simon Pearce are favorites for weddings and other gift-giving occasions. The shop also includes beautiful linens, wooden bowls and serving pieces, and other items that complement the simple elegance of the handmade pieces, most of which are heirlooms in the making.

Chinatown, South End & Roxbury

This chapter is about the constant renewal that makes a city (and its culinary landscape) great. The South End may have Boston's densest concentration of foodies per block and the biggest brunch scene for miles around, yet the increasingly upscale neighborhood of brick town houses has a pre-gentrification history as a magnet for newcomers to the city. When the South End was first built in the 1870s, bank failures forced real estate developers to subdivide fancy residences into what became tenement houses—just in time for a huge influx of immigrants from Europe and the Middle East. Drawn by railroads and by factory work, many African Americans moved from the South into the South End in the early 20th century, only to move farther west into Roxbury in the years after World War II. In more recent decades, Roxbury has become a magnet for

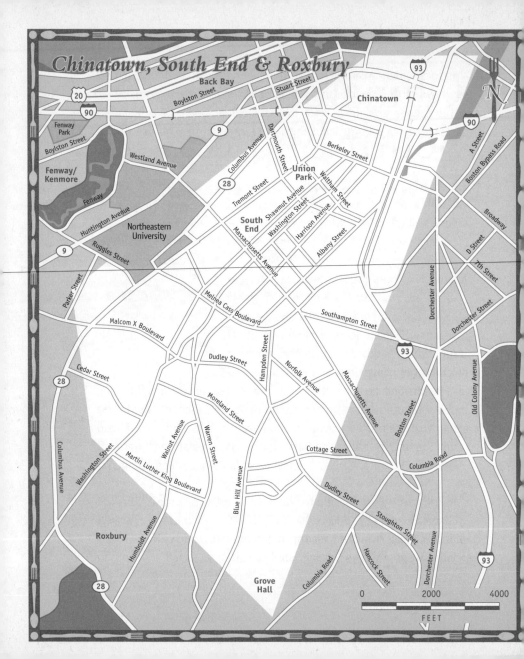

Chinatown, South End & Roxbury

Back Bay

Chinatown

Stuart Street

Boylston Street

95

20

90

Fenway Park

Boylston Street

Berkeley Street

9

Fenway/ Kenmore

Westland Avenue

Columbus Avenue

Dartmouth Street

Union Park

Fenway

28

Tremont Street

Waltham Street

Huntington Avenue

Shawmut Avenue

South End

Washington Street

Harrison Avenue

Albany Street

A Street

Boston Bypass Road

Broadway

90

Northeastern University

Ruggles Street

Massachusetts Avenue

D Street

9

Parker Street

Melnea Cass Boulevard

7th Street

Southampton Street

Dorchester Avenue

Dorchester Street

Malcom X Boulevard

Hampden Street

93

Cedar Street

Dudley Street

Norfolk Avenue

Massachusetts Avenue

Boston Street

Old Colony Avenue

28

Moreland Street

Columbus Avenue

Walnut Avenue

Warren Street

Cottage Street

Columbia Road

Washington Street

Martin Luther King Boulevard

Blue Hill Avenue

Dudley Street

Dorchester Avenue

Humboldt Avenue

Stoughton Street

Roxbury

Columbia Road

Hancock Street

93

28

Grove Hall

N

0   2000   4000

FEET

immigrants from the Caribbean, and even more recently, from east Africa. On the other side of the South End, Chinatown sprang up in the years after the Civil War as Chinese laborers arrived to lay the wires for Alexander Graham Bell's newfangled telephone company. Although many generations of Chinese immigrants have passed through Chinatown and moved to Boston's suburbs, the district still has an Asian caste—as much Vietnamese and Cambodian as Chinese. And even Chinese restaurateurs who left Chinatown have been returning to open new establishments. Somehow there's no place like home. But you don't need a history book: Just follow your nose to the kitchens of a hundred cuisines.

Foodie Faves

Addis Red Sea, 544 Tremont St., South End, Boston, MA 02116; (617) 426-8727; addisredsea.com; Ethiopian; $; T: Back Bay Station. Like its sister restaurant in Cambridge (see p. 233), this branch also Americanizes service by precombining ingredients in dishes rather than leaving that to the diners. They make their own *teff* (the sourdough bread used in lieu of utensils and plates), and the semi-underground location provides the feeling of a romantic hideaway. The staff has had a lot of practice in explaining the cuisine, so if you're eager to learn the difference between *wot* and *tibs,* this is a good place to begin.

Ali's Roti Restaurant, 1035 Tremont St., Roxbury, Boston, MA 02119; (617) 427-1079; Trinidadian; $; T: Ruggles. For the uninitiated, roti are big rounds of flatbread about 14 inches across into which whole East/West Indian meals are rolled. Ali's has been serving spicy Halal meals at this location a few blocks west of the South End since 1989, and Boston's Trinidadian community comes here often for a fix of curry goat, curry shrimp, or stewed oxtail. You can also get stewed fish, stewed chicken thighs, or vegetarian curries—either rolled in a roti or served on a plate with rice, chickpeas, and *dhal* (yellow split peas). There are some booths for eating on premises, but many customers call in their orders and pick them up to go.

Aquitaine, 569 Tremont St., South End, Boston, MA 02118; (617) 424-8577; aquitaineboston.com; French; $$$; T: Back Bay Station. It's hard to go wrong serving such Parisian bistro classics as onion soup with sherry, chicken liver mousse terrine with mustard and cornichons, lemon sole meunière, and filet au poivre with cream and green peppercorns. Lest the kitchen become stuck in a rut, Aquitaine offers daily *plats du jour* that can range from barbecue braised brisket to pan-roasted trout with almond puree, green beans, and figs. The *pommes frites* (French for french fries) come with a delicious basil-garlic aioli—a French-Italian mixed marriage of pesto and mayonnaise. The wine list represents most of the regions of France while also plumping for some of the bigger names in California.

Ashur Restaurant, 291 Roxbury St., Roxbury, Boston, MA 02119; (617) 427-0599; Somalian; T: Roxbury Crossing. Open all day to feed hungry worshippers coming from or going to the Islamic Cultural Center literally around the corner, Ali Ashur's restaurant serves only Halal food, topping it off with sweet, aromatic Somali tea. While the printed menu lists a number of dishes, the real menu is a chalkboard near the counter where you order. Stewed beef, stewed goat, stewed fish, stewed lamb, and stewed chicken are usually available and are served with a choice of rice or spaghetti noodles—or both. (Somalis call the combination "Federation.") In the evenings you can often get a sandwich filled with grilled vegetables and served with french fries. Hot soups are available every day, though the Moroccan *harira* (spicy tomato, lentil, and chickpea soup) is dependably available only during Ramadan, when it's a favorite way to break the fast after sundown.

B&G Oysters, 550 Tremont St., South End, Boston, MA 02116; (617) 423-0550; bandgoysters.com; Seafood; $$$; T: Back Bay Station. This subterranean modern take on the classic oyster bar is a great place to hang in the South End. Hunker down around the marble bar surrounding the open kitchen in the winter; eat on the back patio in the summer. There's always a selection of a dozen different oysters drawn from America's three coasts, local classics like lobster and clam rolls, and a menu of Mediterranean seafood dishes such as pollock (aka "blue cod") with saffron-braised beans. Barbara Lynch's partner in wine, Cat Sillerie, selects some classic Muscadets, Chablis, and Champagnes, then complements them with fish-friendly reds and a nice Austrian Grüner Veltviner ("Cuvée Cat") served exclusively at Lynch-Sillerie restaurants. The restaurant also offers its seafood shack items (like the BLT with lobster) for takeout.

Beehive, 541 Tremont St., South End, Boston, MA 02116; (617) 423-0069; beehiveboston.com; New American; $$$; T: Back Bay Station. One of the liveliest spots in town to hear jazz and contemporary music also happens to be one of the best spots to get a bite to eat, cabaret style. The lamb-filled phyllo spring rolls (called "Moroccan cigars") are a fabulous starter, though sharing a meze platter makes more sense if your party is larger than two. The main dishes tend to be straightforward grill and oven food: seared Scottish salmon, grilled lamb chops with smoked eggplant, pan-roasted cod with tomato fennel broth, and even a simple chicken piccata. There's a pretty extensive wine list with some real surprises from the Balkans. Cocktails lean to the classics.

Best Little Restaurant, 13A Hudson St., Chinatown, Boston, MA 02111; (617) 338-4988; Chinese; $; T: Chinatown. Like many restaurants in Chinatown, this spot a few steps below sidewalk level specializes in mild Cantonese cuisine—and has an overwhelmingly long menu. When faced with too many choices, one of our strategies is to peruse the tables to see what other diners seem to be particularly enjoying. At Best Little Restaurant that is almost always the heaping plate of minced meat and string beans with lettuce wrap. Particularly good for those who are not adept with chopsticks, it involves scooping a spoonful of meat and beans into a crisp lettuce leaf, wrapping it tightly, and eating almost like a taco. By the way, the pork spareribs (served with garlic, sweet and sour, or black bean sauce) are also great finger food.

Butcher Shop, 552 Tremont St., South End, Boston, MA 02118; (617) 423-4800; thebutchershopboston.com; Mediterranean; $$; T: Back Bay Station. Rustic French and Italian cuisines—especially charcuterie—dominate the menu at this wine bar and full-service butcher shop modeled by Barbara Lynch on the *boucheries* of France. In practice, that means lots of nibbles, with appetizer and entree plates about the same size. The menu is always changing, but expect seasonal salads like roasted beets with chèvre in winter or sliced tomatoes with fresh mozzarella in summer, along with pastas tossed with meat sauces, and whole sausages that can range from a house hot dog to a *merguez* (lamb) sausage with preserved anchovies. Sommelier Cat Sillerie pulls out the stops for reds here, the way she does with whites at nearby **B&G Oysters** (see p. 127).

Charlie's Sandwich Shoppe, 429 Columbus Ave., South End, Boston, MA 02116; (617) 536-7669; Casual American; $; T: Back Bay Station. Don't bother to bring a newspaper or book if you head to Charlie's alone. Minutes after you're seated you will be chatting with the person on the next stool at the long counter or with your fellow diners at one of the communal tables. "We have a lot of regulars who sit at the same table every day," says Marie Fuller, daughter of Christi Manjourides, who started working at Charlie's when it opened in 1927. "In 1946 he bought half ownership for $1,000," says Fuller. She and three siblings now preside over this quintessential neighborhood breakfast and lunch joint. Breakfast, including turkey hash with eggs, blueberry griddle cakes, and omelets with home fries, is served all day. But you might opt instead for a chicken club or meat loaf sandwich, a plate of franks and beans, or fish and chips for lunch. In 2005 the James Beard Foundation recognized Charlie's as one of its America's Classics eateries.

Chau Chow City, 83 Essex St., Chinatown, Boston, MA 02111; (617) 338-8158; Chinese; $; T: Chinatown. The modest street entrance of this beloved Cantonese restaurant hides the fact that it is *huge* inside, though the tendency to open levels only as needed tends to keep the tables packed. It's equally esteemed for reasonably priced plates that can be so soothing after a night of too much drinking and for the dim sum scene on weekends that draws many Chinese families from the suburbs.

China King, 60 Beach St., Chinatown, Boston, MA 02111; (617) 542-1763; Chinese; $; T: Chinatown. For more than a decade when Chef-Owner Erwin Mei and his wife, Doris, ran King Fung Garden,

Boston's non-Chinese chefs always came in to eat on their nights off. Not only was Chef Mei adept with Chinese classics, he made what everyone agreed was the best Peking duck in Boston. After a several-year hiatus, the Meis returned to Chinatown in early 2012 with China King, serving that Peking duck as well as Chef Mei's other specialties, including his scallion pie, sweet pickled jellyfish, rice cake with pork and pickled cabbage, and the all-time top cure for a hangover, salt-and-pepper fried squid. Reserve ahead, as China King seats only 24. One-day advance notice is necessary for the Peking duck, which is presented in three courses (skin, stir-fry, and soup).

Coppa, 253 Shawmut Ave., South End, Boston, MA 02118; (617) 391-0902; coppaboston.com; Italian; $; T: Back Bay Station. Small Italian-inspired plates make this South End *enoteca* a perfect spot for grazing and sipping. A joint project of restaurateur Ken Oringer and charcuterie master Jamie Bissonnette, Coppa seats but 40 people, which means the wait for a table can be long if you're not in the first seating. But the prices on the small plates, the pizza, pastas, and *salumi* make it all worthwhile. The all-Italian wine list is broad-ranging and reasonably priced, even by the glass. Given the high-energy ambience, count on making several new friends before the night is over. You can even get egg dishes at the Sunday brunch.

Darryl's Corner Bar & Kitchen, 604 Columbus Ave., Roxbury, Boston, MA 02118; (617) 536-1100; darrylscornerbarboston.com;

Southern; $$; T: Massachusetts Avenue. Darryl Settles has been bringing folks together for decades now, and the latest iteration of his restaurant/bar/music venue at the intersection of Roxbury and the South End preserves many of his beloved menu standards (the Glorifried Chicken and what might be Boston's best jambalaya) and pairs the grub with live music, often from jazz students who attend Berklee College of Music, just down the street. It's one of the rare lounges that actually welcomes children and even has a small menu of kiddie food (chicken strips and fries, mac and cheese). Settles refers to the place as having "soul, spice, and all that jazz," and that pretty much sums it up. On Sunday Darryl's offers a jazz buffet brunch laden with soul food like collard greens, candied yams, and (of course) grits.

Dumpling Cafe, 695–697 Washington St., Chinatown, Boston, MA 02111; (617) 338-8858; dumplingcafe.com; Chinese; $; T: Chinatown. This restaurant is a good bet for a light meal of the namesake dumplings. They are made fresh every day by one chef, who fills the beautiful little pockets with vegetables, beef and cabbage, pork and leek, seafood, or chicken. For a light, healthy meal and pretty presentation in a bamboo basket, order them steamed, or opt for fried to add a nice crispy edge to the wrapper. Scallion pancakes with beef and buns filled with pork, pork and crabmeat, or duck are equally popular. Of course, the menu also features a range of soups, noodle dishes, and larger plates such as sautéed squid with chives, chicken with eggplant, or pork belly with bean curd.

East Ocean City, 25–29 Beach St., Chinatown, Boston, MA 02111; eastoceancity.com; Chinese/Seafood; $; T: Chinatown. Cantonese-style seafood is truly excellent here, where the cooks get 600 pounds of fresh fish daily. A lot of that is trucked in from New York, but the squid mostly hails from Point Judith (Rhode Island), and you can't beat the lightly breaded salt-and-pepper squid. Many Chinese diners like to order live fish from the tanks near the entrance—don't hesitate to follow suit if you see glass shrimp swimming around. If you wait, they will almost certainly be gone. There are some meat and straight vegetable dishes available for non–fish eaters, but the kitchen's heart lies with the ocean.

El Centro, 472 Shawmut Ave., South End, Boston, MA 02118; (617) 262-5708; Mexican; $$; T: Massachusetts Avenue. Chef-Owner Allan Rodriguez hails from the state of Sonora, and he opened El Centro to bring authentic Mexican food to the South End. He makes his own masa dough from scratch daily for tortillas and tamales. Said tamales are usually found on the appetizer menu and they're stuffed with roasted poblano chile peppers and a good fac-simile of Mexican fresh cheese. While Rodriguez does resort to flour tortillas for the quesadillas (try those filled with corn fungus, or *huitlacoche*), most of his dishes hail from farther south of the border. The grilled steak is Tampico style, accompanied by a large enchilada, while the shredded roast pork is Yucatecan, or *pibil*. On a chilly winter day, there's no more soothing lunch than a bowl of his *sopa de*

tortilla: tortilla soup with chunks of roast chicken and slices of avocado. The beer list includes most of the Mexican favorites, including
Bohemia. The staff will even humor gringos and serve beer with a
slice of lime.

Estragon Tapas Bar, 700 Harrison Ave., South End, Boston, MA
02118; (617) 266-0443; estragontapas.com; Spanish; $; T: Newton
Street (Silver Line). It's hard to do tapas Spanish style when you
don't have concentrations of tapas bars, so Estagon encourages
diners to sit down and order a bunch of small plates. The
owners are indeed Spanish and the dishes are as well.
When you order a *pintxo* of chorizo and toast at Estragon,
you get a lot more sausage than you would in a bar in
Pamplona. Most of the dishes are more typical of northern
Spain than of the south, so even sautéed chicken livers (a
staple in Jerez) come with a dab of crème fraîche,
and the menu includes such northern favorites as
grilled leeks with romesco sauce. Still, it's a good
spot for expats to stop by and get a slice of potato
omelet (*tortilla española*) and a *copa de tinto* (glass of red wine) to
allay a bout of homesickness.

Franklin Cafe, 278 Shawmut Ave., South End, Boston, MA 02118;
(617) 350-0010; franklincafe.com; New American; $$; T: Back Bay
Station. Ask almost anyone in the Boston restaurant business
where they go out to eat and the answer will be Franklin Cafe.
That's because they serve dinner until 1:30 a.m., so staff from

other restaurants can eat after their shifts, and because the food is both good and reasonably priced. Some of the early classics of New American cooking remain on the menu here, like the salad of baby greens, roasted walnuts, figs, and blue cheese, or the home-made roasted pumpkin ravioli with sage–brown butter. Add a few French classics like steak-frites and a reasonable, less-rich version of coq au vin, and there's no reason to ever go hungry again. Even vegetarians can eat well on vegetable casseroles or potato gnocchi. This South End original has also spawned a South Boston location, **Franklin Southie** (see p. 190) and a Gloucester edition.

The Gallows, 1395 Washington St., South End, Boston, MA 02118; (617) 425-0200; thegallowsboston.com; New American; $$; T: Back Bay Station. The "gallows humor" can wear a little thin (the stuffed raven, the Halloween lighting) but it's true that Boston's gallows stood on this spot—about 300 years ago. Fortunately, the trying-too-hard schtick ends with the food, which features honest-to-goodness locally sourced ingredients prepared for people who like to eat. Many dishes are meant to be shared, from the fries-cheese-gravy poutine to big cheese and charcuterie platters. The Gallows serves excellent if often restrained burgers (the Kenny Powers version with patty *and* pulled pork is an exception to the restraint), and often features beef soup as an entree. Lest that sound too light, keep in mind that it includes short ribs, oxtail meatballs, and pickled macombers.

Gaslight Brasserie du Coin, 560 Harrison Ave., South End, Boston, MA 02118; (617) 422-0224; gaslight560.com; French; $$; T: Back Bay Station. Little sister to **Aquitaine** (see p. 126), the Gaslight is a real neighborhood restaurant—assuming your neighborhood is a Parisian *arrondisement*. Roomier than Aquitaine, the Gaslight is more thoroughly bourgeois (and that's not a bad thing). We're always happy where we can order a properly executed salade niçoise or get a plate of chewy duck confit with orange gastrique, a chard-orange salad, and roasted garlic potatoes. Like Aquitaine, there are *plats du jours*. It's worth checking the website to find out what night has been designated for the *choucroute garni*. Seating is catch as catch can—a mix of bar stools, cafe tables, large family tables, and a few booths and banquettes. Twenty wines are available by the glass or carafe, and 40 more by the bottle.

Ginza Boston, 16 Hudson St., Chinatown, Boston, MA 02111; ginza-boston.com; Japanese; $$; T: Chinatown. Perhaps it's ironic, but Ginza is at its best when there's an absolute crush on the weekends. For one thing, that's when they put on their most experienced servers who can quickly explain the different types of rolls or the cuts of the sashimi. Warm sake is usually the better bet here, and the salmon snow white *maki* is a favorite of most of the regulars. Service on the weekends continues until 3:30 a.m., which makes Ginza a popular place after the clubs close at 2. If you're dining on a weekday, the sashimi dinner package, where the sushi chefs pick the best cuts of fish, is an especially good deal.

Great Taste Bakery & Restaurant, 61–63 Beach St., Chinatown, Boston, MA 02111; (617) 426-8899; Chinese; $; T: Chinatown. We always turn directly to the last page of the long menu at Great Taste. The bustling restaurant is a good bet for the ultimate Chinese comfort food, congee, a porridge-like rice dish. The creamy rice can be enhanced with little bits of flavor, and Great Taste offers a number of good options, including minced beef, fish fillet, chicken, and scallops with vegetables.

Hamersley's Bistro, 553 Tremont St., South End, Boston, MA 02118; (617) 423-2700; hamersleysbistro.com; French/New American; $$$$; T: Back Bay Station. It is only a slight exaggeration to say that Gordon Hamersley's restaurant launched the renaissance of the South End when it opened in 1987. That reservations at Hamersley's remain some of the most sought-after in the city speaks to the high standards the maestro has managed to maintain, not to mention the enduring appeal of French provincial preparations of great American ingredients. Two of the restaurant's signature dishes are the roasted garlic and lemon chicken and the souffléed lemon custard. In fact, if you can't get a table seat, we recommend settling for a bar stool and ordering those two homey favorites for a meal you won't soon forget. On the way out, pick up a copy of Gordon Hamersley's cookbook, *Bistro Cooking at Home.*

House of Siam, 542 Columbus Ave., South End, Boston, MA 02118; (617) 267-1755; houseofsiam boston.com; Thai; $; T: Massachusetts Avenue. You won't be mistaking the South End for Bangkok when you dine at the House of Siam, but vegetarians are especially pleased with the nine fresh-flavored dishes on the small veggie corner of the otherwise lengthy menu. If you can take the heat of Thai chiles, try the assorted sautéed vegetables with minced hot peppers, garlic, and Thai basil.

Jae's, 520 Columbus Ave., South End, Boston, MA 02118; (617) 421-9405; jaescafe.com; Asian; $–$$; T: Massachusetts Avenue. Jae Chung launched this pan-Asian cafe back in the days when the South End was just becoming gentrified. His other restaurants around the city have closed, but the neighbors keep the original going strong. It might be odd in Boston to think of having a neighborhood sushi joint, but Jae's fits that bill. Sushi sets just barely edge into the $$ category. Jae's may also sell more plates of pad thai than any of the Thai restaurants around. The best winter warmer is the bowl of kimchee *jigae,* a spicy Korean soup of kimchee, pork, and tofu.

Masa Restaurant, 439 Tremont St., South End, Boston, MA 02116; (617) 338-8884; masarestaurant.com; Southwestern; $$$; T: Back Bay Station. Refined Southwestern cuisine had a big run in the 1980s after Mark Miller opened Coyote Cafe in Santa Fe. Miller's moved on, but a few smart chefs have kept the torch burning for one of the most quintessentially indigenous American cuisines. Neither Chef-Owner Phillip Aviles nor Chef de Cuisine José Cardoza goes in for tokenism, so you won't see a lot of "blue corn this" and "hotter than hell that" on the sophisticated menu. Think blackened shrimp and goat cheese quesadilla as a starter, or perhaps skillet-roasted sea scallops and barbecued duck with a sweet corn cream. The cowboy cut, chile-rubbed steaks are about as close as they get to cliché, but by the time you've tasted the accompanying ranchero salsa, grilled baby corn, and chile onion rings, you might be ready to head for the upper Rio Grande.

Mela Modern Indian Cuisine, 578 Tremont St., South End, Boston, MA 02118; (617) 859-4805; melaboston.com; Indian; $$; T: Back Bay Station. Just barely edging into $$ territory, Mela offers Indian cuisine for South Enders striving to still fit into last year's tight leather jacket. Although the selection is nearly as exhaustive as the typical Indian menu, Mela skips a lot of the oil-heavy dishes in favor of curried lamb and goat, spicy Goa preparations of fish, and all manner of proteins roasted in the searing heat of the tandoor oven. If you enjoy drama and are in a DIY mood, order either the meat or seafood hot stone platter. You get a tray of marinated lamb or a combo of scallops and salmon and a lightly oiled hot stone slab on which to cook them.

Metropolis Cafe & Wine Bar, 584 Tremont St., South End, Boston, MA 02118; (617) 247-2931; metropolisboston.com; French; $$; T: Back Bay Station. This wine bar with food launched the

Aquitaine (see p. 126) empire in what now seems like ages ago. As its spawn learned to speak real French in the kitchen, Metropolis has veered more Riviera to even Italian, featuring the likes of potato gnocchi with brussels sprouts, rigatoni with crumbled fennel sausage and Parmigiana Reggiano cheese, and tagliatelle with braised beef and roasted butternut squash. With rib-sticking and reasonably priced food like that, there's no sense quibbling over which cuisine can claim it. As a friend of ours always says with a shrug, "It's all good."

Mike's City Diner, 1714 Washington St., South End, Boston, MA 02118; (617) 267-9393; mikescitydiner.com; Casual American; $; T: Massachusetts Avenue or Worcester Square (Silver Line). **Nobody** has a bad word to say about Mike's, so we'll offer a few: It closes at 3 p.m., far too early for those of us who'd gladly eat three squares a day there. Second, it takes only cash, though that's mitigated by the cheap prices. And third, there are nowhere near enough seats for the weekend brunch rush between 10 a.m. and 1 p.m. The food, however, is great, and even includes ham sliced from the bone on the breakfast menu, as well as a choice between home fries and  grits on most breakfast specials. During the week you can order sandwiches at lunch-time, but just like the faux gruff "cash only" policy, the menu allows "no substitutions." Mike's isn't a place for folks who want everything "on the side." One other bad thing: The place crawls with politicians and their media entourage during election season. Cash only.

Myers + Chang, 1145 Washington St., South End, Boston, MA 02118; (617) 542-5200; myersandchang.com; Asian; $; T: Back Bay Station. The tastes are all Asian—Chinese, Taiwanese, Thai, and Vietnamese—but the concept is something like the intersection of dim sum and tapas. Plates are on the small side and they can add up, but the diner atmosphere is spot-on for the South End and the flavors are amazing. It's no surprise that this place is directly across the street from Boston's most accessible Asian grocery store, **Ming's** (see p. 158), since Chef Karen Akunowicz's menu features easily understood dishes like braised pork belly buns, baby bok choy with wok-roasted shiitake mushrooms, and tamarind-glazed cod with a salad of jicama, mint, and grapefruit.

New Shanghai, 21 Hudson St., Chinatown, Boston, MA 02111; (617) 338-6688; newshanghairestaurant.com; Chinese; $; T: Chinatown. Boston's first Chinatown celebrity chef, C. K. Sau, moved on to run **CK Shanghai** in Wellesley (see p. 365) some years ago, but not before he put his stamp on the New Shanghai. His signature classical dishes—like the unbelievably good tea-smoked duck, made in a wok—remain on the menu, and while it's no longer a safe bet to walk in and just ask the chef to make whatever he feels like, you can put together a great repast of largely northern Chinese dishes by ordering from the "Chef's Special" section. The peppery twice-cooked pork belly is often a good bet. It doesn't hurt to ask, though, if anything special has come in that day—say, fresh local pea tendrils for sautéeing with garlic, or maybe a great fish that can be roasted whole.

Oishii Boston, 1166 Washington St., South End, Boston, MA 02118; (617) 482-8868; oishiiboston.com; Japanese; $$$; T: Back Bay Station. Many regulars here claim that Chef Ting's crew produces the best sushi in the country. We haven't eaten enough sushi around the country to know for sure, but the quality of the fish at this Japanese stalwart (since 1998) is unparalleled, the presentation is exquisite, and the prices are not high for premium Japanese fine dining. The sushi and sashimi are the main attractions at this restaurant sometimes frequented by Tom Brady and Gisele Bündchen. But Oishii also offers tempura and other traditional Japanese fine dining dishes. Sushi-making classes are offered at noon on the second Sunday of the month—lunch included.

Orinoco: A Latin Kitchen, 477 Shawmut Ave., South End, Boston, MA 02118; (617) 369-7075; orinocokitchen.com; Venezuelan; $$; T: Massachusetts Avenue. The original of three Venezuelan restaurants (the others are in Brookline, p. 212, and Cambridge, p. 269), this branch of Orinoco sits kitty-corner across from **El Centro** (p. 133), making this intersection the liveliest Spanish-speaking dining corner in the South End. It's inspired by Venezuelan roadside *taqueritas* and aims to reproduce the feeling of a casual, family-run food shop in the urban setting of the South End. Warning: The place is packed on weekend nights.

O Ya, 9 East St., Leather District, Boston, MA 02111; (617) 654-9900; oyarestaurantboston.com; Japanese; $$$$$; T: South Station. There are no bargains at O Ya—in fact, the typical meal here is probably the most expensive in Boston. But the exquisitely elegant 37-seat restaurant is a rarity in Boston, offering sure-handed innovation of traditional Japanese dishes. Six chefs are constantly at work producing perfect little morsels for the bite-size portions. Half the menu is sushi and sashimi, the other half pork, chicken, beef, and vegetarian. One national reviewer named O Ya for the best *omakase* (tasting) menu in the US. If you're an aficionado, let head chef Tim Cushman treat you to the meal of a lifetime.

Penang Malaysian Cuisine, 685–691 Washington St., Chinatown, Boston, MA 02111; (617) 451-6373; Malaysian; $; T: Chinatown. Malaysian food is the mother cuisine of Southeast Asia, but there are few Malay restaurants in Boston. Penang won't win prizes for its fluorescent-and-Formica dining room, but it serves some excellent inexpensive fare, including its signature clay pot curries and a sweet and sour mango shredded chicken dish served in a mango shell. Penang is very popular for lunch but tends to have plenty of open seats at dinnertime.

Pepper Pot, 208 Dudley St., Roxbury, Boston, MA 02119; (617) 445-4409; pepperpotrestaurant.com; Jamaican; $; T: Dudley Station

(Silver Line). Owner Stanley Byfield smiles widely if you ask him how hot he makes his food. The jerk chicken, he allows, is pretty hot, but when it comes to dishes like the curried goat or curried chicken, "I cook them more mild. I used to do them hot but I think I was losing customers." After more than a decade in Dudley Square, he knows his clientele well. "But I can make it hot for you if you want!" he says. Byfield keeps a lot of stewed dishes simmering, including some less common Jamaican specialties like oxtails and butterbeans, and he will prepare brown stewed fish or callaloo and saltfish (salt cod and greens) to order. All meals are served with rice and pigeon peas, fried plantain, and the steamed vegetable of the day.

Petit Robert Bistro, 480 Columbus Ave., South End, Boston, MA 02118; (617) 867-0600; petitrobertbistro.com; French; $$; T: Back Bay Station. This edition serves the same menu as the Kenmore Square original (see p. 106), proving that Jacky Robert's formula of reliable French bistro classics can be replicated wherever he can install a great crew in the kitchen. Over time the menu has evolved, of course, so vegetarians can order something like the quinoa, farro, and lentil cake, while Francophiles can still tuck into the cassoulet with lamb, pork sausage, duck confit, and navy beans.

Pho Pasteur, 682 Washington St., Chinatown, Boston, MA 02111; (617) 482-7467; phopasteurboston.net; Vietnamese; $; T: Chinatown. This soup house introduced *pho* to Boston back in the days when the only people who had tasted *pho* were either

Vietnamese immigrants or veterans of the Vietnam War. The Vietnamese are such great cooks that they conquered the French (some of the best inexpensive restaurants in Paris) and Pho Pasteur certainly has a strong foothold in Chinatown. The food is terrific: warming soup, nicely sliced meat, and gigantic heaps of bean sprouts and basil to add. Service is minimal, but it gets the job done.

Q Restaurant, 660 Washington St., Chinatown, Boston, MA 02111; (857) 350-3968; thequsa.com; Chinese; $$; T: Chinatown. Superbly cut and beautifully presented sushi is one extreme at Q, while the other is Mongolian hot pot where you cook your own meat or seafood in a nearly bubbling broth. "We make 12 different kinds of broth," says restaurateur Ming Zhu. "Spicy *mala* and blackbone chicken are the most popular. Since the food arrives at the table raw, it all has to be very fresh and healthy." There's also a choice of a vegetarian platter and vegetarian broth. All this is served at bargain Chinatown prices in an upscale setting on the ground level of a luxury apartment complex. Ming Zhu started small in Quincy, but his Boston offspring has been the hit of Chinatown with Chinese and non-Chinese alike.

Quic Pic BBQ, 50 Beach St., Chinatown, Boston, MA 02111; (617) 426-1110; Chinese; $; T: Chinatown. It is hard to pass Quic Pic without experiencing sudden pangs of hunger from the aroma of the barbecued

meats. Mind you, it's not going to win any decor prizes, but you can get a big meal of soup, fried rice, and a selection of barbecued meat for a single-digit price. Here's the catch: Most people get takeout, though there are a few tables where you can sit. Fans of Chinese barbecue are always debating which spot is best. Quic Pic wins all arguments for its crispy pork, not so many for its barbecued chicken.

Shabu-Zen, 16 Tyler St., Chinatown, Boston, MA 02111; (617) 292-8828; shabuzen.com; Japanese; $; T: Chinatown. For the Japanese take on Mongolian hot pot (with shorter chopsticks and different condiments) try this restaurant's shabu-shabu, or "swish-swish," which is pretty much what you do when you swirl raw meat and vegetables in hot broth. Far more casual than **Q** (see p. 145), Shabu-Zen is especially popular at lunch. All main courses come with a vegetable plate, dessert, and a choice of jasmine rice, *udon* noodle, or rice noodles.

South Street Diner, 178 Kneeland St., Leather District, Boston, MA 02111; (617) 350-0028; southstreetdiner.com; Casual American; $; T: South Station. Originally built in 1947 as the Blue Diner to serve factory workers in the Leather District between South Station and Chinatown, the South Street has seen all the factories and most of the residences in its immediate neighborhood disappear, yet it persists like a beloved dinosaur as Boston's only 24-hour diner. So who do you see lingering over the bottomless cup of coffee? Construction and road workers, cops and EMTs, scholars and coders who inhabit nearby lofts, and a certain number of just-folks who get hungry for steak and eggs at 3 a.m. It's also one of the last places in Boston serving a genuine frappé (a milk shake with ice cream, for the uninitiated).

Stella, 1515 Washington St., South End, Boston, MA 02118; (617) 247-2900; bostonstella.com; Mediterranean; $$; T: Back Bay Station. We've been supporters of Evan Deluty since he opened his first Boston restaurant on Charles Street back in the 20th century, but he's found legions of new supporters in the SoWa section of the South End. It helps that Deluty is ready to cook at all hours. You can get breakfast and lunch on weekdays, brunch on weekends, and dinner and late-night dining until 1:30 a.m. every night. You can go casual with pizza or pasta, or hearty with a seafood risotto filled with shrimp, calamari, mussels, and bites of swordfish. Nor is Deluty's chicken merely a "safe" choice, since the roasted bird comes with a ragù of wild mushrooms, crispy onions, and whipped potatoes suffused with gorgonzola. The restaurant is really divided into Stella and **Stella Cafe,** which is the part of the operation open for breakfast, brunch, and lunch.

Taiwan Cafe, 34 Oxford St., Chinatown, Boston, MA 02111; (617) 426-8181; Chinese; $; T: Chinatown. In a Chinatown where the oldest restaurants are either Szechuan or Cantonese, Taiwan Cafe was a real anomaly when Jessica Wang opened it in 1998. Slowly but surely it has won a real following among English-speakers and Mandarin-speakers alike. All the food is served family style, and it's always worth starting with the hot and sour soup. The Taiwan-style noodles, a kind of flat egg noodle, are always good. The waitstaff is friendly, if not always fully conversant in English, and the tired decor got a major overhaul in early 2012. There are very few seats but devotees gladly wait on the street, as the kitchen is quick and turnover is rapid.

Teranga Restaurant, 1746 Washington St., South End, Boston, MA 02118; (617) 266-0003; terangaboston.com; Senegalese; $$; T: Massachusetts Avenue. *Teranga* is the Wolof word for hospitality, and Senegal is known all over Africa as "the land of *teranga*." Chef-Owner Marie-Claude Mendy picked the name for her restaurant, she says, because *teranga* is a way of life in her homeland and she's determined to share it in her adopted Boston. There's a modern African overtone to the restaurant with its zebrawood accents and contemporary African paintings hanging on one exposed-brick wall. The food is modern and sophisticated, too—a reminder that Senegal was once a French colony and that many Senegalese picked up a taste for Vietnamese food when they fought a few generations ago in French Indochina. Among the popular appetizers are *nems*, a Senegalese version of the Vietnamese spring roll. Be sure to order the *thiebou djeun*, a complex plate that is more or less the national dish of Senegal. Along with herb-stuffed whole fish, it includes

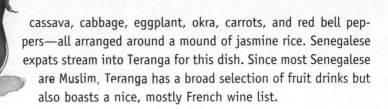

cassava, cabbage, eggplant, okra, carrots, and red bell peppers—all arranged around a mound of jasmine rice. Senegalese expats stream into Teranga for this dish. Since most Senegalese are Muslim, Teranga has a broad selection of fruit drinks but also boasts a nice, mostly French wine list.

Toro, 1704 Washington St., South End, Boston, MA 02118; (617) 536-4300; toro-restaurant.com; Spanish; $; T: Massachusetts Avenue (Orange Line) or Worcester Square (Silver Line). Ken Oringer (**Clio,** p. 97) and Jamie Bissonnette (**Coppa,** p. 131) combined forces for this nonstop hit of a reinterpreted tapas bar. None of the dishes is very expensive, but you'll spend plenty by the time you're full. Nonetheless, you get what you pay for, with hot tapas like smoked duck drumettes with a quince glaze, grilled corn with aioli and aged cheese, or Jonah crab with piquillo peppers. Like genuine Spanish food, it tends to be a bit salty—all the better to encourage you to drink, my dear. The wine list (save one Madeira) is strictly Spanish and includes one of our favorite Tempranillos from the town of Toro.

Tremont 647, 647 Tremont St., South End, Boston, MA 02118; (617) 266-4600; tremont647.com; New American; $$; T: Back Bay Station. This neighborhood restaurant with the extensively illustrated Chef-Owner Andy Husbands at the helm is almost fanatical about using local produce, fish, and meat. It's hard to order badly when the menu features the likes of the house signature hoisin-glazed pan-seared hake, a lemon-garlic spit-roasted half chicken, or fried catfish with bacony collard greens. Husbands is locally famed for his tater tots stuffed with blue cheese. On Saturday and Sunday the restaurant has a "pajama brunch" that extends to its adjunct room next door, Sister Sorel. And yes, people do show up in their pj's.

Wai Wai Restaurant, 26 Oxford St., Chinatown, Boston, MA 02111; (617) 338-9833; Chinese; $; T: Chinatown. This might be the perfect restaurant for diners who like to feel that they have discovered a literal hole-in-the-wall eatery that is an unpolished gem. Wai Wai isn't quite that, but it is a basement operation without air conditioning where most patrons speak Cantonese. Do the smart thing and order what everyone else does: the rice plates with some form of barbecued meat that's been chopped on a big wooden block by a scary guy with a huge knife. Roasted duck or chicken are excellent and the roast pork is a good second place to the crispy pork at **Quic Pic** (see p. 145).

Winsor Dim Sum Cafe, 10 Tyler St., Chinatown, Boston, MA 02111; (617) 338-1688; Chinese; $; T: Chinatown. This is the place for people who like to be in control of their dining destiny. Rather than waiting to see what dim sum delights roll past on the steaming carts, Winsor allows diners to select their favorites from a menu and have them prepared to order. Congee (rice soup) is part of the menu of larger plates, but you can also get a small order with lean pork and preserved egg from the dim sum selection. Shrimp dumpling remains the test of the dim sum chef, and Winsor's are made fresh in the kitchen. A few pieces are weekend specialties: the baked roast pork bun and the egg custard.

Landmarks

Jacob Wirth Restaurant, 31–37 Stuart St., Chinatown, Boston, MA 02116; (617) 338-8586; jacobwirth.com; German/Casual American; $$; T: Boylston. With its knockwurst, sauerkraut, potato salad, and beers, Jacob Wirth keeps up appearances as a German restaurant. A survivor in its neighborhood since 1868, the restaurant is at least as well known for its sing-along piano bar as for its cuisine. The neighborhood around it has become Boston's Theater District, making Jacob Wirth a popular spot for a quick supper before a show or nibbles, beers, and tunes afterward. Wiener schnitzel, jager schnitzel, and sauerbraten are available, but most diners opt for American comfort food: burgers, the signature sandwiches, mac and cheese, steak tips, or fish and chips.

Specialty Stores, Markets & Producers

Bao Bao Bakery & Cafe, 77 Harrison Ave., Chinatown, Boston, MA 02111; (617) 988-8191; Bakery; T: Chinatown. Some of the prettiest decorated cakes in town can be found at Bao Bao, and while they are hardly French or Viennese tortes, they're as sweet and tasty as they are fancy. The selection of bubble tea makes Bao Bao almost irresistible. Get a slice of fancy cake and a big cup of bubble tea and enjoy the sheer sugar high.

Brix Wine Shop, 1284 Washington St., South End, Boston, MA 02118; (617) 542-2749; brixwineshop.com; Wine, Beer & Spirits; T: Back Bay Station. The South End version of Brix (there's another in the Financial District, see p. 81) has a great program of wine tastings from 6 to 8 p.m. Friday and Saturday. But in addition to a superb selection of wines from across Europe, the West Coast, and around the globe, Brix also carries the Signatory line of vintage scotch. The company buys single-barrel lots from various scotch distilleries, then releases them in austere bottles for the discerning whiskey drinker. Each year's selection ($60–$200 per bottle) comes in shortly before Christmas. By summer it's all gone.

Chocolee Chocolates, 23 Dartmouth St., South End, Boston, MA 02116; (617) 236-0606; chocoleechocolates.com; Chocolatier; T: Back Bay Station. A self-taught pastry chef, Lee Napoli worked in some of Boston's finest restaurants before going into business for herself. She sells handmade candy and pastries from what has to be the smallest shop in Boston. (Two customers make it crowded.) If you're lucky enough to arrive some morning when she's just made her chocolate-filled beignets, you will swear undying allegiance.

Check the store or website for her classes, suitable for ambitious home cooks or beginning professionals.

C-Mart Supermarket, 686–692 Washington St., Chinatown, Boston, MA 02111; 617-338-1717; Grocery; T: Chinatown. Almost hidden among shops and restaurants, the nondescript door leads into an almost overwhelming food emporium. C-Mart stocks all the rices, teas, canned fruits and vegetables, snack foods, dried fish, and sauces that you might expect, including more than 60 shelf feet devoted to soy sauce alone. But the market also excels at fresh foods including meat, clear-eyed fish on ice, and tanks for live eel,

codfish, shrimp, rock lobster, and crab. Fresh fruits and vegetables in season might include bok choy, sweet pea tips, Japanese pumpkin, kohlrabi, and numerous varieties of oranges and grapefruit. You might even find durian, the notoriously smelly fruit from Southeast Asia.

Flour Bakery + Cafe, 1595 Washington St., South End, Boston, MA 02118; (617) 267-4300; flourbakery.com; Bakery Cafe. Every time we visit Flour, we silently thank Harvard-educated Chef-Owner Joanne Chang for forsaking applied mathematics and economics for Midnight Chocolate Cake and Lemon Lust Tarts. Opened in 2000,

Eastern Journey

Many non-Chinese find Chinatown's culinary scene a bit daunting, to say the least. The sheer density of the neighborhood and the unfamiliarity of ingredients in the market can be a little overwhelming. Master chef and Mandarin-speaker Jim Becker helps overcome those obstacles on the three-and-a-half-hour **Chinatown Market Tour** that he operates twice daily on Thursday and Saturday. The tour covers a lot of culinary ground, with a crash course in some of the cuisines of China, a guided walk through the exotic produce, seafood, and spices of a market, and sampling at a barbecue shop and a Chinese bakery. The tour winds up with a dim sum meal, included in the fee. The tour is part of **Michele Topor's Boston Food Tours** (p. 42, Mangia! sidebar), which otherwise specialize in Italy and the North End. For information call (617) 523-6032. Tickets must be purchased in advance from Zerve: zerve.com/MicheleTopor/BCMT.

this bakery cafe has spawned two siblings in Cambridge (see p. 253) and Fort Point (see p. 83). Breakfast treats include oatmeal maple scones, chocolate brioche, sticky caramel buns, and sour cream coffee cake. Lunchtime sandwiches feature elegant fillings such as roasted lamb, tomato chutney, and goat cheese or smoked turkey with cheddar and cranberry chutney. Be sure to leave room for a Belgian chocolate brownie or chocolate chip macaroon or take home a whole Boston cream pie or caramel nut tart for a great dinner-party dessert. By the way, Flour staff pull out all the stops with

Valentine's Day cookies with R-rated messages. Ask them to bring the cookies out from hiding under the counter.

Foodie's Urban Market, 1421 Washington St., South End, Boston, MA 02118; (617) 266-9911; foodies-market.com; Grocery; T: Back Bay. Shopping here could turn anyone into a foodie. This full-service store has made a real commitment to stocking New England products, including cheese, eggs, butter, ice cream, bread, chocolate, pizza, pasta, maple syrup, seafood, beer, cider, and handmade sodas. The in-house products are no slouches either. The meat department makes it own sausages and grinds meat fresh daily. The deli turns out such dishes as chicken quesadillas, stuffed shells, baby back ribs, and cornmeal-crusted tilapia. By the way, the popular lunchtime salad bar even offers oatmeal from 8 to 11 a.m.

Hafun Cafe, 51 Roxbury St., Roxbury, Boston, MA 02119; (617) 427-6300; Bakery Cafe; T: Dudley Station (Silver Line). You won't always run into Owner Hussein Hussein, because he's busy doing all the baking for this super-friendly Dudley Square Wi-Fi cafe that serves assorted pastries, including some Somali special-ties. One of those treats is a pastry triangle called a *sambuse*. It's filled with either stewed crumbled ground beef or fish. "We used to eat it with a little Somali tea to break the fast of Ramadan," says Hussein's brother Abdi Yassin with a smile. "But it is so good that now we eat it all the time. It's delicious."

We concur. The Somali tea is a mild, sweet infusion redolent of aromatic spices like cinnamon, cardamom, and cloves. In the evenings Hafun also has beef and vegetable stew, which is served either with bread or with *malawax,* the traditional griddle cake similar to Ethiopian *injera.*

Haley House Bakery Cafe, 12 Dade St., Roxbury, Boston, MA 02119; (617) 445-0900; haleyhouse.org; Bakery Cafe; T: Dudley Square (Silver Line). It was a breath of fresh air for Dudley Square and Haley House alike when the agency moved its bakery cafe from cramped quarters in the South End (now occupied by **Chocolee**

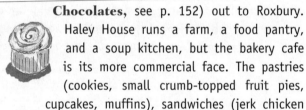

Chocolates, see p. 152) out to Roxbury. Haley House runs a farm, a food pantry, and a soup kitchen, but the bakery cafe is its more commercial face. The pastries (cookies, small crumb-topped fruit pies, cupcakes, muffins), sandwiches (jerk chicken quesadilla, for example), and soups (spicy chicken and potato) all set a high standard. Although the cafe is open until late afternoon, breakfast is one of the most popular meals, with many customers favoring the Haley House Slop. That's a plate of cheesy grits, scrambled eggs, and chicken sausage.

Hamdi Halal Market & Fresh Produce, 1433 Tremont St., Roxbury, Boston, MA 02120; (617) 606-7108; Grocery; T: Roxbury Crossing. This small neighborhood grocer on the Mission Hill side of Roxbury has a significant Halal meat selection in the back, separated from the dried pulses and seeds and general east African/ Middle Eastern groceries in the front. It's a very friendly place, but tends to run out of goat and lamb over the weekend, so buy early or wait until Tuesday.

Hing Shing Pastry, 67 Beach St., Chinatown, Boston, MA 02111; (617) 451-1162; Bakery; T: Chinatown or South Station. Opened in the 1980s, Hing Shing is one of Chinatown's oldest bakeries and also one of the most traditional. It's most busy in the early morning and at lunchtime. Stop in when the crowds have thinned and the friendly staff will point out the specialties, including a ham and egg bun that's a breakfast favorite and a roast pork bun that makes a great quick lunch. Almond cookies are popular, but do not overlook the modest-looking coconut butter roll, which may be Hing Shing's most popular item. Last time we stopped in, we were tempted by a square of red bean pie. "It's very heavy," the young woman behind the counter warned us. "Take the mixed nut pie instead."

Las Ventas, 700 Harrison Ave., South End, Boston, MA 02118; (617) 266-0905; lasventasspain.com; Grocery; T: Newton Street (Silver Line). Las Ventas (the market next to **Estragon Tapas Bar,** see p. 134) specializes in food products from Spain, and one of the best ways to sample them is to order some of the *bocadillos,* or sandwiches. You might opt for *butifarra* sausage with Manchego cheese and mixed greens or Spain's famous dry-cured mountain ham, *jamon serrano,* with tomato. You can also buy the pricey ham from the deli, along with Palencios chorizo from León, cabrales blue cheese from Asturias, or the long, thin Basque sausage known as *txistorra*. Las Ventas also stocks such Spanish essentials as smoked paprika, saffron, olive oil, rice, and canned tuna, sardines, and anchovies (they make great appetizers). You can even pick up a seafood paella mix and a paella pan.

Ming's Supermarket, 1102 Washington St., South End, Boston, MA 02118; (617) 338-1588; Grocery; T: Back Bay Station. This Asian supermarket is one of the easiest we have ever encountered for Westerners to navigate. Once you pass the wall of 20-pound bags of jasmine, Thai, brown, sushi, and sweet rices and peruse the huge tea selection, you'll find that the aisles are clearly labeled: "Southeast Asian Food and Condiments," "Japanese and Korean Foods," and the like. There is even a whole aisle of instant noodle soups, and another of spices. Still overwhelmed? Take a tip from the chefs at **Myers + Chang** (see p. 141), who often stop by for ramen noodles and Chinese black vinegar, which adds a smoky depth to soups and marinades. Ming's also has a huge selection of fresh produce, meats, and fish, and a hot deli with such dishes as roasted fish, preserved duck, spicy beef tendon, and pork with mustard.

Morse Fish Company, 1401 Washington St., South End, Boston, MA 02118; (617) 262-9375; morsefish.com; Fishmonger; T: Back Bay Station or Union Park (Silver Line). This neighborhood fishmonger has stood across the street from Holy Cross cathedral since 1903, which was no doubt convenient in the days of fish on Friday. But now it's fish every day, and Morse keeps up with all the local fresh catch as well as fried fish meals to eat at the few tables or take home. The most popular lunch dish is the fried haddock sandwich.

New Saigon Sandwich Banh Mi, 696 Washington St., Chinatown, Boston, MA 02111; (617) 542-6296; Sandwich Shop; T: Chinatown. Every Chinatown needs a great *banh mi* joint to complement the one good *pho* house, and New Saigon is it. In fact, the shop was selling Vietnamese sandwiches (which they call French submarines) for decades before they bothered to put up any English signage. It doesn't matter—it's probably the single most popular lunch spot for all the staff and students at nearby Tufts Medical campus. Not only do they love the shredded pork or barbecued beef sandwiches piled high with a veritable salad of vegetables, they also scarf up the vegetarian and the chicken box lunches with rice. Bubble tea is another plus.

Render Coffee, 563 Columbus Ave., South End, Boston, MA 02118; (617) 262-4142; rendercoffeebar.com; Coffee Shop; T: Massachusetts Avenue. Tall and looming with a few days' beard and a knit cap, Barista-Owner Chris Dadey looks like a man from American coffee culture. He's mum about where he worked before, but opened Render in October 2011 because he was tired of cutting corners. Here he's trying "to take coffee to a new level." Along with the espresso machine drinks, Render serves three or four single-origin pour-overs—drip coffee made fresh by the cup, which many connoisseurs feel is the *only* way to brew good joe. "We don't do 20-ounce lattes," Dadey says drolly. He offers a smattering of food: quiches made in cups of phyllo dough, a few good cookies, scones, and croissants. The shop has ample seating at marble-topped tables, including a terrarium room for winter sunshine, and free Wi-Fi—that other coffeehouse essential.

Siena Farms, 106 Waltham St., South End, Boston, MA 02116; (978) 261-5365; sienafarms.com; Farmstand; T: Back Bay Station. This tiny shop serves as the urban "farmstand" for Siena Farms, a 50-acre farm about 25 miles west of Boston. Farmer Chris Kurth grows beautiful produce for farmers' markets and restaurants, including wife Ana Sortun's **Oleana** (see p. 267) and **Sofra** (see p. 300). In fact, Sortun, one of the area's top chefs, established the South End shop. It's open year-round and also stocks produce from other farms, along with cheese, eggs, chocolate, cider, milk, coffee, and other goods from New England producers.

South End Buttery, 314 Shawmut Ave., South End, Boston, MA 02118; (617) 482-1015; southendbuttery.com; Bakery Cafe; T: Back Bay Station. "Buttery" is not only an adjective that might describe a particularly good cookie or slice of cake. In British universities, "buttery" is a noun, used for places that serve the kinds of comfort food that students crave. Richard Gordon, a former criminal prosecutor, had the latter in mind when he and a partner opened this bakery cafe that serves everything from breakfast burritos to Szechuan noodle salad or a PBJ sandwich with organic homemade peanut butter and homemade jam on sourdough bread. But come to think of it, the former might also apply to the cupcakes, including chocolate cake with coffee buttercream frosting or vanilla cake with fresh strawberry buttercream.

South End Formaggio, 268 Shawmut Ave., South End, Boston, MA 02118; (617) 350-6996; southendformaggio.com; Cheesemonger; T: Back Bay Station. Ihsan and Valerie Gurdal opened this smaller off-shoot of **Formaggio Kitchen** in Cambridge (see p. 291) in 1999. As befits the neighborhood, SEF functions not only as a top-notch cheesemonger but also as a general gourmet shop packed with chocolates, olive oils, honeys, jams, craft beer, and a highly select group of wines. The kitchen does a bang-up lunch business in sandwiches and prepares salads and ready-to-heat entrees for quick meal prep. Tastings are offered almost every week and classes in cheese *affinage* or cooking with cheese are sometimes available.

South End Pita, 473 Albany St., South End, Boston, MA 02118; (617) 556-2600; Sandwich Shop; T: Broadway. One look at the silvery teapots and delicate painted glasses used to serve mint tea should tell you that this is not a slapdash falafel joint. South End Pita is run by a brother-and-sister team from Morocco and almost all the items on the short menu are made from scratch. Stop in and you might encounter staff from the nearby Boston Medical Center enjoying such healthy fare as hummus and pita bread, vegetarian lentil soup, grape leaves stuffed with rice, or grilled lamb shish kebabs.

Syrian Grocery Importing Co., 270 Shawmut Ave., South End, Boston, MA 02118; (617) 426-1458; Grocery; T: Back Bay Station. When Syrian Grocery opened in 1940, it provided the food staples from home for the South End's large Middle Eastern community. The shop has been in Ramon Mansour's family since 1967 and still stocks such essentials as Arabic allspice, a blend of seven spices that is used in stews and is the "secret spice" in kibbe, and *mahlab*, which is used in sweet breads instead of vanilla. As the neighborhood has become gentrified, he has noted a broader interest in his products. "People visit Morocco and then they want to re-create the food at home," says Mansour, who always carries beautiful clay tagines, preserved lemons, and Morocco's all-purpose seasoning blend, *ras al hanout*. He's always ready to provide advice as culinary trends veer toward the Middle East. "Right now we are having a run on farro and farik," he says. "People want to try these new grains." Pomegranate seed oil is also in demand. "It's been used in the Middle East for ages to flavor meat or drizzle on eggs. Now the chefs are using it in different ways."

Tropical Foods, 2101 Washington St., Roxbury, Boston, MA 02119; (617) 442-7439; tropicalfoods.net; Grocery; T: Dudley Square (Silver Line). Also known by its Spanish name, El Platanero, Tropical has been Roxbury's neighborhood supermarket since 1974, making sure that its African-American and Caribbean clientele are equally well fed. The frozen food aisle appeals to both with black-eyed peas, okra, mustard greens, chopped collard greens, and butter beans. Puerto Rican frozen specialties include fried plantains (*tostones*), baked ripe plantains, chicken croquettes, and empanadas. Goya's Hispanic products abound, including a wide range of sausages and the whole line of soup bases and seasonings (including one with culantro and achiote). Goya's *sofrito* (tomato-based) and *recaito* (cilantro-based) cooking sauces are readily available. In the dry goods, one side of an entire aisle is devoted to dried beans, peas, and other pulses, and an entire section of the fresh vegetables is devoted to root crops, ranging from yautia and cassava to African and Japanese yams. Tropical is the place to find Demarara sugar at a non–gourmet shop price, or to pick up smoked goat meat, salted pig's feet, or cross-sectioned oxtail for making an unctuous stew.

Wholy Grain, 275 Shawmut Ave., South End, Boston, MA 02118; (617) 277-1531; wholygrain.com; Bakery Cafe; T: Back Bay Station. Although Boston's homegrown department store, Jordan Marsh, morphed into a Macy's in 1996, generations still remember the bakery's almost legendary blueberry muffins. The fruit-filled, sugar-coated muffins live on at this small bakery, thanks to a recipe passed on from a former Jordan's baker. And if that's not enough, the shop also turns out pecan and peach raspberry bars, cinnamon chip and blueberry almond scones, Toll House cookie pie, luscious fruit tarts and quiches, and a range of sandwiches. Ironically enough, the bakery's signature dish is gluten free. The "wholy bowl" is a mix of brown rice, red and black beans, avocado, olives, cilantro, fresh salsa, grated cheese, and sour cream. Think of it as a burrito without the confines of a tortilla.

Wine Emporium, 607 Tremont St., South End, Boston, MA 02118; (617) 262-0379; T: Back Bay Station; and 474 Columbus Ave., South End, Boston, MA 02118; (617) 536-5545; T: Massachusetts Avenue; thewineemporiumboston.com; Wine, Beer & Spirits. Although neither iteration of the Wine Emporium is destination shopping in and of itself, Tremont Street carries about 1,300 labels, while Columbus Avenue has about 1,000 stacked on the new staggered shelving. The strengths of both shops are everyday drinking wines and wines you'd bring as a gift when invited to dinner—that is, respectable but hardly superstars. We like such wines because you can uncork and enjoy them without having to build a dinner around them. In practice, this means excellent second-tier producers in major wine areas, or top wines from underappreciated areas. Wine Emporium has a flurry of soft, youngish Piemontese wines made from the Nebbiolo grape, for example, but only a few Barolos. It carries a handful of Riojas, but mostly young reds to accompany food rather than oaky aged Riojas better suited to contemplating while smoking a cigar. Staff at both places are knowledgeable and helpful, willing to steer a novice wine drinker or cater to the requests of an aficionado.

Farmers' Markets

Boston Medical Center Farmers' Market, 840 Harrison Ave., Boston. Fri from 11:30 a.m. to 2:30 p.m., mid-June through mid-Oct.

Mission Hill Farmers' Market, Brigham Circle, intersection of Huntington Ave. and Tremont St., Roxbury. Thurs from 11 a.m. to 6 p.m., June through Oct.

Roxbury/Dudley Farmers' Market, Town Common, Dudley St. and Blue Hill Ave., Roxbury. Tues and Thurs from 3 to 7 p.m., June through Oct.

Roxbury/Frederick Douglass Square Farmers' Market, corner Tremont and Hammond Streets, Roxbury. Sat from 11 a.m. to 5 p.m., July through Oct.

South End Farmers' Market, South End Open Market, end of Thayer St., Boston. Sun from 10 a.m. to 4 p.m., May through Oct (closed holiday weekends).

South End Winter Farmers' Market, 485 Harrison Ave., Boston. Sun from 10 a.m. to 2 p.m., late Nov to late Apr.

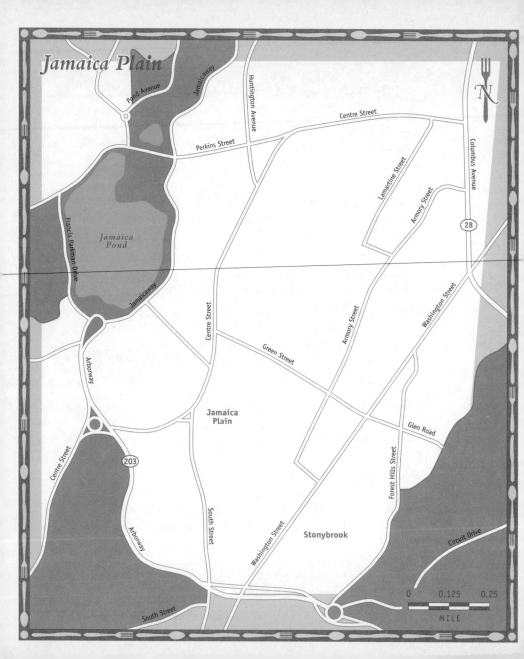

Jamaica Plain

Bracketed by Jamaica Pond and the Arnold Arboretum, two of the gems of Boston's Emerald Necklace of parks designed by Frederick Law Olmsted, Jamaica Plain was one of Boston's first streetcar suburbs, developing as a working-class residential district in the mid-19th century. By 1880 it was also Boston's beer-making center, boasting several breweries that continued to thrive until the advent of Prohibition. Today the Boston Beer Company, maker of the Samuel Adams line of ales and lagers, occupies a portion of the former Haffenreffer Brewery. The surrounding neighborhood is a funky mix. Central American and Caribbean immigrants whose first language is Spanish account for the restaurants that are hangouts for Hispanic players from the Red Sox and visiting teams. Art-school and college students from MassArt, the Museum School, and Northeastern can be spotted at all hours soaking up the free Wi-Fi in the coffee shops. Young professionals, many of whom are raising families in the condos carved out of old triple-decker tenements, make JP a child-friendly place to dine. Many establishments even offer separate kiddie menus. Jamaica Plain also has a strong GLBT contingent, and—most important for its cuisine—an unusually high percentage of vegetarians.

Foodie Faves

Bella Luna Restaurant and Milky Way Lounge, 284 Amory St., Jamaica Plain, Boston, MA 02130; (617) 524-3740; milkywayjp .com; Casual American; $–$$; T: Stony Brook. This hybrid lounge, restaurant, and club relocated a few years ago to the Brewery building and it's still a place where a certain 20-something and 30-something crowd hangs out, bringing their kids on Saturday afternoons and leaving them with the sitter at night when there might be live music or a DJ dance scene. Local artists show on the walls, and no one gets excited if you order a burger for dinner instead of one of the more expensive entrees like steak with chimichurri sauce and cumin-roasted sweet potatoes, or homemade meatballs and marinara sauce on linguine. That burger might be the Big Easy Black Bean Burger, with a patty of black beans, portobello mushroom, and bulgur topped with lime *crema* and a choice of cheeses, caramelized onions, avocado, or for baconarians (vegetarians who think bacon doesn't count), applewood-smoked bacon. There are a dozen beers on draft (including various Harpoon and Sam Adams ales), plus a few dozen more in the bottle.

Blue Nile Restaurant, 389 Centre St., Jamaica Plain, Boston, MA 02130; (617) 522-6453; bluenilejp.com; Ethiopian; $; T: Jackson Square. While Blue Nile serves plenty of fish and meat dishes, vegans and vegetarians also flock here for the Ethiopian home cooking that celebrates fresh vegetables. In fact, Blue Nile offers vegetarian combo plates of four vegetable dishes, or six vegetable main dishes and one appetizer. One of the tastiest vegetarian plates is the stew called *yatakitt wet,* which consists of fresh veggies (carrots, green peas, potatoes, and hot peppers) sautéed with caramelized onions, garlic, and ginger. The kitchen makes its own *teff injera,* a buckwheat flatbread that doubles as the primary eating utensil (the other is fingers) in Ethiopian cuisine. It's almost worth eating dinner here to catch the background music of Ethio-jazz as played by the great vibraphonist Mulatu Astatke, who has been known to collaborate with Cambridge's Either/Orchestra.

Bukhara Indian Bistro, 701 Centre St., Jamaica Plain, Boston, MA 02130; (617) 868-8311; bukharabistro.com; Indian; $–$$; T: Green Street. Part of the same group that includes Diva in Somerville, Bukhara is nicely tailored for Jamaica Plain. While it does serve a number of traditional dishes, the main thrust of the menu is Westernized Indian cuisine, which can include such dishes as tandoori duck Kadahi (tandoori duck pan-roasted with onions, tomatoes, and aromatic spices). The luncheon buffet is a steal, especially for the pleasure of dining in such a pretty, light-filled room.

Canary Square, 435 South Huntington Ave., Jamaica Plain, Boston, MA 02130; (617) 524-2500; canarysquare.com; New American; $–$$; T: Stony Brook. If Al Gore, Bill McKibben, and Ed Norton were to go out for a drink, they'd probably come to Canary Square, where they could park their bicycles in the rack outside, plunk down amid the brick-walled recycled factory decor, and order a plate of charcuterie served on a plank of wood recycled from church pews. When they decided on the wood-grilled burger (family farm, grass-fed, local), the seared local scallops (from New Bedford), and the SLT (made with local smoked salmon), they could rest assured that few carbon offsets would be necessary to justify their meal. They would probably drink Notch's Session Ale, brewed in Ipswich. Part of the appeal of Canary Square is eating and drinking without having to worry if you're politically and environmentally correct. The bar-restaurant has taken care of that for you, but still has fun by serving such nutritionally incorrect snacks as a mean deep-fried Twinkie, best accompanied by the Bourbon Root Beer Float.

Centre Street Cafe, 669A Centre St., Jamaica Plain, Boston, MA 02130; (617) 524-9217; centrestcafe.com; Eclectic; $–$$; T: Green Street. Chef-Owner Felicia Sanchez has been buying produce and meat from local farmers since she opened back in 1988, and the

REVOLUTIONARY BREW

When Jim Koch (pronounced "cook") and company launched the **Boston Beer Company** in 1984, they essentially reinvented a category of beer that had been absent from the American scene since Prohibition: the local craft brew. Indeed, there are many who credit the company with launching the renaissance of fine ales in America. Samuel Adams Boston Lager was the revolutionary brew, based on a recipe in Koch's family that was developed in 1860. The rest, as they say, is history. The Boston Beer Company is a certified American Craft Brewer, but it is the 800-pound gorilla of the group. Major production is farmed out to contract brewers across the country, but the original Jamaica Plain facility still develops new brews (some of which are trialed at nearby **Doyle's,** see p. 179). The brewery offers tours, taking a small suggested contribution for local charities.

Boston Beer Company, 30 Germania St., Jamaica Plain, Boston, MA 02130; (617) 368-5080; samueladams.com; T: Stony Brook.

restaurant even dries Sanchez's garden tomatoes for use throughout the winter. There are only 15 tables, and if none is free, you wait in the line that stretches out the door until a table opens up. Brunch is a major, very busy scene as hipsters in black and paunchy ex-freaks with tiny gray ponytails queue up for the organic oat and cornmeal waffles. Lunch and dinner are rather more laid-back.

Fill Belly's, 3381 Washington St., Jamaica Plain, Boston, MA 02130; (857) 417-3535; facebook.com/FillbellysRestaurant; Southern; $; T: Green Street. Perhaps best known for chicken and waffles, this Southern soul food restaurant started out as a food truck before setting down roots in JP in 2011. Chef-Owner Boswell Scott, better known as "Chef Bos," offers such comfort fare as mac and cheese loaf in slices with extra cheese sauce, and a variant that adds sweet potato and collards. (That's the Mac 'n' Soul Casserole.) He also serves fried chicken, Southern style, and a series of empanadas that he calls Bosalitos. Fillings vary but include shredded curry chicken, salmon with hot peppers, and spicy bean-and-pea.

Grass Fed, 605 Centre St., Jamaica Plain, Boston, MA 02130; (617) 553-2278; grassfedjp.com; Casual American; $; T: Green Street. Operated by Krista Kanyak of **Ten Tables** (see p. 177), this burger bar offers handheld cuisine perfectly suited to JP folks who crave her New American food at Ten Tables but can't afford to eat there often. Some inspired burgers (sure to be copied) are on the menu, including the Oyster Burger: 5 ounces of ground beef, a fried oyster, and homemade tartar sauce. Like all the burgers, it can be ordered on a bun or "on the grass," that is, minus the bun. Classic hamburgers, cheeseburgers, and bacon cheeseburgers are available, but so are a ground chicken burger with mozzarella and pesto (the Italian Stallion) and a chickpea burger with cucumber, roasted red pepper, shredded lettuce, and *harissa* aioli. Other sandwiches range from a po'boy of fried whitefish or fried shrimp with Cajun aioli to pastrami on rye with sauerkraut and house-made Thousand Island dressing. The small space is furnished in contemporary Italian streamline style, with counters and stools where folks can chow down if they're not getting the burgers to go.

The Haven, 2 Perkins St., Jamaica Plain, Boston, MA 02130; (617) 524-2836; thehavenjp.com; Scottish; $$; T: Jackson Square. It is an American tradition to look down on English food, and an English tradition to look down on Scottish food. What fools we be! The food here is lovingly executed and is just different enough from any other pub's fare to catch your attention. You don't have to be a fan of haggis—which is made weekly here and, as the staff will remind you, is just another form of charcuterie—to enjoy the sausages made in-house. Everything except the sandwich breads is made from scratch, including the delicious oat cakes served with butter before the meal. JP residents flock here for the burger alone, which is a massive ½-pound of beef with Huntsman cheese, house-made pickle sauce, and bacon-onion marmalade. House-made ketchup is available for smearing the accompanying "chips," which are Scottish chips: deep-fried chunky wedges of potato. A delicate flaky pastry makes the "bridies" (a turnover that brides traditionally serve to guests at the wedding) a sensational snack or starter. Yet the single most popular item on the lunch, dinner, and bar menus is the Scotch egg—a deep-fried, sausage-wrapped, hard-boiled egg cut in half and served with mustard. The Scottish beers, both on tap and in bottle, are a treat, and the sound track ranges from bagpipe skirls to ethereal heathery folk songs to English Beat (revival ska) and Glasgow's own unclassifiable Camera Obscura. There's open-mic acoustic music some nights, live bands others. You know you're in the right place when you see a portrait of young Sean Connery as James Bond on the bar. Among the desserts is the deep-fried candy bar of the week.

J. P. Seafood Cafe, 730 Centre St., Jamaica Plain, Boston, MA 02130; (617) 983-5177; jpseafoodcafe.com; Korean/Japanese/ Seafood; $; T: Green Street. Come for the sushi, stay for the bibimbap bowl of steamed rice, various vegetables, miso broth, and fiery Korean chile paste served with a fried egg and choice of meat or tofu. An elegant alternative for Jamaica Plain, J. P. Seafood Cafe has cultivated a loyal following since it opened in 1996. While the interior is beautifully minimalist, it's not as showy as some newer sushi restaurants, but it's also more modestly priced. Try the unconventional Sunshine Maki roll of salmon, lemon, cilantro, and cucumber. Tempura dishes are so light they seem like they will float right off the plate.

James's Gate Restaurant & Pub, 5 McBride St., Jamaica Plain, Boston, MA 02130; (617) 983-2000; jamessgate.com; New American; $–$$; T: Forest Hills. Named for the Dublin neighborhood where the Guinness brewery stands, James's Gate is more Irish than the Irish when it comes to the bar and the music. Chef Erik

Wunderlich's food, however, is more contemporary, ranging from a coq au vin blanc (chicken leg braised in white wine and vegetables) to a glistening rack of lamb with caramelized onions and a red-wine demi-glace, accompanied by potatoes cooked in duck fat and a small spinach salad. That's for dinner in the restaurant. For more casual fare, many diners stick to the pub menu, nibbling chips (as in fries) with curry sauce, the artisanal cheese plate, or a classic toastie (ham or turkey, swiss or cheddar, tomato) melted in the oven. Pub entrees are handsome and hearty versions of such classics as meat loaf, fish and chips, and bangers and mash.

Miami Restaurant, 381 Centre St., Jamaica Plain, Boston, MA 02130; (617) 522-4644; Caribbean; $; T: Jackson Square. Part of the stretch of Centre Street that might be called the Costa de JP, Miami dukes it out with **El Oriental de Cuba** (see p. 176) over which place serves the better Cubano sandwich and which attracts the most Spanish-speaking professional baseball players. We give a slight edge for the sandwich to El Oriental de Cuba, but Miami's is probably more authentic, from what we've been told by people who grew up eating the real thing. We do know that you get a heap of food when you order a plate here, including mounds of maduros (ripe plantains) and yucca. The *carne guisada con papas* (beef stew with potatoes) might eclipse *ropa vieja* as the best Caribbean treatment of beef.

El Oriental de Cuba, 416 Centre St., Jamaica Plain, Boston, MA 02130; (617) 524-6464; elorientaldecuba.com; Cuban; $–$$; T: Jackson Square. While the majority of JP's Hispanic population hails from either Central America or the Dominican Republic, there remains a strong Cuban strain from the migrations of the 1960s. They all come here for braised beef tongue, *bistec a caballo* (grilled skirt steak with a fried egg on top), and *ropa vieja de res,* the Cuban national dish of shredded flank steak in tomato sauce. By necessity the kitchen compromises tradition in favor of freshness, so a dish usually associated with grouper becomes haddock in coconut sauce. It's a huge plate served with rice, beans, and a choice of fried ripe or green plantain.

Sorella's, 388 Centre St., Jamaica Plain, Boston, MA 02130; (617) 524-2016; Casual American; $; T: Jackson Square. Be forewarned: The breakfast menu is six pages long and includes more pancake variations than we can shake a spatula at. If you can't choose, opt for the ginger blueberry walnut, which landed Sorella's on an AOL list of best pancakes nationwide. French toast—either the corn bread version or the oatmeal raisin walnut—is an equally sweet selection. This being JP, Sorella also offers breakfast burritos with an option of substituting tofu or tempeh for the eggs.

Tacos El Charro, 349 Centre St., Jamaica Plain, Boston, MA 02130; (617) 983-9275; Mexican; $; T: Jackson Square. For

Americans weaned on the Southern California interpretation of Mexican food, Tacos El Charro can seem a little off. Hint: Don't order the burritos. This is basically a home-cooking joint where "home" is Jalisco. So the tacos *el pastor* (braised pork and pineapple) are authentic and deeply flavored, the fried tortilla chips and chunky salsa are crispy-salty and *muy picante* (very hot), respectively, and the chicken enchilada with mole sauce, while not authentic to Puebla, is very much in line with the northern Mexican interpretation of that dish. The mariachi decor is a little kitsch, but there used to be an authentic mariachi band associated with the restaurant.

Ten Tables, 597 Centre St., Jamaica Plain, Boston, MA 02130; (617) 524-8810; tentables.net; New American; $$; T: Green Street. Krista Kanyak founded Ten Tables in 2002 in a space that a succession of other restaurants had outgrown. Her solution to success was to open another in Cambridge (see p. 274), expand into a bar space next door in JP to add more seating, and then add a third TT in Provincetown. The strategy worked to keep the JP original as intimate as originally intended—kind of a community dining room focused on produce from nearby farms and seafood from local fishermen. Kanyak now has a chef in charge of each location—Sean Callahan, in this case. The intimacy does not mean the food is homey (unless your mom was Julia Child). Even when winter means the fields are dormant, Callahan serves up seasonality in the likes of a *bourride*—a fish stew with hake, clams, and grilled bread—or pappardelle made on the premises and served with braised rabbit, baby brussels sprouts, and shaved Parmigiana Reggiano. Ten Tables always offers a bargain-priced four-course tasting menu (and an even cheaper four-course vegetarian tasting menu), with optional

 wine pairings. Desserts are less pastry than savory chef's desserts. But who can criticize a ginger pound cake with blood orange sherbet and candied blood orange? Or a chocolate terrine finished with flake sea salt and Thai basil ice cream?

Tres Gatos, 470 Centre St., Jamaica Plain, Boston, MA 02130; (617) 477-4851; tresgatosjp.com; Spanish; $; T: Stony Brook. One of the stranger combinations in JP, Tres Gatos is partly a book and music shop, and partly a tapas bar that serves real Spanish bar food. A lot of the charcuterie (which the place insists on spelling in Catalan as "xarcuterie") is imported from Spain, and ranges from serrano and *ibérico* air-dried hams to chorizo from La Rioja. They take a little artistic license with tradition, for example, injecting Moroccan spices into the *albóndigas* (meatballs). North African *harissa* perks up the slow-roasted pork with turnip puree. The very traditional grilled lamb's tongue is accompanied by very untraditional (but inspired) grits and a soft-boiled egg. Wines are all Spanish, and feature fascinating options from lesser-known districts where some of Spain's most cutting-edge vinification is taking place.

Doyle's Cafe, 3484 Washington St., Jamaica Plain, Boston, MA 02130; (617) 524-2345; doylescafeboston.com; Traditional American; $–$$; T: Green Street/Forest Hills. Founded in 1882, just 8 years after Boston annexed Jamaica Plain, Doyle's is possibly the most Irish-American of Irish bars and restaurants in the city. It was long the unofficial headquarters of the Hibernian contingent of the Massachusetts Democratic Party, and the sort of place to celebrate the election and reelection of Irish-American mayors. Doyle's makes frequent appearances in films and TV shows as representative of blue-collar Boston, and tourists often stop by to see "real" Boston Irish characters. The collection of more than two dozen beers on tap makes it a mecca for beer drinkers as well, and the proximity to the **Boston Beer Company**'s headquarters (see p. 171) means that Doyle's often serves experimental batches of Sam Adams. Doyle's also serves a large menu of simple American fare, ranging from barbecued steak tips to broiled rainbow trout to a German sausage plate or spaghetti and meatballs.

Alex's Chimis, 358c Centre St., Jamaica Plain, Boston, MA 02130; (617) 522-5201; alexschimisrestaurant.com; Sandwich Shop; $; T: Jackson Square. There are actually 12 seats where you can chow down on this authentic Dominican fast food, though most customers take their food to go. The *chimis* (strangely translated as "Dominican hamburger") are sandwiches on a soft sub roll. The *chimi super* consists of several very thin hamburgers laid end to end and topped with pickles, lettuce, onions, tomatoes, and a tomato-mayo dressing with bits of chopped pickle. (A Dominican version of Thousand Island dressing, perhaps?) The *chimi de pierna* piles the same veggies and sauce on slow-roasted pork shoulder. But most steady customers opt for a fried or roast chicken combo plate of one form or another, piling on *pastelitos* (fried turnovers filled with cheese, beef, or chicken), *relleno de yucca* (a meat-filled cassava pastry), or fried plantains, potatoes, or sweet potatoes. A lot of folks call in for the whole rotisserie chickens, which the server chops into big serving pieces with a few fierce whacks of a cleaver.

BMS Paper, 3390 Washington St., Jamaica Plain, Boston, MA 02130; (617) 522-1122; bmspaper.com; Grocery/ Housewares; T: Green Street. Largely serving restaurants and catering firms, BMS happily sells to anyone who needs #10 cans (around 6 pounds) of baked beans, ketchup, pizza sauce, or peaches in heavy syrup. It's a great place to equip your arsenal of baking pans, as you can find cake pans and cookie sheets in every imaginable size and shape, along with industrial kitchen aluminum pots and pans that include stock pots that will hold 50 gallons. Envy the squeeze bottles for ketchup and mustard that you see at fast food joints? They are cheap here, as are paper and plastic plates, plastic tableware, and even sugar dosers. If you ever find yourself in need of disposable aluminum lasagna pans with foil or plastic lids—or cardboard boxes designed for transporting cakes—you know where to come.

Blanchards Wines & Spirits, 741 Centre St., Jamaica Plain, Boston, MA 02130; (617) 522-9300; blanchardsliquor .com; Wine, Beer & Spirits; T: Green Street. One of greater Boston's wine merchants most focused on affordability, Blanchards manages to turn up extraordinary finds in the $12–$15 range while still carrying a nice selection of higher-end Bordeaux, Burgundies, and Napas. The displays as you enter the wine section of the store include a lot of relatively unknown vineyards that offer good value. It's no coincidence that you'll find many of these same wines on restaurant lists for about the same price per glass that Blanchards charges per bottle.

Canto 6 Bakery and Cafe, 3346 Washington St., Jamaica Plain, Boston, MA 02130; (617) 983-8688; canto6jp.com; Bakery Cafe; T: Green Street. Flaky croissants, fun-to-pull-apart monkey bread,

salade niçoise sandwiches on seven grain bread, great coffee, a strong Wi-Fi signal, and plenty of company—what more could a JP hipster ask? How about a crème fraîche, caramelized onion, and herb tart? Or cornmeal lemon sable cookies that melt in your mouth?

City Feed and Supply, 672 Centre St., Jamaica Plain, Boston, MA 02130; (617) 524-1700; cityfeedandsupply.com; Grocery; T: Green Street. "Local" is the watchword—nay, the mantra—here. In fact, shelf tags advising "Keep it local" abound, pointing out mustard from Raye's Mustard Mill in Maine, smoked wild kippers from Bar Harbor, and whole wheat and white pita from **Samira's Homemade** (see p. 354) in Belmont. Almost all the cheeses and sausages come from farms or smokehouses we profiled in companion volumes in this series, *Food Lovers' Guide to Massachusetts* and *Food Lovers' Guide to Vermont & New Hampshire.* But that's just the supply side of CFS. The feed aspect pops up in the deli line, where fresh sandwiches can be ordered from 6 a.m. to 10 p.m., and you can select salads and soups as well as baked goods, coffee, tea, and herbal infusions.

Harvest Co-Op, 57 South St., Jamaica Plain, Boston, MA 02130; (617) 524-1667; harvest.coop; Grocery; T: Green Street. Sister operation to the one in Cambridge (see p. 292), this grocer carries some foods with processed ingredients (breakfast cereals, for example) that it might never have allowed in earlier, more doctrinaire days. Like the Cambridge location, the store offers a wide range of spices, nuts, pastas, grains, and flours from bulk bins for significant savings over prepackaged foods. When the season permits, the store buys a lot of its produce locally.

J. P. Licks, 659 Centre St., Jamaica Plain, Boston, MA 02130; (617) 524-6740; jplicks.com; Ice Cream/Yogurt; T: Green Street. Think of it as ice cream and frozen yogurt with a distinctly local flavor. One of the few survivors of the Premium Ice Cream Wars of the 1980s, J. P. Licks got some of its original offbeat character from the hordes of tattooed, pierced, and ultimately polite art-school kids who worked at this first store. The ice cream and hard frozen yogurt show admirable restraint by rarely mixing more than two flavors (mint chip, say, or coffee Oreo) and the shop now roasts its own coffee and serves a variety of pastries, including spinach and cheese croissants. There are 10 more outlets, but JP will always be home base for J. P. Licks.

Kitchenwitch, 671 Centre St., Jamaica Plain, Boston, MA 02130; (617) 524-6800; Housewares; T: Green Street. How did we ever live without the cream canoe set to make our own Twinkies? Or the pizza peel? While we are proponents of the less-is-more kitchen, even we get seduced by kitchen gadgets that do a particular job very well. Indeed, we're not sure what we would do without our Cuisinart stick blender, or the Chinese bamboo steaming boxes for preparing dim sum.

Prices are very good here and the selection of kitchen gadgets rivals that of much larger shops.

Tostado Sandwich Bar, 300 Centre St., Jamaica Plain, Boston, MA 02130; (617) 477-8691; tostadosandwichbar.com; Sandwich Shop; T: Jackson Square. Tony Tavarez, ex-Telemundo executive, operates this Dominican sandwich shop across from the Stop & Shop. It serves some of the healthiest Caribbean fare we've seen, including a Cubano that competes nicely with **Miami** (see p. 175) and **El Oriental de Cuba** (see p. 176). Part of what sets this tiny take-out joint apart is that every order is made from scratch, and the fruit and vegetable smoothies are as big a hit as the sandwiches. Regulars also swear by the *tres golpes* freshly extracted juice of carrots, beets, and oranges.

Ula, the Brewery, 284 Amory St., Jamaica Plain, Boston, MA 02130; (617) 524-7890; ulacafe.com; Bakery Cafe; T: Stony Brook. Spacious enough to serve as a meet-up spot and inventive enough to make you want to keep nibbling, Ula is a modern take on the old-fashioned coffee shop and the old-fashioned bakery. For starters, the place serves New Harvest Coffee from Pawtucket, Rhode Island, a line of artisanal coffees not generally found in these parts. It's hard to choose among all the baked goods, but a warm popover smeared with Nutella might take the prize. All sandwiches are made to order on artisan breads from Fornax in Roslindale, and several vegetarian/vegan options are available, including roasted sweet potato with avocado, Jack cheese, sweet red pepper, red onion, sprouts, and a tahini–poppy seed spread.

When Pigs Fly, 613 Centre St., Jamaica Plain, Boston, MA 02130; (617) 522-4948; sendbread.com; Bakery; T: Green Street. This Maine-based baker produces more than two dozen artisanal breads a day, some of which are available at natural foods stores. The JP outlet—as well as branches in Brookline, p. 228, and Somerville, p. 337—carries the whole line, as well as freshly baked cookies and bread pudding cakes. You can also load up on jams, honeys, and dipping oils, and if you become a real fan, the hats, shirts, and aprons bearing the When Pigs Fly logo.

Farmers' Markets

Jamaica Plain Community Servings Farmers' Market, 18 Marbury Terrace, Jamaica Plain. Wed from 4 to 7 p.m., mid-July to mid-Oct.

Jamaica Plain Farmers' Market, 677 Centre St., Jamaica Plain. Tues from noon to 5 p.m. and Sat from noon to 3 p.m., May through late Nov.

Jamaica Plain/Loring-Greenough Farmers' Market, 12 South St., Jamaica Plain. Thurs from noon to dusk, early July to late Oct.

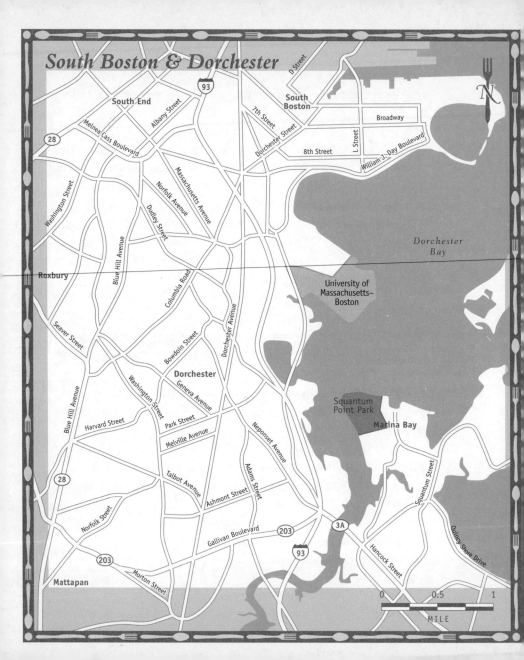

South Boston & Dorchester

Irish pubs have been a mainstay of South Boston and the Irish corners of Dorchester since the 19th century, and you'll find some wonderful eating and drinking establishments in the Bars, Pubs & Lounges chapter (p. 386), including some operated by a new wave of Irish immigrants. Just as good beer pushed out bad at the end of the 20th century, good food has become more prevalent in the old neighborhoods. Even humble bars and bakery cafes began to serve plates like lobster mac and cheese or herb-roasted chicken with polenta. As gentrification raised a head of steam in South Boston, adventurous restaurants and gourmet grocers began to pop up to serve a new clientele. A little farther south, some of the Dorchester neighborhoods remain distinctly immigrant enclaves with Vietnamese *pho* restaurants on practically every street corner. Pockets around the Savin Hill and Ashmont MBTA stations have begun to gentrify, but even they exhibit greater ethnic and cultural diversity than almost anywhere else in the city. Walk in any night to restaurants around the Ashmont T station, and you'll be dining with a cross section of the new Boston—once you can get a table.

Ashmont Grill, 555 Talbot Ave., Dorchester, Boston, MA 02124; (617) 825-4300; ashmontgrill.com; New American; $$; T: Ashmont. We suspect that half the residents of the South End donned black and went into mourning when Chris Douglass closed his long-running Icarus restaurant that had helped pioneer that neighborhood's fine dining. But the South End's loss was Dorchester's gain. Douglass, a longtime Dorchester resident, was finally persuaded by his friends and neighbors to open this sassy, chic, and affordable restaurant in 2005. It's been mobbed ever since, and for good reason. Every Thursday is buck-a-shuck night for oysters, and Monday evenings are "give-back" nights when part of the sales support a neighborhood charity. But bargains and bonhomie abound every night, with tasty starters like wood-grilled lamb sliders on focaccia with cucumber *raita* and crispy onion strings, and American bistro entrees like a roasted half chicken or oven-roasted flounder in a parsley-garlic sauce. The succinct wine list is packed with value-priced fun wines that are as unpretentious and delicious as the food. See Pastry Chef Clare Garland's recipe for **Nanny Sheila's Carrot Cake,** p. 439.

Cafe Polonia, 611 Dorchester Ave., South Boston, Boston, MA 02127; (617) 269-0110; cafepolonia.com; Polish; $–$$; T: Andrew. The light-wood tables and chairs create the feeling of a country cottage in Poland—the perfect setting to sample such comfort food classics as borscht served with a mushroom-filled ravioli; cabbage stuffed with rice and pork; or potato and cheese, cabbage and mushroom, or meat pierogi with caramelized onions. Hearty eaters might try the beef goulash baked in a clay pot and then served in a bread bowl, and everyone should save room for a slice of apple cake. If you're inspired to try your hand at making Polish specialties at home, you can stock up on all the essential ingredients at **Baltic European Deli** almost directly across the street (see p. 198).

dbar, 1236 Dorchester Ave., Dorchester, Boston, MA 02125; (617) 265-4490; dbarboston.com; New American; $$; T: Savin Hill. This Dot Ave bar-restaurant-nightclub epitomizes the ongoing transformation of Dorchester. The gleaming dark mahogany woodwork harks back to the bar's days as an old-school Irish pub but the leather banquettes and little candles glowing on all the tables signal that this is no longer Uncle Paddy's haunt. The menu is packed with full-flavored dishes like braised pork tacos in corn tortillas with poblano pepper sour cream and pico de gallo, or lemon-glazed seared day-boat scallops served with a cumin-carrot risotto, asparagus spears, and pureed celery root. Starting around 10 p.m. dbar begins to transition from dining room to nightclub as the sound system is cranked up, people start ordering neon cocktails, and the shameless flirting begins. Although dbar welcomes customers of all gender identifications and has more waitresses than waiters, Out.com consistently names it one of the 50 best gay bars in the world.

Franklin Southie, 152 Dorchester St., South Boston, Boston, MA 02127; (617) 269-1003; franklincafe.com; New American; $$; T: Broadway. Just as friendly as its South End counterpart (see p. 134), Franklin Southie serves inventive comfort food way into the late evening. Bar-hoppers can end the night here over a plate of slow-braised beef cheeks with braised greens or a roasted vegetable and polenta torte with local goat cheese. This restaurant has probably done more to popularize quinoa than anyone since Simon Bolivar, thanks to its addictive quinoa salad with pine nuts, candied kalamata figs, feta, and arugula. You can get cocktails here, but in-the-know regulars drink bargain-priced Pabst Blue Ribbon longnecks.

KO Catering and Pies, 87 A St., South Boston, Boston, MA 02127; (617) 269-4500; kocateringandpies.com; Australian; T: Broadway. Sam Jackson opened KO to introduce the meat pies of his native Australia to Boston. The delicious individual-serving pies feature a short crust base filled with braised lamb shank, Irish beef stew, beef and cheese, or curried vegetables, and then topped with puff pastry. For an authentic experience, douse your perfect little pie in ketchup. "It's an Australian thing," Jackson says with a shrug. So are his sausage rolls, spicy shrimp on the barbie over rice, and grilled fish sandwiches. For dessert? Lamingtons, an Aussie childhood favorite of sponge cake covered with chocolate icing and rolled in grated coconut. Bostonians have so embraced KO that Jackson has opened a second outlet in East Boston (see p. 24).

Local 149, 149 P St., South Boston, Boston, MA 02127; (617) 269-0900; local149.com; New American; $$; T: Broadway. Opening right around St. Patrick's Day in 2011, Local 149 reflects the changes in Southie. Taking the space of an ancient shot-and-a-beer Irish bar, this genuinely American pub styles itself as a neighborhood joint. It bustles with a largely youthful crowd all afternoon and evening, and features a slew of local beers on tap, a taut wine list, and a kitchen where Chef Leah Dubois's cooking keeps regulars both well fed and amused. Dubois is a master of raw foods as well as cooked ones, so don't be too surprised when pickled green beans pop up as a side dish with seared sea scallops and cheesy grits, or the eggplant "bacon" she makes in the dehydrator tops the yellowfin tuna burger. She's a master of conventional charcuterie as well, making her own duck prosciutto and pastry-encased pâté. This is one bar restaurant where vegetarians feel more than comfortable, whether it's snacking on the fried brussels sprouts with chipotle lime sauce and homemade blue cheese dressing or chowing down on the vegan Badass Risotto of seasonal local vegetables.

Lucky Cafe, 1107 Dorchester Ave., Dorchester, Boston, MA 02125; (617) 822-9888; Chinese; $; T: Savin Hill. Mainly a take-out operation, Lucky Cafe offers real Chinese barbecue along with more traditional Chinese-American fare from a menu written in Chinese, English, and Vietnamese. (This is Little Saigon, after all.) To sample Lucky Cafe's best dishes, try the rice plate of roast duck, crispy barbecued pork, and steamed chicken over rice and pak choi (Vietnamese for bok choy). Many customers come in to order a whole roast duck to take home for the family. In addition to the barbecue, Lucky Cafe also cooks an addictive plate of salt-and-pepper calamari.

McKenna's Cafe, 109 Savin Hill Ave., Dorchester, Boston, MA 02125; (617) 825-8218; mckennascafe.com; Casual American; $; T: Savin Hill. It sometimes seems like almost everyone in the Savin Hill neighborhood eats breakfast and lunch here—or at least stops in to order takeout. Cheerful and friendly, McKenna's has a gigantic menu of breakfast combinations, including both corned beef hash *and* Irish rashers and black-and-white pudding. (They don't serve sad little breakfast tomatoes, offering only the good parts of Irish morning fare.) The sandwich list for lunch is nearly as extensive and the "extreme" salads are generous enough to feed two hungry people. On Friday only, McKenna's offers three fresh fish specials: fish and chips, baked haddock, and a crispy fried haddock sandwich.

Paramount, 667 E. Broadway, South Boston, Boston, MA 02127; (617) 269-9999; paramountboston.com; Casual American; $–$$;

T: Broadway. The Paramount has been serving hot breakfasts and soothing comfort food dinners on Beacon Hill (see p. 65) for generations. The same formula of cafeteria-style service for breakfast and lunch and table service for dinner holds true at this stylish Southie offshoot, which opened in late 2011 and sports prints of old South Boston on its exposed-brick walls. Locals embraced it from the moment it opened. After all, it's hard to find fault with a buttermilk fried chicken sandwich at lunch or coconut fish curry at dinner. The big, juicy Paramount Burger (with smoked bacon, melted cheddar, and onion rings on the side) is great anytime. The bar can pull three **Harpoon** (see p. 200) drafts along with Sankaty Light from Nantucket's Cisco Brewers.

Pho Le, 1356 Dorchester Ave., Dorchester, Boston, MA 02122; (617) 506-6294; Vietnamese; $; T: Fields Corner. It's not surprising in this Little Saigon stretch of Dorchester that Pho Le sits right across the street from a chain *pho* restaurant. But every time we visit, Le's is full of Vietnamese from the neighborhood. It's certainly not the cheapest *pho* spot around, but the whole experience feels more like restaurant dining than grabbing a quick bowl of soup. The chopsticks are fancy, the staff is in uniform, and the bilingual (probably trilingual) servers are both friendly and helpful. In addition to excellent beef and chicken soups, consider the shredded duck salad, the grilled pork spring rolls (*goi cuon nem nuong*), and the roasted quail. Although it operates with a slightly different menu, Pho Le is owned by the same restaurateur (Duyen Le) who operates **Le's Vietnamese Restaurant** (see p. 262) in Harvard Square.

Savin Bar & Kitchen, 112 Savin Hill Ave., Dorchester, Boston, MA 02125; (617) 288-7500; savinbarandkitchen.com; New American; $$; T: Savin Hill. Something of a case study in slow-track gentrification, SBK replaced a beloved Savin Hill bar in early 2011 and came on strong with upscale bistro fare. The neighbors stayed away in droves, and SBK righted its ship by focusing on affordable New American comfort food like slow-braised lamb shank, a nicely brined beer-can chicken, and meat loaf enlivened with a shot of chipotle pepper, smoked mozzarella, and gruyère cheese. Smaller plates appease the bar crowd with the likes of Cajun fried dill pickle spears, flatbread topped with whiskey barbecued pork, and mussels steamed in a *fra diavolo* sauce. House desserts are big sweet treats, like the ice cream sandwich of chocolate or vanilla ice cream between chocolate chip cookies. You don't have to pick it up—it is drizzled with chocolate sauce and slathered with whipped cream.

Tavolo, 1918 Dorchester Ave., Dorchester, Boston, MA 02124; (617) 822-1918; tavolopizza.com; Italian; $$; T: Ashmont. You could simply order an excellent pizza here, but then you'd miss out on the creative cuisine of Chef Nuno Alves, a veteran of Jody

Adams's kitchen at **Rialto** (p. 271). Alves has unerringly good taste and invents dishes that seem so logical that you'd think they were part of the Italian canon. On Wednesday night Tavolo offers a regional pasta tour—a three-course, set-price meal focusing on a pasta characteristic of a given region. For Sardinia, Alves invented a dish of Squid Three Ways: squid ink *malloreddus* pasta (a half-inch-long, ridged pasta like small fat worms); tender squid bodies stuffed with bread crumbs, herbs, and mint; and crisply fried tentacles. With a few dollops of tomato *sugo,* it was a dish to have made any Sardinian grandmother proud. Do not miss the *frico* appetizer. This "pancake" of crisped Montasio cheese, potato, and onion is served with arugula and a dollop of applesauce. Alves works similar magic with pastas, tossing pappardelle noodles with braised lamb, preserved lemon, fennel, and sweet, bright green Castelvetrano olives. It's a small kitchen, but Alves and staff also make all the desserts. His panna cotta with marinated red cherries and a bit of tart cherry preserve actually redeemed that often bland and rubbery dessert for us. See Chef Nuno Alves's recipe for **Beer-Braised Lamb Shoulder,** p. 433.

224 Boston Street Restaurant, 224 Boston St., Dorchester, Boston, MA 02125; (617) 265-1217; 224bostonstreet.com; New American; $$; T: JFK/UMass. A pioneer in modern dining in Dorchester, 224 Boston Street has been a neighborhood favorite since the early 1990s. It's just about a perfect match to the diversity around it—even the silverware seems to have come from a dozen different yard sales, and the clientele is young, old, gay, straight, multiracial, native-born, and recent immigrant. They all come for one thing: the no-nonsense bistro comfort food (burgers, meat loaf, Cajun mac and cheese, pan-seared scallops with red pepper–potato hash, grilled swordfish with lobster risotto). The wine list veers away from California and Europe to find bargains from South America and South Africa.

Van Shabu & Bar, 1156 Dorchester Ave., Dorchester, Boston, MA 02125; (617) 436-8100; vanshabubar.com; Japanese; $$; T: Savin Hill. With hot pot stations at the bar, a line of gleaming two-tops down the middle, and small padded booths by the windows, this smart but small operation on Dot Ave replicates the hottest concept food bars of the Asian rim—do-it-yourself shabu-shabu cookery combined with stylish sushi, glowing cocktails, and big televisions turned to every sport that is broadcast. Lest it all seem too precious, Van runs all-you-can-eat specials on Monday (hot pot) and Wednesday (sushi).

Landmarks

Amrheins Restaurant, 80 W. Broadway, South Boston, Boston, MA 02127; (617) 268-6189; amrheinsboston.com; Traditional American; $$; T: Broadway. With the shamrocks in the windows and the polished dark wood of the interior, Amrheins has been the sentimental Southie favorite since 1890. The classic wiener schnitzel has probably been on the menu since the place opened, and it rivals the seafood Alfredo in popularity. The all-you-can-eat Sunday brunch buffet with fancy carving station is a major event. Don't show up without a reservation. To beat the parking difficulties of this corner of Southie, inquire about the free shuttle service for dinner and brunch customers.

Sullivan's, 2080 Day Blvd., South Boston, Boston, MA 02127; (617) 268-5685; sullivanscastleisland.com; Casual American; T: Broadway. When Sullivan's opens on the last weekend in February, South Boston knows that spring is around the corner. Young and old alike turn out for the first "trifecta" of the season: a hot dog, fries, and ice cream cone, which is properly followed by a stroll around Pleasure Bay. First opened in 1951, Sullivan's has its own custom-made, natural casing hot dogs, known locally as "Sully's snap dogs." They are half price on opening weekend and for the entire month of November. Open last weekend in Feb through last weekend in Nov.

Specialty Stores, Markets & Producers

American Provisions, 613 E. Broadway, South Boston, Boston, MA 02127; (617) 269-6100; americanprovisions.com; Grocery; T: Broadway. This farm-to-table gourmet grocer is perhaps the surest sign of gentrification in South Boston. Linni Krall, who does much of the buying for the shop, features local products whenever possible. "I encourage customers to check the address on anything they buy," she says. "My favorite new find is BOLA granola from the Berkshires. And I eat Narragansett Creamery yogurt for breakfast every day." The cheese case—the store's most popular area—features a number of local producers. But the deli area adds an international flavor with chorizo from Spain and prosciutto and salami from Italy. The short list of take-out sandwiches includes the Grilled Pig, with Black Forest ham, brie, and French butter on crusty sourdough bread.

Baltic European Deli, 632 Dorchester Ave., South Boston, Boston, MA 02127; (617) 268-2435; balticeuropeandeli.com; Grocery; T: Andrew. Baltic Deli sits in the once-vibrant "Polish Triangle," defined by Boston Street, Dorchester Avenue, and Columbia Road, that swelled with immigrants after World Wars I and II. Although many of the original residents have died and their descendants have moved to the suburbs, this market continues to provide a vital link to the foods of the old country. Refrigerator and freezer cases are stocked with soups (sour pickle, beef tripe, chicken, borscht), pierogies (potato and cheese, plum, mushroom), and blintzes (cheese, blueberry, strawberry). The deli case includes smoked and plain kielbasa or liver sausage, hard salami, and countless other hams and sausages. You can sample them in sandwiches, such as kielbasa with sauerkraut or the popular pork loaf. Pick up some dark rye bread and jars of sauerkraut, grated beets, and pickled mushrooms to round out a meal.

Blue Tierra Chocolate Cafe, 258 W. Broadway, South Boston, Boston, MA 02127; (617) 268-4900; bluetierrachocolate.com; Chocolatier/Bakery; T: Broadway. Jen Turner's signature truffle has an elegant simplicity: a crème fraîche milk chocolate filling is enrobed in dark chocolate. But Turner loves to experiment with bolder flavors as well, such as mixing spearmint and green tea with milk chocolate. To dark chocolate she might add blood orange and Grand Marnier, bacon and maple syrup, or a combination of chile pepper, cinnamon, cumin, and clove. She also makes French *macarons* and decadent tortes, such as the Sticky Sweet: a concoction of dark chocolate cake, dulce de leche mousse, and chocolate ganache. Enjoy them in the lounge area at the back of the shop, along with an espresso, raspberry tea Creamsicle, or—for the true chocoholic—a chocolate frappé.

Greenhills Irish Bakery, 780 Adams St., Dorchester, Boston, MA 02124; (617) 825-8187; greenhillsbakery.com; Bakery Cafe; T: Ashmont. Greenhills is one-stop shopping for Boston's many Irish immigrants who crave a taste of home. True to its name, the bakery is known for its Irish soda breads, made with white or whole wheat flour. They are available plain, with raisins, with raisins and caraway, or made with treacle, a dark sugar syrup. The bakery

SUDS BY THE SHORE

The return of breweries to Boston in the 1990s was a cause for celebration among beer drinkers across New England. The products of South Boston's **Harpoon Brewery** have become the standby beers for many Boston pubs and bars, especially those in Southie. Harpoon makes eight year-round beers, four seasonal brews, and occasional specials in its 100-barrel limited edition series and its high-alcohol Leviathan series. Complimentary tastings are held twice each weekday afternoon, while guided tours and tastings for a fee are offered on weekends.

Harpoon Brewery, 306 Northern Ave., South Boston, Boston, MA 02210; (617) 574-9551; harpoonbrewery.com; Brewery; T: Northern Avenue & Harbor Street (Silver Line SL2).

turns out a number of other breads and rolls that are also used for breakfast and lunch sandwiches. Perhaps the most traditional—and filling—is the Irish breakfast sandwich of Irish or American bacon, Irish sausage, white and black pudding, and scrambled egg on a roll. Good lunch options include Irish sausage rolls and fresh soups. Desserts include simple bars (fig, lemon, raspberry), cupcakes and cakes, fruit pies, and sherry trifle. Guinness beef stew, traditional lamb stew, and chicken stew are always available for takeout and a few shelves hold such British and Irish grocery staples as HP Sauce, Bird's Custard, Barry's Tea, and Ready Brek Porridge.

Joseph's Italian Bakery, 258–260 K St., South Boston, Boston, MA 02127; (617) 268-1133; josephsbakerydeli.homestead.com; Bakery; T: Broadway. It's no surprise that this old-fashioned bakery is known for such Italian sweets as cannoli, lobster tails, *zeppole,* and *sfogliatelli,* along with pizza slices and calzones. But you can also pick up Irish bread and hot cross buns, and all-American favorites such as cupcakes and whoopie pies. In March look for cupcakes decorated with green sprinkles and shamrocks.

Kam Man Farmers' Market, 101 Allstate Rd., Dorchester, Boston, MA 02125; (617) 541-2288; Grocery; T: Andrew. When we enter this large grocery store with wide, well-marked aisles, we usually head straight to the freezer cases in the rear to assemble a DIY dim sum feast of frozen dumplings (crabmeat, chicken and lotus root, lamb with oyster sauce), potstickers (shrimp, vegetable, beef) and steamed buns. Then we head to the sauce aisle to pick up dipping sauces that range from plum to peanut, and chile-garlic to lemongrass. But we have to admit that we are most fascinated by the corner of the store devoted to more variations of noodles than we had ever imagined: stick, pan-fried, lo mein, *udon,* wonton, soft tofu, silken tofu, Shanghai, Vietnamese. The fish display is one of the most extensive (and best) in the city, and the range and quality of the produce is outstanding.

Liberty Bell, 170 W. Broadway, South Boston, Boston, MA 02127; Sandwich Shop; T: Broadway. Liberty Bell opened in 1976 and Harry Kanellos's family has owned this sandwich shop with a big parking lot since 1979. Over the years, they have expanded the menu to include pizza, subs, fried seafood, Italian specialties, and barbecue dinners. But most customers stick to the original roast beef sandwiches, which are made with choice roast beef cooked on the premises, and properly topped with spicy barbecue sauce.

Sweet Tooth Boston, 371 W. Broadway, South Boston, Boston, MA 02127; (617) 268-2555; sweet toothboston.com; Bakery; T: Broadway. "We are not a cupcake shop," insists David Venter, co-owner of this bakery that specializes in custom cakes for any imaginable occasion. That said, Sweet Tooth does make dynamite cupcakes, including a vanilla cake filled with lemon curd and a scaled-down version of a Boston cream pie. You'll also find cinnamon buns, strudel, napoleons, brownies, pecan and blueberry pies, and even a chocolate pizza.

Farmers' Markets

Dorchester/Bowdoin Geneva Farmers' Market, Bowdoin Street Health Center, Bowdoin St., Dorchester. Thurs from 3 to 6:30 p.m., July through Oct.

Dorchester/Codman Square Farmers' Market, Codman Commons at Washington St. and Talbott Ave., Dorchester. Thurs from 1 to 6 p.m., late June through Oct.

Dorchester/Dorchester House Farmers' Market, 1353 Dorchester Ave., Dorchester. Tues from 11:30 a.m. to 1:30 p.m., July through Sept.

Dorchester/Fields Corner Farmers' Market, Park Street Shopping Center, Dorchester. Sat from 9 a.m. to noon, July through Sept.

Dorchester/Grove Hall Farmers' Market, next to 461 Blue Hill Ave., Dorchester. Tues from 3 to 7 p.m., mid-July through mid-Oct.

Dorchester/Peabody Square Farmers' Market, Ashmont Station Plaza, Dorchester. Fri from 3 to 7 p.m., early July through mid-Oct.

Dorchester Winter Farmers' Market, 6 Norfolk St., Codman Square Health Center, Dorchester. Sun from noon to 3 p.m., early Jan through late Mar.

South Boston Farmers' Market, W. Broadway municipal parking lot, South Boston. Mon from noon to 6 p.m., May through late Nov.

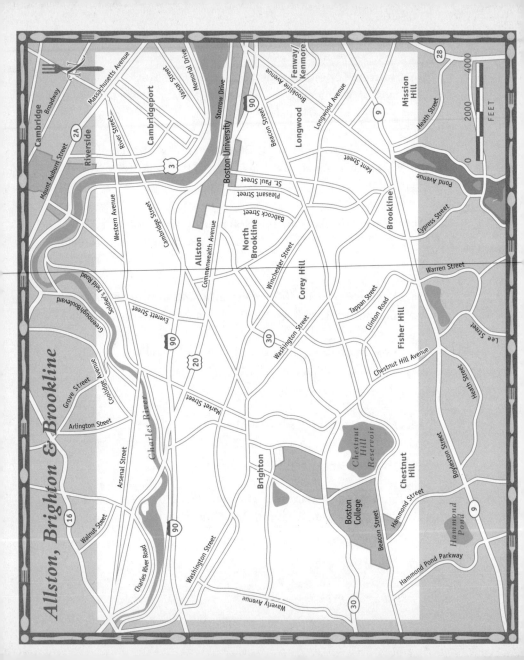

Allston, Brighton & Brookline

Allston, Brighton & Brookline

These Green Line streetcar suburbs offer something of a global gastronomic adventure. Even one single block in Allston—Brighton Avenue between Parkvale and Harvard Avenues—has tiny storefront restaurants serving Japanese teriyaki dishes, Salvadoran/Mexican combo plates with tortillas and rice, sushi, Italian pasta, Thai rice bowls, Middle Eastern kebabs, and Italian-American pizza. We ran into the landlord one Saturday, and he told us he never lacks for potential renters, but always samples the food first. The proximity of Boston University and, to a lesser extent, Boston College, guarantees a strong student clientele for inexpensive ethnic restaurants. In Brookline, literally just down Harvard Street, the restaurants are more likely to be New American or represent earlier waves of immigrants from Europe. They are fancier, more polished, a little more expensive, but often still very good bargains.

The Abbey, 1657 Beacon St., Brookline, MA 02445; (617) 730-8040; abbeyrestaurant.com; New American/Casual American; $; T: Washington Square. Something of a spinoff from the more proper **Washington Square Tavern** (see p. 217), the Abbey is a neighborhood gastropub where the food is so good that it outshines the excellent beer. Everyone talks about the bison Bolognese sauce, but the real genius lies in the "small plates" of bar food, including scallop and ricotta dumplings that come three to a plate with micro greens and constitute a new food fusion: Italian dim sum. (They're very good with wheat beer.) Roasted chicken and roasted fish are finished in cast-iron frying pans, emphasizing the rough-and-ready bar mystique as well as simply delicious flavors. Think of it as comfort food dressed up to go out.

BonChon, 123 Brighton Ave., Allston, MA 02134; (617) 254-8888; bonchonallston.com; Korean; $; T: Harvard Avenue. We haven't included many chain restaurants in this book, but we couldn't ignore the loyal local following for BonChon's Korean-style fried chicken. Pieces are cooked to order and the strips, wings, and drumsticks are crisp on the outside and juicy on the inside. Either soy garlic or hot sauce is brushed on during cooking to give the chicken a subtle, slightly exotic flavor.

Cafe Brazil, 421 Cambridge St., Allston, MA 02134; (617) 789-5980; cafebrazilrestaurant.com; Brazilian; $–$$; T: Harvard Avenue.

You can order a chicken- and olive-stuffed savory pastry, a fresh fish stew, or a sizzling platter of steak, chicken, and linguiça on any day. But Brazilian families head to this popular restaurant Friday through Sunday when the kitchen prepares *feijoada*, Brazil's national dish of black beans and mixed meats that's slow-simmered in a clay pot and served with rice and greens.

Camino Real Restaurant, 48 Harvard Ave., Allston, MA 02134; (617) 254-5088; caminorealrestaurant.com; Colombian; $; T: Packard's Corner. In the United Nations of Brighton, Camino Real represents the cuisine of Colombia. In Camino Real's interpretation, it's not so different from Central American fare: shrimp with yellow rice and veggies, fried plantains, or the South American version of a cowboy steak—a small grilled sirloin with Creole sauce and a pair of fried eggs, served with sides of rice, beans, and green plantains.

Cognac Bistro, 455 Harvard St., Brookline, MA 02446; (617) 232-5800; cognacbistro.com; French/New American; $$; T: Harvard Avenue. Nelson and Joanne Cognac have made the most of their bistro's past by painting the brick walls and installing a stunning oyster bar up front but otherwise leaving the gas-station architecture alone. At the Brighton edge of Coolidge Corner, the quirky venue is a sheer delight, and the menu emphasizes Cognac's love of fish. Preparations come and go with the seasons, but you can always count on bistro dishes built on salmon, trout, swordfish, monkfish, and whatever might be the catch of the day. Yet the plates are hardly predictable. Cognac might accompany the trout with pumpkin seeds rather than the traditional almonds, and he could ladle a lobster thermidor over the swordfish brochettes. Other bistro dishes, such as steak-frites, roast chicken, and homemade sausages, are available. The wine list is short and French (mostly), offering an excellent range of food-friendly wines by the glass and half-carafe as well as the bottle.

Daily Catch, 441 Harvard St., Brookline, MA 02446; (617) 734-2700; dailycatch.com; Seafood; $–$$; T: Harvard Avenue. If you can't make it to the original North End location (see p. 20) or the waterfront (p. 55), you can enjoy the signature Sicilian-style seafood here, including fried calamari, still served as it was when the restaurant opened in 1973.

Dorado Tacos & Cemitas, 401 Harvard St., Brookline, MA 02446; (617) 566-2100; doradotacos.com; Mexican; $; T: Harvard Avenue. Not far out of Coolidge Corner, this Mexican quick food joint is *the* place to find a great Baja California fish taco or a Puebla-style *cemita*—a sandwich on an eggy roll with avocado, Oaxacan cheese, cilantro, chipotles *en adobo*, and your choice of grilled pork or chicken cutlet, thin beefsteak, chorizo sausage, or grilled portobello mushroom (for the vegetarians in the crowd). Dorado is a model of cheerful efficiency.

The Fireplace, 1634 Beacon St., Brookline, MA 02446; (617) 975-1900; fireplacerest.com; New American; $$$; T: Washington Square. The dinner menu here always reads like the table of contents for an issue of *Food & Wine* magazine, and when the plates come out, they look like they were styled there, too. The emphasis on fresh produce (local when possible) and the extensive use of a wood grill and rotisserie to prepare meat and fish dishes make The Fireplace an exemplar of contemporary American bistro style. Don't look for fussy preparations: Most meats and fishes are simply roasted and served with side dishes and limited sauces. (A significant exception is the rib eye steak, served with the restaurant's signature steak sauce.) The actual fireplace faces the bar and provides flickering warmth and a certain woodsmoke scent, at least in the winter. But when the weather turns warm, diners can also sit at outdoor tables.

Garlic 'n Lemons, 133 Harvard Ave., Allston, MA 02134; (617) 783-8100; garlicandlemons.com; Lebanese, Vegetarian Friendly; $; T: Packard's Corner. Many of the roll-ups and plates (with rice and side dishes) on the menu are built around the spit-roasted chicken and beef that give this mom-and-son eatery such a mouth-watering aroma, and most are even better when paired with the shop's plain or spicy whipped garlic sauce. Vegetarians won't be disappointed with a falafel or hummus and vegetable roll-up and lots of folks simply opt to make a meal of the tasty side dishes such as tabbouleh, stuffed grapes leaves, and baba ghanoush.

JoJo Taipei, 103 Brighton Ave., Allston, MA 02134; (617) 254-8889; jojotaipeiboston.com; Chinese; $; T: Packard's Corner. It's rare to find Taiwanese Hoklo cooking in greater Boston, but the gigantic menu at JoJo Taipei includes a lot of dishes no one else seems to serve, including pork chitterlings with long rice noodles, fried taro rolls, and white-turnip pastries. The aggressively spiced sour and spicy fisherman soup is a wonder, though many homesick Taiwanese at Boston University come here for the green onion pancakes and the Taiwanese beef noodle soup.

Kaju Tofu House, 56 Harvard Ave., Allston, MA 02134; (617) 208-8540; Korean; $–$$; T: Harvard Avenue. Kaju opened just as we were finishing research for this book and was immediately embraced by Korean students and Korean-Americans for its *sundubu,* or soft tofu soups. Each bowl features a flavorful broth and meltingly soft tofu. Diners can choose their spiciness comfort level and select from a number of options, such as tofu with vegetables, mushrooms, kimchee and beef, or with seafood. The soups are accompanied by a small pot of rice and a raw egg to swirl into the hot broth. For those with heartier appetites, Korean barbecue is also available.

La Morra, 48 Boylston St., Brookline, MA 02445; (617) 739-0007; lamorra.com; Italian; $$; T: Brookline Village. Josh Ziskin may come from Brookline but he absorbed most of what he needed to know about cooking by working in a restaurant in the Piemonte town of La Morra. His wife, Jennifer Ziskin, the restaurant's wine director, studied there, too. Between them, they re-create a mom-and-pop northern Italian *osteria*, right down to the prices lower than most comparable restaurants in greater Boston. The menu begins with the little Venetian-style small bar dishes known as *cicchetti*: fried sage leaves with white anchovy, salt cod seasoned with garlic and lemon, meatballs with porcini mushrooms and prosciutto . . . Pastas (available as a first course or an entree) include such classics of the North as pappardelle with braised rabbit, green olives, toasted almonds, and golden raisins. Most of the *secondi* dishes are wood-grilled, whether it's the Cornish hen under a brick with polenta, the leg of lamb with fava beans, or the swordfish with the fregola pasta of Sardinia (rather like Israeli cous-cous). The location just off Route 9 is out of the way, making La Morra a true hidden gem.

Lineage, 242 Harvard St., Brookline, MA 02446; (617) 232-0065; lineagerestaurant.com; New American; $$; T: Coolidge Corner. The fish is so good at Lineage that it's no surprise that it dominates the menu. In fact, Lineage offers a bargain-priced three-course seafood tasting menu in addition to Island Creek oysters that are half price early in the evening if you eat them at the bar. The wood-fired oven gets a workout, and not just with the pizzas. Roasted baby octopus is among the oven-cooked appetizers, and regular customers are big fans of the baked stuffed quahogs. One of the nicer simple plates is pasta tossed with Maine lobster and carrots cooked in brown butter. There are a few turf dishes among all that surf: roast chicken, grilled steak, and a burger.

Matt Murphy's Pub, 14 Harvard St., Brookline, MA 02445; (617) 232-0188; mattmurphyspub.com; Irish/New American; $$; T: Brookline Village. One of the first of the Irish pubs opened in the Boston area by Irish immigrants with a taste for good food, Matt Murphy's remains a reliable haunt for a trencherman's feast (rib eye steak with wild mushroom ragù, or duck leg confit with roasted pears and savory bread pudding) and a frothy pint of Guinness. It's a small place, barely accommodating 50 people, so make a dinner reservation if you have a party of 4 or more. Cash only.

Orinoco, 22 Harvard St., Brookline, MA 02445; (617) 232-9595; orinocokitchen.com; Venezuelan; $$; T: Brookline Village. The appeal of all three Orinoco restaurants (for the South End see p. 142, for Cambridge p. 269) is that they serve inexpensive Venezuelan street food. The arepas—a corn cake similar to an extra-thick Mexican tortilla—are always a hit. One of the best is the Domino, which is filled with black beans and a pale white melting cheese. The entrees draw from both the Caribbean coast and the Andean high country, with some surprises like the salmon marinated in brown sugar and served with quinoa tossed with a yellow chile sauce.

Osaka Japanese Sushi & Steak House, 14 Green St., Brookline, MA 02446; (617) 732-0088; osakabrookline.com; Japanese; $$; T: Coolidge Corner. This bright and attractive restaurant embodies the yin and yang of Japanese dining. On one side is the serene world of colorful, beautifully plated sushi rolls and slivers of artistically cut sashimi. Service is hushed and diners are subdued. The other half of the restaurant is reserved for the madcap antics of hibachi chefs who make flames jump, steam billow, and food sizzle while diners sit around the hot steel grill. Kabuki or wrestle-mania: The choice is yours. Either way, the food is both good and reasonably priced.

Petit Robert Bistro, 1414 Commonwealth Ave., Brighton, MA 02135; (617) 274-8687; petitrobertbistro.com; French; $$; T: Allston Street. The bistro was born as a neighborhood restaurant serving French comfort food. This version of Jacky Robert's network of bistros serves the neighborhood of Allston and Brighton with the signature dishes of the French kitchen: coq au vin, steak-frites, cassoulet . . . For other locations see pp. 106 and 144.

Punjab Palace, 109 Brighton Ave., Allston, MA 02134; (617) 254-1500; punjabpalace.com; Indian; $; T: Packard's Corner. This Sikh-operated Indian restaurant is the Allston-Brighton leader in its cuisine, never failing to satisfy with reasonably priced entrees like the chicken or lamb *biryani* or the aggressively hot shrimp vindaloo.

The range of breads cooked in the tandoor oven is impressive, and it's worth ordering the unusual *keema* naan, which is stuffed with minced lamb and spices. For another unusual dish, try the chicken *methi,* which contains boneless chicken pieces stewed with onion, tomato, herbs, spices, and lots of slightly bitter fenugreek greens.

The Regal Beagle, 308 Harvard St., Brookline, MA 02446; (617) 739-5151; thebeaglebrookline.com; New American; $$; T: Coolidge Corner. When you see all the young fathers wheeling their kids around Coolidge Corner on Saturdays, you can find the young mommies sipping wine and enjoying lunch at The Regal Beagle, named for the hangout on the '70s sitcom *Three's Company.* By evening, though, the scene shifts to couples, and the salads-and-sandwiches daytime menu switches to American bistro fare: slow-roasted chicken, seared scallops, grilled lamb, pan-roasted salmon, and (of course) a voluptuous burger and a gooey mac and cheese. Chef Laura Henry-Zoubir's food is friendly and soothing, and the wines by the glass are the same.

Regina Pizza, 353 Cambridge St., Allston, MA 02134; (617) 783-2300; reginapizza.com; Italian/Pizza; $–$$; T: Packard's Corner. Perhaps not as atmospheric as the original North End shop (see p. 32), this 1886 former train depot gives diners a lot of room to spread out and enjoy a Regina's pizza, baked pasta or plate of eggplant Parmesan, or grilled sausages and peppers. Big television screens tuned to sports are visible from every angle, but kids prefer to take a window table and watch the Amtrak and commuter trains rumble by.

Rubin's, 500 Harvard St., Brookline, MA 02446; (617) 731-8787; rubinskosher.com; Casual American/ Jewish; $$; T: Harvard Avenue. Opened in 1927, Rubin's has served up the taste of home for generations of Eastern and central European immigrants. The full-service deli sells superb brisket, pastrami, chopped beef or chicken liver, knockwurst, latkes, potato kugel, beet salad, and even the school lunchbox standard of tuna salad. Sit-down meals can range from simple (a cup of borscht and a couple of spinach knishes) to hearty (barbecue brisket sandwich with homemade potato salad) or comforting (a chicken thigh and leg with matzo ball, noodles, and kreplach in broth). Best for sharing is a smoked fish sampler of whitefish, sable, smoked salmon, and herring. Pick up more of your favorites at the deli on your way out. Closed Saturday.

Steve's Kitchen, 120 Harvard St., Allston, MA 02134; (617) 254-9457; steveskitchen.net; Casual American; $; T: Coolidge Corner. Overheard at a table of a half-dozen college students eating giant breakfasts on a Saturday morning: "I will never drink again." He meant until evening. A classic Greek-American eggs-and-burgers grill, Steve's provides big servings of mostly healthy food, transitioning from omelets and pancakes in the morning (always with the option of gyros, of course) to burgers, gyros, and souvlaki at lunch to kebabs, meat loaf, and fish cakes in the evening. The clientele does skew heavily to the collegiate demographic, but three eggs with gyros should cure any hangover. Cash only.

Taberna del Haro, 999 Beacon St., Brookline, MA 02446; (617) 277-8272; tabernaboston.com; Spanish; $$; T: St. Mary's Street. Chef-Owner Deborah Hansen spent eight years living and working in Spain and she brings an understanding of the Spanish cuisine of La Rioja to her tavern, named for one of the most famous Iberian wine towns. Almost everything on the menu is a *pincho* or *racion* small plate, giving diners lots of different tastes as they compile a meal. That might include such classic Spanish tapas as potato omelet, garlic soup with a poached egg, or ham croquettes. Hansen offers a few more substantive plates, such as roasted sea bass; chicken stewed with sherry, saffron, almonds, and Spanish ham; or grilled organically raised rib eye steak. More than 240 Spanish wines are available, easily the most comprehensive Spanish cellar in greater Boston.

Umami, 1704 Beacon St., Brookline, MA 02446; (617) 879-9100; umamiboston.com; Asian; $$; T: Tappan Street. Chef-Owner Yoshi Hakamoto may be Japanese, but there's no sushi at his Asian fusion bistro, nor are there any dishes that could be called Japanese, Chinese, Korean, or even Malaysian. He's cooking a true fusion cuisine with the formal elements of a European plate (steak au poivre) with Asian flavors (Szechuan pepper mixed with the black peppercorns). When preparing salmon, Hakamoto applies a sweet Japanese miso glaze that is traditional with black cod. He combines fresh basil with *udon* noodles and cubes of tofu spiked with five-spice powder for a Marco Polo pasta. It's a fun place to dine, since Hakamoto likes to confound expectations. The style is bistro but the flavors are global.

@Union Breakfast Cafe, 174 Harvard Ave., Allston, MA 02134; (617) 779-0077; unionallston.com; Casual American; $; T: Harvard Avenue. We love places that serve breakfast all day, especially when they have good corned beef hash, lots of fresh ingredients for build-your-own omelets, and the option of home fries with your eggs. At @Union, you also get a side of Wi-Fi, at least during the week. To discourage lingering during the breakfast-brunch rush, management shuts off the router on weekends until 2 p.m.

Washington Square Tavern, 714 Washington St., Brookline, MA 02445; (617) 232-8989; washingtonsquaretavern.com; New American; $$; T: Washington Square. Shelves of books and dark woodwork help contribute to a cozy look for this tavern that was a hit when it opened in 1999 and remains one of the favorite neighborhood dining spots. And why not? The kitchen does all the charcuterie in-house, including the delicious duck sausage served in Madeira wine sauce as an appetizer. That and the spice-rubbed skirt steak (also available as an app) would make a fine meal. But then you'd be missing the eggplant and spinach ravioli and the pan-roasted local cod. The beer list is good; the wine list is even better. This is an American bistro that even a Parisian could love.

Yasu Japanese Sushi & Korean BBQ, 1366 Beacon St., Brookline, MA 02446; (617) 738-2244; yasuboston.com; Korean/Japanese; $–$$; T: Coolidge Corner. Having outlasted a whole string of Asian restaurants in its space, Yasu strikes a good balance between sushi and barbecue. The house rolls are good and the sashimi perfectly cut. But for hearty eating, sit down at one of the grill tables, order some meat dishes, and enjoy the great spread of small side dishes that come as a standard accompaniment: kimchee, cucumber salad, pickled seaweed, and a number of other vegetable combos that most diners would be hard-pressed to identify but nonetheless love.

Zaftig's Delicatessen, 335 Harvard St., Brookline 02446; (617) 975-0075; zaftigs.com; Casual American/Jewish; $; T: Coolidge Corner. Zaftig's is a little bit of Brooklyn in Brookline, serving the favorites of Ashkenazi Jewish-American cuisine. So, yes, you can have blintzes, and latkes, and kugel for breakfast, matzo ball chicken soup at lunch, and braised brisket for supper. You can also get cheese fries with turkey gravy, salad niçoise, and french toast all day. There have been lines out the door since Zaftig's first opened in 5757 (that's AD 1996).

Zenna Noodle Bar, 1374 Beacon St., Brookline, MA 02446; (617) 566-0566; zennanoodle.com; Vietnamese/Thai; $; T: Coolidge Corner. Zenna kicks traditional Vietnamese street food up a notch, serving a version of *pho,* for example, that is filled with enough vegetables (onions, carrots, peapods, broccoli, scallions) to qualify as an Asian minestrone. The *banh xeo,* a sort of half-crepe, half-omelet filled either with vegetables or with a combo of shrimp and chicken, is far richer in flavor than any egg dish has a right to be. The restaurant is as beautiful as the plates, making for an aesthetically agreeable dining experience only enhanced by the small size of the bill.

Specialty Stores, Markets & Producers

Allandale Farm, 259 Allandale Rd., Brookline, MA 02467; (617) 524-1531; allandalefarm.com; Farmstand. Allandale is Boston's last working farm, and work they do, starting vegetables (including multiple varieties of tomatoes) in greenhouses so that the summer growing season can get off to a fast start. The produce is for sale in a seasonal farmstand, and is augmented with the harvest from other farms, and coffee, ice cream, baked goods, and other good foods from local producers. Open Apr through late Dec.

LAUNCHING PAD FOR GOURMET GROCERS

Brookline has been in the vanguard of Boston-area foodie-dom from the beginning. The first Bread & Circus store opened in 1975 on the Brighton-Brookline line. The company grew into the largest organic food retailer in the Northeast by 1992, when it was acquired by Whole Foods. Ten Whole Foods stores serve greater Boston:

15 Washington St., Brighton, MA 02135; (617) 738-8187

181 Cambridge St., Beacon Hill, Boston, MA 02114; (617) 723-0004

15 Westland Ave., Fenway, Boston, MA 02115; (617) 375-1010

200 Alewife Brook Pkwy., Fresh Pond, Cambridge, MA 02138; (617) 491-0040

115 Prospect St., Central Square, Cambridge, MA 02139; (617) 492-0070

340 River St., Cambridgeport, Cambridge, MA 02139; (617) 876-6990

413 Centre St., Jamaica Plain, MA 02130; (617) 553-5400

Berezka International Food Store, 1215 Commonwealth Ave., Allston, MA 02134; (617) 787-2837; Grocery; T: Harvard Avenue. In this case, the international foods are Russian and Eastern European and it's amazing how much can be packed into a small space—from canned borscht and tins of caviar to frozen dumplings and a dozen or more varieties of salami. Dried and smoked fish choices include

916 Walnut St., Newton, MA 02461; (617) 969-1141

647 Washington St., Newton, MA 02458; (617) 965-2070

442 Washington St., Wellesley, MA 02482; (781) 235-7262

When California-based Trader Joe's looked to expand to the east coast, the company also opened its first store in Brookline. That was 1996. Now six Trader Joe's outlets serve greater Boston:

1317 Beacon St., Coolidge Corner, Brookline, MA 02446; (617) 278-9997

899 Boylston St., Back Bay, Boston, MA 02115; (617) 262-6505

748 Memorial Dr., Cambridgeport, Cambridge, MA 02139; (617) 491-8582

211 Alewife Brook Pkwy., Fresh Pond, Cambridge, MA 02138; (617) 498-3201

1427 Massachusetts Ave., Arlington, MA 02476; 781-646-9138

1121 Washington St., West Newton, MA 02465; (617) 244-1620

salmon, Sevruga, Nova lox, rainbow trout, herring, and shad. A fresh pastry case is filled with tortes, mousses, and chocolate balls, while the deli case has potato pancakes, stuffed cabbage, and chicken Kiev to go, along with beet, carrot, and mushroom salads. Those really craving a taste of home can even find ice cream bars from Russia.

Blanchard's Liquors, 103 Harvard Ave., Allston, MA 02134; (617) 782-5588; blanchards.net; Wine, Beer & Spirits; T: Harvard Avenue. With its full-service attitude and extensive parking lot, Blanchard's could be mistaken for a simple high-volume liquor store. It does sell an awful lot of cases of beer to a largely collegiate clientele, and the stacks of two-liter plastic bottles of inexpensive vodka are enough to give fine wine lovers pause. But Blanchard's has an immense climate-controlled wine cellar that extends beneath the parking lot, and an almost hidden tasting room. Wine ranges from Shafer Hillside Select Cabernet (a Parker 100 points) all the way down to jug wines. What interests us most about Blanchard's are the wines in between—all those great drinking bottles in the $12–$25 range.

BLM Wine + Spirits, 1354 Commonwealth Ave., Allston, MA 02134; (800) BLM-WINE; blmwine.com; Wine, Beer & Spirits; T: Allston Street. The unofficial motto at BLM (the store formerly known as Brookline Liquor Mart) is "expertise without attitude." We've certainly found it to be true over the years and have long depended on BLM for good buys in *negociant* Burgundies, hard-to-find varietals from Alsace, and great selections of Italian and Spanish reds. Tastings are truly educational sessions, including the periodic samplings of wines from the eastern Mediterranean, where some great neglected bargains are still to be found.

The Butcherie, 428 Harvard St., Brookline, MA 02446; (617) 731-9888; butcherie.com; Butcher; T: Harvard Avenue/Coolidge Corner. The Rabbinical Council of New England supervises this glatt kosher shop where the shelves are piled high with US and Israeli kosher canned and dry goods. But kosher goods are available in lots of stores. What is unusual at The Butcherie is the range of fresh kosher meats, sausages, fish, latkes, and composed salads. Closed Saturday.

Clear Flour Bread, 178 Thorndike St., Brookline, MA 02446; (617) 739-0060; clearflourbread.com; Bakery; T: Packard's Corner. The bakers at Clear Flour find endless satisfaction and variety concentrating on breads from France and Italy. All the breads are made with unbleached flour, and many of the flours are organic and stone ground. Rustic French baguettes, buckwheat walnut loaves, onion focaccia, and seeded deli rye are available every day. But we'd bet that Brookline neighbors mark the calendar by the specialty breads, such as porter pumpernickel on Wednesday, fire-roasted-tomato rolls on Thursday, and challah on Friday. They have to wait for the weekend for the soft German pretzels.

Cutty's, 284 Washington St., Brookline, MA 02445; (617) 505-1844; cuttyfoods.com; Sandwich Shop; T: Brookline Village. Cutty's is a mom-and-pop sandwich shop with a twist. Owners Rachel and Charles Kelsey trained at the Culinary Institute of America and raise the simple sandwich to new heights. All their meats are roasted in-house and they make their own potato chips, pickles, and sauces.

Some fans make a special trip for lunch on Saturday—the only day that slow-roasted pork sandwiches with pickled fennel or with sautéed broccoli rabe are offered. But it's not exactly a hardship to settle for roast beef with crispy shallots and Thousand Island dressing or egg salad with radishes, olives, and cilantro during the week.

Gimbel's Liquors, 1637 Beacon St., Brookline, MA 02146; (617) 566-1672; Wine, Beer & Spirits; T: Washington Square. Sometimes liquor stores are like bistros—it's all about the neighborhood. Gimbel's has been around for a very long time and has evolved with the neighborhood. Look past the obvious big sellers and you find some of the specialties, like a nice selection of fine ports. Take the time to engage the staff and you'll get sage recommendations on a wine for dinner. Two lesser-known facts: the store has a parking lot out back for customers, and Gimbel's delivers even small orders.

Hong Kong Supermarket, 1 Brighton Ave., Allston, MA 02134; (617) 787-2288; Grocery; T: Packard's Corner. Shopping here is a bit like cruising all the little markets of Chinatown under one roof. Fortunately, the aisles are clearly marked so it's easy to find the specialty ingredients from Japan, China or Thailand, and Vietnam, for example, or to locate entire aisles of tea and coffee, oil and vinegar, or snack foods. Fresh vegetables are up front, while the back wall is devoted to meat and fish, including a broader selection of finfish than most Chinese grocers carry. For a little punch of flavor, we like to pick up some of the small jars of rice seasonings, such as sesame seed and seaweed, kimchee, salmon, or roasted wasabi.

Japonaise Bakery, 1020 Beacon St., Brookline, MA 02446; (617) 566-7730; japonaisebakery.com; Bakery; T: St. Mary's Street. Though Owner Hiroko Sakan specializes in blending Japanese flavors with European pastry traditions, she doesn't overlook the all-American donut. Her offerings include plain and chocolate cake-style donuts, as well as her version of a jelly donut filled with sweet red-bean paste. The shop's namesake pastry features layers of green-tea sponge cake filled with green-tea mousse. A similar concoction of strawberries, sponge cake, and vanilla Bavarian cream is one of the most popular treats.

Kupel's Bakery, 421 Harvard St., Brookline, MA 02446; (617) 566-9528; kupelsbakery.com; Bakery; T: Harvard Avenue/Coolidge Corner. This certified kosher bakery specializes in bagels and makes more than 20 flavors from onion to poppy, whole wheat raisin to cinnamon glaze. There's an art to pairing bagel with cream cheese. Kupel's choices include garlic and herb, green olive, strawberry, dill, honey walnut, and of course plain for those who prefer not to obscure the flavor of the bagel. Kupel's also bakes breads and makes strudel, rugalach, babkas, and other pastries. Closed Saturday.

Martignetti Liquors, 1650 Soldiers Field Rd., Brighton, MA 02135; (617) 782-3700; martignettiliquors.net; Wine, Beer & Spirits. Set out on a highway, this warehouse-size wine and liquor store is the retail outlet for one of the biggest importers in Massachusetts. We've always found it a useful place to peruse Tuscan, Piemontese, and Puglian red wines, in particular. In truth, Martignetti carries almost every wine available in the Massachusetts marketplace.

Michael's Deli, 256 Harvard St., Brookline, MA 02446; (617) 738-3354; delitogo.com; Sandwich Shop; T: Coolidge Corner. Michael's calls itself the "corned beef king" and a corned beef Reuben with Swiss cheese, Russian dressing, and sauerkraut tops the sandwich menu. You can substitute coleslaw for the sauerkraut if you want or have the corned beef served with salami and chopped liver. But there are plenty of other choices, such as mango chicken salad, hot cooked tongue, Romanian pastrami, or a BLT with 10 slices of bacon. Cash only.

Sakanaya Japanese Fish Market, 75 Linden St., Allston, MA 02134; (617) 254-0009; sakanayaboston.com; Fishmonger; T: Harvard Avenue/Packard's Corner. The best way to learn about good sushi is to eat it, and Sakanaya sells excellent sushi at bargain prices. Whenever you walk in, there will be a sushi chef patiently preparing more. But the next best way to understand sushi is to make it yourself, and Sakanaya has the incredibly good fresh fish to make that easy. A significant portion of the clientele is Japanese.

Serenade Chocolatier, 5 Harvard Square, Brookline, MA 02445; (617) 739-0795; serenadechocolatier.com; Chocolatier; T: Brookline Village. Serenade is steeped in the Viennese chocolate-making tradition, so it's no surprise that the signature sweet is the wonderfully old-fashioned Viennese with alternating layers of dark and milk chocolate blended with hazelnut butter. The shop also makes more conventional filled chocolates and truffles with centers of blood orange, dulce de leche, kirsch, and even marzipan. For a thoroughly modern treat, opt for a made-to-order, chocolate-dipped ice cream bar with vanilla or chocolate ice cream or mixed berry yogurt from **J. P. Licks** (see p. 183).

Tatte Fine Cookies & Cakes, 1003 Beacon St., Brookline, MA 02446; tattecookies.com; Bakery Cafe; T: St. Mary's Street. Owner Tzurit Or is a genius at baking with nuts. Starting with family recipes, she has expanded her repertoire to include nut-studded XXL biscotti, butter pistachio cookies, crisp almond biscuits, cashew or hazelnut tarts, walnut coffee cake, and her trademark nuts box of buttery pastry with a caramelized filling and toasted nut topping.

She also makes a wonderful strawberry walnut roll, beautiful fruit tarts, an elegant peach bundt cake, and a homey cherry *clafouti*.

Twin Donuts, 501 Cambridge St., Allston, MA 02134; (617) 254-9421; Bakery; T: Allston Street. We think that the best way to judge a donut shop is to sample the donut classics: plain cake and yeasted honey dip. This small shop excels on both counts with a cake donut that boasts a nicely crisp crust and moist, fine crumb, and a raised donut with a rather chewy, yeasty texture. Unlike the products of the donut chains, donuts at Twin actually have the flavor of pastry. The shop also has an iconic neon sign that, alas, is not always functioning.

When Pigs Fly, 1378A Beacon St., Brookline, MA 02446; (617) 232-1077; sendbread.com; Bakery; T: Coolidge Corner. Even with all the excellent local bread bakeries, this Maine-based company has found a following for its multigrain anadama, New York rye, maple walnut banana, and other loaves. They are also available in Somerville (see p. 337) and Jamaica Plain (see p. 185).

Wulf's Fish Market, 407 Harvard St., Brookline, MA 02446; (617) 277-2506; Fishmonger; T: Harvard Street/Coolidge Corner. What distinguishes Wulf's is that they buy their fish fresh daily from Fish Pier and cut all their fillets from whole fish. The salt smell of the sea pervades the shop and the whole fish laid out on beds of ice are as clear-eyed a lot as you'll find anywhere. One of the great pleasures of shopping at Wulf's, which dates from 1926, is watching the gents in white aprons cut your order.

Yi Soon Bakery, 112 Brighton Ave., Allston, MA 02134; (617) 254-3099; Bakery; T: Harvard Avenue/Packard's Corner. The woman behind the counter paused when we pointed to the case full of tiger skin rolls. "It's not real tiger skin," she said with a smile before explaining that a mixture of egg white and egg yolk is baked onto a thin cake layer to create the distinctive spotted pattern. The "skin" wraps around sponge cake with chocolate, strawberry, coffee, or orange fillings. Regulars stop in on weekends for specials such as scallion and cheese buns, hot dog and cheese buns, or *mochi*, a flaky pastry filled with sticky rice. On weekdays you can opt instead for a big bun filled with peanut butter, coconut, or cheese.

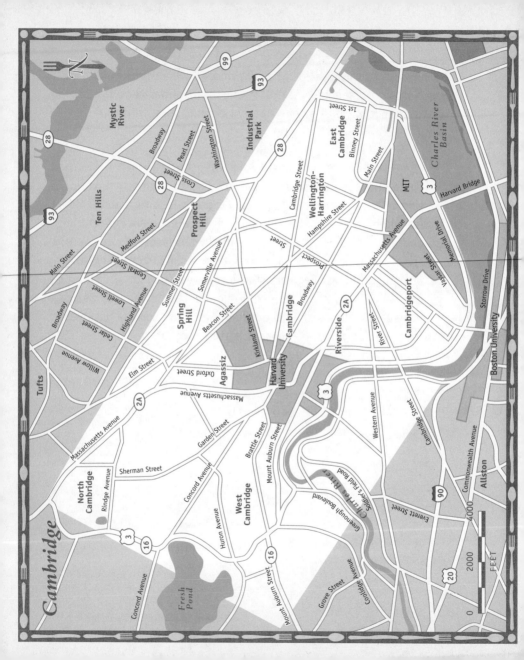

Cambridge

As Cantabrigians, we understand that Cambridge is often accused of thinking it is a world unto itself. We smugly refer to our two major universities as proof of superiority. We could also point to our restaurants. Taken together, the many neighborhoods of Cambridge (each identified in the address in the listings below) have far more places to eat than any single neighborhood of Boston proper. We are a city of villages. Most outsiders think of Cambridge as Harvard Square. As a dining neighborhood in the orbit of Harvard University, it naturally has restaurants suitable for everyone from students on a cheap date to professors celebrating a Nobel Prize. But Harvard Square barely scratches the surface. Central Square used to be the city's ethnic cheap-eats specialist, but even Central is gentrifying and raising the bar on casual dining. Porter Square is only one subway stop out of Harvard, yet it is rich with ethnic dining, including a strong concentration of Japanese eateries. Inman Square boasts both one of the region's last delis and a vibrant casual dining scene that functions as a form of nightlife. East Cambridge remains calmly Portuguese (though even that is changing) and, to some extent, Brazilian. Head in that direction on a weekend and you'll find large families pushing restaurant tables together so three generations can spend the afternoon eating and socializing. Perhaps the biggest change in 21st-century Cambridge dining is the emergence of Kendall Square, home of the techno-geek ascendancy thanks to Massachusetts Institute of Technology (MIT) and corporate biotech and robotics. Top restaurateurs have discovered Kendall in the past few years, and others have discovered it's worth cooking lunch for all the office workers who refer to themselves as the biotech working class. The happy result has been a number of reasonably priced bars and restaurants (and venues that defy pigeonholing) in very modern, soaring spaces. And the food is very good indeed.

Foodie Faves

Abigail's Restaurant, 291 3rd St., Kendall Square, Cambridge, MA 02142; (617) 945-9086; abigailsrestaurant.net; New American; $$; T: Kendall Square. A neighborhood favorite of the generation of coders and tech entrepreneurs who have colonized the stretch between MIT and Portuguese East Cambridge, Abigail's embodies the Cambridge casual fine dining aesthetic, offering all-day sandwiches like barbecued brisket with fried egg and, at dinnertime, cassoulet, spice-rubbed roast chicken, and a few other comforting entrees. (The winter veggie entree is often roasted stuffed acorn squash, which is comforting indeed.) For late-night dining, a short version of the dinner menu is available at the bar.

Addis Red Sea, 1755 Massachusetts Ave., Porter Square, Cambridge, MA 02140; (617) 695-3677; addisredseacambridge.com; Ethiopian; $; T: Porter Square. There's no questioning the authenticity of the dishes at Addis Red Sea, but the Americanized service of combining ingredients in each dish rather than letting diners do it themselves frustrates some traditionalists. Service can be slow, but the food is tasty, the price is right, and using bread rather than utensils for eating lends a touch of exoticism. Addis Red Sea has almost as many vegan main dishes as meat and fish. Two preparations of the proteins dominate: a spicy version simmered in red pepper sauce with ginger, garlic, and cardamom, or a milder dish with the protein simmered in a sauce of butter, onions, ginger, and turmeric. Addis also has a branch in the South End (p. 125).

Algiers Coffee House, 40 Brattle St., Harvard Square, Cambridge, MA 02138; (617) 492-1557; Middle Eastern; $; T: Harvard Square. In the old days the Algiers could pass for a North African hookah joint since the air was always blue with tobacco smoke as beatnik wannabes hunched over their bitter little cups of espresso. The espresso is much better, thank you, and the falafel and merguez sausage both taste better in the clear light of smoke-free dining. Admittedly, the Algiers no longer looks like the set for a spy movie, but it is still a good place to relax with a coffee or tea and maybe enjoy a bowl of *mujaddara* (a lentil-rice dish with sautéed onions).

All Star Sandwich Bar, 1245 Cambridge St., Inman Square, Cambridge, MA 02139; (617) 868-3065; allstarsandwichbar.com; Casual American; $. The proprietors of this busy shop are convinced that sandwiches remind us of the simpler days of childhood. But our moms' tuna salad and bologna and cheese on white bread literally pale in comparison to All Star's Beef on Weck (roast beef and extra-strong horseradish sauce on a kimmelweck bun) or Atomic Meatloaf Meltdown with Jack cheese, hot sauce, and red onion jam. Daily specials include Friday's Krispy Fried Local Fish Po'Boy with Tabasco remoulade, lettuce, tomatoes, and pickle relish. The gigantic sandwiches are served with a pickle spear and coleslaw —but go ahead and order a side of hand-cut fries anyway. This spot is popular even with neighborhood dogs, who appreciate the jar of dog biscuits outside the front door.

Amelia's Trattoria, 111 Harvard St., Kendall Square, Cambridge, MA 02139; (617) 868-7600; ameliastrattoria.com; Italian; $; T: Kendall Square. Chef-Owner Delio Susi grew up in the restaurant trade, making sausage in his parents' restaurant before he even entered high school. He and wife Rebecca run this marvelous little trattoria, where they've been dishing up traditional Italian cooking since 1999. Susi is particularly known for his delicate gnocchi and his handmade pastas. Don't miss his homage to his mother, Amelia: Fettuccine Mama is tossed with sautéed chicken, broccoli, sun-dried tomatoes, and a garlic butter–white wine sauce. At lunch Amelia's also offers panini for the coders and administrators who have to rush back to their desks at MIT, Lincoln Labs, and the Whitehead Institute.

Area 4, 500 Technology Sq., Kendall Square, Cambridge, MA 02139; (617) 758-4444; areafour.com; New American; $; T: Kendall Square. The terrific postindustrial space is the equivalent of Mom's kitchen for slews of MIT folk. They start the day at the bakery–coffee shop, where everyone is typing on a laptop, but no one is writing the Great American Novel—they're all writing code. The cafe (which closes around dinnertime) flows into the bar area, which steps up to the raised "dining room." Truthfully, the distinctions between the rooms are almost as fluid as the meals, and most menu items are offered at all hours. (Coders never know whether it's night or day anyway.) None of the 30 wines at the bar comes from a bottle— they're all on tap (a more eco-sensitive way to drink, the proprietors claim). They can be ordered by the glass, half carafe, or carafe. There's also a selection of 30 whiskeys (scotch) and whiskeys (all the others). The dining area faces the ovens, and most of the service is direct oven to table, whether it's one of the many pizzas, a roasted half chicken, or roasted squid and mussels with fennel sausage. For a good lunch at the bar, try the large plate of house charcuterie (including a country terrine and chicken liver mousse) with one of the New England brews. Like the food, the beer is sourced as locally as possible.

Asmara Restaurant, 739 Massachusetts Ave., Central Square, Cambridge, MA 02139; (617) 868-7447; asmararestaurantboston .com; Ethiopian; $$; T: Central Square. You'll want to visit this restaurant with close friends or family members since dining in the small, welcoming space is an intimate experience. The food is served family style in a large woven basket and diners use a traditional bread called *injera* as their utensils. The dishes may be familiar from the Ethiopian food that has been popularized by star chef Marcus Samuelsson. As he notes, the cuisine relies heavily on spices, and Asmara's kitchen is especially adept at seasoning with berbere, a combination of 14 spices and blends. Many of the meat, fish, and vegetable dishes are cooked in mild or spicy sauces. Meat or vegetarian combination plates are the best introduction to the cuisine.

Atasca Restaurant, 50 Hampshire St., Kendall Square, Cambridge, MA 02141; (617) 621-6991; atasca.com; Portuguese; $$; T: Kendall Square. Located at the intersection of Portuguese East Cambridge and polyglot Kendall Square, Atasca specializes in elegant Portuguese food prepared and served with more finesse than in the neighborhood's more casual home-style Portuguese restaurants. There's a distinctly Azorean cast to the cuisine—such as the chicken breast sautéed with San Jorge cheese, linguiça, and white wine—but mainland classics are also a good bet. The *cataplana*, for example, is actually steamed in the copper vessel that gives the combo of clams, mussels, shrimp, onions, red peppers, prosciutto, and linguiça its name. True to its Portuguese roots, Atasca serves at least three *bacalhau* (salt cod) dishes every evening: *de cebolada* (with caramelized onions and a side of fried potatoes), *á lagareiro* (charcoal grilled and drizzled with olive oil and garlic), and *com natas* (in a light cream sauce with garlic mashed potatoes).

Baraka Cafe, 80½ Pearl St., Central Square, Cambridge, MA 02139; (617) 868-3951; baraka.com; North African; $; T: Central Square. Chefs Alia Radjeb Meddeb and Krimo Dahim preside over a pretty dining room that almost feels like a private home. But they bring a sure-handed sophistication to their North African dishes. Start with a cold appetizer of smoky eggplant with roasted peppers or a warm dish of chickpea custard with a tapenade of *harissa* (a hot chile sauce) and you'll still have room for a traditional couscous of vegetables, lentils, chickpeas, and fava beans or for baby lamb chops marinated in the Moroccan spice mix *ras el hanout*. Baraka is particularly known for its *bastilla torte,* but you'll have to plan ahead to enjoy it. This dish of phyllo dough layered with almonds, spices, and either marinated squab or chicken must be ordered 36 hours in advance. By the way, Meddeb grew up outside Paris, which may explain why the menu also features a rich and complex seven-spice flourless chocolate torte. No alcohol is served, but Algerian-style lemonade with rose petals and spices is a worthy substitute. Cash only.

The Blue Room, 1 Kendall Sq., Kendall Square, Cambridge, MA 02139; (617) 494-9034; theblueroom.net; New American; $$; T: Kendall Square. This pioneer of good eating in Kendall Square seems to have a life of its own. These days the Blue Room has lots of company in the immediate neighborhood, but it wasn't always so. Over the years a number of very talented chefs have presided over the kitchen, always emphasizing wonderful grill-based, mostly locally sourced fresh food with the occasional quirky kick of spice. The wine list is affordable and carefully selected, and you'll be in the company of a lot of people having a good time dining in the dimly lit basement room. Classic starters here include the wood-grilled octopus, the duck leg confit, and a gruyère-laden bowl of French onion soup. The wood-grilled meats are nothing short of spectacular.

Bondir, 279A Broadway, Central Square, Cambridge, MA 02139; (617) 661-0009; bondircambridge.com; New American; $$$; T: Central Square. Bondir is one of those restaurants that can sneak up on you. It's located in an out-of-the-way hole-in-the-wall spot that is only coincidentally zoned for a restaurant, and Chef Jason Bond, while celebrated by the local food scribes, is not among the media stars of greater Boston. Nor does he bang you over the head with his cooking, where the pleasures are likely to be fairly subtle ones of complex, married flavors and meticulous plating. Moreover, he is gung-ho about sourcing his food locally, which can limit the menu, especially in the winter. It also means that the menu literally changes daily, based on availability. One night he might serve the roasted duck with corn cakes and beans; the next night the leftover duck is featured in a plate of handmade pasta. Many dishes are offered in half and full portions, which is great for tasting a lot of things, not so great if you have trouble making up your mind. One thing we really love is that Bond offers a stunning cheese every night as a dessert option, usually accompanying it with something like his own pickled grapes.

Cafe Barada, 2269 Massachusetts Ave., Porter Square, Cambridge, MA 02140; (617) 354-2112; cafebarada.net; Lebanese; $; T: Porter Square. This little cafe is a favorite for homemade Middle Eastern food, especially the stuffed grape leaves that, in deference to American preferences, are served warm instead of cold. Chef Claude Salameh makes dynamite falafel with a blend of chickpeas and fava beans that she soaks overnight and grinds with onion, garlic, Aleppo pepper, and other spices. The fried falafel balls are big and hearty, and they're served by smashing them flat in pita and rolling up with tomatoes, pickles, a little tahini, and parsley. Claude's son Charbel runs the dining room, and extends both a heartfelt welcome and discreet assistance to diners unfamiliar with the cuisine. Cash only.

Cafe Pamplona, 12 Bow St., Harvard Square, Cambridge, MA 02138; (617) 492-0352; Spanish/Casual American; $; T: Harvard Square. As far as we know, Ernest Hemingway never ate here, but apart from the lack of alcohol, it would have been his kind of place. A fixture at the edge of Harvard Square since 1959, the cafe was opened by Spanish refugee Josefina Yanguas to replicate the cafe scene of her native Pamplona. For years it was one of the few places where you could get a good cup of espresso and a *sopa de ajo* (garlic-chicken soup) and argue anti-fascist politics while wearing a beret and still—somehow—not look ridiculous. Pamplona served pressed ham sandwiches decades before panini became mall food. Josefina is gone but Pamplona persists—gritty as ever (thanks to dim light and crumbling plaster walls). The low-ceilinged basement room can be claustrophobic, but the sidewalk tables are always in demand when the weather shows the slightest warmth.

Casa Portugal, 1200 Cambridge St., Inman Square, Cambridge, MA 02139; (617) 491-8880; restaurantcasaportugal.com; Portuguese; $$. Chef-Owner Fernando Gomes hails from the Algarve, and his cooking at this favorite of the Cambridge Portuguese community reflects that region's relatively straightforward approach to dining. He often grills or fries pork and beef steaks, serving them with a vegetable-based sauce. The *escalopes de porco a casa* are the perfect example. He fries pork with thinly sliced onions (which caramelize) and sliced linguiça, then deglazes the pan with wine to make a sauce. The house version of *carne de porco a Alentejana*—practically the national dish of Portugal after *bacalhau* and *cataplana*—is a rich stew of marinated cubes of pork with fresh littleneck clams and diced potatoes. Gomes stocks a terrific list of wines from the Dao and the Alentejo and also offers a wide variety of ports in different ages and styles.

Catalyst, 300 Technology Sq., Kendall Square, Cambridge, MA 02139; (617) 576-3000; catalystrestaurant.com; New American; $$$; T: Kendall Square. **Chef-Owner William Kovels's last major gig in Boston before opening Catalyst was directing the fine dining at the Four Seasons Hotel, but he's really come into his own with this fine-casual room in the heart of Kendall Square. The lunch business really hops, with service so well planned that you can get in and out in under an hour while enjoying a leisurely sit-down meal. In the evening, though, you might prefer to linger, if only because the food is so good. Kovels understands that the point of an appetizer is to awaken your hunger, not to show off what can be done in a small plate. So the house pickled vegetables are just right—tart, slightly crisp, brightly colored. A lobster strudel might have a small pool of bisque, but the dressing on the accompanying greens immediately cleanses the palate. That's all the better to get you ready for well-rounded and satisfying main dishes like the roasted "blue cod" (pollock) served with a chowder of mussels, bacon, and herbs, or the cider-glazed pork chop with mustard spaetzle.**

Central Kitchen, 567 Massachusetts Ave., Central Square, Cambridge, MA 02139; (617) 491-5599; enormous.tv/central/index1.html; New American; $$$; T: Central Square. Chef-Owner Gary Strack runs a decidedly American kitchen where he celebrates all that is great about local food while still indulging the taste spectra of the Mediterranean. Thus he serves *gambas pil pil*—a Basque dish of spiced shrimp using rock shrimp with local tomato, garlic, and hot peppers—and a *bouillabaisse* that employs the local catch. We remember fondly a molasses-glazed pork chop with smoked ham grits, fava beans, and grilled local ramps. The broad and quirky wine list is organized by grape and ranges far and wide. It includes some terrific Spanish, Greek, and Sicilian choices as well as less obvious French and West Coast wines. Even Massachusetts is represented by Westport Rivers. The upstairs bar, **Brick & Mortar** (see p. 389), strives for suave with upscale cocktails and a very buttoned-down look, encapsulating the ongoing gentrification of Central Square.

Chez Henri, 1 Shepard St., Harvard Square, Cambridge, MA 02138; (617) 354-8980; chezhenri.com; French; $$$; T: Harvard Square. Chef Paul O'Connell had never been to Cuba when he started serving empanadas and Cubano sandwiches at his bistro's tiny front bar. Then people started coming just for the Cuban snacks and he had to expand the bar area. Slowly but surely, Latin accents have crept into the French dishes of the main dining room and O'Connell now bills Chez Henri as "a modern French bistro with a Cuban twist." Maybe the best example of the fusion of French technique and Latin spice is his criollo bouillabaisse, which piles Latin spices in a saffron fish soup full of New England shellfish and served with a chipotle-garlic rouille. Just when you think that the chef has waded a little deep into the Caribbean, he comes back with a strict French dish like *blanquette de lapin*—pasta tossed with white-wine-braised rabbit, cream, and Provençal herbs.

Clover HSQ, 7 Holyoke St., Harvard Square, Cambridge, MA 02138; no phone; T: Harvard Square; and **Clover HUB,** 1075 Cambridge St., Inman Square, Cambridge, MA 02141; no phone; cloverfoodlab .com; Casual American; $. The Clover folks operate some of Boston's most popular food trucks (p. 13). They have expanded their mini-empire with these two fixed sites that maintain the bare bones and casual attitude of the trucks, but give customers a chance to sit down and enjoy the mostly healthy versions of American comfort food, including pancakes and waffles at breakfast and sandwiches and burgers (chickpea and bean, among others) at lunch. Clover communicates by Twitter (@cloverHUB and @cloverHSQ) and people track down the trucks just for the fried-rosemary french fries. (They deep-fry the fresh rosemary for 15 seconds, then mix the crisped herb into the fries.)

Court House Seafood Restaurant, 498 Cambridge St., East Cambridge, Cambridge, MA 02141; (617) 491-1213; courthouse seafood.com; Seafood; $; T: Lechmere. The motto—"quality fresh fish since 1912"—actually refers to the fish market next door, but this no-nonsense restaurant carries on the same tradition. More than half the orders are phoned in for takeout, especially at lunchtime when the city workers would otherwise overwhelm the small restaurant. The Portuguese influence shows through—who else would offer a fried seafood dinner of mackerel or a side order of fried smelts?—but most plates are simple fried or broiled fish with sides of french fries or onion rings. The restaurant does offer some grilled meats (hamburger, chicken breast, linguiça) as well as deep-fried chicken, but you wouldn't come here for a burger any more than you'd go to a burger joint for great fish.

Craigie on Main, 853 Main St., Central Square, Cambridge, MA 02139; (617) 497-5511; craigieonmain.com; New American; $$$; T: Central Square. Chef Tony Maws trained in Burgundy and has essentially reinvented the Lyon *bouchon* for American food. His style is big and bold and roasted meats figure heavily on the menu. Many a Cantabrigian foodie grazes at the bar here, where you can load up on fried pig tails (probably the favorite bar snack), roasted bone marrow (they split the bone for you), and a pricey burger that could be the best beef you've ever eaten. And those are just the snacks. Dinner ramps up the scale of the food. Most diners opt for the three-course prix fixe, but you can order a la carte for nearly the same price. (All dishes in a given course are priced the same.) Maws is famous for using all but the pig's squeal. You might find a salad of pig's ears paired with beets or an entree of roasted swordfish wrapped with house-cured pig's cheek (*guanciale*) and served

CHOCOLATE AS BRAIN FOOD

To set itself apart from other student groups at the Massachusetts Institute of Technology, the **Laboratory for Chocolate Science** notes that it is the only organization on campus that orders more than 500 pounds of chocolate a year. The club was founded in 2003 and members are certainly more well-versed in the chemical properties of *Theobroma cacao* than the average chocoholic. But even at MIT taste usually trumps science and the public is invited to many of the group's tastings, classes, and scientific demonstrations. Truffle-making classes are particularly popular and fill up quickly. Check the website (chocolate.mit.edu) for details.

with pine nuts and golden raisins in a robust Sicilian style. One of the house specialties is the confit and roasted suckling pig head for two, which is far more savory than it sounds, thanks to accompaniments of Peking pancakes, spicy pumpkin chile paste, *boudin noir*, and hoisin sauce. Maws, by the way, does all the charcuterie in-house.

Cuchi Cuchi, 795 Main St., Central Square, Cambridge, MA 02139; (617) 864-2929; cuchicuchi.cc; Eclectic; $$; T: Central Square. Between the three Victorian stained-glass windows behind the bar, and the early Hollywood references to Carmen Miranda and exotic dancer/nude model Dita von Teese, there's no question that Cuchi

Cuchi shoots for camp and hits it dead on. But the food is seriously fun—a sampler of small dishes from around the globe. (No, they're *not* tapas, as the staff will explain. One of the owners is also co-owner of Spanish restaurant **Dalí**, see p. 312, and knows the difference.) Tasty treats range from fingerling potatoes with crisp-fried oysters, crème fraîche, salmon roe, and Champagne sauce (aka Caspian Heaven) to grilled Indian-spiced lamb served with a beet salad, grilled fennel, and cumin-impregnated crisp flatbread (*poppadom*). Enough vegetarian dishes are available that non–meat eaters will leave full as well. The wine list is as interestingly eclectic as the menu, but Cuchi Cuchi really shines with its cocktails. As you might hope, given the devotion to old-time decadence, the vintage cocktail list is long and strong, ranging from the French 75 (cognac, lemon juice, simple syrup, and Champagne) to a Corpse Reviver (gin, Cointreau, Lillet blanc, lemon juice, and absinthe).

Dante Restaurant, Royal Sonesta Hotel, 40 Edwin Land Blvd., East Cambridge, Cambridge, MA 02142; (617) 497-4219; restaurant dante.com; Italian; $$$; T: Lechmere or Science Park. Like its more casual sibling in Belmont, **Il Casale** (p. 342), Dante specializes in a modern interpretation of classic Italian (not Italian-American) food. Chef Dante de Magistris makes sure that a huge array of antipasti is available, but rather than order an assortment, each little plate is available separately. It's tempting to make a whole meal out of the *sfizi,* as they're called on the menu. Who would want to miss the tiny pork burger (the Mini Maiale) with cheddar cheese and pancetta, or skip over the *tuffo* of roasted eggplant dip, sweet peppers, and fennel with crostini and potato toast? But if you stick to *sfizi*, you'll miss the tagliatelle tossed with rabbit cacciatore, the gnocchi with truffle fonduta and sweet red peppers, or the pan-roasted scallops with Meyer lemon marmalade. Even the vegetable sides are special, like the lentils with escarole and crispy pancetta, or the steamed zucchini with mint and olive oil. Six- and nine-course personalized chef's tasting menus (with and without wine) are also available.

Desfina Restaurant, Bar & Grill, 202 3rd St., East Cambridge, Cambridge, MA 02141; (617) 868-9098; desfina.com; Greek; $-$$; T: Lechmere. Cambridge doesn't have the strong Greek population it once had, but those who remain seem to go to Desfina to eat. With low ceilings and a busy bar, it fits the image of a neighborhood bar and grill. Then you see the first order of Saganaki OPA! come out of the kitchen. The waiter flicks his cigarette lighter and the piece of sheep's milk cheese goes up in a blue flame, which you douse by squeezing lemon on it. And that's the appetizer. Are we having fun yet? A lot of the menu is conventional American fare like steak tips, grilled pork chops, and even mussels steamed in wine. Look farther afield for the Greek taverna dishes, like the slow-roasted lamb, the meat- and rice-stuffed dolmades drizzled with egg-lemon sauce, and the moussaka (the Greek casserole of eggplant, potato, ground meat and béchamel sauce).

Dosa Factory Indian Street Food, 571 Massachusetts Ave., Central Square, Cambridge, MA 02139; (617) 868-3672; dosafactory .com; Indian; $; T: Central Square. This pocket-size eatery at the rear of **Shalimar Gourmet Foods & Spices** (see p. 300) has a surprisingly long menu. But for a quick and filling meal, stick with a signature *dosa* (a crisp crepe made with rice flour) filled with spiced shrimp and swordfish or with lamb and potatoes. Larger entree plates, such as beef with herbs and nuts in cream sauce or tandoori-style chicken in tomato cream sauce, are served with rice and salad. Vegetarians can select from more than a dozen dishes, including spiced cauliflower florets and potatoes, baked eggplant, or braised lentils with herbs and spices. There are a few tables for dining, but most people take their food to go.

East by Northeast, 1128 Cambridge St., Inman Square, Cambridge, MA 02139; (617) 876-0286; exnecambridge.com; Chinese; $. It might sound counterintuitive to cook Chinese food with New England ingredients, but Chef-Owner Phillip Tang more than makes it work—he makes it sing. In his unpretentious small-box restaurant at the edge of Inman Square, Tang brings together his French training, years in fancy Boston restaurants, and experience with his family's Washington, DC–area dim sum palaces to craft a highly personal cuisine. The roots of Tang's dishes are either northern Chinese (roasted meats, hot spices, steamed breads) or Taiwanese (pork bun cooking), but the execution is all his own. That pork bun, for example, is filled with his own crispy cured pork belly (local pig, naturally) combined with bean paste and barely pickled onions. He is likely to add duck confit and pickled mustard greens to congee (perhaps echoing Shanghai's French concession) or cross cultures with smoked cod and pork wontons in a hot and sour broth (a bit of the Portuguese influence on Macao). All the dishes are small plates meant for sharing—if you can bring yourself not to lick up every morsel. Sunday brunch adds a delightful Asian wrinkle to the Inman Square brunch scene that started at **East Coast Grill** and spread.

East Coast Grill, 1271 Cambridge St., Inman Square, Cambridge, MA 02139; (617) 491-6568; eastcoastgrill.net; New American; $$. When East Coast Grill opened in 1985, casual fine dining was considered an oxymoron, and no serious restaurant did most of its cooking on an open wood grill. But it has proved such a winning formula that diners are still willing to line up and wait for a table. The menu is always loaded with fish specials, depending on the season, and they're usually done in a tropical way, reflecting founder Chris Schlesinger's youthful obsession with warm beaches and big waves. You might find mahimahi seasoned with a hot pepper rub, grilled, and served with rice and beans, grilled avocado (amazingly delicious), pineapple salsa, and fried plantains. The restaurant's eastern North Carolina shredded pork platter sets the bar for that BBQ style in greater Boston. A grilled veggie plate is always available for the non-meat eater in the party. On Sunday East Coast Grill features a whole smoked pig in rotating styles from around the world, including Latin American, Southeast Asian, and Hawaiian. If you haven't already guessed, eating here is fun.

Elephant Walk, 2067 Massachusetts Ave., Porter Square, Cambridge, MA 02140; (617) 492-6900; elephantwalk.com; Cambodian/French; $$; T: Porter Square. French Indochina may have been a debacle of imperialism, but it certainly yielded some of the world's great fusion cuisines. Elephant Walk, which also has locations in Boston (p. 99) and Waltham (p. 367), serves upscale Cambodian food, including the signature *amok*. This spicy dish suspends fresh crab, shellfish, and catfish fillets in a coconut-milk custard laced with aromatic Khmer spices. Yet the same menu also contains a Parisian-style steak-frites with Roquefort sauce. We like the in-between dishes, too, like the crispy wontons layered with warm pear and scallions and topped with shrimp flambéed in white wine. The restaurant also offers a complete vegetarian menu and breaks out an entire page of gluten-free dishes.

Emma's Pizza, 40 Hampshire St., Kendall Square, Cambridge, MA 02139; (617) 864-8534; emmaspizza.com; Pizza; $$; T: Kendall Square. Emma's is a Cambridge original. On one hand, it bears no relation to chain pizza or even old-school American pizza. On the other, it's also far from Neapolitan. All the pizzas start with a thin, cracker-like crust that can be topped with a classic oregano-tomato sauce, a zestier tomato sauce with lots of rosemary, or plain garlic-infused olive oil. The 32 toppings range from pepperoni, sausage, and roasted red peppers to sliced potato, dried cranberries, or (our favorite) thyme-roasted mushrooms. There are also six types of cheese. The possible combinations exceed our math ability to calculate. Maybe that's why Emma's also has a list of 25 suggested combinations. (We usually get a small #9, which has the mush- rooms, baby spinach, garlic, feta, traditional sauce, and mozzarella.) Service is good, but as you can imagine, it takes almost as long to order as it does to cook.

EVOO Restaurant, 350 3rd St., Kendall Square, Cambridge, MA 02142; (617) 661-3866; evoorestaurant.com; New American; $$$; T: Kendall Square. It was a sad day when EVOO moved out of our neighborhood after a 10-year run. But Peter and Colleen McCarthy just took their splendid food and warm hospitality a mile or so down the street to East Cambridge, where they have many more seats. There's never much question where your food has come from, as the McCarthys were listing their suppliers down the side of the menu long before "locavore" became a dining mantra. The dishes tend to confound expectation. The "surf and turf" might well be braised veal and cornmeal-crusted fried catfish, and the vegetarian special could easily be a sweet potato *tamal* filled with braised onion, raisin, and roasted sweet red pepper. In the fall and winter, Peter offers an outstanding lobster-parsnip bisque with leeks, hedgehog mushrooms, and tarragon butter as a starter. Meals are priced as a 3-course prix fixe (with a modest additional charge for wine pairing) with choice of each course, although courses are technically available a la carte. The chef's whim tasting menu is an elaborate set menu available Monday through Thursday. Lunch has many of the dinner dishes (which change constantly), along with good sandwiches like the ABC (apple, bacon, and cheddar).

Finale Desserterie & Bakery, 30 Dunster St., Harvard Square, Cambridge, MA 02138; (617) 441-9797; finaledesserts.com; Bakery Cafe; $; T: Harvard Square. This version of Finale (another is found at Park Plaza in Boston, see p. 100) functions as a lunchroom for many Harvard Square workers, who enjoy the fresh daily soups and line of made-to-order sandwiches. But dessert is the point of Finale, and many of the sweets are far more elaborate (and more expensive) than the sandwiches. Still, it's worth splurging for the Manjari Mousse, which is served between layers of chocolate buttermilk cake and garnished with a scoop of napoleon blackberry Cabernet sorbet. The future is uncertain, so begin with dessert.

Firebrand Saints, 1 Broadway, Kendall Square, Cambridge, MA 02142; (617) 401-3399; firebrandsaints.com; Casual American; $; T: Kendall Square. A collaboration between MIT and the chef-owner of **Central Kitchen** (p. 242), Firebrand Saints has the feel of a cyberprep restaurant as Hollywood might interpret one of the early William Gibson novels. Scratch the warehouse-y surface and ignore the people punching code on various devices, and the menu is surprisingly old-fashioned but mostly well-executed bar food focused on several burger variations (beef, veal and pork, lamb and beef, haddock, or mushroom), or "hand-carved rotisserie," which is another way of saying sliced chicken, beef, or roast pork. The pork comes Roman style—as *porchetta* with soft polenta and braised kale. The *porchetta* can also be ordered as a sandwich. Diners who like their pork lean and mild will be pleased, but those who like it salty and/or greasy may be disappointed. Not surprisingly, the beer selection is top-notch.

Flat Patties, 33 Brattle St., Harvard Square, Cambridge, MA 02138; (617) 871-6871; flatpatties.com; Casual American; $; T: Harvard Square. In the new hamburger wars, Flat Patties seems to be gaining turf on the other upstarts trying to unseat the golden arches and the big head in a crown. Burgers still rule (South of the Border, with jalapeño relish, avocado, cilantro aioli, and melted Jack cheese, is *very* popular), but the joint also offers grilled chicken sandwiches, pulled pork, fish and chips, and even salads. The only downside of Flat Patties is that it's often hard to get a seat, which means taking the burger to go.

Flour Bakery + Cafe, 190 Massachusetts Ave., Central Square, Cambridge, MA 02139; (617) 225-2525; flourbakery.com; Casual American; $; T: Central Square or Kendall Square. Just follow the crowd to find this version of Flour, which sits at the intersection of Central Square and the MIT campus. (For the original, see p. 153.) Master Baker Joanne Chang makes some of the city's favorite scones and muffins in the morning, and packs the customers in for lunchtime sandwiches such as roasted lamb with tomato chutney and goat cheese. Don't forget to pick up a tart for dessert. They're scaled from bite-size to individual to 5-, 8-, and 10-inch sizes for sharing (or not).

Four Burgers, 704 Massachusetts Ave., Central Square, Cambridge, MA 02139; (617) 441-5444; fourburgers.com; Casual American; $; T: Central Square. The original location of the Four Burgers mini-chain is as simple as its name. The menu consists of a beef burger using local grass-fed beef; a vegan black bean burger served with guacamole and salsa or with mango barbecue sauce; a turkey burger with cranberry chutney on the side; or a wild salmon burger with sesame coleslaw. Think of the place as fast food minus the nagging guilt.

Fuji at Kendall, 300 3rd St., Kendall Square, Cambridge, MA 02142; fujiatkendall.com; Japanese; $$; T: Kendall Square. The Asian students and faculty at MIT probably have no problem navigating the menu at this upscale Japanese and sushi restaurant just a few blocks from campus. For the rest of us, the menu actually explains most dishes and suggests more than a dozen preselected assortments of nigiri and sashimi entrees. If you're ordering sashimi, nigiri, or *maki* for a whole table, you can get the combos as "boats." But don't miss one of the most talked-about dishes: the

Philly Cheese Bomb, which packages assorted fish, flying fish roe, crabmeat, and Philadelphia Brand Cream Cheese in a nori wrapper. Then the whole thing is deep fried and served with a jalapeño *ponzu* sauce. This is definitely not Uncle Hiro's sushi bar. Only nonalcoholic beverages are served.

Garden at the Cellar, 991 Massachusetts Ave., Harvard Square, Cambridge, MA 02138; (617) 230-5880; gardenatthecellar.com; New American; $$; T: Harvard Square. Easy to overlook unless you're shopping for home decor at BO Home Concepts, DWR, or Crate & Barrel, the Garden at the Cellar styles itself as a gastropub, which is another way of saying "American bistro" but without the paper tablecloths. In fact, the tables are clad in copper, which wipes off just as nicely as Formica and looks much cooler. The lunch business revolves around sandwiches—an excellent burger, a generous mound of pulled pork, and a Reuben with house-made sauerkraut. All come with much-vaunted crisp, freshly cooked rosemary-truffle shoestring fries. The grilled cheese comes with the classic pairing of tomato soup. The same sandwiches are available in the evening but they're augmented by larger, more expensive plates like steak-frites, roasted mahimahi with coconut rice, or smoked chicken with caramelized artichoke. The wine list is limited but offers good value by skipping California, Bordeaux, and Burgundy in favor of less pricey locales.

Grafton Street Pub & Grille, 1230 Massachusetts Ave., Harvard Square, Cambridge, MA 02138; (617) 497-0400; graftonstreetcambridge.com; New American; $$; T: Harvard Square. Grafton Street opened in 1996 as part of a wave of Irish-inspired bars and restaurants. The wave crested and receded, but Grafton Street stands tall. The seasonally changing beer list of 75 quaffs certainly helps, but the pub is also immensely popular for weekend brunch and lunch. The kitchen produces some tasty dinner plates as well, ranging from a beef short rib pot roast to pan-roasted duck breast or seared sea scallops with chorizo. And since it is, at least nominally, Irish, you can get a fine ale-battered fish and chips. Big windows open to the sidewalk in nice weather, making for quasi-alfresco dining.

Grendel's Den, 89 Winthrop St., Harvard Square, Cambridge, MA 02138; (617) 491-1050; grendelsden.com; Eclectic/Vegetarian; $; T: Harvard Square. Many a Harvard or Radcliffe grad has fond memories of a date at this Cambridge icon back in the days when a grilled chicken breast qualified as gourmet cooking. The menu is much the same, including the beloved "beggar's banquet." Pick an entree and get spinach pie, hummus, pita, and choice of pasta or salad. Think of it more as glorious cafeteria food rather than restaurant fare and you'll be in the right mood to enjoy dinner. There's a good selection of beers (Grendel's had to sue to overturn the Massachusetts law that let nearby churches veto its liquor license), and the cheese fondue for two is an enduring bargain (and still a good choice on a date).

Hana Sushi, 2372 Massachusetts Ave., Porter Square, Cambridge, MA 02140; (617) 868-2121; hanasushicambridge.com; Japanese; $–$$; T: Porter Square. Sashimi here is very good, but the sushi rolls are where this little storefront restaurant in North Cambridge stands out. All made fresh throughout the day and crafted both for the eye and the taste buds, the artistry of the sushi stands in contrast to the Formica-and-fluorescents decor. Some diners rate the miso soup as among the best they've ever tasted. Don't overlook the cooked entrees as well, including tempura and teriyaki.

Harvest, 44 Brattle St., Harvard Square, Cambridge, MA 02138; (617) 868-2255; harvestcambridge.com; New American; $$$; T: Harvard Square. A culinary landmark since 1975, Harvest was Cambridge's first restaurant to adopt market-driven cuisine. It was Julia Child's favorite restaurant in her later Cambridge years, and served as a launching pad for chefs who transformed the Boston-area dining scene, including Chris Schlesinger (former chef-owner of **East Coast Grill,** see p. 249), Lydia Shire (Scampo and **Towne Stove and Spirits,** see p. 113), and Frank McClelland (**L'Espalier,** see p. 103). Now under the direction of Mary Dumont, Harvest serves contemporary farm-to-table dishes in a comfortable but classy setting. If you want to really taste the seafood of the Northeast, order the Grand Banks sampler from the raw bar. It includes local oysters (Island Creek, Duxbury), Jonah crab claws, and local fish ceviche along with Gulf shrimp. Seared Atlantic halibut with a saffron broth and a squid ink–Pernod sauce is a perennial favorite. Bar snacks include a mini Maine lobster roll—the perfect bite to accompany a cold beer in the outdoor summer courtyard bar.

Helmand Restaurant, 143 1st St., East Cambridge, Cambridge, MA 02142; (617) 492-4646; helmandrestaurant.com; Afghani; $$; T: Lechmere. This authentic restaurant operated by Afghan president Hamid Karzai's older brother is our ace in the hole for entertaining couples with conflicting dietary limitations. Since the menu covers the gamut of Afghani cooking, there are about a zillion vegetarian dishes, including the platter of baked pumpkin, fried eggplant, sautéed spinach, and okra and tomatoes. All dishes can be made gluten-free, and carnivores can sink their teeth into all manner of beef and lamb dishes. A lot of the spicing (cardamom, garlic, mint, turmeric, coriander) may remind some diners of Indian and Pakistani food. Dishes are usually offered with rice prepared one of two ways: boiled, seasoned with oil and cumin and baked (called *challow*), or treated in a similar fashion but seasoned with warm spices like cardamom, cinnamon, nutmeg, cumin, and black pepper (called *pallow*). There's a magical air about the restaurant, as luxurious handwoven rugs are draped everywhere and in the winter a fire crackles in the fireplace.

Henrietta's Table, Charles Hotel, 1 Bennett St., Harvard Square, Cambridge, MA 02138; (617) 661-5005; henriettastable.com; New American; $$; T: Harvard Square. Chef Peter Davis made this service restaurant for the Charles Hotel into a dining destination in its own right—no small feat when you share a building with **Rialto** (see p. 271) and **Legal Sea Foods** (see p. 262). Henrietta is the fictitious pig mascot who is meant to suggest the farm-to-table philosophy that the restaurant adopted literally decades before it became a fad. Sunday brunch is a veritable groaning-board all-you-can-eat buffet that includes a stupendous raw bar of Wellfleet oysters and jumbo shrimp. Yet the evening meal is called supper, rather than dinner—an indicator of lower prices and smaller portions. The New American cooking owes a lot to traditional American fare, so Yankee pot roast, baked scrod, and rotisserie chicken share the menu with more unusual offerings such as pulled lamb shank and farro. Many of Davis's recipes are corraled in his cookbook *Fresh & Honest: Food from the Farms of New England and the Kitchen of Henrietta's Table.*

Hungry Mother, 233 Cardinal Medeiros Ave., Kendall Square, Cambridge, MA 02141; (617) 499-0090; hungrymothercambridge .com; Southern; $$; T: Kendall Square. This tiny spot located near the Kendall Square cinema complex gets its share of dinner-and-a-movie date nights, but it also has its adherents who could care less about film as long as they get their fill of cornmeal-battered fried oysters or catfish—or for that matter, during the season, fried green tomatoes. Chef Barry Maiden hails from Virginia, so there is a Tidewater gentility that tempers the Southern flavors. Perhaps the best marriage of classical French technique with down-home ingredients is the crispy cylinder of head cheese accompanied by a succotash of hominy and pinto beans, pureed celeriac, and homemade pickled vegetables. Even the snacks are Southern, though the boiled Virginia peanuts are dusted with Maine sea salt. Maiden bakes a different pie daily for dessert, offering it plated at the restaurant, or packaged to take home for later.

Jasper White's Summer Shack, 149 Alewife Brook Pkwy., Alewife, Cambridge, MA 02140; summershackrestaurant.com; Seafood; $$; T: Alewife. The original of seafood master Jasper White's casual restaurants, Summer Shack seems about the size of an airplane hangar. It's not quite that big, but it is rather like a beachside fish shack on steroids (and, alas, far from the water). The size and the location at the edge of town near the Alewife T parking garage mean that White can keep the prices down, which is no mean feat. On top of traditional treatments like steamed clams with drawn butter, or plain steamed whole lobster, he offers surprises like lobster pot stickers with ginger; a pumpkin, corn, and lobster bisque; and a killer Shack Bouillabaisse that contains lobster, mussels, littleneck clams, fish, and squid in a saffron-tomato-fennel broth. It's served with jasmine rice and red pepper aioli. White is a very tall chef who used to be rather heavy but trimmed down decades ago. Each day he offers the "be good to yourself special" of a 6-ounce portion of high-omega-3 fish grilled and served with salad and brown rice. It lets you be virtuous while everyone around you is dipping lobster in drawn butter or scarfing down fried clams dredged in tartar sauce.

Kika Tapas, 350 3rd St., Kendall Square, Cambridge, MA 02142; (617) 245-6030; kikatapas.com; Spanish; $; T: Kendall Square. Next door to **EVOO** (see p. 251) in the Watermark Building at the corner of Broad Canal Way, this Spanish small-plates restaurant dizzies us with the mixed Spanish nomenclature for its plates (confusing *pintxo* for *tapa, tapa* for *ración,* etc.) but the food is on the mark, right down to the imported Spanish ham and sausages, the cold octopus stewed with paprika, and the slices of pork loin drizzled with a creamy sauce of mushrooms and cabrales blue cheese. Most dishes are under (many way under) $10, but you'll want to eat a few to make a meal. For a more substantial dish, consider one of the three versions of paella or *fideuá* (like a paella but made with crushed angel-hair pasta). They offer one with sausages, chicken, and seafood; another with cod, squid, and shellfish; and a strictly vegetarian version. Really hungry diners might consider the beef tenderloin cooked with dried prunes and apricots and served with a brandy cream sauce. Kika also does a booming lunch business, with many diners ordering sandwiches or meal-size salads.

Koreana, 158 Prospect St., Central Square, Cambridge, MA 02139; (617) 576-8661; koreanaboston.com; Korean; $$; T: Central Square. Located in a residential neighborhood rather than right in the square, Koreana attracts Korean diners from all over greater Boston. The place is packed every night of the week, so if you want to try the Korean barbecue menu when it's a little less hectic, plan a weekday lunch. The tabletop barbecue is the main lure (single diners cannot get a table with a grill). The most popular order is *yuksu bolgoki,* which includes thinly sliced rib eye beef and enoki mushrooms and clear noodles in a soy and sesame broth. (One order serves two.) Many diners opt for the vegetable barbecue of a couple of kinds of mushrooms, red and green peppers, eggplant, and zucchini—all of which you grill to taste. In lieu of grilled food, you can opt for a hot pot like the kimchee *chigae,* a stew of kimchee, pork, tofu, scallions, and sliced rice cake.

Le's Vietnamese Restaurant, 35 Dunster St., Harvard Square, Cambridge, MA 02138; (617) 864-4100; lescambridge.com; Vietnamese; $; T: Harvard Square. Part of a small local chain of restaurants serving the traditional noodle soup of Vietnam, *pho,* this casual spot in the Garage at Harvard Square does a smashing business at lunch, less so at dinner time. A bowl of *pho* spiked with chile pepper and lime juice and heaped high with bean sprouts and Thai basil is the perfect pick-me-up on a winter's day. There are also meat and fish entrees available and the whole steamed striped bass makes an impressive dinner for two to share.

Legal Sea Foods, Charles Square, 20 University Rd., Harvard Square, Cambridge, MA 02138; (617) 491-9400; legalseafoods.com; Seafood; $$–$$$; T: Harvard Square. Like the branches of this seafood empire found all over the city, the Charles Square Legal serves the chain's excellent clam chowder and all manner of fresh fish. The big attraction here is plaza dining in the summer.

Life Alive Urban Oasis & Organic Cafe, 765 Massachusetts Ave., Central Square, Cambridge, MA 02139; (617) 354-5433; life alive.com; Vegetarian; $; T: Central Square. The folks behind Life Alive take the relationship between food and health seriously, using only ingredients that are fresh, unprocessed, and "as close to 100 percent organic as possible." But their whimsical side shines through in the names of their dishes. The Sufi Poet salad, for example, features red lentil hummus whirling atop cranberries, cashews, apples, carrots, and spring greens. The Hot & Healthy Bachelor brings together cheddar cheese, hard-boiled egg, greens, and nutritional yeast in a whole wheat tortilla. Even kids can eat healthy with the Feisty Child, a tortilla topped with peanut butter, strawberry jelly, banana, and honey. Life Alive is easy to spot by the big window full of herb plants. Some dishes use eggs, as well as Cedar Grove raw cheddar cheese, which is made with vegetable rennet, but the majority of plates are fully vegan.

Middle East Restaurant, 472–480 Massachusetts Ave., Central Square, Cambridge, MA 02139; (617) 864-3278; mideastclub.com; Middle Eastern; $; T: Central Square. More people come here for the music than the food, as the Middle East is one of the must-stops for indie musicians on their way to the top. But it never hurts to have a meal before the show, especially if you're planning on serious drinking while you rock out. In blessed contrast to most bar food, much of the food is vegetarian, lots of it vegan, and you will get your vegetables, even if you're a carnivore and order the grape leaves stuffed with ground meat. The baba ghanoush is properly smoky and the lentil stew is deeply warming on a cold night. Couscous is available with tofu, chicken, beef, lamb, shrimp, tuna, or spicy kofta meatballs. Pretty much the same menu is available in the evenings upstairs in the ZuZu Bar (which morphs into **Z Rant,** see p. 281, at lunch) or in the downstairs dining room.

Midwest Grill, 1124 Cambridge St., Inman Square, Cambridge, MA 02139; (617) 354-7536; midwestgrillrestaurant.com; Brazilian; $$. We always enjoy the theatrical nature of dining on Midwest's Brazilian-style *rodizio*. After you select from a buffet of hot and cold dishes, you simply sit back and wait as servers circulate with skewers of meat hot off the grill. But try to pace yourself for the steady stream of beef, pork, lamb, chicken, kielbasa, ribs, chicken heart, and Brazilian sausage. To make a night of it, start your meal with a *caipirinha,* Brazil's national cocktail of lime, sugar, and *cachaça,* a liquor made from fermented sugarcane juice.

Moksa, 250 Massachusetts Ave., Central Square, Cambridge, MA 02139; (617) 661-4900; moksarestaurant.com; Asian; $; T: Central Square. Chef Patricia Yeo calls Moksa a Pan-Asian *izakaya,* a style of Japanese drinking establishment that serves food to go with the booze. There's also a nightclub in the back of the space, so food is not entirely front and center here. But Yeo has become famous in New York and Boston for reinventing Asian street food, and she continues that trend at Moksa with dishes like Vietnamese rice paper rolls stuffed with spice-spiked tuna, or Indian roti filled with ingredients as disparate as *paneer* and avocado, lamb breast and crisp anchovies, or lobster and mango. Most dishes are available until midnight.

Mr. Bartley's Gourmet Burgers, 1246 Massachusetts Ave., Harvard Square, Cambridge, MA 02138; (617) 354-6559; mrbartley .com; Casual American; $; T: Harvard Square. You have to love a restaurant that aspires to do one thing well in a single location. Under slightly different names, the Bartley family has been making great burgers here since 1960. The formula is simple: Grind the beef daily and use 7 ounces per patty. This being a college town, Bartley's has celebrity, political, and punning names for its various combos. The Tom Brady (with cheddar, guacamole, lettuce, tomato, onions, and fries) has the notation "ladies, make a pass at this." The Jersey Shore is denoted as "over the top," which it is with bacon, cheese, grilled mushrooms, and onions, accompanied by onion rings. These are meaty beasts—fistsful of beef on big buns. Yielding to changing times, Bartley's also permits the substitution of veggie and turkey burgers for the beef patties in any combo.

Muqueca, 1008 Cambridge St., Inman Square, Cambridge, MA 02141; (617) 354-3296; muquecarestaurant.com; Brazilian; $$. We've never met restaurateurs with more pride in their native cuisine than Fatima and Antonio Gomes, who serve the dishes they ate while growing up in Brazil. To ensure the authenticity of their signature seafood stew, or *muqueca,* they use handmade clay pots from their home state of Espírito Santo and neighboring Bahía to simmer fish and shellfish with cilantro, tomato, and onion. The finished dishes, such as a *muqueca* of fish, shrimp, and mussels, are served with rice. Muqueca's menu is heavy on fish, including deep-fried red snapper or *bacalhau* (salt cod) with hard-boiled eggs, cilantro, plantain, and coconut milk. But meat eaters have a number of good options including *feijoada,* the Brazilian national dish of stewed black beans with pork, sausage, and bacon, served with collard greens and fried plantain. The Gomeses may be sticklers for authenticity, but they depart from tradition with their delightful original creation of lasagna made with plantains, cheese sauce, and oregano.

Nubar, Sheraton Commander Hotel, 16 Garden St., Harvard Square, Cambridge, MA 02138; (617) 234-1365; nubarcambridge.com; New American; $$; T: Harvard Square. The Commander is one of the original Sheraton hotels, and its service restaurant has been a modest part of the Cambridge dining scene for nearly a century. This latest incarnation is a chic bar with adjunct dining rather than the other way around, and the fare is comfort food that's gone to school to learn proper manners. So the potato gnocchi are sautéed with chanterelle mushrooms, the grilled salmon comes with sides of lentils and glazed root vegetables, and the steak-frites is accompanied by a watercress salad. Even if you're not eating here, it's worth stopping at the bar for any number of specialty cocktails, including the Nubar Rouge of Lillet Rouge, St. Germain elderflower liqueur, and a splash of cava.

Olé Mexican Grill, 11 Springfield St., Inman Square, Cambridge, MA 02139; (617) 492-4495; olerestaurantgroup.com; Mexican; $$. Chef-Restaurateur Erwin Ramos might be Filipino by birth, but he has a Mexican soul, a devotion to the deep traditions of Mexican cooking, and the will to do things right. Chicago's Mexican food guru Rick Bayless told him that all his effort would be wasted if he used tasteless commercial tortillas, so now Olé makes tortillas nightly from fresh *masa*. The menu offers main-dish plates but most of the best flavors are available only in small dishes. In practice, this is a great way for everyone at the table to taste the *cuitlacoche* crepes, the street-vendor-style grilled corn with chile and lime, the sautéed scallops with roasted garlic, and the chicken *tamal* topped with mole negro dark chile-pepper sauce. If you want to see what you've missed at conventional "Mexican" restaurants, order the enchilada plate. You can get it filled with grilled diced chicken, braised pork, or mixed vegetables. It's served with rice and black beans (very Yucatecan), and a choice of *ranchera,* mole negro, or salsa verde.

Oleana, 134 Hampshire St., Inman Square, Cambridge, MA 02139; (617) 661-0505; oleanarestaurant.com; Mediterranean; $$$; T: Central Square. Ask most diners what region is covered in

Mediterranean cuisine and they suggest an arc of countries from Spain to Greece. Ask Ana Sortun, chef-owner of Oleana, and she's more likely to think of a similar arc that runs from Morocco to Turkey. Sortun is the spice mistress of Boston-area chefs. She even wrote a cookbook of dishes grouped by predominant flavors called *Spice: Flavors of the Eastern Mediterranean*. It's tempting to make an entire meal of the meze dishes—like the grape leaves stuffed with lentils, rice, chestnuts, and prunes, or the beans and chickpeas with green chard and orange aioli—but then you'd miss some of the great entrees. These dishes vary with the season but might well include flattened lemon chicken with zaatar spices and Turkish cheese pancakes, or fish roasted with grapes and olives and served with salami and a polenta cake. In case the meze do appeal most, Oleana offers a vegetable tasting menu of five meze and dessert.

Olecito!, 12 Springfield St., Inman Square, Cambridge, MA 02139; (617) 876-1374; olerestaurantgroup.com; Mexican; $. Last time we popped in for lunch, all the staff was Guatemalan, but this tiny, mostly take-out offshoot of Olé across the street serves wonderfully reimagined Mexican street food. There's a limited selection of terrific tacos (including the delicious *carnitas,* with braised pork, salsa verde, pineapple salsa, and pickled cabbage); quesadillas with a choice of chicken, steak, or braised pork; and tortas—Mexican-style sandwiches. The most popular lunch choice is a burrito, with the same choice of meats or grilled vegetables wrapped in a flour tortilla with rice, beans, guacamole, pico de gallo, Jack cheese, and sour cream. If you have a sweet tooth, Olecito also offers the strips of fried dough known as churros. There are only a handful of stools at a bar, since most business is takeout. Cash only.

Orinoco, 56 JFK St., Harvard Square, Cambridge, MA 02138; (617) 354-6900; orinocokitchen.com; Venezuelan; $$; T: Harvard. The third of the Orinoco Venezuelan restaurants has brightened up the hideaway held down for decades by the beloved Basque restaurant Iruña. Orinoco's cuisine draws from both the Caribbean coast and the high country of the Andes for dishes like fried red snapper with a mojo sauce of roasted pepper and culantro (a Caribbean herb with similar flavor to fresh coriander). The original Orinoco is in the South End (p. 142), while its other offspring is in Brookline (p. 212). But Cambridge has a hidden secret: outdoor garden dining in the summer.

Portugalia, 723 Cambridge St., Inman Square, Cambridge, MA 02141; (617) 491-5373; portugaliaincambridge.com; Portuguese; $$. On weekend afternoons this unprepossessing little restaurant is packed with families from the local Portuguese-American neighborhood. And you can bet that every table will order the pitch-perfect *caldo verde* (potato-kale soup with a slice of linguiça), and someone will have one of the many *bacalhau* (salt cod) dishes for which Portugalia is well known. It's said that Portuguese cuisine has 365 *bacalhau* dishes—one for each day—but Portugalia serves only 6 of them. The casserole of shredded salt cod, onions, potatoes, and

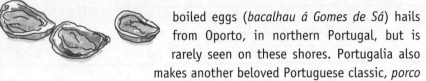

boiled eggs (*bacalhau á Gomes de Sá*) hails from Oporto, in northern Portugal, but is rarely seen on these shores. Portugalia also makes another beloved Portuguese classic, *porco Alentejana,* which consists of marinated pork cubes cooked with small clams and topped with cubed potatoes. Wines are reasonably priced, with some excellent reds from the Alentejo and a few of the top *vinhos verdes.*

Rendezvous, 502 Massachusetts Ave., Central Square, Cambridge, MA 02139; (617) 576-1900; rendezvouscentralsquare.com; Mediterranean; $$$; T: Central Square. Chef-Owner Steve Johnson has been a tireless advocate for local farmers and fishermen since long before it was fashionable and sources almost everything he can from the immediate local region. In the summer, that includes the garden on the restaurant roof. But his dishes take their inspiration from the western Mediterranean cuisines of Italy, coastal France, Spain, and North Africa. For example, he'll break down a 6-pound locally foraged hen-of-the-woods mushroom into smaller pieces to sauté and serve with fried orecchiette, sautéed black kale, and Piave cheese (or with fried pasta and his signature braised pork and veal meatballs). The olive oil and Piave come from Italy, everything else from New England. His winter dish of crispy roast chicken with brussels sprouts, butternut squash, apples, and fried sage is a classic in Gascony and nearby Catalonia, but it too is pure New England. Johnson runs consumer-friendly promotions on what are usually off-nights for restaurants. Sunday usually has a bargain prix fixe as well as a bargain cassoulet in winter, while Monday nights are tapas nights with all Spanish-inspired small dishes and a different sherry featured each week.

Rialto, Charles Hotel, 1 Bennett St., Harvard Square, Cambridge, MA 02138; (617) 661-5050; rialto-restaurant.com; Mediterranean; $$$–$$$$; T: Harvard Square. Jody Adams's taste has kept marching east across the Mediterranean. In her early days as Gordon Hamersley's sous-chef at **Hamersley's Bistro** (p. 137), she favored the sunny dishes of southern France. In more recent years, her taste has broadened to incorporate fish dishes from Sardinia and the earthy flavors of Sicily. She has an impeccable palate, and mixes and matches flavors from different regions with great panache. Thus, her grilled swordfish might come with a Friulian bean stew, braised cabbage, and house-cured bacon, but it also gets a palate-refreshing blast of juniper berry. The slow-roasted duck with braised escarole is unctuous, but sharp Sicilian green olives cut through the heaviness. The menu is always in flux because Adams responds to the seasonality on a daily basis. In fall and winter, don't miss her warm crispy lobster salad with beets, chestnuts, apples, and horseradish.

S&S Restaurant, 1334 Cambridge St., Inman Square, Cambridge, MA 02139; (617) 354-0777; sandsrestaurant.com; Casual American; $. This Inman Square gathering spot was founded in 1919 and takes its name from the Yiddish word *es,* which translates as "eat." And that's exactly what patrons do at this institution known for its generous portions. You'll still find what S&S calls the "deli traditions" of potato pancakes, cheese blintzes, pearl knockwurst and beans, lox or smoked whitefish on a bagel, or chopped liver on rye. (Many top Boston chefs come here to order chopped liver sandwiches.) But the restaurant has changed with the times and the multi-page menu features everything from rack of lamb and fried haddock to gourmet pizzas and barbecued baby back ribs. Saturday and Sunday brunch is served until 4 p.m. and the roasted salmon hash, steak and eggs, or poached eggs on potato pancakes with crabmeat, asparagus, and béarnaise sauce could be the only meal you need to eat all day.

Salts, 798 Main St., Central Square, Cambridge, MA 02139; (617) 876-8444; saltsrestaurant.com; New American; $$$; T: Central Square. Great food has come out of the kitchen at 798 Main St. since the late 1970s, when it was a collaborative restaurant involving several of the then-young chefs who went on to dominate the local culinary scene. Since early 2004, though, it's been home to the French-inspired American cooking (think Thomas Keller as the model) of Gabriel Bremer, with his gracious Uruguayan-born wife, Analia Verolo, running the front of the house. They produce a wonderfully civilized dining experience—very *soigné,* as the French would put it. But civility doesn't undercut the intense flavors of, say, a starter of bergamot-cured ocean trout with compressed cucumber (a neat trick to partially dehydrate cuke slices), French breakfast radishes, and pea greens. Nor does the French accent mask the local flavors of wild striped bass roasted with small clams, spring peas, wild ramps, and smoked ham. For dessert, Salts serves ice creams and sorbets (made in-house) with one of our favorite cookies, brown-butter-almond *financiers*. The wine list is craftily chosen and features several value choices from Spain's Valdeorras region as well as some of the superb wines of Uruguay.

Sandrine's Bistro, 8 Holyoke St., Harvard Square, Cambridge, MA 02138; (617) 500-3055; sandrines.com; French; $$–$$$; T: Harvard Square. We've always had a soft spot for Raymond Ost's Alsatian bistro, but then we're big fans of Alsatian wines and beers and his food is the perfect match. Admittedly, diners hoping for a Mediterranean meal may be disappointed, because Ost concentrates on the cuisine of northern France. Anything with pork products will be fantastic (including the bacon on the *flammekueche,* an Alsatian hearth flatbread), as will anything cold-weather French (like the mussels steamed in Riesling wine). If you're drinking beer, you can't go wrong with the Alsatian *choucroute garnie*: a big plate of slow-cooked sauerkraut with juniper berries, three kinds of sausage, smoked pork loin, ham hock, and hickory-smoked bacon. Did we mention anything with pork is great?

Tanjore, 18 Eliot St., Harvard Square, Cambridge, MA 02138; (617) 868-1900; tanjoreharvardsq.com; Indian; $; T: Harvard Square. Tanjore is proof positive that one should never judge an Indian restaurant by its lunch buffet. The midday buffet is frankly . . . predictable. But come instead at dinnertime and you can eat your way across India. The menu is laid out by geography, giving diners a chance to sample the cuisine of some of the more overlooked regions, such as southern India, with its emphasis on Portuguese spices, potato dishes, and wonderful fish. Dosas are served with coconut chutney and a lentil stew (*sambhar*). Spice lovers might opt for the vindaloo from Goa.

Ten Tables, 5 Craigie Circle, Harvard Square, Cambridge, MA 02138; (617) 576-5444; tentables.net; New American; $$; T: Harvard Square. Chef David Punch runs the Cambridge version of Ten Tables, oddly located in the basement of a condo complex on the edge of Harvard University's sphere of influence. But this same spot has launched many a great restaurant over the years, and Ten Tables is full all the time with diners looking to savor the farm-to-table menu. Punch has a flair for sensitive spicing, so his *glandulat*—a Gascony dish of red beans with carrots and pork—is spiked with Armagnac and brightened with a hint of cinnamon. The perfect appetizer? A bowl of Catalan garlic soup with paprika croutons and a soft-boiled egg. Like its two sibling restaurants in Jamaica Plain (p. 177) and Provincetown, this Ten Tables buys almost all its produce from local organic farmers when the season permits.

BLUE RIBBON SPECIAL

Le Cordon Bleu, which has a branch in Cambridge, has been teaching would-be chefs to cook for more than 100 years. While the school's name is common knowledge, its teaching restaurants are a surprisingly well-kept secret. They offer lunch and dinner Monday through Friday, and charge about half what a non-teaching restaurant would. (Dinner guests have a choice of a three- or four-course meal.) The main dishes are presented by the technique used to cook them. Thus, halibut with corn and fava bean succotash might appear under the *sauter* heading, a filet mignon steak under *griller,* and veal shank under *braiser.* All the food is prepared and served by students at the school under the watchful tutelage of instructors. Wine is extra but is extremely reasonable. **Technique Restaurant,** Le Cordon Bleu College of Culinary Arts, 215 1st St., East Cambridge, Cambridge, MA 02142; (617) 218-8088; techniquerestaurant.com; New American; $; T: Kendall Square.

Thelonious Monkfish, 524 Massachusetts Ave., Central Square, Cambridge, MA 02139; (617) 441-2116; theloniousmonkfish.com; Asian; $$; T: Central Square. This Asian fusion upstart sports an exceedingly polished look for funky Central Square, with wooden tables, leather-upholstered chairs, and walls covered in warm colors and stone tiles. Then there's the cool jazz soundtrack, which is so smooth it might have made the Monk launch into a cacophony of dis-chords but certainly makes the dining experience serene. Think of it as sushi jazz—fitting enough for a menu filled with sushi, sashimi, *maki,* and nigiri. But there's far more going on here than the creations of the sushi chefs. The kitchen mixes and matches Japanese, Chinese, Korean, Malaysian, and Southeast Asian traditions with American tastes and comes up with hits like smoky bacon pad thai, grilled cod and zucchini with miso and garlic-flavored rice, and a fig-jam fried rice. Flavors are crisp and bold and service is friendly and efficient.

Think Tank Bistroteque, 1 Kendall Sq., Kendall Square, Cambridge, MA 02142; (617) 500-3031; thinktankcambridge.com; New American; $$; T: Kendall Square. Definitely a different kind of bar restaurant, Think Tank turns into a dance floor after 10 p.m. Wednesday through Saturday, yet has singer-songwriter night on Tuesday. The layout creates conversation pods all around the space (with the dance floor in the middle). But this isn't just a bar. The dining program emphasizes New American comfort food with a few global accents. Thus, one of the burgers is Korean BBQ-marinated beef with lettuce and tomato, a fried egg, and aioli. Instead of pizza, there are flatbreads topped with the likes of grilled chicken, red onion, roasted peppers, and goat cheese. Mains could include a grilled swordfish steak with a green olive tapenade. The cocktail list is long and sweet and the beer list outshines the wine. Mostly Think Tank is a place to have a fun night out and get a good meal at the same time.

Tupelo, 1193 Cambridge St., Inman Square, Cambridge, MA 02139; (617) 868-0004; tupelo02139.com; Southern; $$. Before ordering, remember to leave room for dessert. Renee "Petsi" McLeod of **Petsi Pies** (see pp. 298 and 335) also owns Tupelo and features her delicious pies on the menu. Chef Rembs Layman, however, is the one who idolizes Elvis (from Tupelo) and has a mama from New Orleans. That no doubt plays a role in the authenticity of the Cajun gumbo, the "red" jambalaya with smoked andouille sausage and tiger shrimp, and the Cajun-spiced blackened catfish over creamy cheddar grits. Consider starting with Southern spiced turkey meatballs (with French bread for mopping up), or fried oysters with green Tabasco aioli and house pickle. As for those Petsi Pies desserts, how could you go wrong with a brown-butter pecan pie served with vanilla ice cream from **Toscanini's** (see p. 303).

T. W. Kitchen, 377 Walden St., Huron Village, Cambridge, MA 02138; (617) 864-4745; twfoodrestaurant.com; New American; $$$. Chef Tim Wiechmann's credentials read a little like a who's who of great French cooking. He even worked under Joël Robuchon

at Atelier in Paris—one of his last gigs before opening this tiny mom-and-pop fine dining restaurant in an essentially residential corner of Cambridge. Wiechmann is, shall we say, ingredient obsessive, and makes other locavore chefs look like they shop at the airport. The technique is pure French, but the ingredients are so local that it's hard to call the dishes anything but American. The restaurant serves only New England fish, which means Wiechmann has to get creative with lemon sole and winter flounder across the cold months (Moroccan spices are one answer), and he can come out blasting with a bold bluefish and mustard sauce in the summer. Winter menus are full of earthy vegetables like kohlrabi, rutabaga, and celeriac, while summer menus burst first with green peas and keep going through tomatoes and corn right into the squashes of autumn. In addition to the nightly changing a la carte menu, grand tasting menus are available most weeknights. They feature seven courses—with a separate, parallel menu for vegetarians. The wine list skews heavily French.

Upstairs on the Square, 91 Winthrop St., Harvard Square, Cambridge, MA 02138; (617) 864-1933; upstairsonthesquare.com; New American; $$$–$$$$; T: Harvard Square. "Exuberant" is an understatement when talking about Upstairs, which looks like it was designed by the team of Hieronymus Bosch and Salvador Dalí. In fact, it's the product of the team of Mary Catherine Deibel and Deborah Hughes, who have pretty active imaginations of their own.

own. If you're trying to keep the cost down, best bet is to eat in the downstairs Monday Club Bar, where dishes like tagliatelle with pork jowl Bolognese are available in small and entree-size portions. Monday Club has all the over-the-top desserts for which Upstairs is known—like the Zebra Cake of chocolate layer cake, dulce de leche buttercream, and malted chocolate ice cream. Dinner is bigger and bolder upstairs in the Soirée dining room, where a charcoal-grilled sirloin might be served with coconut-scented parsnips and a gratin of macomber turnip. Tasting menus (including an all-vegetarian) are available, with and without selected wine pairings.

Veggie Galaxy, 450 Massachusetts Ave., Central Square, Cambridge, MA 02139; (617) 497-1513; veggiegalaxy.com; Vegetarian; $; T: Central Square. Boston vegetarian guru Didi Emmons brings a meat-less approach to diner food at this bakery-cum-diner in Central Square. There's not a whiff of pizza here (for that you'll have to go to her **Veggie Planet** in Harvard Square, see p. 280), but tempeh bacon, bean- or mushroom-chickpea-based burgers, and seitan-laced hash fill in all the usual protein gaps in veggie cooking. The bakery-diner has such a fun, retro vibe that we can almost imagine the cast of *Happy Days* sitting in a booth washing down their burgers and fries with coconut-based vegan frappés. The breakfast menu is also available all day, if you'd rather have an omelet with corn and apple salsa or french toast with mixed berries and coconut whipped cream.

Veggie Planet, 47 Palmer St., Harvard Square, Cambridge, MA 02138; (617) 661-1513; veggieplanet.net; Vegetarian; $; T: Harvard Square. When legendary folk music venue Club Passim invited local vegetarian guru Didi Emmons to serve food, little did they know that years later Veggie Planet would be the headliner and people would say that its dining room turns into Club Passim by night. (They keep serving through the music, by the way.) Ordering is simple. You start by selecting the starch base—vegan pizza dough, brown rice, or coconut rice—and then choose what goes on top. That could be a peanut curry or tomatoes, broccoli, and grilled cheese. There are also soups, salads, and vegan desserts.

Wagamama, 57 JFK St., Harvard Square, Cambridge, MA 02138; (617) 499-0930; wagamama.us; Asian; $; T: Harvard Square. This Harvard Square outpost of the London-based noodle house is popular at lunchtime but quiets down in the evening. It's probably the smallest of the 3 area Wagamamas. The others are at Faneuil Hall (p. 75) and Prudential Center (p. 116).

West Side Lounge, 1680 Massachusetts Ave., Harvard Square, Cambridge, MA 02138; (617) 441-5566; westsidelounge.com; New American; $$; T: Harvard Square. We've been big fans of West Side practically since it opened, in part because it's more a restaurant with a good cocktail program than a bar that serves food. Funny thing is, the cocktails tend to be pricey, while the food comes in generous and reasonably priced portions. Pretty much the whole menu is bistro comfort food with a bit of panache, like the truffle-Parmesan fries appetizer. The fries go nicely with the steamed mussels as a DIY *moules-frites*. They are also served as a steak-frites main dish. West Side is extremely popular with residents of the immediate neighborhood, so tables are often at a premium. The two outside tables (summer only) are first-come, first-served.

Z Rant, 474 Massachusetts Ave., Central Square, Cambridge, MA 02139; (617) 864-3278, ext. 237; zrant.com; Casual American; $; T: Central Square. What a great idea! From 10 a.m. to 3 p.m. daily, upstart Z Rant serves brunch and sandwiches in the space occupied in the evening by Central Square stalwart ZuZu Bar restaurant and dance club. And we're not just talking any sandwiches. The slow-roasted duck with chicken liver and fig pâté has an almost cult-like following. Weekday brunch items are fairly simple, such as a sandwich of sunny-side-up egg, applewood-smoked bacon, cheddar cheese, and avocado smash, or the Go Green! scramble of eggs with basil-marinated portobello mushroom, fried green tomatoes, fresh mozzarella, and basil-cashew pesto. The kitchen gets fancy on Saturday and Sunday with several variants of eggs Benedict (the Sour New Yorker has roasted Roma tomatoes and sliced flank steak) and waffles that scream "sugar overload" (including one with Nutella ice cream). Pack back on

The Rising Sun in Porter Square

The 1920s Art Deco–style building in Porter Square is definitely not your grandfather's Sears & Roebuck. The retailer occupied it until 1985 and Lesley University now has classrooms, art and dance studios, and offices on the upper level. Lesley's lucky students and professors can enjoy healthy, budget food in the thriving enclave of Japanese restaurants and food stalls that fill much of the street level. The bustling scene so resembles a Japanese street market that it also attracts homesick Asian students from all over the city for noodle soups at **Sapporo Ramen** (617-876-4805; $), teriyaki-style rice bowls at **Ittyo** (617-354-5944; $) or scorpion and dragon rolls at **Masa's Sushi** (617-492-4655; $). Before leaving, many stop at **Japonaise Bakery & Cafe** (617-547-5531) for the specialty *an* donut filled with red bean paste or, for a change of pace, a thoroughly Western almond croissant. The complex even offers the option of a more formal dinner, complete with fine linens, at **Bluefin** (617-497-8022; bluefin-cambridge.com; Japanese; $$). Porter Square Exchange, 1815 Massachusetts Ave., Porter Square, Cambridge, MA 02140; Japanese; T: Porter Square.

all the calories you danced off the night before. For something simpler, try the oat waffles with apple cashew butter or lemon and thyme waffles with fresh blueberries.

Specialty Stores, Markets & Producers

Abodeon, 1731 Massachusetts Ave., Porter Square, Cambridge, MA 02138; (617) 497-0137; abodeon.com; Housewares; T: Porter Square. Cooks who favor the clean lines of modern design will find lots of practical and well-designed kitchen utensils in this shop that stocks both new and vintage merchandise. Vintage selections are unpredictable but might include Danish teak trays or rosewood peppermills, along with iittala glasses made in Finland. Contemporary products with a modern sensibility range from cheese slicers and graters to beautiful glass teapots. Those with small kitchens should check out the clever nesting set of mixing bowls, colander, strainer, and measuring cups—all in brightly colored plastic.

Au Bon Pain, aubonpain.com; Bakery Cafe. You can count on flaky croissants, tasty soups and sandwiches, and rich cookies at all branches of this local chain. The store at 1360 Massachusetts Ave., next to Holyoke Center in Harvard Square, is perhaps the most colorful. Street performers often stake out a spot near the outdoor tables—one of which is usually held down by the Chess Master as he waits for worthy opponents. Locations: 1360 Massachusetts Ave., Harvard Square, Cambridge, MA 02138, (617) 497-9797, T: Harvard Square; 1100 Massachusetts Ave., Harvard Square,

Cambridge, MA 02138, (617) 354-4144, T: Harvard Square; and 684 Massachusetts Ave., Central Square, Cambridge, MA 02139, (617) 492-0884, T: Central Square.

Berry Line, 3 Arrow St., Harvard Square, Cambridge, MA 02138; (617) 868-3500; and 1668 Massachusetts Ave., Harvard Square, Cambridge, MA 02138; (617) 492-3555; berryline.com; Ice Cream/ Yogurt; T: Harvard Square. Harvard Square is the first location of this frozen yogurt mini-chain founded by former graduate students in biochemistry and molecular biology. Science's loss is yogurt lovers' gain. The "original" is such a perfect mix of yogurt's tang with ice cream's, well, creaminess that it can easily stand on its own. But the shops offer a range of healthy fruit and nut toppings, along with chocolate chips and crushed Oreos. True to the spirit of scientific experimentation, the proprietors have developed more than 100 other flavors, two of which (blueberry, basil, green tea, salted caramel, Fluffernutter . . .) are always available along with the original.

L. A. Burdick Chocolate Shop & Cafe, 52 Brattle St., Harvard Square, Cambridge, MA 02138; (617) 491-4340; burdickchocolate .com; Chocolatier; T: Harvard Square. One of our consolations for cold winter days is indulging in cups of Burdick's milk-based hot chocolate made with dark or white chocolate or even single-source dark chocolate that, like wine, develops a distinctive flavor as a result of where it's grown. Those same rich drinks are also served iced, so we can continue to indulge during the summer—even without a weather-related rationale. This outlet of the Walpole, New Hampshire–based chocolatier also offers pastries to eat in the shop or take home along with chocolate bonbons (such as cherry and cumin or fig and port), truffles (lemon pepper or cognac), and traditional and salted caramels. For all the elegance of his handmade chocolates that use organic ingredients when possible, founder Larry Burdick retains a sense of fun. His signature product is a chocolate mouse with a colorful ribbon tail.

Capone Foods, 2285 Massachusetts Ave., Porter Square, Cambridge, MA 02140; (617) 354-0599; caponefoods.com; Grocery; T: Porter Square. This child of the Somerville original (p. 329) has outgrown its original conception as a fresh pasta store that also sells sauce to become not quite, but almost, a full-service gourmet grocery. In addition to Capone's excellent pasta, the shop carries some otherwise hard-to-find charcuterie, including Spanish chorizo from Palacios in La Rioja. This shop does a big business in heat-and-eat meals like lasagna, mushroom napoleon, spinach and mushroom strata, and other one-dish delights. For a quick snack, try the sweet pastry empanadas filled with ricotta cheese and dulce de leche or with ricotta and Nutella. See Capone's recipe for **Al's Favorite Quick Tomato Sauce** on p. 428.

Cardullo's Gourmet Shoppe, 6 Brattle St., Harvard Square, Cambridge, MA 02138; (617) 491-8888; cardullos.com; Grocery; T: Harvard Square. "Vienna sausages" still passed as gourmet food when this pioneering shop opened in Harvard Square in 1950. It remains the go-to place for tins of caviar or duck leg confit, Italian truffle sauce, Swedish lingonberry preserves, Spanish smoked paprika, or sweet Bavarian mustard. We've never failed to find a chocolate assortment to suit any gift-giving occasion, but often just pop in for a Cadbury Flake or other hard-to-find British candy bar. As might be expected, many of the sandwiches made to order in the deli rise above the ordinary, including country pâté with fig spread or Spanish cured ham with Manchego cheese and quince paste. Cardullo's also has a small wine selection of good, if obscure, bottles in the moderate price range and its own line of Italian products, such as pastas, sauces, and olives.

Central Bottle Wine + Provisions, 196 Massachusetts Ave., Central Square, Cambridge, MA 02139; (617) 225-0040; central bottle.com; Wine, Beer & Spirits; T: Central Square. Barely on the civilian side of Massachusetts Avenue from MIT, Central Bottle is a wine store for people who either have taste or would like to develop it. Founded by four friends who were inspired by the *enotecas* of Venice, this shop focuses on interesting yet reasonably priced fine wines from all over Europe and California, with a few nods to the southern hemisphere. The real strength tends to be in southern French and Italian producers, but the buyers do a great job of rooting out some of the less-expected regions of Spain, too. The owners take the "provisions" part of the name seriously as well: Look for top-notch artisanal cheeses (many of them regional) along with charcuterie from near and far. From 5 to 9 p.m. on Thursday, Central Bottle turns into a wine bar with free tastings and weekly promotions to encourage you to take home a bottle or two.

China Fair, 2100 Massachusetts Ave., Porter Square, Cambridge, MA 02140; (617) 864-3050; chinafairinc.com; Housewares; T: Porter Square. This shop next to the **Cambridge School of Culinary Arts** (see p. 411) is smaller and less-encompassing than the immense shop in Newton (p. 374). But it still stocks most of the utensils, small appliances, glassware, and dishware that you might need to equip a small Cambridge kitchen.

Christina's Homemade Ice Cream, 1255 Cambridge St., Inman Square, Cambridge, MA 02139; (617) 492-7021; christinasicecream.com; Ice Cream/Yogurt. There are always about 50 flavors of ice cream waiting to be scooped at Christina's, and staff experiment with new flavor combinations all the time. Coffee Oreo, burnt sugar, and pistachio are among the favorites, along with fresh rose, a delicate specialty offered only when rose petals are available.

You'll certainly find cookie dough, maple walnut, mint chocolate chip, and other standards, but many of Christina's rich ice creams have more subtle flavorings, such as ginger molasses, green tea, honey lavender, adzuki bean, or fresh mint. They stand on their own or can be made into a variety of sundaes and other concoctions. Cash only.

Christina's Spice & Specialty Foods, 1255 Cambridge St., Inman Square, Cambridge, MA 02139; (617) 576-2090; Grocery. This offshoot of the ice-cream shop (above) carries just about any spice you can imagine from *amchur* powder (made from tart unripe mango) to zaatar (a mix of thyme, sumac, and toasted sesame seeds). You'll also find lots of loose teas, dried chile peppers, hot sauces, oils (including grapeseed, walnut, and avocado), flours, and grains. Wondering what the canned mango puree tastes like? Go next door and try a scoop of mango ice cream. Cash only.

Court House Seafood Fish Market, 484 Cambridge St., East Cambridge, Cambridge, MA 02141; (617) 876-6716; Fishmonger; T: Lechmere. East Cambridge has a decidedly Azorean cast and this venerable fish market definitely caters to the first- and second-generation Portuguese clientele. It carries all the fresh catch from Boston Fish Pier as well as New Bedford and Gloucester, and flies in fresh sardines from Portugal twice a week, stickleback once a week, and cockles and other European shellfish as needed. If you want to make an authentic bouillabaisse, this is the spot to source the prescribed Mediterranean and eastern Atlantic fish.

Dado Tea, 50 Church St., Harvard Square, Cambridge, MA 02138; (617) 547-0950; T: Harvard Square; and 955 Massachusetts Ave., Cambridge, MA 02139; (617) 497-9061; dadotea.com; Tearoom. Coffee fanatics and tea lovers can meet on neutral territory in these two shops that feature clean-lined, vaguely Asian design but give equal weight to drinks deriving from beans or leaves. For everyone else there's always a smoothie. Dado offers baked goods at breakfast along with a range of healthy and vegetarian-friendly sandwiches and salads throughout the day, including the Dado Wrap of multigrain rice, marinated soy-ginger tofu, and greens in a whole wheat wrap.

Darwin's Ltd., 148 Mount Auburn St., Harvard Square, Cambridge, MA 02138; (617) 354-5233; and 1629 Cambridge St., Harvard Square, Cambridge, MA 02138; (617) 491-2999; darwinsltd.com; Bakery Cafe; T: Harvard Square. On opposite sides of Harvard Square, both shops are attuned to the rhythms of their neighborhoods, offering their breakfast sandwiches until 3 p.m. on Saturday and Sunday so that late sleepers can still enjoy a breakfast burrito of scrambled eggs, chouriço, onion, cheddar cheese, and Tabasco sauce, or a fried egg sandwich with cream cheese, smoked salmon, red onions, and tomato. During the week, workers on lunch break are as likely to grab a tuna salad sandwich with Jamaican relish as a hot pastrami with coleslaw, Swiss cheese, and Russian dressing on pumpernickel to go. Both locations offer a great selection of cookies to round out the meal, but the Mount Auburn Street shop has a greater selection of pastries—from chocolate mousse towers to pear ginger tarts—along with fresh fruits and vegetables and a selection of wine and beer.

The Fishmonger, 252 Huron Ave., Huron Village, Cambridge, MA 02138; (617) 661-4834; Fishmonger. Cheryl Williams has operated this pioneer foodie shop in Huron Village for more than 20 years, and knows just how to win over customers. The moment you walk in the shop you're presented with a display of beautifully trimmed fish nestling in beds of crushed ice. Off to one side is a large open kitchen where Williams or her staff is preparing meals to order as well as the ready-to-heat dishes to take home. The board above the fish display indicates which plates of The Fishmonger repertoire are available that day. One of the most popular, Williams admits, is an "old-fashioned tuna noodle casserole. But you can be sure that we don't use cream of mushroom soup." Poached salmon is another favorite—a dish she started offering one summer as a convenience for customers who didn't want to buy a whole salmon. Now she sells 4- to 5-inch sections of a large fish to singles and couples. She also touts her Mediterranean fish stew, which she explains is "low fat, no dairy, no shellfish—and it tastes good!" We'll second that.

Follow the Honey, 1132 Massachusetts Ave., Harvard Square, Cambridge, MA 02138; (617) 945-7356; followthehoney.com; Specialty Shop; T: Harvard Square. "We're like a little secret spot," says sales clerk Pauline Mallea, "but a lot of people are getting into honey and there's a huge subculture of beekeepers." Many of them have found their way to this shop on the edge of Harvard Square that stocks honeys from around the world along with such "bee-inspired" products as candles, beauty products, soaps and lotions, mustards, jams, and even fudge sauces. But the honeys themselves are a revelation and if you think they all taste the same, you are in for a sweet surprise at the tasting table. According to Mallea, the most popular is Volcano, a white honey from Hawaii. "The bees only pollinate one type of tree that grows on volcanos," she says, "and the honey has a very smooth consistency." Other favorites include a more granular honey made by killer bees in Brazil and Nicaragua and gathered by rural communities and a rich molasses-like honey from Zambia that is gathered by a women's cooperative. As for the acacia honey with white truffle—"it flies off the shelf," says Mallea.

Formaggio Kitchen, 244 Huron Ave., Huron Village, Cambridge, MA 02138; (617) 354-4750; formaggiokitchen.com; Cheesemonger/ Grocery. We can remember when this gourmet shop juggernaut was just a modest (but wonderful) cheese shop. Now it is one of the

region's true treasures, as Ihsan Gurdal seeks out great cheeses of the world and brings them here, often to age in the cheese cave under the store. But once Gurdal started bringing in artisan sausages and other charcuterie and opening up to fresh fruits and veggies as well as breads, the whole place morphed into a jam-packed jewel box of all manner of precious foods. The shop also sells chocolates, olive oils, honeys, jams, craft beer, and a highly select group of wines. Tastings are offered almost every week and classes in cheese *affinage* or cookery are sometimes available.

Harvest Co-Op, 580 Massachusetts Ave., Central Square, Cambridge, MA 02139; (617) 661-1580; harvestcoop.com; Grocery; T: Central Square. This survivor of the culture wars of the 1960s has moved way beyond granola and tofu to embrace a broad vision of healthy foods that even includes some with processed flour and/ or sugar, as well as beer and wine. The store's strength, however, remains its bulk bins of spices, herbal tea ingredients, fair-traded coffee, pastas, nuts, rices, and different kinds of flour. (The savings over prepackaged foods are phenomenal.) The co-op also buys as much of its produce as it can from local farmers. See recipe for **Green Bean and Summer Squash Ratatouille with Couscous** on p. 431.

hi-rise, 1663 Massachusetts Ave., Harvard Square, Cambridge, MA 02138; (617) 492-3003; T: Harvard Square; and 208 Concord Ave., Huron Village, Cambridge, MA 02138; (617) 876-8766; hi-risebread

.com; Bakery Cafe. If you stop in any morning at the Huron Village branch, you can see the aproned, flour-dusted staff of hi-rise making your daily bread. Half the facility is the open bakery, the other half an exceedingly casual cafe where you can get breakfast sandwiches in the morning; lunchtime sandwiches, soups, and chili; and ready-to-heat dinner entrees in the afternoon. Those meals can run the gamut from veal and mushroom stew to pork loin wrapped in pancetta, to broccoli rabe with roasted onions and olives. But the hi-rise breads are always the big stars, from the dense potato bread to the daily challah to the specialty loaves available only a few days per week, like olive bread, walnut bread, or the cheddar-pepper bread.

Iggy's Bread of the World, 130 Fawcett St., Alewife, Cambridge, MA 02138; (617) 924-0949; iggysbread.com; Bakery. You'll find Iggy's breads and rolls in many grocery stores and specialty shops throughout greater Boston, but it's worth seeking out this shop at the baking facilities in a small industrial park for the fullest and freshest selection, including the sweet pastries (apple pie, bread pudding) and cookies (caramel, linzer) not distributed to the company's wholesale customers. At lunch there are also slices of pizza and such sandwiches as speck and brie, or ham with sun-dried tomatoes. There are usually about a half-dozen loaves cut for samples, so you might be able to taste the dark rye, cranberry pecan, or olive bread. Probably the most popular breads are the pillowy-soft brioche dinner rolls and the salt-crusted Francese loaves.

J. P. Licks, 1312 Massachusetts Ave., Harvard Square, Cambridge, MA 02138; (617) 492-1001; jplicks.com; Ice Cream/Yogurt; T: Harvard Square. The Harvard Square venue of this popular local ice cream chain nearly always has a line, but it moves quickly. See the Jamaica Plain chapter (p. 183) for the shop that started it all.

Lotte Market, 297 Massachusetts Ave., Central Square, Cambridge, MA 02139; (617) 661-1194; Grocery; T: Central Square. We're guessing that many of the young Asian shoppers at this Korean supermarket near MIT are students eager for the taste of home—and that they know exactly what to do with the 40 kinds of dried seaweed and the pickled radish, lotus root, and kimchee in the refrigerator case. Fortunately, there are plenty of tempting convenience foods for the rest of us—pork and vegetable dumplings, fried fish cakes, shrimp or vegetable spring rolls, or beef, shrimp, pork, or chicken pot stickers. The meat case includes beef cut for *bulgogi*, the Korean version of marinated barbecued beef, while the fish case is heavy on fresh catch from Norway such as sardines and mackerel. Since some goods move slowly in this small shop, be sure to check expiration dates on packages.

Lyndell's Bakery, 74 Prospect St., Central Square, Cambridge, MA 02139; (617) 576-3530; lyndells.com; Bakery Cafe; T: Central Square. This Cambridge branch of the Somerville 1887 original is our personal occasion of sin, since we live nearby. Suffice it to say that we've learned to assuage our guilt by splitting a Half Moon (a 5-inch disk of cake topped half with chocolate, half with white frosting) between us. See the Somerville chapter (p. 333) for the original.

Market in the Square, 60 Church St., Harvard Square, Cambridge, MA 02138; (617) 441-2000; Grocery; T: Harvard Square. Market is Harvard Square's 24-hour food source, stocking everything a student might crave while pulling an all-nighter: salsa and chips, ice cream, pastas and sauces, packaged soups, Indian meals in a pouch, and lots of fancy breakfast cereals from Weetabix or Familia Swiss Balance to Cherry Almond All Natural Peace Cereal. The deli has prepared wrap sandwiches and sushi, and those craving a quick, hot meal can turn to the hot food buffet (open until 10 p.m.) for Korean soft tofu, macaroni and cheese, and a dozen or so other choices.

Mayflower Poultry Company, 621 Cambridge St., East Cambridge, Cambridge, MA 02141; (617) 547-9191; mayflower poultry.com; Butcher; T: Lechmere. The sign out front says "Live Poultry, Fresh Killed," but you'll have to show up Saturday morning if you really want to pick a bird and have it slaughtered, plucked, and dressed to your specifications (with or without the head and feet, for example). Although the chickens are slaughtered in the humane Halal manner, that's probably too close for comfort for all but the most dedicated carnivore foodie, so Mayflower also sells dressed birds and parts. The shop also carries a full line of fresh and frozen beef, pork, lamb, goat, rabbit, and game birds, although it's wise to place special requests a few days ahead, especially if you're looking for a whole lamb, kid, or piglet. Mayflower is also known for carrying super-jumbo eggs, which are larger than a standard jumbo and often contain two or even three yolks. They're especially sought after by commercial bakers who measure their eggs by volume rather than number.

Miso Market, 1963 Massachusetts Ave., Porter Square, Cambridge, MA 02140; (617) 945-7789; misomarketasian.com; Grocery; T: Porter Square. Not far from the Japanese food court in **Porter Square** (p. 282), this grocery store has fresh sushi available every day—along with all the ingredients for those who want to roll their own. For a quick and easy meal, you can select instant soups or check the refrigerated cases for steamed buns (teriyaki chicken, pork and chicken curry), dumplings (with crab or shrimp), and spring rolls. There's also a good chance that the frozen and dried fish, beautifully packaged condiments (pickled eggplant, garlic, or cucumber, for example), range of sauces (sweet chile or black bean garlic), vinegars, rices, and noodles will inspire you to attempt some more serious cooking.

Montrose Spa, 1646 Massachusetts Ave., Harvard Square, Cambridge, MA 02138; (617) 547-5053; Grocery; T: Harvard Square. The Cuban-American owners of this neighborhood variety store offer a long list of take-out sandwiches, but the standout is their Cubano, a grilled sandwich of French bread filled with pork, ham, mortadella, swiss cheese, pickles, and mustard. It's a more than satisfactory option if you're in the mood for a Cubano at lunch or before the bar opens in the evening at **Chez Henri** (see p. 242).

New Deal Fish Market, 622 Cambridge St., East Cambridge, Cambridge, MA 02141; (617) 876-8227; newdealfishmarket.com; Fishmonger; T: Lechmere. A neighborhood fixture since 1928, New Deal is our go-to fishmonger in the summertime when we want to grill tuna kebabs for a fresh version of salade niçoise. The market sells the trim from its beautiful tuna steaks for about half price. The variety of tuna, of course, varies through the summer, depending on what's being landed at Boston or Chatham. New Deal also features the delicious Point Judith (Rhode Island) squid, and a full range of the catch being landed at New England ports.

Pemberton Farms & Garden Center, 2225 Massachusetts Ave., Porter Square, Cambridge, MA 02140; (617) 491-2244; pemberton farms.com; Grocery; T: Porter Square. In the summer, flats of plants fill the patio area in front of the store, and any time of year you can grab a table in the greenhouse to enjoy a grilled cheese sandwich, Greek-style veggie wrap, cup of soup, or slice of pie. But cuisine augments horticulture in this spacious emporium full of fresh produce, extensive lines of oils, vinegars, mustards, rices and other grains, barbecue and hot sauces, and imported dried pastas. Both cheese and wine selections are broad—covering Europe and the US in equal measure—and the deli covers the globe with broccoli and Parmesan *arancini,* Tuscan potato salad, General Gao's tofu, and the good old Southern comfort standby of chicken and dumplings.

Petsi Pies, 31 Putnam Ave., Harvard Square, Cambridge, MA 02138; (617) 499-0801; petsipies.com; Bakery Cafe; T: Harvard Square. The main bakery is in Somerville (p. 335), but this little neighborhood cafe carries most of every given day's pies, albeit only in the large size. Not to worry—individual pieces are available for a snack or to take home. The cafe also has sandwiches, soups, and coffee.

Prospect Liquors, 1226 Cambridge St., Inman Square, Cambridge, MA 02139; (617) 876-9409; Wine, Beer & Spirits. This tiny shop has a little something for everyone, from the 40-ounce malt liquor for the neighborhood panhandler to an amazing selection of Portuguese table wines and liqueurs. This isn't the place to head for a big selection of fine ports, but if you're looking for a premium *vinho verde* (yes, there are some outstanding Alvarinho-based whites), a full-bodied Douro red, or a voluptuous, soft Alentejo red, Prospect has some of the best selections in the region. Much of the time, though, there's only one guy working the register, so you may have to find the wines without his assistance.

Rosie's Bakery, 243 Hampshire St., Inman Square, Cambridge, MA 02139; (617) 491-9488; rosiesbakery.com; Bakery. Judy Rosenberg (aka Rosie) has unapologetically titled her latest cookbook *Rosie's Bakery All-Butter, Cream-Filled, Sugar-Packed Baking Book.* And that pretty much tells you all you need to know about the treats that fill the cases of her original retail location in Inman Square. Rosenberg has built her mini-empire on the simple goal of giving people the goodies they loved as children, from chocolate sour cream cupcakes to peanut butter chocolate chunk cookies. But her fame rests most firmly on her very adult Chocolate Orgasms—rich brownies topped with a smooth and silky chocolate ganache. If you really want to gild the lily, stop at **Christina's Homemade Ice Cream** (see p. 287) for a scoop of ice cream (Rosenberg likes chocolate chip, coffee, or mint) to top it off.

Savenor's, 92 Kirkland St., Inman Square, Cambridge, MA 02138; (617) 576-6238; savenorsmarket.com; Grocery/Butcher. Located right on the Cambridge-Somerville line, this original outlet of Savenor's was Julia Child's favorite butcher shop, in part because it could supply the cuts of meat (or even whole animals) not usually available in traditional supermarkets. Savenor's is definitely the best retail outlet for exotic meats like elk, bison, alligator, kangaroo, ostrich, and yak, and for offal and game animals as well. But it's also a great place to get the very best in grass-fed, pastured, and humanely raised beef, pork, and poultry. The company also cures its own bacon. Savenor's supplies whole suckling pigs, roasting pigs, and even hogs for open-pit barbecue, though you usually have to order a week ahead. If you have a yen to learn butchering, basic classes are offered periodically in breaking down a carcass into primal and subprimal cuts.

Shalimar Gourmet Foods & Spices, 571 Massachusetts Ave., Central Square, Cambridge, MA 02139; (617) 868-8311; shalimar indianfoods.com; Grocery; T: Central Square. There are plenty of Indian restaurants in Central Square, but if you want to create Indian food at home, check out Shalimar, the self-proclaimed first Indian grocery store in Cambridge. You can shop for herbs and spices, along with frozen samosas (with lamb, cheese, or vegetable fillings) and Indian breads including naan, roti, and paratha. We're particularly fond of the packaged gourmet spice blends with recipes on the back. They take most of the guesswork out of dishes such as chicken vindaloo, a spicy, garlicky stew seasoned with the vindaloo masala blend. Look also for a whole range of teas, chutneys, and canned soups, and bag upon bag of basmati rice.

Sofra Bakery and Cafe, 1 Belmont St., West Cambridge, Cambridge, MA 02138; (617) 661-3161; sofrabakery.com; Bakery Cafe. Practically on the Watertown line, this busy, casual spot opened by Chef Ana Sortun and Pastry Chef Maura Kilpatrick, both of **Oleana** (p. 267), draws a young crowd who often bring their babies. It is almost as if they're all homing in on Mama's kitchen, if Mama were from the Middle East and cooked like a dream. Sure, you can buy lots of dips and spreads and finger food to go, but many customers hang out on the banquettes in the windows to eat the meze off copper-clad low tables while sipping coffee, tea, or juice. Stuffed flatbreads are especially popular at lunch, especially those filled with spinach, three cheeses, and herbs, though it's hard to resist the green olive and walnut salad, or the dish of smoky eggplant with pine nuts. Sweets? You bet. Probably the single most tempting is the "sandwich" called a Maureo—crisp chocolate wafers spread with milk jam. Sortun and Kilpatrick pack the shop with temptations to take home, from produce grown by Sortun's husband at **Siena Farms** (see p. 160) to specialty fresh cheeses made for Sofra by Fiore di Nonno (like a zaatar *burrata*!) to date and rose petal truffles to small containers of *muhammara* (a puree of walnuts, sweet red peppers, scallions, and pomegranate molasses).

1369 Coffee House, 1369 Cambridge St., Inman Square, Cambridge, MA 02139; (617) 576-1369; and 757 Massachusetts Ave., Central Square, Cambridge, MA 02139; (617) 576-4600; T: Central Square; 1369coffeehouse.com; Coffee Shop. Oh yeah, 1369 serves bagels and sandwiches, two kinds of cookies, and the occasional slice of cake. But the main reason to head to either location (except to hang out with all the other beanheads) is the drinks. In addition to the whole Jedi barista espresso scene, 1369 sells a lot of its homemade chai and a perfect winter warmer, the London

HEALTHY, SPICY, EASY

The line on the box sums it up: "A Fast Way to Slow Food." Working with a Newton health care company, Chef Ana Sortun has developed a line of meal kits that supply the grain, seasonings, spices, nuts, and even garnishes for a healthy meal. Each **Chef Set** comes with instructions and tells you which protein to buy (chicken or salmon, most often) and how to prepare it. Sortun confesses to always being the kid who was on a diet, and felt strongly that she wanted to develop healthy meals that were treats rather than punishments. One Chef Set, for example, contains couscous with almonds and North African spices. You supply pieces of cooked chicken, diced carrot and onion, and a little olive oil. The kits are available at **Oleana** (see p. 267) and **Sofra Bakery and Cafe** (see p. 300) and some gourmet shops.

Fog (steamed milk, Earl Grey tea, and vanilla). Top summer cooler is the zillion-calorie Mocha Slide (cold-brewed coffee, milk, cream, and chocolate syrup). The Central Square branch has outdoor tables that host a sort of ongoing *tertulia* of hipster discussions on politics, film, acoustic music, and the plight of street people (some of whom join in).

Tealuxe, Zero Brattle St., Harvard Square, Cambridge, MA 02138; (617) 441-0077; tealuxe.com; Tearoom; T: Harvard Square. There's an art to brewing a perfect cup of tea and this small shop seems to have it down to a science—and advises on the amount of tea, water temperature, and brewing time for black, white, green, Darjeeling, oolong, herbal, and other teas. You can enjoy a cup in the shop or select from more than 80 loose teas to take home, along with an elegant teapot or utilitarian tea ball.

Toscanini's, 899 Main St., Central Square, Cambridge, MA 02139; (617) 491-5877; tosci.com; Ice Cream/Yogurt; T: Central Square. We have friends who stock their freezer with Toscanini's deeply flavored burnt caramel ice cream in fear that they will arrive at the shop and find it sold out. Others find perfection in the simple French vanilla or the seasonal strawberry. But we like to keep an open mind. You could close your eyes and point to the chalkboard list of flavors and not be disappointed, whether your finger fell on Kenyan *khulfee*, salty caramel, lemon espresso, or goat cheese brownie. And yes, in a twist of Euro perfection, there is a Belgian chocolate to go with that French vanilla.

University Wine Shop, 1739 Massachusetts Ave., Porter Square, Cambridge, MA 02138; (617) 547-4258; universitywineshop.net; Wine, Beer & Spirits; T: Porter Square. This venerable wine shop offers affordable value. Inexpensive wines surround the checkout area, but the better deals are to be found in the regionally arranged shelves. Strengths include northern Italy, South Africa, the Pacific Northwest, and even, to a lesser extent, Spain. Expect to walk out with an exceptional dinner wine for around $15.

Verna's Coffee and Donut Shop, 2344 Massachusetts Ave., Cambridge, MA 02140; (617) 354-4110; vernaspastry.com; Bakery; T: Porter Square. This North Cambridge institution crafts terrific traditional cake and raised donuts, available hot from 5:30 a.m. almost every day. (You have to wait until 7 a.m. on Sunday.) The raised donut dipped in a liquid glaze is known as the Honey "Tip" in honor of Thomas P. "Tip" O'Neill, the late speaker of the US House who hailed from the 'hood. The cake donut dipped in the same glaze, however, might be the best sugar high in Cambridge. It's called an old-fashioned glazed.

Zinneken's, 1154 Massachusetts Ave., Harvard Square, Cambridge, MA 02138; (617) 876-0836; Bakery Cafe; T: Harvard Square. Belgian waffles are typically a little larger and lighter than their American cousins and have bigger indentations—all the better to absorb the variety of delicious toppings offered at this little shop in Harvard Square. You might choose bananas, whipped cream, and caramel, or strawberries and Belgian chocolate. But the best bet is to opt for Zinneken's signature waffle topped with whipped cream, Belgian chocolate, and a caramel-ginger spread made with another Belgian treat, *speculoos* cookies. The smooth spread melts into the waffle, adding a layer of rich, spicy flavor.

Farmers' Markets

Cambridge Center Market, Cambridge Center Plaza, Main St., Cambridge. Wed from 11 a.m. to 6 p.m., mid-May through late Oct.

Cambridge/Central Square Farmers' Market, parking lot No. 5, Bishop Allen Dr., Central Square, Cambridge. Mon from noon to 6 p.m., late May through mid-Nov.

Cambridge/Charles Square Farmers' Market, Charles Hotel Courtyard, Harvard Square, Cambridge. Fri from noon to 6 p.m., early June to mid-Nov and Sun from 10 a.m. to 3 p.m., late May through mid-Nov.

Cambridge/Harvard University Farmers' Market, corner of Oxford and Kirkland Streets, Cambridge. Tues from noon to 6 p.m., mid-June through Oct.

Cambridge/Kendall Square Farmers' Market, 500 Kendall St., Cambridge. Thurs from 11 a.m. to 2 p.m., June through early Sept.

Cambridge Winter Farmers' Market, 5 Callender St., Cambridge Community Center, Cambridge. Sat from 10 a.m. to 2 p.m., Jan through Apr.

Cambridgeport Farmers' Market, Morse School parking lot, Magazine Street and Memorial Drive, Cambridge. Sat from 10 a.m. to 2 p.m., June through late Oct.

Arlington & Somerville

These two commuter communities that border on Cambridge have their own distinct characters, influenced to a great extent by the international community that inevitably accretes around universities like Harvard, MIT, and Tufts. Both the town of Arlington and the city of Somerville boast some of the more interesting ethnic dining in the suburbs, and they also have wonderful places to shop, including some of the best meat markets in the whole metropolitan area. Both communities are particularly rich in relaxed, even casual dining. Most of what you'll be looking for in Arlington can be found along the length of Massachusetts Avenue. Somerville's principal squares, at least as far as foodies are concerned, are the Portuguese-, Brazilian-, and Korean-influenced Union Square (also home to some top gastropubs) and the more diverse, Tufts-influenced Davis Square, which blossomed as a dining and nightlife destination after the MBTA Red Line subway station opened in late 1984.

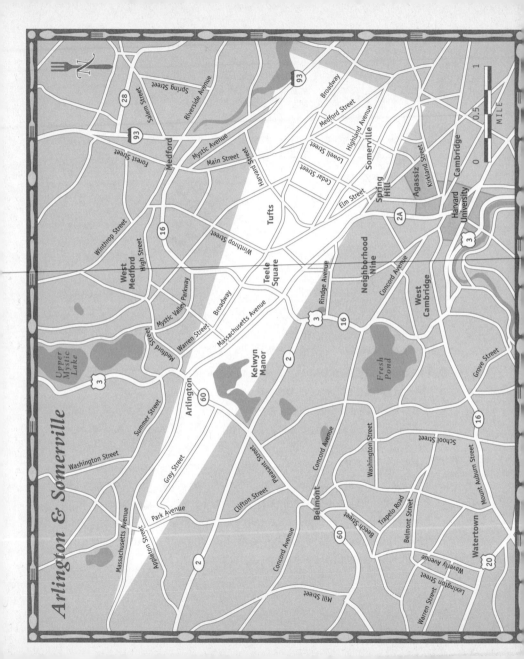

Arlington & Somerville

Acitrón Mexican Bistro, 473 Massachusetts Ave., Arlington, MA 02474; (781) 777-2839; acitronrestaurant.com; Mexican; $$. All the regional cuisines of Mexico have found their way to the capital, where they've been adapted in many cases to Spanish, French, and Italian culinary traditions to produce a distinctly *criollo* cuisine that most *norteamericanos* rarely associate with Mexican food. Acitrón serves this *criollo* food using the fresh produce, meat, and fish of New England. It's a highly sensible approach, though Owner Gotu Hule and his staff have to import certain ingredients—most notably chile peppers, cactus pads, citrus fruits, and tamarind—that don't grow around here. It's nice to find some of the Federal District standbys, like chiles *en nogada,* which are roasted poblano peppers stuffed with finely ground meat and served in a creamy sauce that includes ground walnuts. The Yucatecan dish of pork *pibil,* very popular in the capital, is a standout thanks to the marinade of Seville oranges and achiote. Fans of more familiar Mexican fare will be relieved to find enchiladas *de tinga*—stewed chicken in soft corn tortillas served with a choice of red or green chile sauce and melted cheese.

Amelia's Kitchen, 1137 Broadway, Somerville, MA 02144; (617) 776-2800; ameliaskitchen.com; Italian; $$; T: Davis Square. The sister restaurant of Cambridge's **Amelia's Trattoria** (see p. 234), this was the original Susi family restaurant, established on Teele Square in 1995 and named in honor of Delio Susi's mother. Her dish Fettuccine Mama remains a popular choice. It consists of pasta tossed with sautéed chicken, broccoli, sun-dried tomatoes, and a garlic butter–white wine sauce. This location also specializes in small pizzas—most without tomato sauce but with toppings that would make a great antipasti plate: various sausages, cheeses, roasted peppers, and marinated artichoke hearts.

Bergamot, 118 Beacon St., Somerville, MA 02143; (617) 576-7700; bergamotrestaurant.com; New American; $$. You might catch on that Chef-Owner Keith Pooler is doing something a little different when you peruse the appetizers and discover that not only does he offer a traditional charcuterie plate—but he also has a vegetable charcuterie plate of pickled items and terrines. While many other New American bistros are serving great hunks of oven-roasted halibut steak, Pooler opts to batter and fry the fish, serving it with an oregano-mint pesto that makes the succulent flavor really pop. He blithely cuts across cuisine lines to offer delectable ravioli filled with slow-roasted lamb and North African spices. Located on the Cambridge-Somerville line a short distance from Inman Square, Bergamot manages to keep its prices unusually low for such labor-intensive, artistic cuisine. There's also an unusually good list of wines by the glass.

Blue-Ribbon Bar-B-Q, 908 Massachusetts Ave., Arlington, MA 02476; (781) 648-7427; blueribbonbbq.com; Barbecue; $. When it comes to barbecue, we are not purists. Your birth certificate need not read North Carolina, Tennessee, Texas, or Missouri to make good barbecue. All we ask is that you please don't parboil the meat and that you roast everything long and slow over a smoky fire. We like *all* the barbecue at Blue-Ribbon, though we're probably most partial to the Carolina-style pulled pork, which takes a good 14 hours to roast before pulling it apart and simmering in a vinegar sauce. We're also fans of the Kansas City–style burnt ends: slightly charred beef chunks cut from the tougher top of the brisket and simmered in a tomato-based sauce until they disintegrate. Blue-Ribbon has another operation in Newton (see p. 365).

Boston Burger Co., 37 Davis Sq., Davis Square, Somerville, MA 02144; (617) 440-7361; bostonburgerco.com; Casual American; $; T: Davis Square. Be prepared to make a lot of choices at this friendly spot with 24 burger variations. Most begin with 8 ounces of prime beef and purists can stick to the Boston burger, which adds lettuce, tomato, and onion. The options escalate to the jalapeño burger with sliced jalapeños, cheddar cheese, and horseradish sauce, and on to the Kitchen Sink burger with fried egg, ham, bacon, three cheeses, and grilled onions, peppers, and mushrooms. Vegetarian and conch burgers are also available, along with chicken sandwiches, a dozen variations on fries, and eight types of boneless wings.

Casa B, 253 Washington St., Davis Square, Somerville, MA 02143; (617) 764-2180; casabrestaurant.com; Latin American; $$; T: Davis Square. This loose interpretation of a Spanish tavern serves a menu composed entirely of small dishes constructed in the spirit of tapas and pinchos. Almost all can be eaten with your fingers or, in a pinch, with a toothpick, and you'll want at least three per person. We say a "loose" interpretation because the dishes owe a lot more to the native Puerto Rico and Colombia of the husband-and-wife team behind Casa B than to the bar food of Spain. Instead of roasted bonito, Casa B serves sesame-seared yellowfin tuna with sweet plantain. The meatballs come in guava sauce rather than brown gravy, and even the grilled chorizo is the Caribbean style of the sausage served with yucca and coconut sauce. Casa B is bright, buoyant, and rather tropical. It's nothing like Barcelona, but it does offer a peek at what Havana might have been like had history taken a different turn.

Dalí Restaurant & Tapas Bar, 425 Washington St., Somerville, MA 02143; (617) 661-3254; dalirestaurant.com; Spanish; $$$. Decades before the small-dish craze hit America, this restaurant at the border of Cambridge and Somerville launched with a menu of tapas and just a few *platos principales,* or main dishes. If you want to sit down to dinner, we recommend ordering a main plate, like the signature whole fish baked in salt, Cádiz style. There are also vegetable, seafood, and mixed paellas. But it's more fun to stand in the bar area with a glass of wine and order plate after plate of traditional small dishes that could range from a slice of tortilla *española* (potato omelet), *pa amb tomàquet* (toasted bread rubbed with garlic and fresh tomato and drizzled with olive oil), or garlic shrimp. If you were in Spain, you'd have a dish and drink and move on to the next tapas bar. In Somerville you'll have to make do in the same place.

Ebi Sushi, 290 Somerville Ave., Union Square, Somerville, MA 02143; (617) 764-5556; ebisushi.com; Japanese; $-$$. This bright little room may be the only Japanese sushi restaurant run by Guatemalans in greater Boston, but it's something of a revelation. Adolfo and José Garcia know sushi, as they were the sushi chefs for many years in one of the **Porter Square Exchange** Japanese restaurants (see p. 282) for a pretty discerning clientele. The large menu includes an extensive sushi section that highlights José's skills. In fact, the majority of diners order the 12-piece combo that mixes standard sushi rolls with 6 pieces of nigiri and 1 specialty roll. A good specialty choice is the house roll, which is a crispy shrimp tempura with cucumber, *tobiko,* and avocado dabbed with a spicy mayonnaise and drizzled with eel sauce. Cooked Japanese dishes abound for the sushi-averse. One good option is the messy plate known as "Japanese pancake." A pancake of cabbage, pickled ginger, and grated yam provides a base for a sweet barbecue sauce, spicy mayo, and flakes of rehydrated bonito tuna.

The Flatbread Company @ Sacco's Bowl Haven, 45 Day St., Davis Square, Somerville, MA 02144; (617) 776-0552; flatbreadcompany.com; Pizza; $; T: Davis Square. The Flatbread Company began in Amesbury, Massachusetts, in 1998 and its concept of making pizzas in wood-fired ovens using local and organic ingredients has spread as far as British Columbia and Hawaii. But we think no location is as inspired as this pizza parlor in a candlepin bowling alley. You can enjoy a Somerville Community Flatbread with wood-fired cauldron tomato sauce, caramelized onions, mushrooms, mozzarella, Parmesan, and garlic oil, then bowl a few frames, and return for slice of warm gingerbread with pumpkin ice cream. Children's bowling and pizza parties are very popular here.

Flora, 190 Massachusetts Ave., Arlington, MA 02474; (781) 641-1664; florarestaurant.com; New American; $$–$$$. Chef-Owner Bob Sargent was one of those top guns for hire in Boston's high-end restaurant scene, cooking at some of the city's top restaurants before opening this relaxed, friendly bistro in the former Arlington Five Cents Savings Bank in 1996. He and wife Mary Jo have been providing a warm welcome and memorable meals ever since. Plates are available in three sizes. Appetizers range from simple salads to carrot-ginger soup to a house charcuterie plate. So-called medium plates are good for sharing as an appetizer or ordering as a modest main dish. That might include a dish of clams with white beans, braised escarole, and sausage—or a single lamb T-bone chop with green beans, red peppers, and French feta fondue. Flora is also very popular for Sunday brunch, when light streaming in the big windows highlights the elegance of the white linens and gleaming table settings.

Foundry on Elm, 255 Elm St., Davis Square, Somerville, MA 02144; (617) 628-9999; foundryonelm.com; New American; $$; T: Davis Square. Designer Peter Niemitz gets special kudos for turning what could have been a cavernous space into a convivial eating and drinking establishment with several "rooms," very much in the style of a good Parisian brasserie. The food is solidly American, though, from the blueberry barbecue pork belly sandwich (with shaved dill pickles, no less) to the rainbow trout roasted with local apples, chorizo, and brussels sprouts, then served with an apple cider reduction sauce. As much gastropub as restaurant, Foundry on Elm also serves excellent pizzas. The kitchen also supplies the victuals for the downstairs bar, **Saloon** (see p. 403).

Highland Kitchen, 150 Highland Ave., Somerville, MA 02143; (617) 625-1131; highlandkitchen.com; Casual American; $$. Chef-Owner Mark Romano single-handedly made Spring Hill a Somerville dining destination with this pitch-perfect little restaurant that combines the neighborhood's utter lack of pretension with its considerable diversity and sophistication. The menu at Highland Kitchen runs the gamut from a Cuban Reuben sandwich to a spicy coconut curried goat stew to a grilled flat-iron steak with a Gouda version of scalloped potatoes. Starters touch most of the United

Nations bases, from potato-chive pierogies to a North African dip plate to down-home-satisfying shrimp and grits with smoked bacon, mushrooms, and scallions. Romano has also assembled a well-chosen list of food-friendly wines by the glass, six draft beers, and some excellent nonalcoholic drinks that include ginger beer, sparkling limeade, and the Jamaican standby, Ting (grapefruit soda).

House of Tibet Kitchen, 235 Holland St., Somerville, MA 02145; (617) 629-7567; Tibetan; $; T: Davis Square. One of the longest-running Tibetan restaurants in the region, this 25-seat storefront restaurant in Teele Square has never wanted for customers: Tibetans longing for the taste of home, college students and professors curious about the mountain cuisine, and vegetarians eager for a fix of a cuisine where meat is always just an option. In case you're wondering about the authenticity of a given dish, the menu is divided between traditional Tibetan dishes and "Tibet-in-exile" dishes that reflect Nepalese, Indian, Chinese, and even American influences. The restaurant also offers several meat dishes featuring yak, which is lower in calories and cholesterol than beef, pork, chicken, or beefalo.

The Independent, 75 Union Sq., Union Square, Somerville, MA 02143; (617) 440-6022; theindo.com; New American; $–$$. This convivial, noisy pub was an American pioneer among gastropubs. With two bar areas as well as a dining room, it's not surprising that the food is beer-friendly fare like cast-iron roast chicken with spring onions and crispy spaetzle, a grilled pork chop with

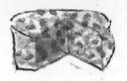

Gorgonzola polenta, or grilled flat-iron steak with bordelaise. On the other hand, it's one of the few bars to take fresh vegetables seriously with salads that might combine arugula, shaved fennel, and Manchego cheese or soups like a spring fresh pea soup with pancetta and shaved Piave cheese. The bar features 32 draft beer lines.

Istanbul'lu, 237 Holland St., Somerville, MA 02144; (617) 440-7387; istanbul-lu.com; Turkish; $–$$; T: Davis Square. We have a friend who loves Turkish cuisine and would follow Chef Huseyin Akgun wherever he goes. This friendly little storefront restaurant in Teele Square serves Turkish home cooking. Eggplant in Akgun's signature light tomato sauce shouldn't be missed. Tops among the starters is the red lentil soup with mint. One of the more unusual (and delicious) plates is *istim* kebab, a baked casserole of steamed lamb shank cooked with vegetables, wrapped with sliced eggplant, and topped with sliced tomatoes and peppers.

Journeyman, 9 Sanborn Ct., Union Square, Somerville, MA 02143; journeymanrestaurant.com; New American; $$$–$$$$. Hidden down a back alley at the edge of Union Square, Journeyman serves a choice of 5 or 7 courses per night in omnivore and vegetarian options. That makes dining here something of an adventure, since the chefs cook with whatever strikes their whim that day and is available from suppliers. As a result, meals are based on fresh and local ingredients, but beyond stating dietary restrictions, you don't really choose any of your courses. Portions tend to be small, so do clean your plate or you could leave hungry. The five- and seven-course menus also have optional wine pairings. Sunday through Wednesday, Journeyman also offers a less expensive four-course menu after 8:30 p.m. (wine pairing not available).

Mr. Crepe, 51 Davis Sq., Davis Square, Somerville, MA 02144; Eclectic; $; T: Davis Square. Crepes are our bargain street food in Paris, so we find it a nice change of pace to actually sit and eat at this Davis Square spot—even if we have to wait for a table. Besides, the options here are too elaborate for handheld dining. Think North African–style spicy lamb sausage with roasted bell peppers, onions, spinach, and feta cheese, or grilled salmon with corn relish, and spinach. Dessert crepe fillings can be as simple as our Paris favorite of lemon juice and sugar or as elaborate as the signature Tiff and Tone with strawberries or bananas, Belgian chocolate, and vanilla ice cream.

Painted Burro, 219 Elm St., Davis Square, Somerville, MA 02144; (617) 776-0005; thepaintedburro.com; Mexican; $$; T: Davis Square. File away any expectations about culinary authenticity. Chef Dante Bua serves unabashedly Americanized Mexican food here—but in this case, that's a compliment, not a canard. Think of it as Mexican cuisine interpreted by a creative New American chef in the same way other chefs reinterpret Italian or French cuisine. Admittedly, certain dishes are direct translations, like the Veracruzana fish, which is wrapped in a banana leaf with tomatoes, olives, capers, and sliced potatoes and then baked. Small plates like the tacos show the most originality, as in a taco of zucchini and nopal cactus with strips of hot chile peppers and mayonnaise made with charred lemons. The decor of this bar-restaurant is far enough over the top to make some people cringe at the visual cliches (including the painting of a burro wearing a Mexican wrestling mask), but it's ironic rather than kitsch and dishes like the ceviche or chilled octopus and shrimp salad are such solid homages to Mexican food that it's easy to see no offense is meant. The bar even shows sufficient restraint to offer only four variations on the margarita.

Pasha, 669A Massachusetts Ave., Arlington, MA 02476; (781) 648-5888; pashaturkish.com; Turkish; $–$$. The Boston area has a half-dozen or so good Turkish restaurants, but Pasha is the prettiest and has the most extensive menu and most extensive list of Turkish wines. The wines are something of an acquired taste, but Turkish food almost always hits the spot. You can start with a little of everything by ordering the plate of mixed appetizers, which includes hummus, stuffed grape leaves, shredded beets in homemade yogurt, and baba ghanoush. We tend to skip kebabs at Turkish restaurants—while they are invariably good, we're usually more curious about sautéed and baked dishes. A good bet at Pasha is to order the *manti,* described on the menu as Turkish-style ravioli. They are more like canneloni stuffed with a mixture of ground lamb and ground beef and served over creamy yogurt with a butter sauce on top.

Pescatore, 158 Boston Ave., Somerville, MA 02144; (617) 623-0003; pescatoreseafood.com; Italian/Seafood; $$; T: Davis Square. Located at the edge of Ball Square, this neighborhood Italian seafood restaurant is the baby of Anna and Luigi Buonopane, who hail from Lazio, the region north of Rome on the Mediterranean coast of Italy. Don't expect the heavy-handed Sicilian-American fried seafood here. The lightly fried calamari come with a bright tomato dipping sauce, not a heavy marinara. Grilled fish is always accompanied by big portions of fresh vegetables. Anna Buonopane makes all the pasta by hand. Alas, the restaurant doesn't have a liquor license, but that shouldn't be an impediment to getting a fix of fresh fish, real Italian style.

Posto, 187 Elm St., Davis Square, Somerville, MA 02144; (617) 625-0600; pizzeriaposto.com; Italian/Pizza; $$; T: Davis Square. Here in the US, we consider pizza the ultimate casual food, but the Associazione Verace Pizza Napoletana begs to differ. Founded in 1984, the "True Neapolitan Pizza Association" has specific guidelines for any parlor that hopes to call itself an "official Neapolitan pizzeria." Posto is the only establishment in New England to pass muster and you'll need a reservation if you want to check out the hand-kneaded pies that are baked at 485°C for 60 to 90 seconds in a wood-fired, domed oven. By the way, the Neapolitans grant authenticity only to marinara and Margherita pizzas. Posto has them both, along with more varied toppings for eclectic American tastes. If your table decides to share a pizza as an appetizer, you can select from a range of pastas (lobster and scallop tortellini, rabbit ravioli) and entrees (wood-roasted chicken, wild striped bass with oven-braised fennel) for your main course.

Redbones, 55 Chester St., Davis Square, Somerville, MA 02144; (617) 638-2200; redbones.com; Barbecue; $–$$; T: Davis Square. Austin meets Boston at Redbones, which is as close to a Texas barbecue roadhouse as you can find in the land of the bean and the cod. All the meats are cooked slow and low except for the grilled sausage and the fried catfish, and the sides are a list of the greatest hits of Southern cuisine, from hush puppies and cat fingers to corn fritters, mac and cheese, succotash, and sweet potato fries. All-meat Texas chili is available, but you can also get a gentle cup of pot likker—the broth from braising greens. Redbones is at its best with big Texas beef ribs, slabs of country-style Arkansas pork ribs, and traditional dry-rub Memphis pork spareribs. In fact, you can order a Barbecue Belt and get some of each along with a serving of smoked beef brisket. All the barbecue is available for takeout, but it's more fun to eat on site, keeping the gullet lubricated with a string of longnecks.

Sabzi Persian Chelow Kabab, 352A Massachusetts Ave., Arlington, MA 02474; (781) 753-0150; sabzikabab.com; Persian; $–$$. We love trying unfamiliar cuisines, but sometimes find it hard to make choices when faced with an almost encyclopedic menu. Sabzi makes it easy by limiting its entrees to kebabs (ground beef, chicken, Cornish hen, vegetables, steak), which are all seasoned with herbs and spices and served with saffron-accented rice. Vegetable-oriented appetizers and side dishes—such as sautéed eggplant spread or yogurt and cucumber dip—are both healthy and tasty.

Sweet Chili, 470–472 Massachusetts Ave., Arlington, MA 02474; (781) 646-2400; sweetchilitogo.com; Thai; $. Thai restaurants abound in greater Boston, but few rise to the level of this Arlington standby that's been around since the 1990s. Some of the best dishes are the village curries, like the Randang curry with a choice of chicken or beef, or the Panang curried duck, which is served as a half duck roasted with vegetables. Fans of spicy Thai food might consider the soft-shell crab with a hot basil chile sauce, or the squid stir-fried in a (basil-free) hot chile sauce. If you're tempted to order pad thai, opt for the more authentic (and fiery) country style.

Tango of Arlington, 464 Massachusetts Ave., Arlington, MA 02474; (781) 443-9000; tangoarlington.com; Argentinian; $$–$$$. Not a restaurant for vegetarians or light eaters, Tango serves huge portions of Argentine beef—exactly as it's served in Buenos Aires. "Small" steaks start at 12 ounces and some are well over a pound. The mixed grill, or *parrillada mixta,* includes enough beef, chicken, sweetbreads, sausages, and pork to provide a week's protein for a small country. Grilled fish—everything from salmon fillets to swordfish kebabs—is also available. Tango also has a good selection of Argentine wines, especially Malbecs, and desserts that feature dulce de leche.

True Bistro, 1153 Broadway, Somerville, MA 02144; (617) 627-9000; truebistroboston.com; Vegetarian; $$; T: Davis Square. We're not sure what the "true" in the name is supposed to stand for, but it should be "true food." This restaurant is hard-core vegan, right down to not using honey because it exploits the bees. True resorts to a lot of spice to replace the depth of flavor provided by animal products, so the cornmeal-crusted oyster mushrooms come with a horseradish-dill aioli and an aji pepper amarillo sauce. Similarly, the Hyderabadi stuffed eggplant is filled with coconut basmati rice with an apricot chutney on the side. Wines are all available by the glass and the menu even suggests pairings with the entree-sized dishes. Desserts are big and gooey and as sophisticated as the savory menu, ranging from a napoleon of phyllo, white chocolate mousse, and fresh berries to a coconut torte with blood orange sauce. Tofu scrambles, crepes, and seitan burgers are the main choices at the very popular brunch.

Tryst, 689 Massachusetts Ave., Arlington, MA 02476; (781) 641-2227; trystrestaurant.com; New American; $$–$$$. Chef-Owner Paul Turano strikes just the right balance of upscale elegance with relaxed style to make Tryst an affair to remember. (The menu is full of such references. Appetizers are labeled "Just a Fling," while small plates are "Not Fully Committed," salads are "Getting Fresh," and main dishes are "Getting Serious.") For all the whimsy, the dishes are serious bistro comfort food, ranging from slow-roasted coq au vin served with Parmesan polenta, tagliatelle Bolognese, or spicy roast duck with black pepper spaetzle. Solo diners can grab a spot at the communal high-top table in the bar. The wine list includes numerous wines by the glass.

Yak & Yeti, 719 Broadway, Somerville, MA 02144; (617) 284-6227; yakandyeticafe.com; Nepali/Indian; $; T: Davis Square. A photo mural of Himalayan peaks in Nepal—simultaneously one of the most beautiful and more forbidding scenes imaginable—wraps around one of the two dining rooms at Yak & Yeti. It's a lot for the Nepalese side of the menu to live up to, but this mountain cuisine is so simple and unpretentious that it just might win you over. Start with some steamed or stir-fried dumplings (chicken or vegetarian), move on to a main dish of tofu and spinach cooked with ginger and garlic or stewed goat meat garnished with fresh coriander (cilantro). The other half of the menu is devoted to Indian dishes, with a great choice of breads: tandoori roti, grilled whole wheat chapati, grilled paratha, and the ever-popular naan, including *peshawari* naan stuffed with coconut, cashews, and raisins. The Indian menu continues at length, even embracing a few South Indian delights that are half a continent apart from the austere Nepalese cooking. Like many Indian restaurants, Yak & Yeti offers an Indian buffet at lunchtime. Wait for dinner and head to the mountains.

Landmarks

Kelly's Diner, 674 Broadway, Somerville, MA 02144; (617) 623-8102; kellysdiner.net; Casual American; $; T: Davis Square. This stainless-steel beauty was manufactured by the Jerry O'Mahony Company in Elizabeth, New Jersey, and was relocated from New Castle, Delaware, to Somerville's Ball Square in 1996. At 55 feet long, it's one of the largest diners manufactured in the 1950s. That means you will have plenty of room to enjoy your breakfast of corned beef hash with toast, eggs, and home fries or your lunch platter of grilled steak with mashed potatoes and vegetable. Cash only.

Rosebud Diner, 381 Summer St., Davis Square, Somerville, MA 02144; (617) 666-6015; rosebudbarandgrill.com; Casual American; $; T: Davis Square. Even as trendier restaurants open in Davis Square, this beautifully restored 1941 Worcester Diner continues to hold its own with a winning strategy of offering something for everyone. Unlike many diners, Rosebud serves three meals a day, so you can order a Western omelet for breakfast, a double-decker BLT for lunch, and roast turkey with all the trimmings for dinner. Rosebud also has a lively bar and music scene in the evening, though you can order Helen's Famous Bloody Mary, with hot sauce made by server Helen DeFrancisco, starting at 8 a.m., 6 days a week, or 11 a.m. on Sunday.

Ball Square Fine Wines & Liquors, 716 Broadway, Somerville, MA 02144; (617) 623-9500; ballsquarefinewines.com; Wine, Beer & Spirits; T: Davis Square. This isn't the most convenient wine store in greater Boston, and it's certainly not the most comprehensive, even with 35,000 bottles. But Ball Square does have a superbly curated selection of wines offering great value at all price points and will do almost anything to please its customers. Best of all, the entire inventory can be searched online, so if you're in a rush, you can select your wine at home, call it in, and pick it up without having to forage through the racks. Ball Square also delivers anywhere in greater Boston and ships throughout Massachusetts. If you join the store's "club," you get extra discounts on wines highlighted in the newsletter and can refer back to your own purchasing history to find that great little wine you bought for Thanksgiving a couple of years ago and can no longer remember. It's a nice touch.

Barismo, 169 Massachusetts Ave., Arlington, MA 02474; (339) 368-7300; barismo.com; Coffee Shop. Coffee nerds love to stop here for great pour-overs, perfectly weighed and timed espresso, and more technical data than anyone needs to know to simply enjoy a cup. The guys behind Barismo are themselves ultimate coffee nerds who obsess about nuances of flavor due to growing conditions, patio techniques, and precision roasting. Somehow they even come up with optimal granule size for the grinds, and when you buy beans for espresso, you'll find the bags also marked with optimal brewing temperature, weight in grams per shot, and weight in grams for extracted shot. All that would make no difference at all, except that the coffee is really, really good.

The Biscuit, 406 Washington St., Somerville, MA 02143; (617) 666-2770; visitthebiscuit.com; Bakery Cafe. You might have already sampled the pastry, bread, or sandwiches of The Biscuit, as the bakery supplies a number of cafes and a few restaurants in the area. But you'll never get fresher food than at the source. Breakfast is a special treat, as The Biscuit makes warm quiches, piping-hot brioche, super-flaky croissants, and cinnamon sticky buns that you can smell a block away. At lunch the cafe side offers pizzas made on focaccia dough and sandwiches assembled on any of the several varieties of yeast breads that the kitchen bakes daily. (Selection changes daily but almost always includes black-olive bread, French baguette, and sourdough country loaves.)

Bloc 11 Cafe, 11 Bow St., Union Square, Somerville, MA 02143; (617) 623-0000; bloc11.com; Bakery Cafe. During nice weather you can enjoy your egg salad, avocado, and tomato sandwich and a raspberry lime rickey on the outdoor patio. In cooler weather you might prefer a roast beef, herbed cream cheese, and shredded beet sandwich and a cup of Stumptown coffee indoors by the huge windows that let in lots of light. Located in a former bank building, with a yoga studio on the floor above, Bloc 11 has become a real gathering place for the denizens of Union Square.

The Boston Shaker, 69 Holland St., Davis Square, Somerville, MA 02144; (617) 718-2999; thebostonshaker.com; Housewares; T: Davis Square. As anyone who has watched a top mixologist at work knows, it takes great ingredients and the right tools to make a craft cocktail. That's where this chic little shop comes in. It's filled with books, tools, glassware, and a few select products including Bittermens Small Batch Bitters. Occasional classes are designed to help amateurs improve their technique.

Cakes, 795 Massachusetts Ave., Arlington, MA 02476; (857) 321-3450; cakesbostononline.com; Bakery Cafe. "We serve salad before dessert," the woman behind the counter joked the last time we visited Cakes. Sure enough, Cakes offers healthy soups (barley minestrone, for example), salads (grilled veggie and hummus), and sandwiches (lemon tuna melt). Just leave room for a blueberry crumble bar, piece of lemon shortbread, or carrot cupcake. If you need a whole cake for a party, the most popular is the Black and White: chocolate cake layered with white chocolate and dark chocolate mousse and covered with chocolate ganache.

THEOBROMA: FOOD OF THE GODS

The **Taza Chocolate** factory takes its organic chocolate from bean to bar and offers tours of the process Wednesday through Sunday. Even if you miss the tour, a factory store is open on the same days and big windows offer a view of the work area, including stone mills similar to the ones that inspired cofounder Alex Whitmore on a trip to Mexico. Better yet, you can sample the end result and discern the differences between the 60, 70, 80, and 87 percent dark chocolate bars. Taza also makes discs of Mexican-style chocolate, either plain or with flavors including cinnamon, coffee, orange, and chile. If you decide to take the tour, be sure to wear closed-toe shoes and avoid perfume, since it might mask the sultry smell of chocolate. (See Taza's recipe for **Molten Spiced Taza Chocolate Cake,** p. 441.)

Taza Chocolate, 561 Windsor St., Somerville, MA 02143; (617) 284-2232; tazachocolate.com; Chocolatier.

Capone Foods, 14 Bow St., Union Square, Somerville, MA 02143; (617) 354-0599; caponefoods.com; Grocery. Albert Capone and his staff use 3,000 pounds of durum wheat every week to make plain, flavored, and filled pastas. A few of the products are served in some of the city's top restaurants, but you'll find the largest selection here in the original shop/kitchen and in a satellite shop in

Cambridge (see p. 285). A true food enthusiast, Capone has developed more than 400 recipes, half of which are in active production. His fresh pastas alone range from squid-ink fettuccine and black pepper pappardelle to artichoke ravioli and tomato tortellini. Add in all the sauces (Alfredo, roasted pepper pesto, white clam, tomato and sausage . . .) and the variations are almost limitless. Capone also makes a richly flavored ricotta and stocks a small assortment of cheeses. He especially likes to introduce customers to his array of olive oils and vinegars, mostly from Italy and Spain. Not surprisingly, his cooking classes fill up quickly. (For Capone's recipe for Quick Tomato Sauce, see p. 428.)

Casa de Carnes Solução Latin Meat Market, 38 Bow St., Union Square, Somerville, MA 02143; (617) 625-1787; Butcher. To be honest, it helps to speak Portuguese if you want a special cut, but this establishment on the west end of Union Square is a full-service butcher shop with everything from freshly ground hamburger to specialty cuts of meat. The dry-aged beef and pork are unusually lean, so don't count on butter-tender steaks for the grill. But if you want real flavor for a hanger steak or a brisket that you're planning to barbecue low and slow over glowing wood coals, this is the place to come. It doesn't hurt that prices are competitive with the least expensive supermarkets in the area while the quality of meat is much higher. The shop also carries Brazilian and Salvadoran breads and specialty foods.

Dave's Fresh Pasta, 81 Holland St., Davis Square, Somerville, MA 02144; (617) 623-0867; davesfreshpasta.com; Grocery; T: Davis Square. Dave's may have started largely as a fresh ravioli shop, but all the other gourmet foods have long since taken over. You can still buy nice ravioli (including the pumpkin ravioli found on half the restaurant menus in town) and sheets of fresh pasta for assembling your own lasagna, but you'll also find seasonal roasted vegetables (beets, brussels sprouts, carrots), the popular artichoke and lemon pesto, and a large array of specialty cheeses and artisanal chocolates. Dave's even has a good selection of unpretentious wines and craft brews.

Diesel Cafe, 257 Elm St., Davis Square, Somerville, MA 02144; (617) 629-8717; diesel-cafe.com; Coffee Shop; T: Davis Square. A grown-up version of a student cafe, Diesel is full at all hours with folks nibbling sandwiches and salads, sipping on coffee drinks, and otherwise entirely engrossed in their laptops. Judging by the number of computer users, Diesel has *really* good bandwidth. It's doubly cool that the cavernous cafe also has pool tables, a vintage coin-operated photo booth, and gluten-free whoopie pies. Design is very Jetsons, i.e., the future as of 1965, long before any of the customers were born.

La Internacional Foods, 318–322 Somerville Ave., Union Square, Somerville, MA 02143; (617) 776-8855; Grocery. Enter La Internacional and you'll think you're in just another bodega, but keep going deeper into the store and you'll discover all manner of foodstuffs imported from Central and South America as well as the Caribbean. The shop carries a full array of dried Mexican chiles (essential if you're going to make some of the lesser-known mole sauces), as well as a great selection of Latin American cheeses. We used to default to fresh cow's milk feta to crumble over mole negro, for example, but now go to La Internacional for authentic Mexican *queso fresco* and *queso* Oaxaqueño. Spice selections include all the flavors of the Indian subcontinent—or of the cooking of Trinidad and Tobago.

J. P. Licks, 4A College Ave., Davis Square, Somerville, MA 02144; (617) 666-5079; jplicks.com; Ice Cream/Yogurt; T: Davis Square. J. P. Licks ice cream has become so popular that shops have spread from its Jamaica Plain base (see p. 183) throughout the area. This Davis Square shop is a fine place to order a scoop of perennially popular cookie dough ice cream or check out the seasonal flavors.

Kickass Cupcakes, 378 Highland Ave., Davis Square, Somerville, MA 02144; (617) 628-2877; kickasscupcakes.com; Bakery; T: Davis Square. The customer favorite at this cupcake shop with attitude is the Mochiatto, a chocolate cupcake with caramel filling and mocha frosting. We're partial to the Lucky Cupcake of lemon cake with white chocolate buttercream. It's topped with candied ginger and comes with a fortune—as if we weren't feeling lucky enough to have such a luscious treat. There's also a flavor of the day, such as Thursday's German chocolate, a chocolate cupcake filled with chocolate buttercream and slathered with coconut pecan frosting.

Pupcakes and Kittycakes ensure that four-legged friends aren't forgotten.

Lakota Bakery, 1375 Massachusetts Ave., Arlington, MA 02476; (781) 646-0121; lakotabakery.com; Bakery. Lakota Bakery cookies are sold in cafes and coffeeshops throughout greater Boston, but the shop next to the baking facility is the best place to see the whole range of handmade and hand-decorated treats. Owner Barbara Weniger learned to bake from her mother and says that the secret to a rich, flavorful cookie is to use more butter and chocolate than sugar. Taste the difference yourself in the strawberry or apricot linzer cookies, the chocolate ginger or orange chocolate chip cookies, or the lemon, mint, chocolate, or vanilla sandwiches.

Lyndell's Bakery, 720 Broadway, Somerville, MA 02144; (617) 625-1793; lyndells.com; Bakery; T: Davis Square. Opened in 1887, Lyndell's claims to be one of the oldest retail "scratch" bakeries in the country. This Ball Square shop is still the place to go for a beautifully decorated cake, but alas, does not have the sandwich menu or cafe tables of the newer Cambridge branch (see p. 294). Both locations, however, offer a full range of fresh baked breads, pies, cookies, and cupcakes. Lyndell's also sets the standard for the Half Moon—a round of golden cake spread half with vanilla frosting and half with chocolate—that they've been baking for more than a century.

McKinnon's Meat Market, 239 Elm St., Davis Square, Somerville, MA 02144; (617) 666-0888; mckinnonsmeatmarket.com; Butcher; T: Davis Square. Like **Casa de Carnes Solução** (see p. 330), McKinnon's is an old-school butcher shop—except that McKinnon's is much larger, employs at least a half-dozen butchers per shift, and is especially known for its marinated meats: garlic and pepper London broil, honey-barbecue baby back ribs, Chinese-style pork tips, boneless chicken breasts teriyaki style, etc. Peek into the freezer case and you might find big bags of frozen chicken parts for under $1 per pound, or a turducken, a duck stuffed inside a turkey breast, ready to defrost and roast for a special occasion. T-bone steaks and filet mignon cost about half as much as at other stores.

The Meat House, 1398 Massachusetts Ave. #4, Arlington, MA 02476; (781) 643-6328; themeathouse.com; Butcher. Rarely do we recommend chain stores, but the Meat House, which has stores in 10 states, is too good to pass up. Most of the meat comes from Pineland Farms in New Gloucester, Maine, and while it does not arrive as a whole carcass, it does come in primal cuts that the staff breaks down to request. Want a porterhouse that's 2 inches thick? No problem. The cases are also filled with marinated meats ready for grilling, and the store carries an extensive line of prepared foods that might range from Red Bliss potato salad to grilled asparagus to barbecue baked beans. Almost everyone on staff, at least at this outlet, has a culinary school degree, so cooking advice comes from people who know what they're talking about. See the recipe for **Grilled Beef with Asian Sesame Dressing** from The Meat House, p. 435.

Penzey's, 1293 Massachusetts Ave., Arlington, MA 02476; (781) 646-7707; penzeys.com; Specialty Shop. Taste and smell are so closely related that it's a real treat to visit this spice emporium and sniff the differences between Turkish and Mexican oregano or between Spanish and Hungarian paprika. It's also a great place to pick up double-strength vanilla or hard-to-find ingredients such as Middle Eastern zaatar or *charnushka* (the tiny black seeds often found on Jewish rye bread). So far this Arlington shop is the only Massachusetts outpost of the Wisconsin-based retailer.

Petsi Pies, 285 Beacon St., Somerville, MA 02143; (617) 661-7437; petsipies.com; Bakery. Less of an eat-in cafe than the Cambridge location (see p. 298), this original Petsi can still set you up for a great meal. Select a savory pie (roasted vegetable and goat cheese or bacon, leek, and gruyère) for dinner and a sweet pie (blueberry, banana cream, bourbon chocolate pecan) for dessert. All pies are sold by the slice or whole. The savory pies are baked in 10-inch pans only, while the sweet pies come in 5-inch, 8-inch, and 10-inch sizes. Petsi also bakes cookies, muffins, and bars, but the pie's the thing.

Quebrada Baking Co., 208 Massachusetts Ave., Arlington, MA 02474; (781) 648-0700; quebradabakingco.com; Bakery Cafe. The folks at Quebrada realize that sometimes you need only a little taste of something sweet, and we're grateful that we can stop in for a mini mocha bean cupcake, blueberry scone, chocolate chip muffin, éclair, or fresh fruit tart. Kids love the whimsically decorated cookies, while their moms snap up the breads of the day, including challah loaf on Wednesday and cardamom coffee bread on Friday.

Reliable Market, 45 Union Sq., Union Square, Somerville, MA 02143; (617) 623-9620; Grocery. If you cook Korean, Vietnamese, Cambodian, Chinese, or even Japanese food and can't get to one of the gigantic Asian supermarkets, chances are that you'll find everything you could possibly want or need at Reliable: fresh local fish, exotic western Pacific fish, all manner of Asian produce, and all the sauces, oils, condiments, dried noodles, and other staples. Prices are surprisingly good.

Sherman Cafe, 257 Washington St., Union Square, Somerville, MA 02143; (617) 776-4944; Bakery Cafe. This bakery cafe is the crunchy-granola sibling to slicker, hipster **Bloc 11** (see p. 327). But if you have a hankering for soy chai latte and a vegan muffin, Sherman is hard to beat. The cafe is completely on board with the "local first" mantra of Sherman Market around the corner (22 Union Sq., 617-666-0179), so non-vegan baked goods use real local butter and you can also get that latte with wholesome real milk from a Jersey herd in western Massachusetts. For what it's worth, the layout makes Sherman one of the more stroller-friendly cafes in the area.

3 Little Figs, 278 Highland Ave., Somerville, MA 02143; (617) 623-3447; 3littlefigs.com; Bakery Cafe. Katie Rooney decorated her shop in blue and white to pay homage to her Greek heritage and crafted a menu of tastes that recall the Greek Isles. Her breakfast scones feature lavender, goat cheese and herbs, or fig and pear, and lunchtime sandwiches include almond butter, banana, and honey or egg, feta, and arugula. The kitchen also turns out spinach pie and Greek cheese pie, along with a delicious olive oil citrus cake and baklava made from Rooney's family recipe. We're not certain if they are Greek, but the Ginger Bomb cookies are amazing!

When Pigs Fly, 378 Highland Ave., Davis Square, Somerville, MA 02144; (617) 776-0021; sendbread.com; Bakery; T: Davis Square. Like its sister shops in Jamaica Plain (see p. 185) and Brookline (see p. 228), this Davis Square outlet stocks the full line of breads from the Maine-based bakery, along with cookies and cute logo T-shirts.

Wine & Cheese Cask, 407 Washington St., Somerville, MA 02143; (617) 623-8656; thewineandcheesecask.com; Cheesemonger/Wine, Beer & Spirits. Straddling the Cambridge-Somerville line across the street from **The Biscuit** (see p. 327) on one side and **Dalí Restaurant & Tapas Bar** (see p. 312) on the other, this deceptively small shop is stuffed to the gills with good wine buys and is particularly strong in French wines of the $15–$25 sort. The monthly bargain bins are really that—wines that would be worth drinking at twice the price. Many bargain-hunters come just for the wines and overlook a great array of New England and Quebec cheeses carefully labeled to indicate which are made from raw milk and which are not.

Farmers' Markets

Arlington Farmers' Market, Russell Common parking lot, Arlington center. Wed from 2 to 6:30 p.m., mid-June through late Oct.

Somerville/Davis Square Farmers' Market, Day and Herbert Streets parking lot, Davis Square, Somerville. Wed from noon to 6 p.m., late May to late Nov (closes 5 p.m. in Nov).

Somerville/Union Square Farmers' Market, Union Square Plaza, Somerville. Sat from 9 a.m. to 1 p.m., June through late Oct.

Somerville Winter Farmers' Market, Center for the Arts at the Armory, 191 Highland Ave., Somerville. Sat from 10 a.m. to 2 p.m., mid-Nov through late May.

Swirl & Slice: Union Square Specialty Food Market, Union Square Plaza, Somerville. Thur from 5 to 8 p.m., mid-June to late Sept. Locally produced refined foods, such as wine, cheese, sausages, jams, breads, and pickles.

Belmont, Lexington & Concord

Despite suburban sprawl, these suburbs west of Boston retain their agricultural roots, so it's not surprising that during the growing season produce in the local stores and restaurants often comes from nearby farms. Yet all three are sophisticated communities with urban tastes and, to a great extent, the wherewithal to support upscale shops and eating establishments. Lexington and Concord lie on the commuter rail from Boston, while Belmont is tucked up on the shoulders of Cambridge, Arlington, and Watertown, giving it the greatest immigrant ethnic diversity of this chapter. All three communities tend to look to Boston and Cambridge for much of their special-occasion dining, but they are unusually rich in suppliers of wine, cheese, fresh produce, and gourmet foods.

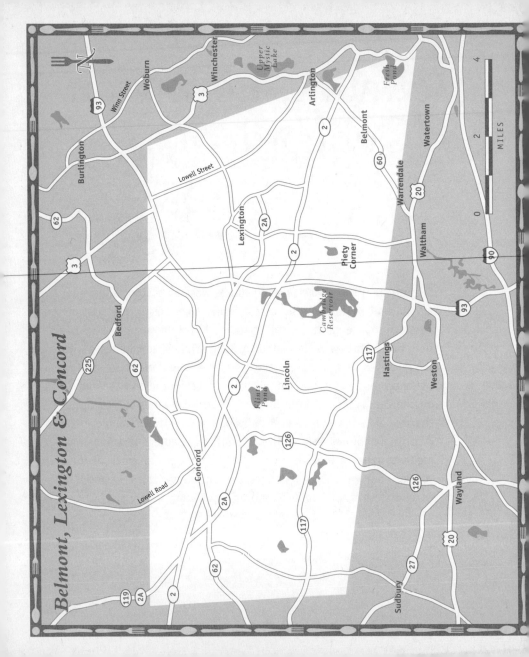

Belmont, Lexington & Concord

80 Thoreau, 80 Thoreau St., Concord, MA 01742; (978) 318-0008; 80thoreau.com; New American; $$–$$$. With **Rialto** (see p. 271) alumna Carolyn Johnson in the kitchen, 80 Thoreau proves that Concord residents need only go to the commuter rail station to get a great meal. They don't need to take the train into the city. Johnson lets seasonal ingredients shine in her cleanly conceived, intensely flavored dishes. Winter starters, for example, favor such plates as a scallop crudo, with the raw shellfish supported by pomegranate, fresh cress, and sea salt. Her tagliatelle with lamb ragù comes with braised fennel seasoned with juniper berries and accented by black olives. In the summer local farms supply all the vegetables. The wooden floors, high-beamed ceiling, and solid white walls bounce sound, so 80 Thoreau often sounds even fuller than it is. Good luck even getting a seat in the bar unless you arrive before the commuter train from North Station does.

Gustazo Cuban Cafe, 289 Belmont St., Belmont, MA 02478; (855) 487-8296; gustazo-cubancafe.com; Cuban; $. Cuban food has a low profile in greater Boston, apart from the Cubano sandwich. Gustazo does a very authentic version of the Cubano, aside from having to put it on French bread because Miami-style Cuban bread is unavailable. Miami expats also favor the *pan con léchon,* a sandwich of slow-roasted pork served with an avocado-pineapple salad. For a heartier plate, try the classic *ropa vieja* ("old clothes"), a

Canary Islands recipe that evolved into the Cuban national dish. It's a hearty plate of shredded skirt steak cooked with *sofrito* (onion, garlic, and diced pepper) in a mild tomato sauce. It's served with white rice, fried plantains, and black beans.

Il Casale, 50 Leonard St., Belmont, MA 02478; (617) 209-4942; ilcasalebelmont.com; Italian; $$–$$$. Dante de Magistris may serve high-end contemporary Italian fare at his eponymous Cambridge restaurant (see Dante Restaurant, p. 246), but this far more casual spot in his hometown focuses squarely on his grandmother's recipes for Italian comfort food. Even the name (which translates as "the country house") suggests home cooking. Of course, few of us ever lived in a huge former firehouse with brick walls and dashing chandeliers. You could just graze on the *sfizi*—little appetizer plates that include terrific meatballs in a tomato ragù and *arancini* made from porcini mushroom risotto. Many pasta dishes are available as appetizers or main dishes. You can dine like Italians and order a bunch of dishes for the table and have them all served family style. The food may be rustic but the kitchen prepares it with exquisite finesse. The "naked ravioli" (*ignudi*), for example, are made by rolling ricotta and Parmigiana cheese into balls, then breading them with egg white and flour, and very gently boiling them so the filling has a barely perceptible skin holding it together. Family-style tasting dinners are available in an economical choice called the Fiat, or a deluxe version called the Ferrari.

Main Streets Market and Cafe, 42 Main St., Concord, MA 01742; (978) 369-9948; mainstreetsmarketandcafe.com; Bakery Cafe; $$. You can eat all day at Main Streets, starting with three-egg omelets and breakfast sandwiches in the morning followed by wraps and a bowl of bean-free beef chili at lunch. The most tempting items might be the afternoon sweet snacks, like red velvet cupcakes, individual Boston cream pies, and old-fashioned lemon bars. In the evening the menu becomes more tavern-oriented with shrimp and scallop risotto, steak-frites, and lobster mac and cheese. There are also six choices of beer on tap, including an ale brewed exclusively for Main Streets. Acoustic musicians entertain Wednesday through Saturday nights.

Mario's Italian Restaurant, 1733 Massachusetts Ave., Lexington, MA 02420; (781) 861-1182; marioslexington.com; Italian; $. With red-and-white checkerboard tablecloths, large murals of Italian scenes, and a menu of Italian-American favorites, it's no wonder that Mario's is full at every meal. It doesn't hurt that the food is generous and inexpensive. You can order chicken, eggplant, or veal Parm (served with spaghetti or shells), ravioli, lasagna, and baked ziti. Most dishes can be ordered with extra meatballs. American-style pizzas (lots of crust, lots of cheese) are especially popular with the high school kids who come in on weekend dates. There's plenty

Putting the J in PB&J

One of the great frustrations of New England's first English colonists was the inability to grow European grapes for table consumption or for making wine or even jelly. Even American grapes of the early 19th century, like Catawba and Isabelle, wouldn't ripen in New England. Enter Ephraim Bull, goldbeater by trade and horticulturalist by calling. After moving from Boston to Concord for his health, he began experimenting in 1843 with growing grapes from seed. He ultimately raised more than 22,000 seedlings before lighting on one that produced large, sweet fruit in the short growing season. Awarded a prize at the Massachusetts Horticultural Fair of 1853, he released seedlings of his grape in 1854 and it soon swept the Northeast. Bull, alas, had no plant patent or other protection and others made money off the grape while he died in near poverty. His tombstone at Sleepy Hollow Cemetery carries the epitaph "He Sowed Others Reaped." But his creation—which he named the Concord grape—lives on as an important table grape and the signature flavor of grape jelly. It's still widely available at area farmstands in the fall.

of take-home food as well, including the ever-popular spaghetti bucket of a half gallon of pasta with sauce, a dozen meatballs, and bread—enough to feed four (at least). Quantity isn't all that Mario's has going for it: The food is delicious and filling.

Nourish Fresh Grill & Bar, 1727 Massachusetts Ave., Lexington, MA 02420; (781) 674-2400; nourishlexington.com; Eclectic; $–$$. You have to admire the great intentions of owners Karen and Kevin Masterson, who seem to be conspiring to make their customers live forever. Nourish has a lot of tofu and tempeh on the menu, brown rather than white rice, and slews of dark green vegetables. That such healthy fare—much of it locally sourced—is also reasonably priced is a big plus. Nourish is very popular with vegetarians, who get equal time with carnivores thanks to veggie quesadillas and chili, falafel, and three of the four pizza options (with sourdough crust made with organic flours). Even so, Nourish will also serve you a delicious grilled steak—from grass-fed New England beef, of course.

Patou Thai, 69 Leonard St., Belmont, MA 02478; (617) 489-6999; patouthai.com; Thai; $–$$. One of the prettiest dining rooms we've seen in ages, Patou Thai holds its own against the juggernaut across the street (**Il Casale,** see p. 342) by offering an entirely different dining experience. Serenity is the signature mood here, and the authentic Thai cuisine teases the palate with a dozen different taste sensations in every dish. Try the tangy salad of julienned carrots and green papaya topped by grilled shrimp as a starter, or the house-special halibut with mango salsa and Thai curry as a main dish. (Just because the cuisine is Thai doesn't mean the kitchen avoids our superb New England fish.) Several dishes of assorted seafood with different sauces (green peppercorns and hot peppers, yellow bean sauce, hot chile sauce over a bed of steamed clams) are always sure bets.

Via Lago Cafe & Catering, 1845 Massachusetts Ave., Lexington, MA 02420; (781) 861-6174; vialagocatering.com; Eclectic; $$. Via Lago is nothing if not versatile. The restaurant caters a lot of business functions in and around Lexington, and it's one of the most dependable "nice" spots for lunches ranging from a good juicy hamburger (or less juicy veggie burger) to a plate of coq au vin or pork cassoulet with roast pork, Polish sausage, and duck confit. In the evening the tables are clad in white linens and the menu is kicked up a notch with daily changing specials like grilled grass-fed rib eye steak or peppercorn-crusted rack of lamb. Via Lago may look like a high-ceilinged bar room, but the broad comfort food menu makes it more a place to eat than drink.

Specialty Stores, Markets & Producers

Cake, 1628 Massachusetts Ave., Lexington, MA 02420; (781) 674-2253; cakeperiod.com; Bakery. As a girl Michelle Ryan learned to love baking and now specializes in creating beautiful custom cakes for all occasions. But she always has an assortment of cupcakes on hand so that prospective clients can sample some of her flavor combinations and the rest of us can satisfy a craving for a sweet bite, such as a chocolate cupcake topped with marshmallow icing and peppermint bits, or a rich red velvet cupcake with cream cheese icing.

The Cheese Shop, 29 Walden St., Concord, MA 01742; (978) 369-5778; concordcheeseshop.com; Cheesemonger. Peter Lovis, the proprietor of this exquisite shop, has been in the cheese business since 1976 and has watched tastes change. "I remember when supermarkets started carrying brie in the mid-1970s," he says. "In the mid-1980s, shops started bringing cheese from Europe by air. That was a huge development." Now he credits both the locavore movement and the interest in organic foods with sparking the production of great artisanal cheeses and laments that he has room to stock only about 150 to 200 cheeses—domestic and imported—at a time. "But over the course of a year, we sell about 1,000 different cheeses. And some of them were milk in a goat only 10 days before," he says. "That's pretty cool." Perhaps the most anticipated cheese is the 400-pound wheel of Crucolo that is delivered to the store and rolled in on a red carpet on the first Thursday after Thanksgiving. The cow's-milk cheese made in the Italian Alps has become so popular that Lovis now has to order two of the giant wheels for the holidays. (He stocks 30-pound wheels the rest of the year.) "It's my favorite for a grilled cheese sandwich, with tomato, bacon, and butter on both sides of the bread," he says. Lovis and his staff can give advice for serving all the cheeses, or for pairing them with the shop's wine selection.

The Concord Shop, 13 Walden St., Concord, MA 01742; (978) 371-2286; concordshop.com; Housewares. If visiting **The Cheese**

Shop (see above) inspires you to make a fondue, stop in this well-stocked kitchenware shop for a fondue pot to bubble your cheese in and a wooden cutting board to slice your bread on. While you're at it, why not add a beautiful wooden salad bowl and serving utensils for the salad to round out your meal? Among the shop's more unusual items are a spaetzle press and a jumbo pancake dispenser. Serious bakers will especially appreciate the wide range of specialty baking pans for mini muffins, scones, shortbread, and biscotti, as well as the giant display of cookie cutters in dozens of fanciful shapes.

Concord Teacakes, 59 Commonwealth Ave., West Concord, MA 01742; (978) 369-7644; concordteacakes.com; Bakery Cafe. Judy Ferth began her baking business with only two recipes, but they were good ones. The chocolate and lemon cakes are still part of her repertoire, but now customers can choose among seven cake flavors and nine fillings for custom cakes. The favorite, by the way, is chocolate cake with white buttercream icing. But the shop, with a few tables for those who can't wait to eat their treats at home, is also known for its cupcakes, scones, coffee cakes, and chocolate brownies. There are also breakfast sandwiches to start the day, prepared sandwiches for a quick lunch, and comfort food classics (chicken potpie, mac and cheese, spinach quiche) to heat at home.

Craft Beer Cellar, 51 Leonard St., Belmont, MA 02478; (617) 932-1885; bostoncraftbeercellar.com; Wine, Beer & Spirits. Suzanne Schlaw and Kate Baker are pretty sure there's nothing in the US quite like their store, and we certainly can't think of any other place that stocks around 1,000 craft beers at fair prices. Schlaw is proud to call herself a beer geek, and she can recite the entire pedigree of every beer (and brewer) represented in the place. Whether your taste runs to a simple pale ale or a Belgian triple, this is the place to go. Schlaw and Baker bring beer sommeliers' palates to the task of guiding your purchases to match your preferences. Check for tastings on Thursday, Friday, and Saturday.

Debra's Natural Gourmet, 98 Commonwealth Ave., West Concord, MA 01742; (978) 371-7573; debrasnaturalgourmet.com; Grocery. While most restaurants like to think of themselves as fostering a sense of community, of "gathering 'round the table," this whole-foods shop in foodie West Concord fosters a gathering around the produce aisle and the bulk food bins. The store's namesake, Debra Stark, opened the store in 1989 and is one of the founders of Stark Sisters Granola (sold at the store, naturally). Debra's stocks as much local product as possible, assuming it meets the store's standards, which tend to exceed the USDA requirements for "organic" or the FDA requirements for "natural." You'll find almost every food group you'd find in a conventional grocery, but the brands may be unfamiliar. Special events highlight herbal medicine, potions and lotions, and frequent product tastings.

Eastern Lamejun Bakers, 145 Belmont St., Belmont, MA 02478; (617) 484-5239; easternlamejun.com; Grocery. An Armenian friend first introduced us to *lamejun,* the so-called Armenian pizza, which she always served at cocktail parties. (She also admitted that she never made them herself since so many good ones were available in bakeries catering to the area's Armenian Americans.) One such place is Eastern Lamejun, which opened in 1942 and is still going strong. They offer the flatbread *lamejuns* with toppings of chicken, ground meat (with or without garlic), or vegetables. They also bake turnovers (meat, cheese, and spinach with cheese) and a variety of pastries including date or pistachio cookies, *ragula* with chocolate and walnuts, and baklava with pistachios or with walnuts, lemon, and cinnamon. The refrigerator case is equally tempting with containers of lentil or bulgur pilaf, baba ghanoush, tabbouleh, roasted red pepper or cumin and chile hummus, and more than a dozen kinds of olives.

Glutenus Minimus, 697 Belmont St., Belmont, MA 02478; (617) 484-3550; glutenusminimus.com; Bakery. We've always felt sorry for people who have to eat a gluten-free diet, but this shop at least offers some sweet consolation. With inspiration from her mother, Natalie McEachern, who has celiac disease, has developed a remarkable range of products that are more than simply imitations of their wheat-based counterparts. Her cookie choices, for example, include chocolate chip, gingerbread white chocolate, and double chocolate mint, while her muffins range from banana chocolate chip to mango vanilla bean. McEachern also offers cakes, cupcakes, coffee cakes, and breads. You can pick up the finished products in her shop, or take home a mix for corn muffins, cinnamon streusel coffee cake, or pizza dough.

Hutchins Farm, 754 Monument St., Concord, MA 01742; (978) 369-5041; hutchinsfarm.com; Farmstand. You can find Hutchins Farm produce at some farmers' markets in Cambridge, Somerville, and Belmont, but it's more fun to visit the farmstand during the growing season. The family farm was a pioneer of conscientious organic farming (since 1973) and all vegetables and herbs are grown from seed or from the farm's own mother plants. You'll find the New England basics of carrots and corn, along with more unusual crops such as daikon and rapini. A terrific chart on the website indicates availability of the more than 50 herbs, fruits, and vegetables. Farmstand open June through Oct. Self-serve on the porch, Apr, May, and Nov.

Macaron Sweeterie, 848 Massachusetts Ave., Lexington, MA 02420; (781) 863-0848; macaronsweeterie.com; Bakery Cafe. Sella Abalian, the proprietor of this sweet little shop, is originally from Montreal and knows her macarons. The delicate meringue-based cookies have migrated from France to French Canada and are gaining ground here in the States. The pastel-colored delights include apricot, lavender, passion fruit, pistachio, coconut, lemon, and rose—filled with buttercream or jam. For a bit of Paris meets Rome, Abalian also serves equally colorful Italian gelatos. Try a scoop of chocolate/hazelnut *bacio* with a salted caramel macaron or order an *affogato* (a cup of espresso and vanilla gelato) to sip along with a black currant macaron.

Nashoba Brook Bakery, 152 Commonwealth Ave., West Concord, 01742; (978) 318-1999; slowrise.com; Bakery Cafe. Nashoba Brook is first and foremost a bread bakery, and you'll encounter their loaves at health food stores and conventional groceries all over eastern Massachusetts. You'll also find them in lots of sandwich shops and delis as the sandwich alternative to **Iggy's** (see p. 293). One of the striking aspects of their slow-rise breads is that none of the sandwich breads use oils, milk, sugar, or eggs, so they tend to have strong, grainy flavors. The brioche hot dog buns (which almost by definition have to use both eggs and butter) might be an exception, but they sure beat spongy white bread for holding frankfurters. This cafe at the bakery carries fresh soups and salads as well as sandwiches. There are also four or five kinds of cookies available as well as blondies, brownies, and other sweet treats.

Rancatore's, 36 Leonard St., Belmont, MA 02478; (617) 489-5090; and 1752 Massachusetts Ave., Lexington, MA 02420; (781) 862-5090; rancs.com; Ice Cream/Yogurt. Gus Rancatore learned the premium ice cream ropes from his brother at **Toscanini's** in Cambridge (see p. 303) before opening his first shop in Belmont in 1985. Among the most popular flavors are Hydrox cookie and ginger snap molasses ice creams, mango sorbet, and *kulfi* yogurt. Rancatore likes to encourage creativity. An employee competition to make the best ice cream yielded the Cocoa Joel, a decadent concoction of milk chocolate and bittersweet chocolate ice cream, chocolate mousse yogurt, crushed Hydrox cookies, and chocolate chips.

Reasons to Be Cheerful, 110 Commonwealth Ave., West Concord, MA 01742; (978) 610-6248; cheerful-reasons.com; Ice Cream/Yogurt. This genuinely cheery spot bills itself as "Concord's dessert cafe," but it would be a mistake to overlook the savory crepes, such as ham or turkey with cheese or smoked salmon with crème fraîche. Suitably fortified, you can sample some of the unusual ice cream flavors, such as the signature Dark and Stormy, a mix of ginger ice cream with rum and a swirl of dark molasses, or Hot Chocolate, with a touch of cinnamon and cayenne pepper. If you prefer yogurt, try the tart blueberry, made with wild berries from Maine.

Ride Studio Cafe, 1720 Massachusetts Ave., Lexington, MA 02420; (339) 970-0187; ridestudiocafe.com; Coffee. We'll admit that it's one of the strangest marriages of businesses that we have encountered, but this shop specializing in high-end bicycles also brews really serious coffee drinks. Lattes and cafe crème are made with organic milk or cream from High Lawn Farms in western Massachusetts. The cafe gets its espresso beans from Portland, Oregon's Stumptown Roasters and the beans for pour-over brews from the legendary **George Howell Terroir Coffee Company** (see p. 377) in Acton. After a couple of cups, you'll be ready to pedal like a bike messenger. It's testament enough to the drawing power of the brews that Ride flourishes with Starbucks and Peet's only a few doors away.

Samira's Homemade, 95 Fairview Ave., Belmont, MA 02478; (617) 489-3400; samirashomemade.com; Specialty Shop. When Samira Hamdoun worked at Harvard University, she used to bring her homemade dips to parties. "Everyone told me I should sell them," she says. Who can argue with Harvard? In 2011 Samira, who is Lebanese, and her husband, Ragab, who is Egyptian, founded their business to make authentic foods the way their mothers and grandmothers made them. They began with hummus and soon put their own stamp on the traditional chickpea-based dip by adding flavors such as roasted red pepper, kalamata olive, and jalapeño. They also make *ful medammes,* a hummus-like dish made with fava beans. "It's the Egyptian national dish," says Samira, explaining that their version is more creamy than the traditional, somewhat watery original. "It's called the 'Egyptian meat,'" she says. "They even have it for breakfast. It's very filling and high protein." She prefers it as a sandwich for lunch with tomatoes and cucumbers. (It's also low calorie.) The couple's other products include muhammara, an almost addictive spicy spread of roasted red pepper, walnuts, and pomegranate molasses, and a delicious baba ghanoush. "We make it smoky, the way it's supposed to be," says Samira.

Sophia's Greek Pantry, 265 Belmont St., Belmont, MA 02478; (617) 489-1371; Grocery. Sophia Georgoulopoulos loves to cook and she loves to introduce people to the specialties of her Greek homeland. "We make all the Greek food," she says, pointing to the cold case full of such dishes as *pastitio*, stuffed grape leaves, moussaka, stuffed peppers and tomatoes, and octopus salad. But she seems most proud of the thick and creamy mixed sheep and goat milk yogurt that she makes from her grandmother's recipe. She makes both 2 percent and nonfat versions as well as one mixed with honey. "I put it over fresh fruit with some nuts," she says. "It's my dinner." She lets her imagination run wild when she dreams up flavor combinations for each day's batch of frozen yogurt. One of the customer favorites is taro, though we find the watermelon to be especially refreshing in the summer and also like the complex flavor of the blueberry, honeydew melon, and green apple blend. Georgoulopoulos's yogurt is used by a number of Boston's top chefs, as is the olive oil from her family's olive press imported by Extra Virgin Foods. (Importer Paul Hatziiliades actually has an olive oil tasting bar at Sophia's. The oils come from his family's and her family's trees.)

The Spirited Gourmet, 448 Common St., Belmont, MA 02478; (617) 489-9463; thespiritedgourmet.com; Wine, Beer & Spirits/ Grocery. A great wine shop with a good case of sausages and cheeses, the Spirited Gourmet carries roughly 300 wines under $15. They are arranged mostly by grape, and the strongest regions represented are Italy and France. Buyer Nick Martinelli doesn't do things in half measure. In early spring he's likely to offer 2 dozen or more terrific rosé wines in prerelease. He also carries high-end box wines when he can find them. "All the boxes I sell," he says, "are from guys who make awesome wines." The shop has tastings on Friday and Saturday.

Sweet Thyme Bakery, 1837 Massachusetts Ave., Lexington, MA 02420; (781) 860-8818; sweetthymebakery.com; Bakery. Baker Cindy Chan brings an Asian taste palate to European-style pastries. She might layer her vanilla and chocolate sponge cakes with green tea and strawberry or with mango fillings or make a cheesecake flavored with green tea and red bean paste. She also makes unusual "cheese bars," which are basically long, thin strips of cheesecake wrapped in paper. "They are uniquely ours," says Julianna Lee, who often works at the counter. The bars come in a range of equally unique flavors, including rose cranberry and mango chocolate. "They freeze very well," says Lee. "Lots of people eat them like an ice cream bar." The shop also makes breads such as raisin, sesame, and seven-grain and offers sandwiches at lunchtime. Chan has a following for her Asian-style sweet rice cakes. They are made with rice flour and flavored with apple or red bean paste for a sticky, chewy treat.

Verrill Farm, 11 Wheeler Rd., Concord, MA 01742; (978) 369-4494; verrillfarm.com; Farmstand. Loyal customers were horrified when Verrill Farms' first farmstand was destroyed in a September 2008 fire. But the family promised to rebuild and the stand they opened a year later was indeed bigger and better than ever. The generous-sized space has more than enough room for produce from the Verrills' 100 acres of farmland, along with local honey, jam, marmalade and other products. Sandwiches and salads are available from the deli, and the bakery turns out a range of cakes, fruit tarts, pies, and *crostatas*—a free-form pastry filled with fruits of the season. You could probably eat Verrill's ready-to-heat meals for a month without repeating a dish. They range from vegetarian lasagna to beef stroganoff, lemon dill salmon to veal wiener schnitzel.

Vicki Lee's, 105 Trapelo Rd., Belmont, MA 02467; (617) 489-5007; vickilees.com; Bakery Cafe. It takes advance planning to make aram sandwiches, one of Vicki Lee's signature specialties. Lavosh cracker bread has to be moistened with water and rolled overnight so that it will be soft enough to wrap around beef or ham or turkey with lettuce, or around salmon. But all the foodstuffs in this elegant shop require a similar attention to detail—from the homemade toasted granola to the Chocolate Symphony torte covered in dark chocolate ganache and decorated with handmade chocolate flowers. Vicki Lee's is a favorite for weekday lunches and Sunday brunch. We also imagine that many people in Belmont plan their week around the nightly take-home entrees. If it's Monday it must be meat loaf . . . The signature Anzac cookie (a mix of oatmeal, coconut, and walnuts) is good enough to be eaten every day!

Vintages, 32 Leonard St., Belmont, MA 02478; (617) 484-4560; and 53 Commonwealth Ave., West Concord, MA 01742; (978) 369-2545; vintagesonline.com; Wine, Beer & Spirits. If you are, like us, a fan of the Nebbiolo grape that forms the basis for Barbaresco, Barolo, Gattinara, Carema, Canavese . . . or at its least prestigious but still very drinkable, Spanna, then Vintages is for you. Both shops have carefully curated collections of quality wines, mostly from Italy and France. You'll be hard-pressed to find mass-market names here, but don't hesitate to ask questions about wines that pique your curiosity.

Wilson Farm, 10 Pleasant St., Lexington, MA 02421; (781) 862-3900; wilsonfarm.com; Farmstand. We imagine that the Irish immigrants who founded Wilson Farm in the late 19th century would be dumbfounded if they saw it today. From their original purchase of 16 acres of farmland, the family now grows more than 125 different crops on 33 acres in Lexington and an additional 500 acres in Litchfield, New Hampshire. The farmstand, which is bigger than many grocery stores, offers the full progression of fresh produce across the seasons, along with artisanal and farmhouse cheeses, fresh meats and seafood, delicious baked goods, soups, salads, and heat-and-eat meals.

Farmers' Markets

Belmont Farmers' Market, Municipal parking lot, Cross Street and Channing Road, Belmont. Thurs from 1:30 to 7 p.m. (6 p.m. after Labor Day), early June through late Oct.

Lexington Farmers' Market, Massachusetts and Fletcher Avenues, Lexington. Tues from 2 to 6:30 p.m., late May through late Oct.

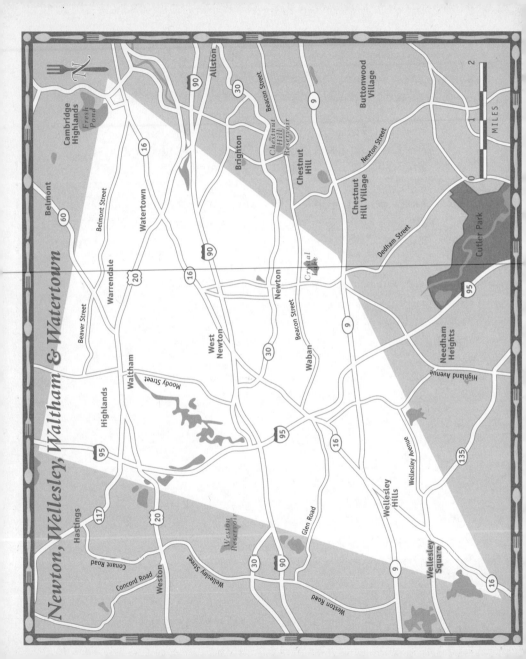

Newton, Wellesley, Waltham & Watertown

N

MILES
0 1 2

Cambridge Highlands
Fresh Pond
Belmont
Belmont Street
60
Allston
90
30
Beacon Street
Brighton
Chestnut Hill Reservoir
9
Buttonwood Village
Watertown
16
Warrendale
20
90
16
Newton Street
Chestnut Hill
Chestnut Hill Village
Beaver Street
Newton
Crystal Lake
Dedham Street
9
95
Cutler Park
Waban
Beacon Street
West Newton
30
Needham Heights
Highland Avenue
Moody Street
Waltham
Highlands
95
Weston Reservoir
95
Weston
20
Hastings
117
Conant Road
Concord Road
Wellesley Street
30
90
Weston Road
Glen Road
16
Wellesley Hills
Wellesley Avenue
135
9
Wellesley Square
16

Newton, Wellesley, Waltham & Watertown

The suburbs have certainly changed since the days when June Cleaver served green bean casserole and TV dinners. These commuter communities are a case in point. They are rich with ethnic diversity—from Eastern European bakeries to Armenian gourmet shops to Indian and Russian supermarkets. Gastropubs, roadhouses, and neighborhood American bistros are popping up within hailing distance of commuter rail stations, and the emphasis on local provender is as strong as anywhere in the city. It is no longer necessary for a suburban foodie to go into the city to shop or to dine. Some of the best tastes available are literally in their own backyards.

Foodie Faves

Aegean Restaurant, 640 Arsenal St., Watertown, MA 02472; (617) 923-7771; aegeanrestaurants.com; Greek; $$. Set on an unlikely corner across the street from the Arsenal Mall, the Aegean is the kind of place that Greek mothers choose when they don't want to cook for the family. It jumps at lunchtime, even though full table service is not inexpensive. At dinner the whole table can share the "house platter" for a taste of spanakopita and some *lokaniko* sausage along with olives, boiled eggs, and other small savories. Grilled seafood, kebabs, and steaks are house specialties, but there are always at least two preparations of lamb and a hefty eggplant moussaka, lest you forget you're in a Greek restaurant.

Alta Strada Restaurant, Pizzeria & Market, 92 Central St., Wellesley, MA 02482; (781) 237-6100; altastradarestaurant.com; Italian; $$–$$$. Michael Schlow of **Radius** (see p. 67) made this "High Street" in Wellesley his first venture into a more casual, community-centric restaurant, and struck a bull's-eye. The Italian menu emphasizes whatever is freshest in the market, and whatever works best in the kitchen's humongous ovens. Even the salads are enough to make most patrons salivate, and the midday pizzas are light and crisp and full of flavors. The reasonably priced pasta plates are always richly flavored: homemade fettucine with wild mushrooms, rosemary, and Parmesan, for example, or hand-rolled cavatelli with spicy fennel sausage and baby broccoli. The *secondi* meat and fish plates at dinner are hearty and simple, like a grilled pork chop, smoky ribs, and agrodolce peppers. For patrons who want to eat the same great food at home (or to pick up some of the great ingredients the restaurant uses), there's a downstairs market with an entrance from the rear parking lot. The entire menu is available for takeout, and some customers have been known to dash in wearing pajamas. For those willing to dress, the Sunday brunch is very popular.

b street, 796 Beacon St., Newton, MA 02459; (617) 332-8743; bstreetnewton.com; New American; $$; T: Newton Centre. We agree with our European friends: The hamburger is the star of American cuisine—nobody does it better. This former bakery converted to a funky small-town American bistro lets the burger star, though it shares center stage with grilled lamb chops, pan-seared local cod, and mushroom ravioli. It's unlikely you'll ever encounter anything terribly exotic at b street, and that sense of familiarity is part of the appeal. But you might be surprised by little touches (the house-made pickle with the burger, for example) that keep you from wondering why you didn't cook the same food at home. Chances are you'd never make that salted peanut turtle tart or lemon cheesecake with gingerbread crust, anyway.

The Biltmore Bar & Grille, 1205 Chestnut St., Newton, MA 02464; (617) 527-2550; thebiltmoregrill.com; New American; $$.

There's a remarkably Southern flavor to the Biltmore, as if to reach into the American past for inspiration means heading south of the Mason-Dixon Line. The tin ceilings and gas station memorabilia meet their match in rockabilly, soul, and retro roots music on the jukebox as well as in the chicken and waffles dish on the late-night menu. Fortunately, the Biltmore takes the Alabama roadhouse theme only so far, stopping this side of greasy collards. In fact, the updated tavern food includes an austere roasted Arctic char with chickpea salad and broccolini and beer-can game hen with sweet potato fries. There's even a separate menu for great cheeses and some local charcuterie. Elvis may have left the building, but the spirit of James Beard has come for dinner.

Blue Ginger, 583 Washington St., Wellesley, MA 02482; (781) 283-5790; ming.com/blueginger; Asian/New American; $$$$. Chef-Owner Ming Tsai, Food Network star and cookbook author, has made Blue Ginger his home base since 1997. Unlike many celebrity chefs, he's in the kitchen on many nights, overseeing the operations of Chef de Cuisine Tom Woods. Known for his matchmaking of Asian and European cuisines, Tsai composes dishes where all the boundaries blur and fabulous flavors emerge. Rack of lamb, for example, is glazed with pomegranate molasses and is served with apple-endive salad, Chinese black-bean creamed spinach, and mashed potatoes. Tsai is also a leader in serving sustainable fish, and his sablefish dishes are invariably big hits. One version marinates the fish (also known as black cod and sometimes as butterfish) in miso and sake, and pairs it with a vegetarian soba noodle sushi. To enjoy the cuisine on a more limited budget, make a lunch reservation (weekdays only).

Blue-Ribbon Bar-B-Q, 1375 Washington St., West Newton, MA 02465; blueribbonbbq.com; Barbecue; $; T: West Newton. The original of the Blue-Ribbon family (the other's in Arlington, see p. 311), this spot surprised us with the authenticity of the food when it opened several years ago. The inspiration is truly Southern, and the recipes span the old Confederacy—leaning strongly on an intense hickory and maple smokiness. Our favorite is the slow-roasted Carolina-style pulled pork, which is pulled before simmering in vinegar sauce (other regions serve the sauce on the side). We also like the Kansas City–style burnt ends—overcooked brisket simmered in a tomato-based sauce. The aromas will tell you that you're in the right spot the moment you walk through the door.

CK Shanghai, 15–17 Washington St., Wellesley Hills, MA 02481; (781) 237-7500; ckshanghai.com; Chinese; $–$$. Eat modern Asian fusion at **Blue Ginger** (see p. 364), or come here and let Chef-Owner C. K. Sau introduce you to the pleasures of world-class traditional Chinese cuisine. The menu is as inscrutable as at any greasy rice bowl restaurant, but Sau's interpretations are exquisite. Focus on the section of the menu called "Shanghai's Specialty Seafood, Meat, and Poultry," which covers the best dishes. Apart from the lobster or the Peking duck, they're remarkably inexpensive. Another good strategy is to fold up the menu, ask what's fresh, and request that the chef cook you a memorable meal. Don't be surprised if it includes Hunan-style whole fish (Sau's special sauce really makes the dish) and some wok-fried scallops with black peppercorn sauce. C. K. Sau is the Chinese chef to whom most of Boston's top chefs doff their toques.

Cabot's Ice Cream & Restaurant, 743 Washington St., Newtonville, MA 02460; (617) 964-9200; cabots.com; Casual American/Ice Cream; $; T: Newtonville. "It's an ice cream world and you're in the middle of it now," proclaims a sign on the wall of this retro parlor that's been a fixture in Newton since 1969. But before you dig into a hot fudge sundae, ice cream soda, or banana boat (all so big they overflow their dishes), you can enjoy a grilled cheese or turkey club sandwich, a burger, or a fish and chips platter. Breakfast choices range from a modest order of cinnamon toast to wild blueberry hotcakes. Belgian waffles do double duty as a breakfast treat with syrup and butter or as the base for a sundae with vanilla ice cream, strawberry fruit topping, and whipped cream.

Deluxe Town Diner, 627 Mount Auburn St., Watertown, MA 02472; (617) 926-8400; deluxetowndiner.com; Casual American; $. One of the things that distinguishes Deluxe as a true diner is that you can get breakfast for all three meals, which, as any traveling salesman or truck driver will tell you, is the safest way to eat on the road. Nobody messes up breakfast. But not everyone does it as well as Deluxe, with dishes such as challah french toast and crab cakes Benedict. Club sandwiches are the stars of the lunch menu, although a pretty authentic New York–style hot pastrami might warrant consideration. The blue plate specials feature diner standards like meat loaf dinner or roast turkey. Young parents from around the region bring their kids here to introduce them to the great American dining car experience, so it's often loud with the sound of excited children.

Elephant Walk, 663 Main St., Waltham, MA 02451; (781) 899-2244; elephantwalk.com; Cambodian/French; $$. With other locations in Boston (p. 99) and Cambridge (p. 250), Elephant Walk reflects the culinary side of French imperialist adventures in Indochina. Elephant Walk serves both upscale Cambodian food, including the house specialty of *amok*—a coconut-milk custard scented with aromatic Khmer spices and filled with crab, shellfish, and catfish fillets. Yet the same menu includes a whole set of Parisian bistro plates along with a list of vegetarian and gluten-free dishes. Should you wish, you can hopscotch courses between Southeast Asia and the French countryside.

51 Lincoln, 51 Lincoln St., Newton Highlands, MA 02461; (617) 965-3100; 51lincolnnewton.com; New American; $$$; T: Newton Highlands. Chef-Owner Jeffrey F. Fournier certainly has all the local bona fides a young chef could ask for, including a stint with Lydia

Shire, but he also spent some of his early days in the trade in and around Santa Monica, giving him a well-rounded and thoughtful approach to contemporary market-driven cooking. So while he poaches lobster in butter and Sauternes, he also serves steamed Asian-style buns, and prepares a lovely seared fluke fillet with sweet-pea risotto. A lot of locals pop in for impromptu dinner at the bar, savoring the excellent but affordable burger or the fish tacos. Intimate and casual, 51 Lincoln is very much a neighborhood trattoria for Green Line commuters.

Fiorella's, 187 North St., Newtonville, MA 02460; (617) 969-9900; fiorellasnewton.com; Italian; $$. Located in a quiet residential area far from public transit, Fiorella's is a suburban favorite for Italian-American food. Moreover, the restaurant claims to make only "Italian-inspired" dishes, which is a subtle way of saying they know the difference and prefer to serve long-simmered red-sauce "gravy," breaded veal cutlets, and chicken with pastas and vegetables. The kitchen also serves American-style pizzas, none of them overladen with mozzarella. A broad selection of value-priced wines is available by the glass.

Il Capriccio, 888 Main St., Waltham, MA 02451; (781) 894-2234; ilcapricciowaltham.com; Italian; $$$. Founded decades ago by a Milanese expat, Il Capriccio was one of the flagbearers for northern Italian cuisine in greater Boston even before meat-centric Tuscan menus became the vogue. The pastas are all available as entrees, but stick with the smaller servings for a first course and enjoy a full meal here. The house *salumi* makes a good starter for sharing, but you'll want your own black risotto with lobster or gnocchi with Ipswich clams before contemplating the meat and fish *secondi*. The semolina-crusted trout stuffed with braised cabbage and speck (and served with mustard sauce and lentils) is a great argument for drinking red (Barbaresco) with fish. The wine list is one of the most extensive in the region, and certainly one of the most discerning. The organization of the list— clumping a group of whites or reds under a single price, then listing by region and grape—is a big help for diners who have an idea how much they can spend but want to see what the selection might be at that price point. Most wines are from northern Italy or France, but Il Capriccio also serves a few from Turtle Creek, a *garagiste* in nearby Lincoln.

Inna's Kitchen, 19 Pelham St., Newton Centre, MA 02459; (617) 244-5345; innaskitchen.com; Jewish/Casual American; $; T: Newton Centre. If you want to order a chicken, brisket, salmon, or vegetarian Shabbat dinner for six, you'll have to order two days ahead. But you can stop in the busy shop for a bowl of chicken matzo soup, a hot pastrami sandwich, a spinach and feta knish, and a slice of apple strudel. You can get cheese blintzes for breakfast or challah french toast for Saturday brunch and take home some stuffed cabbage, latkes, and beet salad for later. Mother and son Inna and Alex Khitrik hold themselves to high standards. Though the shop is not under kosher supervision, they use glatt kosher meat along with organic and local products whenever possible.

The Local, 1391 Washington St., West Newton, MA 02465; (617) 340-2160; thelocalnewton.com; New American; $$; T: West Newton. We bet everybody in West Newton wants to claim Frank Santo and Tom Wynn as their best buds, because eating at Frank and Tom's restaurant feels like being invited to a foodie friend's house for dinner—except you must, of course, pay and chances are good there will be a substantial wait. Everyone in town has discovered how good the food is, from the cult-status fried pickles to the fries liberally dusted with a mixture akin to herbes de Provence (parsley, rosemary, and thyme, it turns out) to the "flatbread pizza things" to Hong Kong noodles with wok-fried peanuts and vegetables. That most of the ingredients come from around New England—as do the craft beers—just adds to the appeal. Tavern dining was meant to be like this.

Lumière, 1293 Washington St., West Newton, MA 02465; (617) 244-9199; lumiererestaurant.com; French; $$$; T: West Newton. Chef-Owner Michael Leviton is one of the good guys—a member of the board of overseers of Chefs Collaborative and a passionate proponent of local and sustainable foods. He's also a heck of a cook with a flair for classical French bistro fare. The local shift to fishing for hake instead of cod suits him perfectly, as he can get day-boat-fresh Gloucester hake to serve with a lentil ragù, just as the French would do. The restaurant does its own charcuterie, which makes a perfect starter—assuming you can pass up the artichoke soup with crème fraîche or a small plate of miso-glazed scallops. The room is classically elegant, even a little formal, which makes it wonderful for a date or special occasion. While Leviton clearly loves fine French wines, he peppers his wine list with outstanding Spanish, Italian, and American finds.

Red Lentil, 600 Mount Auburn St., Watertown, MA 02472; (617) 972-9188; theredlentil.com; Vegetarian; $. Diners with philosophical objections to animal exploitation and/or real food intolerances must be relieved to find Red Lentil, where the menu carefully spells out which of its vegetarian dishes is also vegan or gluten-free or contains nuts. They're probably even happier when they dig into a plate of pistachio- and herb-encrusted tofu with a seared corn cake, Thai peanut noodle salad, or the soothing-spicy ginger miso soup. Red Lentil offers its entire menu for takeout as well as casual dining at the restaurant.

Strip-T's, 93 School St., Watertown, MA 02472; (617) 923-4330; stripts.com; Casual American/New American; $. At lunchtime this pun-named glorified sub shop churns out soup and sandwiches, including the namesake strip sirloin and Caesar salad on a bun. Paul Maslow and a friend opened a simple lunch spot in 1986, but everything was kicked up a notch in 2011, when Paul's son Tim joined the fold, fresh from cooking with New York star chef David Chang. Now the menu includes a striking cioppino fish stew, grilled salmon with a side of cauliflower in green curry sauce, and roasted Cape Cod bluefish with buttery grits. There's no changing the limited seating

(29 chairs plus the take-out room) and the bare-bones decor, but this strip shop doesn't tease: It delivers.

Tuscan Grill, 361 Moody St., Waltham, MA 02453; (781) 891-5486; tuscangrillwaltham.com; Italian; $$. This restaurant built around a simple wood-fired spit put Waltham on the dining map when it opened in 1991, and it has been the anchor of the Moody Street dining scene ever since. The most inventive starter is the shrimp and corn *arancini,* but you won't go wrong sticking to the grill and ordering the grilled calamari with spicy tomato broth. The wood grill dominates the entrees, with the marinated lamb steak, broccoli rabe pesto, and garlic-roasted potatoes leading the way.

Specialty Stores, Markets & Producers

Baza Market, 30 Tower Rd., Newton Upper Falls, MA 02464; (617) 986-8510; Grocery. You'll probably hear more Russian than English being spoken at this very large ethnic supermarket. One look at high-fat sour cream, soft cheeses, and butters from around the world will give you a pretty good idea why Russian food can taste so good. You can try some stuffed cabbage or roasted duck at the hot bar or pick up a beautiful loaf of coriander or sunflower bread, some chicken- or veal-stuffed dumplings, smoked sturgeon, herring in sour cream, and pickled beets and have a feast at home.

Big Sky Bread Bakery & Cafe, 142 Main St., Watertown, MA 02472; (617) 332-4445; bigskybreads.com; Bakery Cafe. Descended from the American school of high-rising bread with tender crusts, Big Sky produces some of the most sophisticated loaves this side of the European-style bakers. The honey whole wheat is a standby sandwich bread in any number of good delis, and the dark and marble rye breads are the perfect complement to hearty soups. While a limited number of Big Sky breads are available in other markets, this shop carries the whole line along with small pastries, cakes, and a full line of challah breads.

Bread & Chocolate Bakery Cafe, 4 Hartford St., Newton Highlands, MA 02461; (617) 795-0500, T: Newton Highlands; and 108 Madison Ave., Newtonville, MA 02460; (617) 243-0500, T: Newtonville; breadnchocolate.com; Bakery Cafe. Of the two shops, Newton Highlands has the larger cafe area for sitting down with a bowl of soup of the day and a slice of quiche or a pesto chicken salad sandwich on ciabatta bread. But both locations have the full range of pastries created by Eunice Feller, a professionally trained artist who now turns her creative eye to delicious baked goods. She's especially known for her Kugelhopf Morning Bun, her Boston cream pie cupcake, and her Hong Kong Ding Dong of green tea sponge cake, marshmallow center, and dark chocolate ganache.

Captain Marden's Seafoods, 270 Linden St., Wellesley, MA 02482; (781) 235-0860; captain mardens.com; Fishmonger. Possibly the Boston area's most respected wholesale fishmonger—there's a hardly a fine restaurant or gourmet shop they don't supply—Captain Marden's also has a comprehensive retail operation. The seafood party platters are especially popular. And you don't have to tell company that you didn't make the lobster quiche from scratch.

China Fair, 70 Needham St., Newton, MA 02461; (617) 332-1250; chinafairinc.com; Housewares. This no-nonsense outlet supplies restaurants, hotels, and culinary schools, so it's a pretty good bet that home chefs will find whatever they might need for the kitchen or the dining table. What's more, they'll get a discount on that Zyliss mandoline, Polder digital kitchen scale, or Swiss Diamond fry pan. Paper plates and plastic cutlery are great for big parties.

Danish Pastry House, 205 Arlington St. #4, Watertown, MA 02472; (617) 926-2747; danishpastryhouse.com; Bakery. Enriched with egg and full of butter, true Danish pastry dough is somewhat like croissant dough, but less flaky. You can taste how good it is in the Danish specialty pastries sold in this small shop at the baking facility. The Spandaver, what most of us think of as a Danish, comes with apple, raspberry, and custard fillings. "Thebirches" mixes the dough with poppy seeds and marzipan to great effect, but perhaps the shop's most extraordinary creation is the Kringle, a perfect combination of pastry, marzipan, and almonds. You can buy it by the slice or take a whole one home to bake in the oven for five minutes and share with friends for breakfast. For dessert try a Mayor Chocolate Snail, which swirls the dough around a big chunk of chocolate. Warm slightly and top with ice cream.

DePasquale's Sausage Co., 325 Watertown St., Newton, MA 02458; (617) 244-7633; Grocery. Sweet and hot Italian sausages are the mainstays of this small shop, along with Chinese sausages, which, says the proprietor, "taste like Chinese spareribs." All the sausages are made in the small kitchen in the back and when you stop in you might also find breakfast sausages and others flavored with maple, tomato and basil, or the extremely popular combination of cheese and garlic. A wall of Italian foodstuffs—pastas, sauces, olive oil, and the like—makes for one-stop shopping.

Fastachi, 598 Mount Auburn St., Watertown, MA 02472; (617) 924-8787; fastachi.com; Specialty Shop. The big machines visible through glass windows at the back of this little shop aren't washing machines. They are nut roasters that turn out the almonds, pistachios, cashews, hazelnuts, pecans, macadamia nuts, and peanuts that are lightly dusted with sea salt and combined into various mixes. The most popular is the tart and salty cranberry nut mix, though purists may stick to their favorite nut sans embellishment, or enjoy it ground into a delicious butter, or savor it enrobed in chocolate. The most popular bark features almonds and dark

ZAATAR, BAKLAVA, AND FETA: LITTLE ARMENIA IN EAST WATERTOWN

The Boston region's largest concentration of ethnic Armenians lives in Watertown, so it should not be a surprise that three shops clustered together in East Watertown are packed with imported goods from Armenia and similar items from Greece, Turkey, and various countries of the Middle East—especially olives, oils, and seasonings that cut across several cultures. **Arax** stands out slightly from the others because the family that operates it is ethnic Lebanese and carries more produce than its competitors. Arax also specializes in hookahs and all their paraphernalia, which brings the shop business from around the region. **Sevan's** is known for its fresh *lamejun* and pita breads as well as a delicate, only lightly smoky baba ghanoush. Sevan's is also the one shop among the three to carry goods from Turkey. **Massis Bakery** carries many of the same breads, baklava, and imported goods (grape leaves, for example) as the others, but also has a good selection of feta cheeses and a mind-boggling assortment of spices in various package sizes.

Arax Market, 585 Mount Auburn St., Watertown, MA 02472; (617) 924-3399; Grocery. **Massis Bakery,** 569 Mount Auburn St., Watertown, MA 02472; (617) 924-0537; massisbakery.com; Grocery. **Sevan's Bakery,** 599 Mount Auburn St., Watertown, MA 02472; (617) 924-9843; sevanboston.com; Grocery.

chocolate, but we're partial to the elegant white chocolate bark with macadamias and lemon peel.

George Howell Coffee, 311 Walnut St., Newtonville, MA 02460; (617) 332-6886; tastecoffeehouse.com; Coffee Shop. The no-compete clause that George Howell signed when he sold his beloved Coffee Connection chain to Starbucks has finally expired, and Howell is once again making his mark on the coffee scene. He started importing beans again under the name Terroir, and in early 2012 made his coffee shop comeback with this small Newtonville location. The baristas are anything but fast, but the coffee is worth waiting for. It's the taste of a legend. You can take it to go, but as staff are quick to say, "It's too good for a paper cup." That you can get delicious croissants or simple sandwiches (fig jam and brie, for example, or turkey with basil pesto) is just a bonus.

Gordon's Fine Wines & Liquors, 894 Main St., Waltham, MA 02451; (781) 893-1900; gordonswine.com; Wine, Beer & Spirits. One of the top wine shops in New England for more than 75 years, Gordon's is operated by the third generation of the founding family, and the depth of its offerings is matched by very few shops in the region. Moreover, Gordon's makes learning about wine fun. First Friday tastings (first Friday of each month) are free and feature 15 or so wines in a two-hour event complete with live jazz and hors d'oeuvres. (Cocktail attire.) Want to know more? The wine education center offers classes ranging from the basics of tasting wine to events highlighting a specific area or style of wine. The third Thursday of every month, two sommeliers square off serving 8 wines paired with four courses of food. Attendees choose the winner of the SomSmack.

Gustare Oils & Vinegars, 90 Central St., Wellesley, MA 02482; (781) 416-2012; gustareoliveoil.com; Specialty Shop. Catherine and Dave Ferraresi developed their interest in olive oil and balsamic vinegars by tasting their way through local markets when they lived in Europe. Their downtown Wellesley shop may not be as colorful as a quaint mountaintop village, but it does offer the opportunity to sample and compare dozens of plain and flavor-infused oils and vinegars. Some of the most interesting of the oils are the single-olive varietals.

International Natural Bakery, 128 Arlington St., Watertown, MA 02472; (617) 923-1224; Bakery. It's hard to predict what will be on the shelves in the outlet store of this wholesale bakery, but the prices can't be beat. The products lean toward the hearty Eastern European style, such as sweet braided challah, big challah rolls, dark rye loaves, or the Borodinsky Gourmet, a dark loaf seasoned with coriander. Some of the staff are recent Russian or Ukrainian immigrants with only a rudimentary command of English, but the same could be said of many of the customers.

J. P. Licks, 4 Langley Rd., Newton Centre, MA 02459; (617) 244-0666, T: Newton Centre, and 63 Central St., Wellesley, MA 02482, (781) 416-1799; jplicks.com; Ice Cream/Yogurt. Jamaica Plain's favorite ice cream (see p. 183) has found a home—or two—in the 'burbs.

Keltic Krust, 1371 Washington St., West Newton, MA 02465; (617) 332-9343; keltickrust.com; Bakery Cafe; T: West Newton. Keltic Krust has made a name for itself with its healthy breakfast bars of nuts, dried fruits, and berries that are both vegan and gluten-free. But, as the name suggests, the bakery specializes in Irish-style breads, including, of course, wheat or raisin soda bread, along with less familiar specialties such as yeasted barm brack bread with raisins and orange and lemon peels, and eccles cakes, a flaky pastry filled with raisins and cinnamon. Best bet for a light lunch? A sausage roll of house-made sausage wrapped in pastry dough.

T. F. Kinnealey, 227 Linden St., Wellesley, MA 02482; (781) 235-8322; kinnealey.com; Butcher. Like adjacent **Captain Marden's Seafoods** (see p. 374), Kinnealey has been a key player in the wholesale meat industry in New England since the mid-20th century. The bulk of the trade is with high-end restaurants, country clubs, and hotels, and most of the meat Kinnealey carries is graded

USDA prime—literally a cut above the best available in supermarkets. Kinnealey acquired the John Dewar stores (including this one) in 2006 and uses them to showcase its best meats and specialty products for discerning home cooks.

La Chapincita Market, 424 Moody St., Waltham, MA 02451; (781) 899-6016; Grocery. Reflecting the Hispanic community of Waltham, La Chapincita focuses mostly on the foods of Mexico, Guatemala, Central America, and Peru. This means a great selection of dried chile peppers, a lot of canned goods from Mexico, fresh Mexican tortillas and Salvadoran arepas, and even dried corn husks for making Mexican tamales. Pick up Mexican sodas (mango, tamarind, pineapple, limón) to wash down your spicy repast.

Lee's Place Burgers, 216 Sumner St., Newton Centre, MA 02459; (617) 795-2022; Sandwich Shop. "Sometimes you just need a good burger," say the proprietors of this mom-and-pop eatery, and they will happily grill one for you even if you arrive a little before they open or a little after they normally close. The 6-ounce sirloin burgers are excellent as they are, but even better with the somewhat spicy house-made special sauce. It's also good on the veggie and turkey burgers, or on the grilled chicken breast sandwich.

Lizzy's Homemade Ice Cream, 367 Moody St., Waltham, MA 02453; (781) 893-6677; lizzysicecream.com; Ice Cream/Yogurt. Customers eagerly await the August treat of fresh peach ice cream, made with fruit from a local farm. The rest of the year, coffee Oreo tends to be the flavor of choice at this homemade ice cream emporium, although Charles River Crunch, a dark chocolate ice cream with almond toffee, has its adherents as well. Lizzy's prides itself on its hot fudge sundaes and even offers a Grab 'n' Go Sundae Party Kit to enjoy at home.

Magnolia Wine Company, 130 Belmont St., Watertown, MA 02472; (617) 924-6040; magnoliawinecompany.com; Wine, Beer & Spirits. Originally a liquor store and market, Magnolia has evolved in the 21st century as a shop devoted almost exclusively to wine and craft beer. Owner Jay Faber is less a wine scholar than an enthusiast, and he cultivates that same sense in his staff. This is the place to go for a friendly recommendation on what to drink.

Marty's, 675 Washington St., Newton, MA 02460; (617) 332-1230; martysfinewines.com; Wine, Beer & Spirits. One of the mega-merchants of wine, beer, and especially spirits, Marty's carries everything from bargain jug wines to $200 bottles of Ornellaia and $500 bottles of Sauternes. Marty's also carries an extensive line of gourmet foods, including dozens of olive oils and balsamic vinegars, all manner of dried pastas and pickled vegetables, and even a line of prepared foods like quiche, meat loaf, or roasted duck leg should you be unable to wait to uncork your latest wine purchase.

New England Mobile Book Fair, 82–84 Needham St., Newton Highlands, MA 02461; (617) 527-5817; nebookfair.com; Specialty

Shop. You'll need several hours to peruse the cookbook section at this big warehouse of a shop. But the clerks help by sorting the titles into all kinds of specialty areas, so you can jump from French Cuisine to Healthy Eating, from Appetizers to Grilling, or from Kids' Cooking to Gluten-Free. There's also an excellent selection of titles on beer, wine, cocktails, and spirits. Best of all: Books are discounted 20 percent off retail. A separate bargain book section offers even greater savings.

Quebrada Baking Co., 272 Washington St., Wellesley, MA 02481; (781) 237-2111; quebradabakingco.com; Bakery Cafe. The beautifully decorated cakes and cupcakes steal the show here and in the original Arlington location (see p. 335). But the fresh-baked breads are the quiet stars, including plain, poppy, sesame, and raisin braided challah, and a slightly sweet Irish soda bread with raisins and caraway seeds that is baked on Wednesday. On Friday customers stock up on the Swedish-style cardamom coffee bread so that they can enjoy it as a toasted breakfast treat on the weekend.

Rosenfeld's Bagels, 1280 Centre St., Newton Centre, MA 02459; (617) 527-8080; Bakery; T: Newton Centre. There are two salient pieces of information about Rosenfeld's Bagels: The folks in Newton swear by them, and the shop is closed Monday and Tuesday. Since no one can resist eating all the Sunday bagels, the two-day closure causes severe withdrawal symptoms in some patrons—but not severe enough to make them buy supermarket bagels. Rosenfelds also makes challah. Cash only.

Stoddard's, 360 Watertown St., Newton, MA 02458; (617) 244-4187; stoddards.com; Housewares. Boston's leading cutlery shop since 1800, Stoddard's has seen every fad in knives come and go. Cooks who like to work with their hands instead of food processors will be like kids in a candy store here, where the selection runs from perfectly functional plastic-handled stamped Victorinox chef's knives ("you'll find them in every restaurant kitchen around the world," says vice president Jeff Grossman) to the perfectly balanced, frighteningly sharp Kikuichi carbon steel knives that Grossman himself prefers. Other small items, like exquisite tweezers, traditional razors and shaving paraphernalia, and mirrors and bath soaps, round out the selections. Stoddard's also offers classes in knife techniques and in care and maintenance of fine knives.

Tutto Italiano, 570 Washington St., Wellesley, MA 02482; (781) 431-2250; tuttowellesley.com; Grocery. The folks at Tutto like to say that all you need to supply is the dinner table and they'll do the rest for a fine Italian family meal. Heat-and-eat entrees run the gamut of Italian-American favorites, from cheese and meat lasagnas to eggplant Parm and stuffed shells to chicken Parm and pasta Alfredo. The shop also makes deli sandwiches to go and carries a limited but good line of canned Italian tomatoes and dried pastas. The deli case also has cannoli and ricotta pie.

Waltham Fresh Fish & Prime, 36 Spruce St., Waltham, MA 02453; (781) 891-1515; walthamfreshfishnprime.com; Sandwich Shop. Subs, salads, and wraps aren't likely to surprise anyone, but a sub shop that specializes in fresh fried seafood and sells both fresh and roasted goat meat—well, that's something else. The place is a smorgasbord of Waltham ethnic cuisines, since they also make lamb and beef gyros and offer baklava for dessert.

Waltham India Market, 315 Moody St., Waltham, MA 02453; (781) 899-6016; walthamindia.com; Grocery. If you're prone to making impulsive purchases on an empty stomach, first head downstairs for a beef or lamb kebab and a glass of fresh juice in the Food Bazaar. It will take you quite a while to peruse the street-level grocery, which we imagine would not be out of place in a neighborhood in Mumbai. And those shoppers would know exactly what to do with snake gourds and long beans, not to mention vegetables with names like *tinda, karela,* and *guvar.* A whole aisle is devoted to dried pulses; dairy cases to cheeses, yogurt, and yogurt drinks; numerous shelves to relishes, chutneys, and hot sauces. One of the best ways to expand your palate and your knowledge of Indian food is to purchase the packaged spice mixes so that you can try your hand at making beef biryani, chicken masala, or fish curry at home.

Wasik's, the Cheese Shop, 61 Central St., Wellesley, MA 02482; (781) 237-0916; wasiks.com; Cheesemonger. The food inspectors in Wellesley must be foodies. While their counterparts in some communities do not permit shops to keep cheeses at the proper temperatures for aging, the Wellesley inspectors do. As a result, Wasik's does a lot of its own *affinage*. In practice, this allows the shop to buy young cheeses at a good price and bring them along to optimal ripeness before selling them. Cheeses here hail from around the world, though an increasing number come from small artisanal New England producers. Wasik's also makes its own cheese spreads and chutneys, and has a terrific selection of cheese gift baskets.

Farmers' Markets

Newton Farmers' Market, Cold Spring Park, 1200 Beacon St., Newton Highlands. Tues from 1:30 to 6 p.m., early July through late Oct.

Newton/Post 440 Farmers' Market, American Legion Post 440, 295 California St., Newton. Tues from noon to 5 p.m., late May through late June. Fri from noon to 5 p.m., mid-June through early Oct.

Waltham Farmers' Market, Sovereign Bank parking lot, Main and Moody Streets, Waltham. Sat from 9:30 a.m. to 2:30 p.m., mid-June through early Nov.

Bars, Pubs & Lounges

Contrary to popular misconception, the Puritan founders did not frown on beer and hard cider. In fact, breweries were among the first industries to spring up in Boston and surrounding communities. By the 19th century, an influx of Germans and Central Europeans to Jamaica Plain made that neighborhood the brewing capital of the region. In the 20th century, Boston was a leader in the craft beer revolution, and the city has always had a strong wine culture. Boston was a latecomer to craft cocktail fever, but the city has established itself as one of the American centers for artisanal cocktail culture. This chapter lists some of the city's notable drinking establishments. Most of them serve food, but that isn't the point. Besides, beer *is* food.

Avery Bar, Ritz-Carlton Boston Common, 10 Avery St., Ladder District, Boston, MA 02111; (617) 574-7100; ritzcarlton.com; T:

Boylston. The Ritz experience is all about the service, and the Avery Bar, even with its Danish modern vibe straight out of the '50s, is no exception. Drinks are pricey, but you *are* putting on the Ritz. The modern craft cocktails include the "Avery 10" list of signature martinis, of which the classic has a nicely refreshing drop of orange bitters that makes the floral qualities of the Beefeater gin bloom in the glass.

Backbar, 9 Sanborn Ct., Union Square, Somerville, MA 02143; (617) 718-0249; backbarunion.com. It's hard to find the door to this speakeasy next to its sister restaurant, **Journeyman** (see p. 317), but once you've arrived you'll feel perfectly at home. Craft cocktails are the point, so you're best trusting the bartender for the drink of the day, drink of the week, or bartender's choice. That said, the menu offers a great local take on the Moscow Mule, here known as a Union Mule: pear-infused gin, St. Germain, citrus, ginger, and spice.

Bar at the Taj, 15 Arlington St., Back Bay, Boston, MA 02116; (617) 536-5700; tajhotels.com; T: Arlington. What is the opposite of a dive bar? A soar bar? Back in the day when the Taj was still the original Ritz-Carlton, this elegant bar and lounge set the standard for ladies who wore wraps and men who wore cufflinks. The Taj has maintained the old-world grace without missing a beat. It's quiet, discreet, and very Don Draper. Bond to the contrary, the martinis are stirred (unless you'd rather have them shaken).

Bleacher Bar, 82A Lansdowne St., Fenway, Boston, MA 02215; (617) 262-2424; bleacherbarboston.com; T: Kenmore. Thanks to a cutout in the centerfield bleachers near the Ted Williams red seat (marking the Splinter's longest home run at Fenway), patrons of this baseball lovers' bar can actually watch games being played. That peekaboo sensation is the bar's main distinction, but not everyone gets a seat with a view. The bar is open all year, which Fenway Park is not. Best strategy is to arrive well before game time and nurse your beers.

Boston Beer Works, 112 Canal St., Downtown, Boston, MA 02114; (617) 896-2337; T: North Station; and 61 Brookline Ave., Fenway, Boston, MA 02215; (617) 536-2337, T: Kenmore Square; beerworks.net. These cavernous brewpubs produce small batches of many beer types, ranging from IPAs to fruit-flavored wheat beers to heavy porters—though the emphasis is on light, American-style brews. They also have pretty good menus, emphasizing pastas, barbecue, salads, and a very hearty mixed-grill plate that will feed one linebacker or an entire table of sports fans. Unlike many brewpubs, these are as popular with women as with men.

Brendan Behan, 378 Centre St., Jamaica Plain, Boston, MA 02130; (617) 522-5386; brendanbehanpub.com; T: Jackson Square. Named for one of Ireland's more talented and garrulous alcoholic playwrights, the Behan is a "talking bar" in the grand Irish tradition of places to tip a pint and converse. Neither televisions nor video games intrude, though musical entertainment (live Irish *seissúns*, rock and roll, alt music) is frequently offered later in the evening. Many beers are on tap and in bottle, and the Guinness flows like water. The late lamented *Sunday Tribune* of Dublin named the Brendan Behan as Boston's best bar.

Brick & Mortar, 569 Massachusetts Ave., Central Square, Cambridge, MA 02139; (617) 491-5599; T: Central Square. With its gleaming fishhook-shaped copper bar and firm seating, Brick & Mortar appeared at the end of 2011 as a sign that Central Square hipsterdom was finally growing up and could let go of the floppy couches and overstuffed chairs that once filled this "secret" bar upstairs from **Central Kitchen** (see p. 242). Some of the male patrons are even clean-

shaven. A socializing spot for 30-somethings equally uncomfortable with the hard-core craft beer culture and glow-in-the-dark cocktails, B&M strikes a sensible middle ground. Nonetheless, there are at least two absinthe drinks on the menu and a special price on four shots of the hard stuff (called Crush on a Stripper)—just so you know it's not all business all the time.

Bukowski Tavern, 1281 Cambridge St., Inman Square, Cambridge, MA 02139; (617) 497-7077; and 50 Dalton St., Back Bay, Boston, MA 02115; (617) 437-9999; bukowskitavern.net. The propriety of naming a bar (let alone two of them) for a brilliant alcoholic lauded as the "laureate of the lowlife" might be suspect, but the Cambridge location has scratched its way onto the list of 100 best beer bars in America, according to *Draft* magazine. Unlike most of the bars in Bukowski's stories and novels, both Bukowski Taverns have real pub grub like shepherd's pie. Thirty taps draw craft beers (well, craft beers plus Pabst Blue Ribbon), including a house pale ale called "The Buk." It's a hophead's straw-colored rye ale brewed by Wormtown Brewery in Worcester. Ask about the cask-conditioned ale of the moment. Cash only.

The Burren, 247 Elm St., Somerville, MA 02144; (617) 776-6896; burren.com. Founded in 1996 by a pair of Irish musicians, the Burren is Somerville's closest thing to a pub from the old sod. Live music is featured most nights, a wide range of pub grub is available for the hungry, and 20 beers and ales are on tap to sate the most powerful thirst.

Cambridge Brewing Company, 1 Kendall Sq., Building 100, Kendall Square, Cambridge, MA 02139; cambrew.com; T: Kendall Square. Will Meyers is the brewmaster at this brewery-cum-brewpub, and he is known for both his skill at executing classic and traditional beers and his enthusiasm for more adventurous suds like his Blunderbuss Barleywine aged in port and sherry barrels, his medieval-style heather-infused Scottish ale, and a pert peculiarity called Sgt. Pepper—which is brewed with three malts, two kinds of hops, and four kinds of peppercorns. While many of the brews are now available in 22-ounce bottles, the best place to drink them is fresh at the brewery, either inside the refurbished mill building or out on the brick patio in the heart of the former industrial square.

Cask 'n Flagon, 62 Brookline Ave., Fenway, Boston, MA 02215; (617) 536-4840; casknflagon.com; T: Kenmore. Probably *the* sports bar for die-hard Red Sox fans, the Cask can get a little rowdy on the weekends, especially in the off-season, as it's also a favorite with barely legal kids from Boston University. It was the closest bar to Fenway for decades before **Game On!** (see p. 394) or the **Bleacher Bar** (see p. 388) opened.

Charlie's Kitchen, 10 Eliot St., Harvard Square, Cambridge, MA 02138; (617) 492-9646; charlieskitchen.com; T: Harvard Square. Long a shot-and-a-beer bar for Harvard Square's blue-collar drinkers, Charlie's spiffed up for the young professionals by opening a terrific outdoor beer garden with space heaters to ease the chill when necessary. Besides the beer garden, Charlie's also has 3 bars distributed on two floors. The upstairs bar music tracks lean heavily toward classic punk (Pixies, Ramones, the Smiths) and the food is diner grub, which goes just fine with the beer. A cocktail at Charlie's Kitchen is a bottle of Mike's Hard Lemonade.

Deep Ellum, 477 Cambridge St., Allston, MA 02135; (617) 787-2337; deepellum-boston.com; T: Allston Street. If you consider beer to be one of the major food groups, then Deep Ellum is your kind of place to drink and eat. The taps spout 28 craft brews, including offerings from local favorites Pretty Things, Clown Shoes, and Idle Hands, and a fair number of Belgian and German brewers. The bar is a shotgun design, looking straight from gritty Cambridge Street out the back door to an urban patio. Food is pretty good, too, with the likes of duck confit hash or pork meatball *banh mi* for brunch, saffron risotto or a plate of house-made sausages (the "best wurst plate") in the evening. You can also get any of a dozen small-batch bourbons straight up, diluted, or on the rocks.

Drink, 348 Congress St., Waterfront, Boston, MA 02210; (617) 695-1806; drinkfortpoint.com; T: Court House/South Station. Getting a drink at Barbara Lynch's upscale lounge Drink is a little like getting a prescription from a doctor. There is no cocktail menu. There are no bottles on display. When you walk in, you'll get a menu of available food. If you want a libation, let the mixologists (there are no mere bartenders here) quiz you about your likes and dislikes, your mood, and your openness to new experiences. If you're lucky, you might even draw Misty Kalkofen, nominee for American Bartender of the Year in 2011, when Drink opened and won Best American Bar. Among her originals is the Sel de la Mar: cognac, manzanilla sherry, green Chartreuse, maraschino liqueur, and celery bitters—garnished, of course, with sea salt. This is cocktail culture at its best.

Druid Restaurant, 1357 Cambridge St., Inman Square, Cambridge, MA 02139; (617) 497-0965; druidpub.com. Like many good Irish pubs, it's hard to figure out what's best at the Druid: the music, the drink, or the food. The place serves the best fish and chips that we've eaten in Boston, and the line stretches down the block for Sunday brunch. Traditional Irish *seissúns* happen twice a week. In the final analysis, the best part is socializing with the crew that comes here to drink properly pumped Guinness from whistle-clean lines.

The Field Pub, 29 Prospect St., Central Square, Cambridge, MA 02139; (617) 354-7345; thefieldpub.com; T: Central Square. At one time The Field held the record for selling more Guinness on draft than any other bar in America. Then they added Murphy's, Bellhaven Scottish Ale, and Newcastle Brown Ale to the taps and lost their crown. No matter. The beauty of The Field is that it's a no-nonsense workingman's pub where it's assumed that there's craft behind even the best-selling major-market beers and that neither solid pub grub nor a pint should cost you a day's wages. You can also toss darts and shoot pool in the back room.

Five Horses Tavern, 400 Highland Ave., Davis Square, Somerville, MA 02144; (617) 764-1655; fivehorsestavern.com; T: Davis Square. With 121 whiskeys (not counting 5 moonshines), 36 rotating taps of craft beers, and roughly 80 more beers in can or bottle, it could take all night to narrow down your choices for a shot and a beer. (A bit over 14,000 by our count.) Five Horses is a pretty swank place—lots of black leather, stone tiles, fieldstone fireplace, dual-level seating areas—and serves some good bar fare, including 10-inch pizzas that are a steal if you order before late afternoon.

Game On!, 82 Lansdowne St., Fenway, Boston, MA 02215; (617) 351-7001; gameonboston.com; T: Kenmore. With 90 HD televisions and a sound system that can outroar an adrenalized crowd, Game On! has the sheer firepower to make it one of the best places in the city to watch a game. Any game. Because it's built into the walls of Fenway Park, fans tend to think of it as a baseball bar, but it also rocks on football Sunday (and Monday and Thursday), and all through the Stanley Cup. Food is a roundup of all the classic bar food.

Good Life, 28 Kingston St., Downtown, Boston, MA 02111; (617) 451-2622; goodlifebar.com; T: Downtown Crossing. Although an awful lot of people come here to dine on the French-Italian-American gastrogrub, plenty more stream in for late-night music (a lot of electronica), a sweet list of wines strong on American pinot noir, and martinis and cocktails with just enough but not too much attitude. If we can't get an Emo (Stoli Blue Berri, lemon, simple syrup, and a twist), just give us the Truth (Hendricks gin, St. Germain elderflower liqueur, and soda).

The Hawthorne, 500A Commonwealth Ave., Fenway, Boston, MA 02215; (617) 532-9150; thehawthornebar.com; T: Kenmore. With **Island Creek Oyster Bar** (see p. 101) on one side and **Eastern Standard** (see p. 98) on the other, the Hawthorne shifts the focus from fine food to fine cocktails. The actual cocktail menu is admirably restrained, but the staff can mix almost anything you've ever tasted and will happily do so. A grown-up bar for adults who can hold their liquor, the Hawthorne is a breath of fresh air in the beery nightlife of Kenmore Square.

Hong Kong Restaurant, 1238 Massachusetts Ave., Harvard Square, Cambridge, MA 02138; (617) 864-5311; hongkong harvard.com; T: Harvard Square. The Comedy Club on the third floor of this Harvard Square institution features young standup comics (except on Tuesday night, when magicians take the stage). You can get drinks with the shows, just as you can get drinks with the Chinese food in the first-floor restaurant. But if you just want to drink—think five straws in a huge scorpion bowl of assorted fruit juices and unnamed liquors—then the second-floor lounge is where you want to be. Most of the drinks are sweet enough to set your teeth on edge and alcoholic enough to have you on the floor before you know what hit you.

Jerry Remy's Sports Bar & Grill, 1 Boylston St., Fenway, Boston, MA 02215; (617) 236-7369; jerryremys.com; T: Hynes. The

Rem Dog has another one of these sport bars with gigantic televisions on the waterfront, but it makes more sense to slop some suds while watching the game within earshot of Fenway Park, where Remy used to turn the double play at second.

John Harvard's Brew House, 33 Dunster St., Harvard Square, Cambridge, MA 02138; (617) 868-3585; johnharvards.com; T: Harvard Square. As far as we know, cleric John Harvard never actually brewed a pint, just as he didn't found the university that now bears his name. But his moniker adds some cachet to one of Boston's first modern brewpubs. The franchise has since spread, but this original location still fashions some tasty craft brews available only on the premises.

Julep Bar, 200 High St., Downtown, Boston, MA 02109; (617) 858-4841; julepbar.com; T: Aquarium. Adjacent to **Blue, Inc.** restaurant (see p. 53), this suave upscale lounge shares Blue's inventive barmaster, Trish LeCount. At Julep, LeCount revives classic cocktails from the '40s and '50s, including an icy version of the bar's namesake. Here's a twist unheard of in the *Mad Men* days: You can reserve a table by text.

Last Hurrah, Omni Parker House Hotel, 60 School St., Downtown, Boston, MA 02108; omnihotels.com; T: State. Once the unofficial headquarters of Boston politics, the elegant bar of the Parker House Hotel has resurfaced in recent years as one of the great whisky (i.e., scotch) bars in Boston, and wins consistent applause for craft cocktails built by Frank Weber around bitters and herbal spirits. One of Weber's signature drinks is a version of the Manhattan named for the hotel's founder, Harvey Parker. It consists of Jameson's Irish whiskey, sweet vermouth, and Angostura bitters served in a martini glass with a maraschino cherry.

Lizzy's, 635 Cambridge St., East Cambridge, Cambridge, MA 02141; (617) 491-9616; T: Lechmere. Josh Velasquez and Lizzy Cannon took over this neighborhood bar in 2011, but the spot has roots that go back to 1933. "We're a bar with good food," explains Lizzy, "but we don't want to be pigeonholed as a gastropub." Josh prepares "finger food of the world," which includes Chinese steamed pork buns, black bean and cheese tamales, Jamaican beef patties, and even snails in puff pastry (escargots *en croute*). He will also build you a sandwich that requires both hands to hold. Lizzy will whip up a Death in the Afternoon (absinthe and Champagne) in a heartbeat. Ready to drink more local? Try her Maine Squeeze (bourbon, blueberry syrup, cinnamon).

Lolita Cocina & Tequila Bar, 271 Dartmouth St., Back Bay, Boston, MA 02116; (617) 369-5609; lolitaboston.com; T: Copley. This subterranean fantasy bar all decked out in whorehouse red and gold (they call it crimson and amber) is dedicated to putting a little spice in your life. The food is Mexican themed and the bar has nine versions of margaritas and three kinds of sangria by the glass or the pitcher. The beers are bottled (except the Tecate) and come with salt, a lime wedge, and Worcestershire and hot sauce on request. It's always party time at Lolita.

Lord Hobo, 92 Hampshire St., Inman Square, Cambridge, MA 02139; lordhobo.com; T: Central Square/Kendall Square. This oddly located bar is where the coders of Kendall Square and the hipsters of mid-Cambridge sit down to clink glasses over New American gastropub fare. Lord Hobo pulls 40 draft lines, mostly craft brews leavened with a few German lagers, Belgian farmhouse ales, and the occasional cask-conditioned English IPA. Craft cocktails abound, including the luminous Soylent Green (green Chartreuse, mint, cucumbers, lemon) and the Sloppy Possum (Fernet Branca, ginger, lemon). When you can nibble a baked raclette plate or hunker down over a mozzarella sandwich with eggplant caponata, there's no need to ever go home—except that they kick you out at closing. How fair is that?

Lucky's Lounge, 355 Congress St., Waterfront, Boston, MA 02210; (617) 357-5825; luckyslounge.com; T: Court House/South Station. With Rat Pack posters and photos on the walls, this basement-level bar really does conjure up smoky subterranean louche lounges of the '50s—minus the smoke. Indeed, you'll catch a lot of Sinatra on the sound system—or even Sinatra impersonators. The joint is very

THE ULTIMATE KEGGER

The all-volunteer organization known as the **Cask-conditioned Ale Support Campaign (CASC)** is a crafty group dedicated to promoting real ale in New England. Each year since the late 1990s, CASC has held the New England Real Ale eXhibition, which is really an excuse for beer lovers to get together and drink cask-conditioned ales, served either by gravity or hand pump. The festival takes place in the spring (March–April) for four days at changing venues. There are usually more than 100 firkins of ale and cider on hand—half from the British Isles, half from the US (mostly New England). For details, visit the website: nerax.org.

popular for Sunday brunch, even with kids in tow, when most diners sip mimosas and a live band plays. Later in the night, you can feel like Don Draper if you sit at the bar and sip an old-fashioned.

Meadhall, 4 Cambridge Center, Kendall Square, Cambridge, MA 02142; themeadhall.com; T: Kendall Square. Located in the heart of Kendall coding country (in the former Quantum Bookstore), Meadhall proves that obsession can extend beyond binary ones and zeros and into the binary interplay of malt and hops. The bar offers 110 beers on tap and 100 more in cans and bottles. There's food, too, which can range from nibbling bowls of olives to snacking bowls of fries to serious oven-roasted striped bass. After all, biological life-forms do not (quite) live by beer alone.

Noir, Charles Hotel, 1 Bennett St., Harvard Square, Cambridge, MA 02138; (617) 661-8010; noir-bar.com; T: Harvard Square. Sultry as a little black dress, Noir is the Charles Hotel's swank cocktail bar where a Periodista (Myers's dark rum, Cointreau, apricot brandy, lime) and a Negroni (Bombay dry gin, Campari, sweet vermouth, twist of orange) never go out of style. Mixologists will, of course, make anything your heart desires, or invent a drink, just for you.

Papagãyo, 283 Summer St., Waterfront, Boston, MA 02210; (617) 423-1000; papagayoboston.com; T: South Station. Both a Mexican restaurant and a tequila bar, Papagãyo impresses with its extensive selection of blanco, reposado, and *añejo* tequilas. For partying, you can also order the house margarita (Agavales tequila, orange liqueur, fresh lime, and agave nectar) by the pitcher. The bar also makes a mean jalapeño cucumber *caipirinha*.

Parlor Sports, 1 Beacon St., Inman Square, Somerville, MA 02143; (617) 576-0231; facebook.com/ParlorSports. American craft brews, shots of rye and bourbon, and standard cocktails help sports fans work up their enthusiasm for whatever is on the big screens. Parlor Sports is an adjunct to **Trina's Starlite Lounge** (see p. 406) next door, and shares the same kitchen, if not the same clientele. That means that sports fans can get good pub grub rustled up by Chef Suzi Maitland.

Playwright Restaurant & Bar, 658 E. Broadway, South Boston, Boston, MA 02127; (617) 269-2537; theplaywrightbar.com; T: Broadway. One of the first of a wave of Irish bars opened by real Irishmen, the Playwright found its place in Southie as a sports bar where the crowd is young, loud, and enthusiastic. Pub fare is good and even healthy (halibut with roasted corn, grilled chicken Marsala), while the popular weekend brunches sport various omelets, various Benedicts, and the option of a full Irish breakfast.

The Plough & Stars, 912 Massachusetts Ave., Central Square, Cambridge, MA 02139; (617) 576-0032; ploughandstars.com; T: Central Square. Sean O'Casey's play *The Plough and the Stars* was about the conflict of a man choosing between his wife and something bigger than both of them. Over the years we've known many a man in Cambridge to choose the Plough over domestic tranquility—and a few happy couples who go to drink and listen to music together. A grand Irish fatalism hangs over the Plough, and it's been the favored watering hole of many a fine poet and many a musician, including some who went on to fame and glory. Good pub fare is available all day, and good if loud music occurs most nights. In between, there's always Guinness.

The Publick House, 1658 Beacon St., Brookline, MA 02446; (617) 277-2880; eatgoodfooddrinkbetterbeer.com; T: Washington Square. The name of the website pretty much says it all. With one of the few kitchens in the city that cooks extensively with beer, Publick House offers artisanal versions of bar food, ranging from four versions of *moules-frites* (steamed in different beers and savories), an honest burger, the requisite local haddock fish and chips, and excellent cheese and charcuterie boards. If you walk up the ramp on the left as you enter, you will be in the Monk's Cell, a small bar where all the taps are reserved for Belgian beers. In all, you'll find 35 drafts—9 from Belgium, a few from Germany, Ireland, and Holland, and a slew of wonderful American craft brews.

Red Lantern, 39 Stanhope St., Back Bay, Boston, MA 02116; (617) 262-3900; redlanternboston.com; T: Back Bay Station. The retro craze for crab rangoon, pupu platters, and scorpion bowls snuck into this corner of Back Bay–by–South End with a flurry of red and gold decor and enough oversize Buddha statues to stock the offensive line of the Patriots. But apart from the über-kitsch, Red Lantern also has a tremendous list of sakes by the glass and some nicely crafted cocktails. The Rose Petal Saketini, for example, is a sweet martini of sorts, composed of vodka, St. Germain, sake, and rosewater.

River Gods, 125 River St., Central Square, Cambridge, MA 02139; (617) 576-1881; rivergodsonline.com; T: Central Square. Another Cambridge bar with Irish roots, River Gods has DJs spinning a range of roots, reggae, hip-hop, funk, and occasional Thai pop and Bollywood sounds. It's all a little tongue-in-cheek, just like the programs of local short films, the gargoyle fixture and granite angels, and the church-pew seating. Excellent food is available at dinner, with a complete second menu for vegetarians and vegans.

We enjoy the Hoegaarden white ale on tap, but you could also opt for classic cocktails, or (on a cold night) warm mulled port or a hot whiskey toddy.

RumBa, InterContinental Boston, 510 Atlantic Ave., Waterfront, Boston, MA 02210; (617) 747-1000; T: South Station. Rum was big in Boston back when the wharves now occupied by the InterContinental were engaged in the nefarious Triangle Trade. This rum-themed cocktail bar has all manner of white, brown, and fine aged rums by the shot and can whip up a mean mojito in minutes—blueberry, cucumber, or clementine. It's also a Champagne bar, with a half-dozen sparklers by the glass and two dozen more by the bottle.

Ryles Jazz Club, 212 Hampshire St., Inman Square, Cambridge, MA 02139; (617) 876-9330; rylesjazz.com. With jazz this hot, you need cool beer, and that's what Ryles delivers in 40 different choices. The downstairs concert room features both local players and national stars. The Sunday jazz brunch (with mimosas, please) is a Cambridge institution.

Saloon, 255 Elm St., Somerville, MA 02144; (617) 628-4444; saloondavis.com; T: Davis Square. We rather like bars that steer away from colorless spirits in favor of brown booze, authentic suds, and lots of dark wood and exposed brick walls. Buried beneath the bistro called **Foundry on Elm** (see p. 315), Saloon aspires to the romance of the Prohibition era—minus the gangsters and the raids by revenue men.

The Sevens Ale House, 77 Charles St., Beacon Hill, Boston, MA 02114; (617) 523-9074; T: Charles/MGH. Most people refer to this old-school Beacon Hill bar as "The Sevens," which causes untold frustration for hard-liquor drinkers lured here by friends. It's an ale house, or in a parlance insufficiently genteel for Beacon Hill, a beer bar. It's the kind of dark, quiet place where it's easy to imagine Robert Parker's detective Spenser enjoying a beer and pretending to mind his own business.

Shenannigans Irish Pub & Restaurant, 332 W. Broadway, South Boston, Boston, MA 02127; (617) 269-9509; shenannigans irishpubbostonma.com; T: Broadway. Name notwithstanding, Shenannigans is Southie's quintessential Irish-American bar. It's the kind of place that serves white chocolate martinis and melon mojitos, a Black Russian topped up with Guinness stout, and that survivor from the dark days of cocktaildom, the Harvey Wallbanger (vodka, orange juice, Galliano, an orange slice, and a cherry, for those too young to remember).

Storyville, 90 Exeter St., Back Bay, Boston, MA 02116; (617) 236-1134; storyvilleboston.com; T: Copley. This is a big space and really functions as two separate venues—a restaurant and lounge, and a dance club. The New Orleans red-light-district theme means too much deep red upholstery and faux mahogany woodwork, but the bar is surprisingly first rate. Best bets are sweet drinks, including a PKNY (Painkiller of New York) with Pusser's rum, and the Red Dress, a New Orleans–style raspberry gastrique with Champagne.

Sunset Grill & Tap, 130 Brighton Ave., Allston, MA 02134; allstonsfinest.com; T: Packard's Corner. A fellow could die of thirst before he makes up his mind. Sunset has 112 active taps and carries 380 more domestic and imported brews. Drink by the mug or by the flight, in case you're of a mind to compare products of different Boston or New York craft brewers, for example. Wild-yeast ales are a specialty, as are lambics and their close relatives, kriek, framboise, and grueze. "Club" membership is offered for patrons who drink their way through a certain number of microbrews or European beers—always served with food. Yeah, they sell food, too.

The Thirsty Scholar, 70 Beacon St., Somerville, MA 02143; (617) 497-2294; thirstyscholarpub.com. Mark Zuckerberg allegedly drank here during his Harvard days, or so the opening scene of *The Social Network* would have you believe. The bar had a brief flash of fame in national media when the movie came out, but after Facebook went public and was no longer cool, Thirsty Scholar reverted to a fine Irish pub with 22 beers on tap (including Guinness) and hardly a Harvard student in sight.

Trina's Starlite Lounge, 3 Beacon St., Inman Square, Somerville, MA 02143; (617) 576-0006; trinastarlitelounge.com. Chicken and waffles with hot pepper syrup won Trina's a spot in a *Bon Appetit* list of 10 best places to order fried chicken in America. It's not quite like being featured on *Slate,* but it helps with Trina's hipster cred. The motif is a 1954 America that was never real, but certainly had its Madison Avenue appeal. There are plenty of craft beers at Trina's, but somehow it's cooler to order a bucket of Miller High Life ponies. Hard-core malt fans swoon for the Clown Shoes.

21st Amendment, 150 Bowdoin St., Beacon Hill, Boston, MA 02108; (617) 227-7100; 21stboston.com; T: Park Street. After a long day of legislating, Massachusetts lawmakers need a place to go. Fortunately for them, the 21st Amendment is right across the street from the statehouse. It's not a flashy bar—more of a middle-of-the-road, reach-across-the-aisle kind of place. Local beer here means Sam Adams and Harpoon, but there are often bargain nights on Narragansett and Pabst tall boys—sometimes on the same night with cheap tacos or wings. Think of it as tax relief.

Wally's Jazz Club, 427 Massachusetts Ave., South End, Boston, MA 02118; (617) 424-1408; wallyscafe.com; T: Massachusetts Avenue. Since 1947 this is where Boston's up-and-coming jazz musicians have cut their teeth and honed their chops. There's live music every night and the bar menu is, shall we say, limited. Get a deal on beer on Blue Mondays. On jazz night, try scotch and soda—mud in your eye optional.

Watch City Brewing Company, 256 Moody St., Waltham, MA 02453; (781) 647-4000; watchcitybrew.com; T: Waltham (commuter rail). You might notice that some of Watch City's brews are on tap elsewhere, which is a tribute to one of the best of the brewpubs in greater Boston. The overall house style favors easy-drinking brews of a deeply golden hue, but seasonal efforts can range from the Sno'Blower Winter Wit (a 7 percent wheat beer made with a Chinese five-spice blend) to the Fenway Fungo Scottish Wee Light Ale (a light hitter indeed at 3.8 percent). Day-to-day drinking, though, is best with the flagship Shillelagh Irish Red Nitro Ale, carbonated with nitrogen for those tiny, creamy bubbles that make it a beer to chew.

Whiskey Priest, 150 Northern Ave., Waterfront, Boston, MA 02210; (617) 426-8111; whiskey-priest.com; T: World Trade Center. This Irish restaurant and bar hasn't evolved into a true Irish local yet because there are very few residences around it. But it's worth treating as a drinking destination for the excellent selection of whiskey (and whisky) from around the globe and for its great deck overlooking the harbor. Naturally, the best selections are Irish, Scotch, and American bourbon. Some creative pairing goes into whiskey flights, like the Aer Lingus (Connemara, Clontorf, and Kilbeggan) or the Whiskey Priests (John L. Sullivan, Michael Collins, John Powers).

White Horse Tavern, 116 Brighton Ave., Allston, MA 02134; (617) 254-6633; whitehorseboston.com; T: Packard's Corner. This neighborhood bar with a pair of 7-foot billiard tables and 15 high-def plasma TVs carefully treads the line between sports bar for grown-ups and game bar for college students. The dozen beers on tap invariably include local favorites (a couple of Harpoons, a few Sam Adams), Guinness, and some sort of fruit ale. By and large, the mixed drinks are very old-school and sweet, favoring the likes of the cosmopolitan, blueberry lemonade, Purple Haze, and a brown sugar old-fashioned.

Woody's L Street Tavern, 658 E. 8th St. #A, South Boston, Boston, MA 02127; (617) 268-4335; T: Broadway. The L Street Tavern is the stuff of legend, some of it fabricated by Hollywood. It gained celluloid fame as the setting for a rather funny scene in *Good Will Hunting* where Minnie Driver tells a smutty joke that still makes the barmen blush. For all the tourists who wander in, the tavern is still a classic Irish-American workingman's bar and one of the last vestiges of the old South Boston. The beer is cold, the TV is on, and the barman will make conversation or not—whichever you prefer.

Les Zygomates, 129 South St., Leather District, Boston, MA 02111; (617) 542-5108; winebar.com; T: South Station. This stylish wine bar–cum–bistro features a huge list of modest wines by the glass, which gives patrons the opportunity to design their own tasting flights. For those who want to go beyond having a couple of glasses at the bar, Les Zyg offers Tuesday-night wine tastings led by Wine Director Nicholas Daddona, sometimes coupled with cooking demonstrations by Chef-Owner Ian Just. Like the bistro itself, the sessions are relaxed and unpretentious, focusing on the simple pleasures of good food and wine. With 150 seats, no one can accuse Les Zyg of being just a wine bar. The bistro fare extends from a good raw bar to seared sea scallops, steak-frites, and Moroccan lamb tagine. There's also live jazz most evenings.

Culinary Instruction

Ever since the establishment of the Boston Cooking School in 1879, Boston has had a wonderful smorgasbord of instructional programs for cooks aspiring to culinary careers as well as home cooks looking to expand their knowledge, techniques, and tastes.

Schools

Boston Center for Adult Education, 122 Arlington St., Back Bay, Boston, MA 02116; (617) 267-4430; bcae.org; T: Arlington. Food and wine classes are so popular that the BCAE built state-of-the-art new kitchens several years ago. Chefs at local restaurants often teach classes and enjoy the top-notch facilities as much as the students. Offerings range from basic and advanced cooking techniques to explorations of world cuisines.

Boston University Programs in Food, Wine & the Arts, 808 Commonwealth Ave., Fenway, Boston, MA 02215; (617) 353-9852; bu.edu/foodandwine; T: Kenmore Square. Courses, classes, and one-off events for the general public range from lectures and seminars on food and drink themes to hands-on cooking to a series of restaurant dinners under the rubric of "Feasts of the World."

Cambridge Center for Adult Education, 42 Brattle St., Harvard Square, Cambridge, MA 02138; (617) 547-6789; ccae.org; T: Harvard Square. Realizing the significant social value of cooking classes, CCAE offers Friday-night wine-tasting classes as well as cooking classes that explore different cuisines from Jamaican-style jerk barbecue to Indian vegetarian dishes.

Cambridge School of Culinary Arts, 2020 Massachusetts Ave., Porter Square, Cambridge, MA 02140; (617) 354-2020; cambridge culinary.com; T: Porter Square. Primarily a professional school of the culinary arts, Cambridge Culinary also offers a wide range of recreational classes.

Create a Cook, 53 Winchester St., Newton, MA 02461; (617) 795-2223; createacook.com. Cooking is fun—that's the premise at Create a Cook, which offers one-time classes for business groups (culinary team building), birthday parties, and other special events. That's in addition to longer courses for kids and teens as well as adults. See p. 425 for Instructor Heather Wish's recipe for **Caramelized Shallot and Goat Cheese Pizza with Savory Chocolate Crust.**

Le Cordon Bleu, Cambridge, 215 1st St., Cambridge, MA 02142; (617) 553-1846; chefs.edu/boston; T: Kendall Square. Part of the nationwide chain of Cordon Bleu campuses, this private two-year school provides a thorough education in culinary technique and theory, combined with an externship as preparation for a professional culinary career. Some classes involve practical skills practice at the school's **Technique Restaurant** (see p. 275).

Newton Community Education, 457 Walnut St., Newton, MA 02460; (617) 559-6999; newtoncommunityed.org. The one-session classes at Newton Community Ed cover a wide range of subjects, from a basic class in making fruit pies to sessions on sharpening and maintaining cutlery to Indian vegetarian finger food.

Stir, 102 Waltham St., South End, Boston, MA 02118; (617) 423-STIR; stirboston.com; T: Back Bay. Master Chef Barbara Lynch's demonstration kitchen and cookbook library serves as an intimate venue for demonstrations of favorite restaurant dishes, "all about" classes on subjects such as mushrooms or shellfish, and a Friday-night "Chef's Table" four-course meal.

More Classes

ArtBar, Royal Sonesta Hotel, 40 Edwin Land Blvd., East Cambridge, Cambridge, MA 02142; (617) 806-4122; artbarcambridge.com; T: Lechmere/Museum of Science. This elegant little riverside bar excels at craft cocktails, and lets consumers in on the fun in once-per-month 45-minute classes.

The Boston Shaker, 69 Holland St., Davis Square, Somerville, MA 02144; (617) 718-2999; thebostonshaker.com; T: Davis Square. Learn the basics of making craft cocktails, working with bitters, and other mixology skills at this shop dedicated to the art of the cocktail (see p. 328).

Capone Foods, 14 Bow St., Union Square, Somerville, MA 02143; (617) 629-2296; caponefoods.com. Albert Capone is probably best known around Cambridge and Somerville for his terrific pastas sold at his shops (see pp. 285 and 329). He offers instruction on making pasta sauces as well as other Italian and Spanish treats. See Capone's recipe for **Al's Favorite Quick Tomato Sauce** on p. 428.

Chocolee Chocolates, 23 Dartmouth St., South End, Boston, MA 02118; (617) 236-0606; chocoleechocolates.com. There are few better ways to spend a Saturday morning or afternoon than learning how to make chocolate barks, truffles, and filled candies. Classes take place in the commercial kitchen adjacent to the **Chocolee** shop (see p. 152).

Dave's Fresh Pasta, 81 Holland St., Somerville, MA 02144; (617) 666-0656; davesfreshpasta.com; T: Davis Square. You could start slow with a class in sauce-making so that you could make your own pestos or tomato sauces to top Dave's fresh pastas (see p. 331).

Elephant Walk, 900 Beacon St., Fenway, Boston, MA 02215; (617) 247-1500, T: St. Mary Street and 2067 Massachusetts Ave., Porter Square, Cambridge, MA 02140; (617) 492-6900, T: Porter Square; elephantwalk.com. Founding Chef Longtiene "Nyep" de Monteiro leads a full-day shopping, cooking, and dining class. Most other hands-on classes run about three hours and reflect the restaurants' skill in executing the cuisines of both France and Cambodia.

Fairmont Copley Plaza Hotel, 138 St. James Ave., Back Bay, Boston, MA 02116; (617) 267-5300; fairmont.com/copleyplaza; T: Copley. The Celebrity Chef series of cooking classes and demonstrations runs for five to six weeks in January and February. Overnight packages and classes can be booked through **Boston Center for Adult Education** (see p. 410).

Flour Bakery + Cafe, 12 Farnsworth St., Waterfront, Boston, MA 02210; (617) 338-4333; flourbakery.com; T: Court House/South Station. Creating great pastry takes a lot of finesse and you can pick up some pointers at the demonstration-only classes held monthly in Flour's Fort Point Channel shop (see p. 83).

Four Seasons Hotel, 200 Boylston St., Back Bay, Boston, MA 02116; (617) 338-4400; fourseasons.com/boston; T: Boylston. Students both observe and get a chance to get their hands dirty in the monthly cooking classes in the hotel kitchen.

Gordon's Fine Wines & Liquors, 894 Main St., Waltham, MA 02451; (781) 893-1900; gordonswine.com. A 1,300-square-foot kitchen at this wine store (see p. 377) is the setting for afternoon and evening hands-on culinary instruction in subjects that might range from making mozzarella cheese at home to planning a dinner party to some of the fine points of, say, German cuisine or basic baking.

Oishii Boston, 1166 Washington St., South End, Boston, MA 02118; (617) 482-8868; oishiiboston.com; T: Back Bay Station. You can get insight into the artistry of making sushi in classes that are offered the second Sunday of every month at this fine restaurant (see p. 142).

Rialto, Charles Hotel, 1 Bennett St., Harvard Square, Cambridge, MA 02138; (617) 661-5050; rialto-restaurant.com; T: Harvard Square. Chef Jody Adams of **Rialto** (see p. 271) offers a limited number of classes that begin in the late morning with coffee and scones and feature instruction and demonstrations before concluding with a multi-course lunch with wine pairings.

Sophia's Greek Pantry, 265 Belmont St., Belmont, MA 02478; (617) 489-1371. Sophia Georgoulopoulos has been giving impromptu cooking advice in her food shop (see p. 355) for years, so it was only a matter of time before she opened a classroom in a new kitchen in the rear of the building.

Verrill Farm, 11 Wheeler Rd., Concord, MA 01742; verrillfarm. com. We can't think of a better place (see p. 356) to get new ideas for how to use the bounty of fresh produce from your home garden or from the farmers' market.

Food Festivals & Events

January

Boston Wine Expo, wine-expos.com/Wine/expo. Most of the events at this full week of wine tastings, seminars, and vintner dinners are held at the Seaport World Trade Center and Seaport Hotel.

Boston Wine Festival, bostonwinefestival.net. Chef Daniel Bruce of the Boston Harbor Hotel founded the Boston Wine Festival in 1989. It's now one of the longest-running and most ambitious wine and food pairing events in the country.

Death by Chocolate, judgechocolate.com. This annual event, held in Newton, encourages good-natured competition among chefs and caterers who vie to create the best cake, cookie, brownie, candy, and unique dessert.

Dorchester Restaurant Week. For the last 2 weeks of January, participating restaurants in Dorchester and adjoining Milton offer fixed-price dinner menus Sunday through Thursday.

Super Hunger Brunch, gbfb.org/super-hunger-brunch.php. More than 20 restaurants offer special brunch menus and donate proceeds to the Greater Boston Food Bank.

Taste of Eastie, ebmainstreets.com. Annual event features East Boston restaurants serving food from South and Central America, the Mediterranean, China, Middle East, Italy, and the US.

March

Restaurant Week Boston, restaurantweekboston.com. More than 200 restaurants in Boston and surrounding towns offer specially priced menus at lunch and dinner.

April

Boston Beer Summit, beersummit.com. For more than 20 years the summit has brought some of the world's best beers to Boston.

Share Our Strength's Taste of the Nation, strength.org/boston. This event benefits Share Our Strength, a national organization dedicated to ending childhood hunger.

Taste of Dorchester, mahahome.org/tasteofdorchester. Sample a wide range of cuisines from Italian to Jamaican, Indian to Vietnamese to support the Massachusetts Affordable Housing Alliance. Look also for pizza, ribs, and ice cream!

Taste of South Boston, tasteofsouthboston.com. To get a taste of the dining renaissance along the waterfront in South Boston, attend this event at the Seaport World Trade Center.

Waltham Food & Wine Festival, crmi.org. More than 30 restaurants participate in this tasting event in Waltham.

June

American Craft Beer Festival, beeradvocate.com/acbf. **Harpoon Brewery** (see p. 200) is a sponsor of the largest celebration of American beer on the East Coast.

A Taste of Allston, allstonvillage.com. This annual event holds true to its promise to deliver "flavors from around the world."

Jimmy Fund Scooper Bowl, jimmyfund.org. This three-day event on City Hall Plaza scoops up ice cream, sorbet, and frozen yogurt to benefit the Jimmy Fund's programs for cancer research and care.

St. Athanasius Greek Festival, saintathanasius.org. Food plays a major role in this three-day festival in early June at Saint Athanasius the Great Greek Orthodox Church in Arlington.

July

Bastille Day, harvardsquare.com. A waiters' race and a Franco-Moroccan dance party are highlights of this festival with French flair held on Holyoke Street in Harvard Square.

Boston Chowderfest, bostonharborfest.com. Chowderfest is one of the highlights of Boston Harborfest, a weeklong celebration leading up to Independence Day.

Festival Betances, iba-etc.org. This celebration of Latino culture includes such Puerto Rican specialties as yellow rice with beans, roasted pork shoulder, beef patties, and fried plantain.

August

Caribbean Carnival Parade & Festival, bostoncarnival.org. Franklin Park food vendors give partygoers their fill of such dishes as Jamaican jerk chicken, Trinidad-style roti or cou-cou, and flying fish from Barbados. There are also lots of curry dishes, fried plantains, and sweets of raisins or coconut rolled in flaky pastry.

Fisherman's Feast, fishermansfeast.com. Founded in 1910, the Fisherman's Feast is the oldest of the North End's religious festivals. Vendors sell Italian sausage subs, slices of pizza, pastries, cannoli, and much more. For a full list of summer feasts, see northend boston.com.

Restaurant Week Boston, restaurantweekboston.com. The economically-priced lunches and dinners at many Boston restaurants are so popular that Restaurant Week is held twice a year (see March, p. 417).

September

Urban Ag Fair, harvardsquare.com. Urban gardeners celebrate the harvest in this Harvard Square event that includes cooking demonstrations by local chefs, talks on gardening, and a spirited competition for biggest and best fruits and vegetables.

What the Fluff?, unionsquaremain.org. Marshmallow Fluff was first made in Somerville, but inventor Archibald Query sold the recipe to Lynn-based Durkee-Mower for $500 in 1920. Somerville stakes its claim with this quirky festival that features entertainment, a Fluff cooking contest, and a variety of Fluff-based foods such as whoopie pies, and Fluffernutters.

October

Boston Vegetarian Food Festival, bostonveg.org. The Boston Vegetarian Society sponsors this weekend event that is not dedicated solely to those who follow vegetarian or vegan diets. It's geared to anyone interested in adding healthy new foods to their diet. It's held at the Reggie Lewis Athletic Center.

Oktoberfest, harvardsquare.org. We usually associate Oktoberfest with Germany, but this annual event at Harvard Square reflects global diversity through food and entertainment.

December

Holiday Bake Sale, cambridgeculinary.com. The instructors and students at the Cambridge School of Culinary Arts bake all the goodies that are offered at this sale to benefit a culinary charity.

Recipes

We always find that re-creating recipes in our own kitchen helps us bring some of the memorable tastes of travel back home. The following recipes reflect some of the diverse flavors of the Boston area, and we are grateful to the chefs and suppliers who shared them with us. We have adapted the recipes for home kitchens and standardized their presentation. Any errors are our inadvertent introductions rather than the fault of our sources.

Caramelized Shallot and Goat Cheese Pizza with Savory Chocolate Crust

We imagine that students at Create a Cook are thrilled to learn the secret of making a richly flavored pizza dough by adding a little chocolate. For an extra pop of flavor, Chef and Instructor Heather Wish suggests adding a pinch of cayenne pepper.

Makes 2 (10-inch) thin-crust pizzas

Chocolate Crust

1 tablespoon active dry yeast

1 cup warm water

1 cup plus 1¾ cup all-purpose flour

3 ounces bittersweet chocolate, chopped

2 tablespoons olive oil

1¼ teaspoons salt

¼ to ½ teaspoon cayenne pepper (optional)

1 tablespoon cornmeal

Toppings

1 tablespoon butter

1 tablespoon olive oil

6 medium shallots, thinly sliced (about 2 cups)

Salt and pepper

2 tablespoons balsamic vinegar

8 ounces goat cheese

6 ounces gruyère cheese, shredded

2 teaspoons minced fresh thyme

2 teaspoons minced fresh rosemary

¼ cup sliced almonds

To make the dough:

In the bowl of a standing mixer fitted with a dough hook, sprinkle yeast over water. Stir in a cup of flour and let stand for 15–20 minutes.

Meanwhile, melt the chocolate and olive oil. Set aside. Once the yeast mixture is foamy, add the melted chocolate, then mix in the remaining flour, salt, and cayenne. Knead in mixer until dough forms a smooth ball, about 5 minutes.

Remove all the dough and knead on a lightly floured countertop until the dough is smooth and elastic. Lightly grease a large bowl with oil. Place dough in bowl and cover with plastic wrap. Let rise in a warm place for 1 hour or until doubled in size.

Set oven at 450°F.

Melt butter and oil together in a sauté pan over medium heat. Add sliced shallots and a pinch of salt. Cook, stirring occasionally, until shallots are softened and brown around the edges. Add balsamic vinegar and cook until reduced and syrupy. Turn off heat and season with additional salt and pepper.

Once dough has risen, divide in half, then roll or toss each section into a 10-inch round. Place each round on a baking sheet dusted with cornmeal.

Spread caramelized shallots over each round, leaving a ½-inch border. Crumble goat cheese and sprinkle shredded gruyère over shallots. Evenly sprinkle on herbs and almonds. Drizzle a little extra oil over the top of each pizza.

Bake until the cheese bubbles and the crust is crisp (10–12 minutes).

Adapted recipe courtesy of Chef and Instructor Heather Wish
of Create a Cook in Newton Highlands, MA (p. 411).

Insalata di Pasta Arrabbiata

Italian food expert Michele Topor cautions that it is essential to use firm, dry, fresh tomatoes that are not too watery. This room-temperature version of pasta arrabbiata is one of her favorite summer dishes. The name translates as "angry pasta," she says, due to the addition of the hot chile pepper.

Serves 6

- ½ cup basil leaves, torn into small pieces
- 1 sprig fresh rosemary, leaves stripped off and chopped
- ¼ cup mint leaves, chopped
- 1 tablespoon dried oregano
- 2 cloves garlic, minced
- ¼ cup capers, rinsed and drained
- ½ cup extra virgin olive oil
- 6 to 8 large ripe plum tomatoes, peeled, seeded, and chopped
- 1 teaspoon hot red pepper flakes, or 1 small fresh chile pepper, seeded and minced
- ¼ cup grated pecorino Romano cheese
- 1 pound penne pasta

Combine the basil, rosemary, mint, oregano, garlic, and capers in a small bowl. Pour on enough olive oil to cover generously. Combine the tomatoes, hot pepper, and cheese in a large serving bowl.

Cook the penne in boiling salted water until al dente. Drain the pasta, shaking the colander to cool it a bit, and transfer it to the serving bowl, mixing it with the tomato mixture. Add the herb mixture and toss again. Let stand for up to 4 hours. Taste before serving and add salt and olive oil if necessary, to taste. Serve at room temperature.

Adapted recipe courtesy of Michele Topor of Boston Food Tours (p. 42, Mangia! sidebar).

Al's Favorite Quick Tomato Sauce

Albert Capone of Capone Foods constantly develops new recipes in his home kitchen. He is particularly fond of this quick sauce (it takes only 15–20 minutes) because it highlights the wonderful flavor that can be achieved with a few good-quality ingredients. Don't forget to save the juice when you drain the tomatoes. Capone says that he usually returns it all to the pan after the tomatoes have reduced and concentrated their flavor. He like's Hunt's tomatoes best for this sauce.

Serves 4–5

1 (29-ounce) can whole
    tomatoes in juice
2 ounces peeled shallots, sliced
¼ cup extra virgin olive oil
4 cloves garlic, sliced thin
3 tablespoons Italian parsley,
    coarsely chopped

¼ cup Burgundy wine
Pinch of dried thyme
¼ teaspoon salt
¼ teaspoon ground black
    pepper

Chop tomatoes coarsely and drain in a bowl with strainer for about 10 minutes. Be sure to save the juice.

Place sauté pan over low to medium heat. While tomatoes drain, slice shallots and begin cooking them in the preheated pan with the oil. Extra virgin olive oil is not generally used for frying, so be sure to cook the shallots gently.

When shallots are translucent (4–5 minutes), add garlic and parsley, turn heat to highest setting, and immediately add drained tomatoes. Stir and scrape bottom of pan frequently and cook at highest temperature to reduce for about 6–7 minutes.

Add wine to sauce and scrape pan with a wooden spoon. Let cook for another minute or two; add enough tomato juice to achieve the consistency you like and cook for 2–3 more minutes. Rub some good-quality thyme in the palm of your hand and add to sauce. Add salt and pepper to taste.

Cook pasta according to directions, drain, and place in a heated bowl. Add sauce and a generous amount of Parmigiana Reggiano or Romano. Pass more cheese at the table.

Refrigerate any unused sauce. It will taste even better the next day!

Adapted recipe courtesy of Albert Capone of Capone Foods in Somerville, MA (p. 329).

Red Lentil Soup (Mercimek Corbasi)

This soup is one of the most popular dishes on the lavish lunchtime buffet tables at Cafe de Boston in the Financial District. We substituted chicken stock for water in the original recipe to give extra flavor and nutrition, and added the Turkish Aleppo pepper because the heat nicely complements the savory lentils and the bright flavor of the mint.

Serves 4 as a main dish

2 quarts chicken stock,
    preferably homemade
1 pound red lentils
½ cup olive oil
½ cup flour

½ cup tomato paste
5 teaspoons dried mint
½ teaspoon Aleppo pepper
salt to taste

In a large pot, bring chicken stock to a boil. Add lentils and bring back to boil. Reduce to simmer and cook covered for about 20 minutes, or until lentils are soft.

Add olive oil to a separate pan. Stir in flour until well mixed. Stirring constantly, cook over medium heat until the raw flour taste is gone and mixture begins to brown. Add tomato paste and stir well until completely blended. Add dried mint and Aleppo pepper and stir.

Add olive oil mixture to lentils, stirring until blended. Heat combined mixture, stirring constantly. If necessary, thin with water. Add salt to taste and serve.

Adapted recipe courtesy of Chef Sezar Yavuz of Cafe de Boston, Boston, MA (p. 55).

Green Bean and Summer Squash Ratatouille with Couscous

Harvest Co-op Market offers produce from many local farms and develops recipes such as this one to celebrate the harvest.

Serves 4

- 1¼ cups vegetable or chicken stock or canned vegetable or chicken broth
- 1 cup couscous
- 1 tablespoon olive oil
- ½ pound green beans, trimmed and cut into ½-inch pieces
- 2 medium zucchini, halved lengthwise and sliced thin
- 1 small yellow pepper, seeded and sliced thin
- ½ small red onion, sliced thin
- 3 medium plum tomatoes, chopped coarse
- 1 (17-ounce) can chickpeas, drained and rinsed
- 1½ tablespoons balsamic vinegar
- Salt and freshly ground black pepper to taste
- Basil leaves, slivered

Bring chicken stock to boil; pour over couscous in medium bowl. Cover and let sit until stock is absorbed, about 10 minutes.

Meanwhile, heat olive oil in skillet, add green beans, and sauté for 3 minutes. Add zucchini, pepper, and onion; sauté until tender, about 5 minutes. Add tomatoes and chickpeas and heat through.

Off heat, season with balsamic vinegar, salt, and pepper. To serve, mound vegetables on couscous on dinner plates. Garnish with basil.

Adapted recipe courtesy of Harvest Co-op Market in Cambridge, MA (p. 292).

Uncle John's Lobster Thermidor

Cooked lobster meat is available fresh from most fishmongers and frozen in most grocery stores.

Serves 8

8 tablespoons butter
½ pound sliced mushrooms
3 tablespoons flour
2 cups heavy cream or milk
¼ cup dry sherry

4 cups cooked lobster meat
Salt
⅓ cup freshly grated Parmesan cheese

Preheat oven to 450°F. Butter a shallow baking dish.

Melt 5 tablespoons of the butter in a saucepan. Add the mushrooms and cook until they are softened. Remove and set aside. Melt the remaining 3 tablespoons of butter, stir in flour, and cook until smooth and blended. Slowly stir in the cream or milk and cook over low heat, stirring until the sauce is smooth and thickened. Add the sherry and cook 1 minute more. Remove from heat and add the lobster and reserved mushrooms. Add salt to taste.

Spoon into the baking dish, sprinkle with cheese, and bake about 10 minutes until the cheese is melted and lightly browned.

Serve over rice or puff pastry with peas on the side.

Adapted recipe courtesy of John Hook of James Hook + Co., Boston, MA (p. 85).

Beer-Braised Lamb Shoulder

This is a great recipe to impress a large party. But Chef Nuno Alves of Tavolo says that it can be halved if you're serving a smaller group. He likes to use black-hops beer from Blue Hills Brewery in Canton, Massachusetts, because the bite of the hops nicely complements the flavor of the lamb.

Serves 12–14

2 fresh lamb shoulders, boned by a butcher

Kitchen twine to secure lamb

Salt and pepper to taste

3 tablespoons canola oil

6 onions, large dice

4 carrots, peeled, large dice

4 stalks celery, large dice

1 head garlic, peeled and smashed

1 tablespoon tomato paste

2 cups canned San Marzano tomatoes, undrained

48 ounces black-hops beer

2 quarts chicken stock

5 bay leaves

1 tablespoon whole juniper berries

1 tablespoon whole pink peppercorns

½ bunch fresh mint

Handful of parsley stems

Remove excess silver skin and fat from shoulders with a sharp knife. Lay shoulders flat and season with salt and pepper. Tie shoulders together with kitchen twine to form one large bundle.

On top of the stove, heat canola oil in large roasting pan and sear the shoulder in oil until browned on all sides, then set aside to rest. Reserve any remaining fat.

In a stockpot, cook the onions, carrots, celery, and garlic in the fat reserved from searing the shoulder until vegetables have caramelized. Add the tomato paste and cook for 5 minutes. Add the canned tomatoes with their juices and the beer, and allow to boil on medium-high heat until liquid is reduced by half.

Add the chicken stock, bay leaves, juniper berries, peppercorns, mint, and parsley. Simmer uncovered until liquid is again reduced by half. Pour resulting liquid over the lamb in roasting pan. It should reach about halfway up sides of pan. Set oven at 300°F. Cover pan with foil and braise meat and liquid in the oven for 3 to 4 hours. Meat should be fork tender.

Remove lamb shoulder to a serving platter, strain the pan juices over the top, and allow to cool slightly before carving.

Adapted recipe courtesy of Nuno Alves, chef de cuisine at Tavolo in Dorchester, MA (p. 194).

Grilled Beef with
Asian Sesame Dressing

This dressing gets its heat by using a small amount of Thai chile sauce (sriracha) or the Indonesian chile sauce sambal oelek, made by grinding hot chile peppers with salt and lime in a basalt mortar and pestle. Both are available in jars from Asian markets or at the Meat House.

Serves 4–6

- 1 teaspoon sriracha or sambal oelek
- 2 garlic cloves
- 2 tablespoons unseasoned rice vinegar
- 1 tablespoon soy sauce
- 1½ teaspoons sugar
- 1 teaspoon Asian sesame oil
- ¼ cup vegetable oil
- 6 large scallions, white and green parts

- 1 pound flank steak, sliced on the bias
- Salt and freshly ground pepper
- 1½ cups (7 ounces) shelled edamame, thawed
- 4 large, thinly sliced radishes
- 1 bunch baby arugula
- Black and white sesame seeds for garnish

Set grill to medium-high. In a blender, combine sriracha (or sambal oelek), garlic, vinegar, soy sauce, sugar, and sesame oil. Process until smooth. Blend in the vegetable oil until incorporated.

Brush the scallions and steak with 2 teaspoons of mixture and season with salt and pepper to taste. Grill over medium-high heat, turning occasionally, about 5 minutes for the scallions and 8–10 minutes for medium rare steak.

Let the steak rest for 5 minutes, then slice. Cut the scallions into ½-inch pieces and transfer into a bowl. Add the edamame, radishes, baby arugula, and about 5 tablespoons of the dressing; toss to coat.

Mound the salad on plates and place the sliced steak on the side. Drizzle any remaining dressing over the steak. Sprinkle with black and white sesame seeds.

Adapted recipe courtesy The Meat House, Arlington, MA (p. 334).

Chocolate Croissant Bread Pudding

This rich bread pudding is one of the most popular dishes at the Langham Boston Hotel's chocolate buffet. Executive Pastry Chef Jed Hackney likes to use Valrhona Manjari chocolate, which has 64 percent cocoa butter and chocolate liquor. Our recipe tester asked the obvious question about this dish: How do you get day-old croissants? If you need to, buy them fresh, tear into pieces, and dry them out in a 250°F oven for an hour.

Serves 6

- 6 large croissants, preferably day old
- 1 pint heavy cream
- 1 pint whole milk
- 6 ounces sugar
- 4 ounces egg yolks
- 16 ounces 60 percent or higher dark chocolate, chopped
- 1 teaspoon vanilla extract

Start by cutting croissants into 1-inch pieces. If fresh, leave on counter to dry for several hours.

In a heavy-bottomed pot bring cream, milk, and sugar to a scald. Temper carefully into egg yolks by adding a tiny bit at first to raise the temperature of the yolks and gradually add more as you proceed.

After dairy and eggs are combined, pour over chopped dark chocolate. Stir to combine as the chocolate melts. Once thoroughly mixed, add the vanilla extract. Mix croissants and chocolate mixture in a large mixing bowl. Allow to soak for at least 45 minutes. If mixture seems dry, you may add additional milk to moisten.

While mixture is soaking, heat oven to 300°F. Once mixture is ready, pour into greased 9 x 9-inch casserole or other ceramic dish. Place dish on a deep jelly roll pan or roasting pan and place in oven on middle rack. Pour hot water to a depth of approximately ½ inch into the bottom pan. This helps insulate the pudding and prevent it from overbaking.

Bake until the pudding has set firm, 50–60 minutes. Be very careful removing the pan from the oven, as the water will be very hot.

Adapted recipe courtesy of Executive Pastry Chef Jed Hackney of
the Langham Boston Hotel's Cafe Fleuri (p. 56).

Nanny Sheila's Carrot Cake

Pastry Chef Clare Garland makes a beautiful version of this classic cake. It's one of the most requested items on the dessert menu at Ashmont Grill.

Serves 12–16

4 large eggs
2 cups light brown sugar
1½ cups canola oil
2 cups all-purpose flour
2 teaspoons baking soda
2 teaspoons cinnamon

1 teaspoon salt
3 cups grated carrots
1 cup golden raisins
1 cup shredded, sweetened coconut
1 cup chopped fresh pineapple

Preheat oven to 350°F. Grease 3 (9-inch) cake pans, then line them with parchment paper.

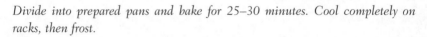

Beat together the eggs, brown sugar, and canola oil until smooth and uniform. In a separate bowl, sift together the flour, baking soda, cinnamon, and salt. Stir dry ingredients into the wet. Next add the carrots, raisins, coconut, and pineapple and stir to combine.

Divide into prepared pans and bake for 25–30 minutes. Cool completely on racks, then frost.

Cream Cheese Frosting

6 ounces unsalted butter, softened slightly

12 ounces cream cheese

2 teaspoons vanilla extract

24 ounces confectioners' sugar

Cream the butter with an egg beater until fluffy, then add the cream cheese and combine both until smooth. Add the vanilla and the sugar and beat again. Makes enough to frost all three layers.

Adapted recipe courtesy Pastry Chef Clare Garland
of Ashmont Grill, Dorchester, MA (p. 188).

Molten Spiced Taza Chocolate Cake

Taza Chocolate of Somerville makes its semisweet baking squares using 70 percent dark stone-ground chocolate. While there is nothing quite like it on the market, you can substitute a very high-grade European bittersweet chocolate (such as Valrhona or Callebaut).

Serves 4

- **4 ounces Taza Chocolate semisweet baking squares**
- **½ cup (1 stick) butter**
- **1 tablespoon Cabernet Sauvignon or other red wine**
- **1 teaspoon vanilla extract**
- **1 cup confectioners' sugar**
- **2 eggs**
- **1 egg yolk**
- **6 tablespoons flour**
- **¼ teaspoon cinnamon**
- **¼ teaspoon ground ginger**

Butter 4 (6-ounce) cups or souffle dishes. Place on a baking sheet.

Set oven at 425°F.

Heat chocolate and butter in a double boiler until butter is melted. Remove from heat and whisk until chocolate is completely melted. Stir in wine, vanilla, and sugar until blended. Whisk in eggs and yolk. Stir in remaining ingredients. Spoon evenly into prepared dishes.

Bake in a preheated oven for 15 minutes or until sides are firm but centers are soft. Let stand 1 minute. Loosen edges with knife. Invert onto serving plates. Sprinkle with confectioners' sugar if desired.

Adapted recipe courtesy of Taza Chocolate, Somerville, MA (p. 329 Theobroma sidebar).

Appendices

Appendix A:
For Further Reading

Bistro Cooking at Home, Gordon Hamersley with Joanne McAllister Smart, 2003.

The Boston Chef's Table, Clara Silverstein, Globe Pequot Press, 2008.

Cooking in Everyday English: The ABCs of Great Flavor at Home, Todd English, 2011.

The Elephant Walk Cookbook, Longteine de Monteiro, 1998.

Flour: Spectacular Recipes from Boston's Flour Bakery + Cafe, Joanne Chang with Christie Matheson, 2010.

Fresh & Honest: Food from the Farms of New England and the Kitchen of Henrietta's Table, Peter Davis with Alexandra Hall, 2008.

Grill It!, Chris Schlesinger and John "Doc" Willoughby, 2010.

In the Hands of a Chef, Jody Adams and Ken Rivard, 2002.

It's About Time: Great Recipes for Everyday Life, Michael Schlow, 2005.

The New Boston Globe Cookbook, Sheryl Julian, Globe Pequot Press, 2009.

The New Legal Sea Foods Cookbook, Roger Berkowitz and Jane Doerfer, 2003.

The North End Italian Cookbook, Marguerite Dimino Buonopane, Globe Pequot Press, 2004.

Rosie's Bakery All-Butter, Cream-Filled, Sugar-Packed Baking Book, Judy Rosenberg, 2011.

Shucked: Life on a New England Oyster Farm, Erin Byers Murray, 2011.

Simply Ming One-Pot Meals: Quick, Healthy and Affordable Recipes, Ming Tsai, 2010.

Spice: Flavors of the Eastern Mediterranean, Ana Sortun, 2006.

Stir: Mixing It Up in the Italian Tradition, Barbara Lynch, 2009.

Sultan's Kitchen: A Turkish Cookbook, Ozcan Ozan, 1998.

The Summer Shack Cookbook: The Complete Guide to Shore Food, Jasper White, 2011.

Wicked Good Barbecue, Andy Husbands and Chris Hart with Andrea Pyenson, 2012.

Wild Flavors: One Chef's Transformative Year Cooking from Eva's Farm, Didi Emmons, 2011.

Wine Mondays: Simple Wine Pairings and Seasonal Menus, Frank McClelland and Christie Matheson, 2008.

Appendix B: Dishes, Specialties & Specialty Food

Bakery/Bakery Cafe

Au Bon Pain, Cambridge, 283

Bao Bao Bakery & Cafe, Chinatown, 151

Big Sky Bakery & Cafe, Watertown, 373

The Biscuit, Somerville, 327

Bloc 11 Cafe, Somerville, 327

Blue Tierra Chocolate Cafe, South Boston, 199

A. Bova & Sons Modern Bakery, North End, 36

Bread & Chocolate Bakery Cafe, Newton Highlands, Newtonville, 373

Cafe Vanille, Beacon Hill, 82

Cake, Lexington, 346

Cakes, Arlington, 328

Canto 6 Bakery & Cafe, Jamaica Plain, 181

Clear Flour Bread, Brookline, 223

Concord Teacakes, Concord, 348

Danish Pastry House, Watertown, 374

Darwin's Ltd., Cambridge, 289

Finale Desserterie & Bakery, Cambridge, 252; Back Bay, 100

Flour Bakery + Cafe, Cambridge, 253; South End, 153; Waterfront, 83

Glutenus Minimus, Belmont, 350

Greenhills Irish Bakery, Dorchester, 199

Hafun Cafe, Roxbury, 155

Haley House Bakery Cafe, Roxbury, 156

Hing Shing Pastry, Chinatown, 157

hi-rise, Cambridge, 292

Iggy's Bread of the World, Cambridge, 293

International Natural Bakery, Watertown, 378

Isabelle's Curly Cakes, Beacon Hill, 85

Japonaise Bakery, Brookline, 225

Japonaise Bakery & Cafe, Cambridge, 282; Fenway, 120

Joseph's Italian Bakery, South Boston, 201

Katz Bagel Bakery, Chelsea, 39

Keltic Krust, West Newton, 379

Kickass Cupcakes, Somerville, 332

Kupel's Bakery, Brookline, 225

Lakota Bakery, Arlington, 333

Lyndell's Bakery, Cambridge, 294; Somerville, 333

Macaron Sweeterie, Lexington, 351

Main Streets Market and Cafe, Concord, 343

Maria's Pastry Shop, North End, 40

Mike's Pastry, North End, 40

Modern Pastry, North End, 41

Nashoba Brook Bakery, West Concord, 352

Panificio Bistro & Bakery, Beacon Hill, 86

A. Parziale's Bakery, North End, 43

Petsi Pies, Cambridge, 298; Somerville, 335

Quebrada Baking Co., Arlington, 335; Wellesley, 382

Rosenfeld's Bagels, Newton, 382

Rosie's Bakery, Cambridge, 298

Sherman Cafe, Somerville, 336

Sip Cafe, Downtown, 84

Sofra Bakery and Cafe, Cambridge, 300

Sorelle Bakery & Cafe, Waterfront, 87

South End Buttery, South End, 160

Sweet Thyme Bakery, Lexington, 356

Sweet Tooth Boston, South Boston, 202

Tatte Fine Cookies & Cakes,
  Brooklilne, 227
Thinking Cup, Downtown, 87
3 Little Figs, Somerville, 337
Twin Donuts, Allston, 228
Ula, Jamaica Plain, 184
Verna's Coffee and Donut Shop,
  Cambridge, 304
Vicki Lee's, Belmont, 357
When Pigs Fly, Brookline, 228;
  Jamaica Plain, 185;
  Somerville, 337
Wholy Grain, South End, 163
Yi Soon Bakery, Allston, 229
Zinneken's, Cambridge, 304

Breakfast/Brunch

Alta Strada Restaurant, Pizzeria &
  Market, Wellesley, 362
Amrheins, South Boston, 196
Angela's Cafe, East Boston, 17
Area 4, Cambridge, 235
Audubon Circle, Fenway, 92
Beacon Hill Bistro, Beacon Hill, 51
Beehive, South End, 128
The Blue Room, Cambridge, 238
Brasserie Jo, Back Bay, 93
Bravo, Fenway, 102
Bristol Lounge, Back Bay, 94
Centre Street Cafe, Jamaica
  Plain, 170
Charlie's Sandwich Shoppe, South
  End, 129
Chau Chow City, Chinatown, 130
Clover HSQ, Cambridge, 243
Clover HUB, Cambridge, 243
Cognac Bistro, Brookline, 207
Coppa, South End, 131
Darryl's Corner Bar & Kitchen,
  Roxbury, 131
Darwin's Ltd., Cambridge, 289
Deep Ellum, Allston, 392
Deluxe Town Diner, Watertown, 366
Druid Restaurant, Cambridge, 393
East by Northeast, Cambridge, 248
East Coast Grill, Cambridge, 249
Eastern Standard, Fenway, 98
Elephant Walk, Cambridge, 250;
  Fenway, 99; Waltham, 367
The Fireplace, Brookline, 209
Flora, Arlington, 314
Flour Bakery + Cafe, Cambridge,
  253; South End, 153;
  Waterfront, 83

Fóumami Asian Sandwich Bar, Downtown, 83

Grafton Street Pub & Grille, Cambridge, 256

Henrietta's Table, Cambridge, 258

The Hungry I, Beacon Hill, 57

Inna's Kitchen, Newton, 369

Kelly's Diner, Somerville, 325

Kinsale Irish Pub & Restaurant, Downtown, 58

Lucky's Lounge, Waterfront, 398

Main Streets Market and Cafe, Concord, 343

Masa Restaurant, South End, 138

McKenna's Cafe, Dorchester, 192

Met Back Bay, Back Bay, 105

Mike & Patty's, Back Bay, 121

Mooo . . . , Beacon Hill, 63

Olé Mexican Grill, Cambridge, 267

Panificio Bistro & Bakery, Beacon Hill, 86

Paramount, Beacon Hill, 65; South Boston, 192

Playwright Restaurant & Bar, South Boston, 401

The Regal Beagle, Brookline, 214

Rosebud Diner, Somerville, 325

Ryles Jazz Club, Cambridge, 403

S&S Restaurant, Cambridge, 271

75 Chestnut, Beacon Hill, 69

Sonsie, Back Bay, 110

Sorella's, Jamaica Plain, 176

Stella, South End, 147

Stephanie's on Newbury, Back Bay, 111

Steve's Kitchen, Allston, 215

Tico, Back Bay, 112

Tremont 647, South End, 149

@Union Breakfast Cafe, Allston, 217

Upstairs on the Square, Cambridge, 278

Veggie Galaxy, Cambridge, 279

Vicki Lee's, Belmont, 357

Warren Tavern, Charlestown, 35

Washington Square Tavern, Brookline, 217

Winsor Dim Sum Cafe, Chinatown, 150

Zaftig's Delicatessen, Brookline, 218

Z Rant, Cambridge, 281

Butcher

The Butcherie, Brookline, 223

Casa de Carnes Solução Latin Meat
Market, Somerville, 330
Haymarket International Food,
Downtown, 84
T. F. Kinnealey, Wellesley, 379
Mayflower Poultry Company,
Cambridge, 295
McKinnon's Meat Market,
Somerville, 334
The Meat House, Arlington, 334
Savenor's, Beacon Hill, 86;
Cambridge, 299
Sulmona Meat Market, North
End, 45

Cheesemonger
The Cheese Shop, Concord, 247
The Cheese Shop, North End, 38
Formaggio Kitchen,
Cambridge, 291
South End Formaggio, South
End, 161
Wasik's, the Cheese Shop,
Wellesley, 384
Wine & Cheese Cask,
Somerville, 337

Chocolatier
Beacon Hill Chocolates, Beacon
Hill, 79
Blue Tierra Chocolate Cafe, South
Boston, 199
L. A. Burdick Chocolate Shop &
Cafe, Cambridge, 284
Chocolee Chocolates, South
End, 152
Hotel Chocolat, Back Bay, 120
Serenade Chocolatier,
Brookline, 227
Taza Chocolate, Somerville, 329

Coffee Shop
Algiers Coffee House,
Cambridge, 233
Barismo, Arlington, 326
Barrington Coffee, Waterfront, 79
Blue State Coffee, Fenway, 118
Cafe Pamplona, Cambridge, 240
Caffè Delo Sport, North End, 36
Caffè Paradiso, North End, 37
Caffè Vittoria, North End, 37
Diesel Cafe, Somerville, 331
George Howell Coffee,
Newtonville, 377

Render Coffee, South End, 159
Ride Studio Cafe, Lexington, 353
1369 Coffee House,
    Cambridge, 301
Zume's Coffee House,
    Charlestown, 46

Dining Cars
Deluxe Town Diner, Watertown, 366
Kelly's Diner, Somerville, 325
Rosebud Diner, Somerville, 325
South Street Diner, Leather
    District, 146

Farmstand
Allandale Farm, Brookline, 219
Hutchins Farm, Concord, 351
Siena Farms, South End, 160
Verrill Farm, Concord, 356
Wilson Farm, Lexington, 358

Fishmonger
Captain Marden's Seafoods,
    Wellesley, 374
Court House Seafood Fish Market,
    Cambridge, 243
The Fishmonger, Cambridge, 290

James Hook + Co., Waterfront, 85
Morse Fish Company, South
    End, 158
New Deal Fish Market,
    Cambridge, 297
North End Fish–Mercato del Mare,
    North End, 42
Sakanaya Japanese Fish Market,
    Allston, 226
Wulf's Fish Market, Brookline, 228
Yankee Lobster Fish Market,
    Waterfront, 88

Grocery
American Provisions, South
    Boston, 197
Arax Market, Watertown, 376
Baltic European Deli, South
    Boston, 198
Baza Market, Newton Upper
    Falls, 372
Berezka International Food Store,
    Allston, 220
BiNA Alimentari, Downtown, 80
BMS Paper, Jamaica Plain, 180
Capone Foods, Cambridge, 285;
    Somerville, 329

Cardullo's Gourmet Shoppe, Cambridge, 286

Christina's Spice & Specialty Foods, Cambridge, 288

City Feed and Supply, Jamaica Plain, 182

C-Mart Supermarket, Chinatown, 153

Dave's Fresh Pasta, Somerville, 331

Debra's Natural Gourmet, West Concord, 349

DeLuca's Market, Back Bay, 119

DePasquale's Sausage Co., Newton, 375

Eastern Lamejun Bakers, Belmont, 350

Foodie's Urban Market, South End, 155

Formaggio Kitchen, Cambridge, 291

Hamdi Halal Market & Fresh Produce, Roxbury, 156

Harvest Co-Op, Cambridge, 292; Jamaica Plain, 182

Hong Kong Supermarket, Allston, 224

La Internacional Foods, Somerville, 331

Kam Man Farmers Market, Dorchester, 201

La Chapincita, Waltham, 380

Las Ventas, South End, 157

Lotte Market, Cambridge, 294

Market in the Square, Cambridge, 295

Massis Bakery, Watertown, 376

Ming's Supermarket, South End, 158

Miso Market, Cambridge, 296

Monica's Mercato, North End, 41

Montrose Spa, Cambridge, 296

J. Pace & Son, North End, 43

Pemberton Farms & Garden Center, Cambridge, 297

Polcari's Coffee, North End, 43

Reliable Market, Somerville, 336

Salumeria Italiana, North End, 45

Savenor's, Beacon Hill, 86; Cambridge, 299

Sevan's Bakery, Watertown, 376

Shalimar Gourmet Foods & Spices, Cambridge, 300

Shaw's, Back Bay, 122

Sophia's Greek Pantry, Belmont, 354

The Spirited Gourmet, Belmont, 355
Syrian Grocery Importing Co.,
    South End, 162
Tropical Foods, Roxbury, 163
Tutto Italiano, Wellesley, 383
Waltham India Market,
    Waltham, 384

Housewares
Abodeon, Cambridge, 283
BMS Paper, Jamaica Plain, 180
The Boston Shaker, Somerville, 328
China Fair, Cambridge, 287;
    Newton, 374
The Concord Shop, Concord, 347
KitchenWares by Blackstones, Back
    Bay, 121
Kitchenwitch, Jamaica Plain, 183
Linens on the Hill, Beacon Hill, 86
Salem True Value Hardware Store,
    North End, 44
Simon Pearce, Back Bay, 122
Stoddard's, Newton, 383

Ice Cream/Yogurt
Berry Line, Cambridge, 284;
    Fenway, 118

Cabot's Ice Cream & Restaurant,
    Newtonville, 366
Christina's Homemade Ice Cream,
    Cambridge, 287
GiGi Gelateria, North End, 39
J. P. Licks, Cambridge, 294;
    Jamaica Plain, 183; Newton,
    379; Somerville, 332
Lizzy's Homemade Ice Cream,
    Waltham, 380
Rancatore's, Belmont,
    Lexington, 352
Reasons to Be Cheerful, West
    Concord, 353
Toscanini's, Cambridge, 303

Sandwich Shop
Alex's Chimis, Jamaica Plain, 180
Al's State Street Cafe,
    Downtown, 78
Cutty's, Brookline, 223
Fóumami Asian Sandwich Bar,
    Downtown, 83
Lee's Place Burgers, Newton, 380
Liberty Bell, South Boston, 202
Michael's Deli, Brookline, 226
Mike & Patty's, Back Bay, 121

New Saigon Sandwich Banh Mi,
Chinatown, 156
J. Pace & Son, North End, 43
South End Pita, South End, 161
Tostado Sandwich Bar, Jamaica
Plain, 184
Waltham Fresh Fish & Prime,
Waltham, 384

Specialty Shop
Boston Olive Oil Co., Back
Bay, 119
DePasquale's Homemade Pasta
Shoppe, North End, 38
Fastachi, Watertown, 375
Follow the Honey, Cambridge, 291
Gustare Oils & Vinegars,
Wellesley, 378
New England Mobile Book Fair,
Newton Highlands, 381
Penzey's, Arlington, 335
Samira's Homemade, Belmont, 354

Tearoom
Bond Restaurant/Lounge,
Downtown, 54
Bristol Lounge, Back Bay, 94

Courtyard Restaurant, Back
Bay, 95
Dado Tea, Cambridge, 289
L'Espalier, Back Bay, 103
Taj Boston, Back Bay, 116
Tealuxe, Cambridge, 302

Wine, Beer & Spirits
Bacco's Wine & Cheese, Back
Bay, 118
Ball Square Fine Wines & Liquors,
Somerville, 326
Beacon Hill Wine & Spirits, Beacon
Hill, 80
Blanchard's Liquors, Allston, 222
Blanchards Wines & Spirits,
Jamaica Plain, 181
BLM Wine + Spirits, Allston, 222
Boston Beer Company, Jamaica
Plain, 171
Boston Wine Exchange,
Downtown, 81
Brix Wine Shop, Downtown, 81;
South End, 152
Central Bottle + Provisions,
Cambridge, 286
V. Cirace & Son Inc., North End, 38

Craft Beer Cellar, Belmont, 349
Federal Wine, Downtown, 82
Gimbel's Liquors, Brookline, 224
Gordon's Fine Wines & Liquors,
   Waltham, 377
Harpoon Brewery, Waterfront, 200
Magnolia Wine Company,
   Watertown, 381
Martignetti Liquors, Brighton, 226
Marty's, Newton, 381
Prospect Liquors, Cambridge, 298

The Spirited Gourmet,
   Belmont, 355
University Wine Shop,
   Cambridge, 303
Vintages, Belmont, West
   Concord, 358
Wine & Cheese Cask,
   Somerville, 337
Wine Bottega, North End, 46
Wine Emporium, South End, 164

Index

Abbey, The, 206
Abigail's Restaurant, 232
Abodeon, 283
Acitrón Mexican Bistro, 309
Addis Red Sea, 125, 233
Aegean Restaurant, 362
Alex's Chimis, 180
Algiers Coffee House, 233
Ali's Roti Restaurant, 126
Allandale Farm, 219
All Star Sandwich Bar, 234
Al's State Street Cafe, 78
Alta Strada Restaurant, Pizzeria
   & Market, 362
Amelia's Kitchen, 309
Amelia's Trattoria, 234
American Craft Beer Festival, 418
American Provisions, 197
Amrheins Restaurant, 196
Angela's Cafe, 17
Antico Forno, 18
Aquitaine, 126

Arax Market, 376
Area 4, 235
Arlington Farmers' Market, 338
ArtBar, 412
Artù Rosticceria & Trattoria, 18
Ashmont Grill, 188
Ashur Restaurant, 127
Asmara Restaurant, 236
Atasca Restaurant, 236
A Taste of Allston, 418
Au Bon Pain, 283
Audubon Circle, 92
Avery Bar, 386

Bacco's Wine & Cheese, 118
Backbar, 387
Ball Square Fine Wines &
   Liquors, 326
Baltic European Deli, 198
B&G Oysters, 127
Bao Bao Bakery & Cafe, 151
Baraka Cafe, 237

Bar at the Taj, 387
Barismo, 326
Barking Crab, 51
Barrington Coffee, 79
Basho Japanese Brasserie, 92
Bastille Day, 419
Baza Market, 372
Beacon Hill Bistro, 51
Beacon Hill Chocolates, 79
Beacon Hill Wine & Spirits, 80
Beehive, 128
Belmont Farmers' Market, 359
Berezka International Food
    Store, 220
Bergamot, 310
Berry Line, 118, 284
Best Little Restaurant, 128
Big Sky Bread Bakery
    & Cafe, 373
Biltmore Bar & Grille, The, 363
Bin 26 Enoteca, 52
BiNA Alimentari, 80
BiNA Osteria, 53
Biscuit, The, 327
Bistro du Midi, 93
Blanchard's Liquors, 222
Blanchards Wines & Spirits, 181
Bleacher Bar, 388

BLM Wine + Spirits, 222
Bloc 11 Cafe, 327
Bluefin, 282
Blue Ginger, 364
Blue, Inc., 53
Blue Nile Restaurant, 169
Blue-Ribbon Bar-B-Q, 311, 365
Blue Room, The, 238
Blue State Coffee, 118
Blue Tierra Chocolate Cafe, 199
BMS Paper, 180
BonChon, 206
Bondir, 238
Bond Restaurant/Lounge, 54
Bon Me Truck, 12
Boston Beer Company, 171
Boston Beer Summit, 417
Boston Beer Works, 388
Boston Burger Co., 311
Boston Center for Adult
    Education, 410
Boston Chocolate Tour, 56
Boston Chowderfest, 419
Boston Medical Center Farmers'
    Market, 165
Boston Olive Oil Co., 119
Boston Public Library, 95, 117
Boston Shaker, The, 328, 413

Boston/South Station/Dewey Square Farmers' Market, 89

Boston/South Station/Dewey Square Winter Farmers' Market, 89

Boston Speed Dog, 13

Boston University Programs in Food, Wine & the Arts, 411

Boston Vegetarian Food Festival, 420

Boston Wine Exchange, 81

Boston Wine Expo, 416

Boston Wine Festival, 416

A. Bova & Sons Modern Bakery, 36

Brasserie Jo, 93

Bravo, 102

Bread & Chocolate Bakery Cafe, 373

Brendan Behan, 388

breweries, 200

Bricco, 19

Brick & Mortar, 389

Bristol Lounge, 94, 117

Brix Wine Shop, 81, 152

b street, 363

Bukhara Indian Bistro, 169

Bukowski Tavern, 390

L. A. Burdick Chocolate Shop & Cafe, 284

Burren, The, 390

Butcherie, The, 223

Butcher Shop, 129

Cabot's Ice Cream & Restaurant, 366

Cafe Barada, 239

Cafe Brazil, 206

Cafe de Boston, 55

Cafe Fleuri, 56

Cafe G, 102

Cafe Pamplona, 240

Cafe Polonia, 189

Cafeteria, 94

Cafe Vanille, 82

Caffè Dello Sport, 36

Caffè Paradiso, 37

Caffè Vittoria, 37

Cake, 346

Cakes, 328

Cambridge Brewing Company, 390

Cambridge Center for Adult Education, 411

Cambridge Center Market, 305

Cambridge/Central Square Farmers' Market, 305

Cambridge/Charles Square Farmers' Market, 305

Cambridge/Harvard University Farmers' Market, 305

Cambridge/Kendall Square Farmers' Market, 305

Cambridgeport Farmers' Market, 306

Cambridge School of Culinary Arts, 411

Cambridge Winter Farmers' Market, 306

Camino Real Restaurant, 207

Canary Square, 170

Canto 6 Bakery and Cafe, 181

Capone Foods, 285, 329, 413

Captain Marden's Seafoods, 374

Cardullo's Gourmet Shoppe, 286

Caribbean Carnival Parade & Festival, 419

Carmen, 20

Casa B, 312

Casa de Carnes Solução Latin Meat Market, 330

Casa Portugal, 240

Cask-conditioned Ale Support Campaign (CASC), 399

Cask 'n Flagon, 391

Catalyst, 241

Central Bottle Wine + Provisions, 286

Central Kitchen, 242

Centre Street Cafe, 170

Charlestown Farmers' Market, 47

Charlie's Kitchen, 391

Charlie's Sandwich Shoppe, 129

Chart House, 76

Chau Chow City, 130

Cheese Shop, The, Concord, 347

Cheese Shop, The, North End, 38

Chef Set, 302

Chelsea Farmers' Market, 47

Chez Henri, 242

China Fair, 287, 374

China King, 130

Chinatown Market Tour, 154

chocolate, 245

Chocolate Bar, 56

Chocolee Chocolates, 152, 413

Christina's Homemade Ice Cream, 287

Christina's Spice & Specialty Foods, 288

Church, 96

V. Cirace & Son, Inc., 38

Citizen Public House and Oyster
    Bar, 96
City Feed and Supply, 182
City Hall Plaza Farmers'
    Market, 89
CK Shanghai, 365
Clear Flour Bread, 223
Clio, 97
Clover Food Truck, 13
Clover HSQ, 243
Clover HUB, 243
C-Mart Supermarket, 153
Cognac Bistro, 207
Concord grapes, 344
Concord Shop, The, 347
Concord Teacakes, 348
Coppa, 131
Court House Seafood Fish
    Market, 288
Court House Seafood
    Restaurant, 243
Courtyard Restaurant, 95, 117
Craft Beer Cellar, 349
Craigie on Main, 244
Create a Cook, 411
Cuchi Cuchi, 245
Cutty's, 223

Dado Tea, 289
Daily Catch, 20, 55, 208
Dalí Restaurant & Tapas Bar, 312
D'Amelio's Off the Boat, 21
Danish Pastry House, 374
Dante Restaurant, 246
Darryl's Corner Bar & Kitchen, 131
Darwin's Ltd., 289
Dave's Fresh Pasta, 331, 413
dbar, 97, 189
Death by Chocolate, 416
Debra's Natural Gourmet, 349
Deep Ellum, 392
DeLuca's Market, 119
Deluxe Town Diner, 366
DePasquale's Homemade Pasta
    Shoppe, 38
DePasquale's Sausage Co., 375
Desfina Restaurant, Bar & Grill, 247
Deuxave, 97
Diesel Cafe, 331
Dorado Tacos & Cemitas, 208
Dorchester/Bowdoin Geneva
    Farmers' Market, 202
Dorchester/Codman Square
    Farmers' Market, 203
Dorchester/Dorchester House
    Farmers' Market, 203

Dorchester/Fields Corner Farmers' Market, 203

Dorchester/Grove Hall Farmers' Market, 203

Dorchester/Peabody Square Farmers' Market, 203

Dorchester Restaurant Week, 417

Dorchester Winter Farmers' Market, 203

Dosa Factory Indian Street Food, 248

Dough, 21

Douzo, 98

Doyle's Cafe, 179

Drink, 392

Druid Restaurant, 393

Dumpling Cafe, 132

Durgin-Park, 76

East Boston Farmers' Market, 47

East by Northeast, 248

East Coast Grill, 249

Eastern Lamejun Bakers, 350

Eastern Standard, 98

East Ocean City, 133

Ebi Sushi, 313

80 Thoreau, 341

El Centro, 133

Elephant Walk, 99, 250, 367, 414

El Oriental de Cuba, 176

El Pelón Taqueria, 99

Emma's Pizza, 250

Erbaluce, 100

Estragon Tapas Bar, 134

EVOO Restaurant, 251

Fairmont Copley Plaza Hotel, 414

Faneuil Hall Marketplace, 50

Fastachi, 375

Federal Wine, 82

Fenway frank, 109

Festival Betances, 419

Field Pub, The, 393

51 Lincoln, 367

Figs, 22, 56

Fill Belly's, 172

Finale Desserterie & Bakery, 100, 252

Fiorella's, 368

Firebrand Saints, 252

Fireplace, The, 209

Fisherman's Feast, 419

Fishmonger, The, 290

Five Horses Tavern, 393

Flatbread Company @ Sacco's
     Bowl Haven, 314
Flat Patties, 253
Flora, 314
Flour Bakery + Cafe, 83, 153,
     253, 414
Follow the Honey, 291
Foodie's Urban Market, 155
food tours, 42, 154
Formaggio Kitchen, 291
Fóumami Asian Sandwich
     Bar, 83
Foundry on Elm, 315
Four Burgers, 254
Four Seasons Hotel, 414
Franklin Cafe, 134
Franklin Southie, 190
Fuji at Kendall, 254
Fusion Foods, 23

Galleria Umberto, 23
Gallows, The, 135
Game On!, 394
Garden at the Cellar, 255
Garlic 'n Lemons, 209
Gaslight Brasserie du Coin, 136
George Howell Coffee, 377
GiGi Gelateria, 39

Gimbel's Liquors, 224
Ginza Boston, 136
Glutenus Minimus, 350
Good Life, 394
Gordon's Fine Wines & Liquors,
     377, 414
Grafton Street Pub & Grille, 256
Grass Fed, 172
Great Taste Bakery &
     Restaurant, 137
Greenhills Irish Bakery, 199
Grendel's Den, 256
Grill 23, 101
Grilled Cheese Nation, 13
Grillo's Pickles, 13
Gustare Oils & Vinegars, 378
Gustazo Cuban Cafe, 341

Hafun Cafe, 155
Haley House Bakery Cafe, 156
Hamdi Halal Market & Fresh
     Produce, 156
Hamersley's Bistro, 137
Hana Sushi, 257
Harborwalk, 84
Harpoon Brewery, 200
Harvest, 257
Harvest Co-Op, 182, 292

Haven, The, 173
Hawthorne, The, 395
Haymarket International Food, 84
Helmand Restaurant, 258
Henrietta's Table, 258
Highland Kitchen, 315
Hing Shing Pastry, 157
hi-rise, 292
Holiday Bake Sale, 421
Hong Kong Restaurant, 395
Hong Kong Supermarket, 224
Hotel Chocolat, 120
House of Siam, 138
House of Tibet Kitchen, 316
Hungry I, The, 57
Hungry Mother, 259
Hutchins Farm, 351

Iggy's Bread of the World, 293
Il Capriccio, 368
Il Casale, 342
Independent, The, 316
Inna's Kitchen, 369
La Internacional Foods, 331
International Natural Bakery, 378
Isabella Stewart Gardner
    Museum, 102
Isabelle's Curly Cakes, 85

Island Creek Oyster Bar, 101
Istanbul'lu, 317
Ittyo, 282

Jacob Wirth Restaurant, 151
Jae's, 138
Jamaica Plain Community Servings
    Farmers' Market, 185
Jamaica Plain Farmers' Market, 185
Jamaica Plain/Loring-Greenough
    Farmers' Market, 185
James Hook + Co., 85
James's Gate Restaurant & Pub, 174
Japonaise Bakery, 225
Japonaise Bakery & Cafe, 120, 282
Jasper White's Summer Shack,
    102, 260
Jerry Remy's Sports Bar & Grill, 395
Jimmy Fund Scooper Bowl, 418
John Harvard's Brew House, 396
JoJo Taipei, 210
Joseph's Italian Bakery, 201
Journeyman, 317
J. P. Licks, 183, 294, 332, 379
J. P. Seafood Cafe, 174
Julep Bar, 396

Kaju Tofu House, 210

Kam Man Farmers' Market, 201
Katz Bagel Bakery, 39
Kelly's Diner, 325
Keltic Krust, 379
Kickass Cupcakes, 13, 332
Kika Tapas, 261
Kingston Station, 57
T. F. Kinnealey, 379
Kinsale Irish Pub & Restaurant, 58
KitchenWares by Blackstones, 121
Kitchenwitch, 183
KO Catering and Pies, 190
KO Prime, 59
KO Pub and Pies, 24
Koreana, 261
Kupel's Bakery, 225

Laboratory for Chocolate
    Science, 245
La Chapincita Market, 380
La Famiglia Giorgio, 25
Lakota Bakery, 333
Lala Rokh, 59
La Morra, 210
Langham Boston Hotel, 56
Last Hurrah, 396
Las Ventas, 157
La Verdad Taqueria, 103

La Voile Boston Brasserie, 104
Le Cordon Bleu, 275, 412
Lee's Place Burgers, 380
Legal Harborside, 60
Legal Sea Foods, 105, 262
Legal Sea Foods Long Wharf, 60
Legal Test Kitchen, 61
Lesley University, 282
L'Espalier, 103, 116
Le's Vietnamese Restaurant, 262
Les Zygomates, 409
Lexington Farmers' Market, 359
Liberty Bell, 202
Life Alive Urban Oasis & Organic
    Cafe, 263
Lineage, 211
Linens on the Hill, 86
Little Armenia, 376
Lizzy's, 397
Lizzy's Homemade Ice Cream, 380
Lobsta Love, 13
Local 149, 191
Local, The, 370
Locke-Ober, 77
Lolita Cocina & Tequila Bar, 397
Lord Hobo, 398
Lotte Market, 294
Lucca, 26

Lucky Cafe, 192
Lucky's Lounge, 398
Lumière, 370
Lyndell's Bakery, 294, 333

Macaron Sweeterie, 351
Magnolia Wine Company, 381
Main Streets Market and Cafe, 343
Mamma Maria, 26
Mantra, 62
Map Room Cafe, 95
Marco, 27
Mare Oyster Bar, 27
Maria's Pastry Shop, 40
Mario's Italian Restaurant, 343
Market in the Square, 295
Martignetti Liquors, 226
Marty's, 381
Masa Restaurant, 138
Masa's Sushi, 282
Massis Bakery, 376
Matt Murphy's Pub, 212
Maurizio's, 28
Mayflower Poultry Company, 295
McKenna's Cafe, 192
McKinnon's Meat Market, 334
Meadhall, 399
Meat House, The, 334

Mela Modern Indian Cuisine, 139
Menton, 62
Meritage, 63
Met Back Bay, 105
Metropolis Cafe & Wine Bar, 139
Miami Restaurant, 175
Michael's Deli, 226
Michele Topor's Boston Food
   Tours, 42
Middle East Restaurant, 263
Midwest Grill, 264
Mike & Patty's, 121
Mike's City Diner, 140
Mike's Pastry, 40
Milky Way Lounge, 168
Ming's Supermarket, 158
Miso Market, 296
Mission Hill Farmers' Market, 165
Mistral, 105
Modern Pastry, 41
Moksa, 264
Monica's Mercato, 41
Montrose Spa, 296
Mooo . . ., 63
Morse Fish Company, 158
Mr. Bartley's Gourmet Burgers, 265
Mr. Crepe, 318
Muqueca, 265

Museum of Fine Arts Boston, 102
Myers + Chang, 141

Nashoba Brook Bakery, 352
Navy Yard Bistro, 29
Neptune Oyster, 29
New Deal Fish Market, 297
New England Mobile Book Fair, 381
New England Real Ale
  eXhibition, 399
New Saigon Sandwich Banh Mi, 159
New Shanghai, 141
Newton Community Education, 412
Newton Farmers' Market, 385
Newton/Post 440 Farmers'
  Market, 385
Nine Zero Hotel, 59
No. 9 Park, 65
Noir, 400
No Name Restaurant, 64
Norman B. Leventhal Park, 84
North End Fish–Mercato del Mare, 42
Nourish Fresh Grill & Bar, 345
Nubar, 266

Oishii Boston, 142, 415
Oktoberfest, 421
Oleana, 267

Olecito!, 268
Olé Mexican Grill, 267
Omni Parker House Hotel, 56
Orinoco: A Latin Kitchen, 142,
  212, 269
Osaka Japanese Sushi & Steak
  House, 213
O Ya, 143

J. Pace & Son, 43
Painted Burro, 318
Panificio Bistro & Bakery, 86
Paolo's Trattoria, 30
Papagāyo, 400
Paramount, 65, 192
Parish Cafe, 106
Parlor Sports, 400
A. Parziale's Bakery, 43
Pasha, 319
Patou Thai, 345
Pemberton Farms & Garden
  Center, 297
Penang Malaysian Cuisine, 143
Penzey's, 335
Pepper Pot, 143
Pescatore, 320
Petit Robert Bistro, 106,
  144, 213

Petit Robert Central, 66
Petsi Pies, 298, 335
Pho Le, 193
Pho Pasteur, 144
Pierrot Bistrot Français, 67
Pigalle, 106
Playwright Restaurant & Bar, 401
Plough & Stars, The, 401
Poe's Kitchen at the
    Rattlesnake, 107
Polcari's Coffee, 43
Pollo Campero, 30
Pomodoro, 31
Porter Square Exchange, 282
Portugalia, 269
Post 390, 108
Posto, 320
Post Office Square Park, 84
Prezza, 31
Prospect Liquors, 298
Publick House, The, 401
Punjab Palace, 213

Q Restaurant, 145
Quebrada Baking Co., 335, 382
Quic Pic BBQ, 145
Quincy Market, 50, 77

Rabia's, 32
Radius, 67
Rancatore's, 352
Reasons to Be Cheerful, 353
Redbones, 321
Red Lantern, 402
Red Lentil, 371
Regal Beagle, The, 214
Regina Pizza, 32, 214
Reliable Market, 336
Render Coffee, 159
Rendezvous, 270
Restaurant Week Boston, 417, 420
Rialto, 271, 415
Ride Studio Cafe, 353
River Gods, 402
Rosebud Diner, 325
Rosenfeld's Bagels, 382
Rosie's Bakery, 298
Rowes Wharf Sea Grille, 68
Roxbury/Dudley Farmers'
    Market, 165
Roxbury/Frederick Douglass Square
    Farmers' Market, 165
Rubin's, 215
RumBa, 403
Ryles Jazz Club, 403

S&S Restaurant, 271

Sabzi Persian Chelow Kabab, 321

Sakanaya Japanese Fish
Market, 226

Salem True Value Hardware
Store, 44

Saloon, 403

Salts, 272

Salty Pig, 108

Salumeria Italiana, 45

Samira's Homemade, 354

Sandrine's Bistro, 273

Santarpio's Pizza, 33

Sapporo Ramen, 282

Saus, 69

Savenor's Market, 86, 299

Savin Bar & Kitchen, 194

Sel de la Terre, 109

Serenade Chocolatier, 227

Sevan's Bakery, 376

Sevens Ale House, The, 404

75 Chestnut, 69

Shabu-Zen, 146

Shalimar Gourmet Foods &
pices, 300

Share Our Strength's Taste of the
Nation, 417

Shaw's, 122

Shenannigans Irish Pub &
Restaurant, 404

Sherman Cafe, 336

Siena Farms, 160

Silk Road BBQ, 14

Silvertone, 70

Simon Pearce, 122

Sip Cafe, 84

slow food, 302

Sofra Bakery and Cafe, 300

Somerville/Davis Square Farmers'
Market, 338

Somerville/Union Square Farmers'
Market, 338

Somerville Winter Farmers'
Market, 338

Sonsie, 110

Sophia's Greek Pantry, 354, 415

Sorella's, 176

Sorelle Bakery & Cafe, 87

Sorellina, 110

South Boston Farmers' Market, 203

South End Buttery, 160

South End Farmers' Market, 165

South End Formaggio, 161

South End Pita, 161

South End Winter Farmers'
Market, 165

South Street Diner, 146

Spirited Gourmet, The, 355

Sportello, 70

Staff Meal, 14

St. Athanasius Greek
    Festival, 418

Stella, 147

Stephanie's on Newbury, 111

Steve's Kitchen, 215

Stir, 412

Stoddard's, 383

Storyville, 405

Strip-T's, 371

Sullivan's, 197

Sulmona Meat Market, 45

Sultan's Kitchen, 71

Sunset Grill & Tap, 405

Super Hunger Brunch, 417

Sweet Cheeks, 111

Sweet Chili, 322

Sweet Thyme Bakery, 356

Sweet Tooth Boston, 202

Swirl & Slice\ Union Square
    Specialty Food Market, 338

Syrian Grocery Importing Co., 162

Taberna del Haro, 216

Tacos El Charro, 176

Taiwan Cafe, 147

Taj Boston, 116

Tangierino, 33

Tango of Arlington, 322

Tanjore, 274

Taranta, 34

Taste of Dorchester, 418

Taste of Eastie, 417

Taste of South Boston, 418

Tasty Burger, 112

Tatte Fine Cookies & Cakes, 227

Tavolo, 194

Taza Chocolate, 329

Tealuxe, 302

tea service, 116

Teatro, 71

Technique Restaurant, 275

Ten Tables, 177, 274

Teranga Restaurant, 148

Thelonious Monkfish, 275

Thinking Cup, 87

Think Tank Bistroteque, 276

Thirsty Scholar, The, 405

1369 Coffee House, 301

3 Little Figs, 337

Tia's on the Waterfront, 72

Tico, 112

Times Irish Pub & Restaurant, 72

Watch City Brewing Company, 407
West Side Lounge, 280
What the Fluff?, 420
When Pigs Fly, 185, 228, 337
Whiskey Priest, 407
White Horse Tavern, 408
Wholy Grain, 163
Wilson Farm, 358
Wine & Cheese Cask, 337
Wine Bottega, 46
Wine Emporium, 164
Winsor Dim Sum Cafe, 150
Woodward at Ames, 75
Woody's L Street Tavern, 408

Wulf's Fish Market, 228

Yak & Yeti, 324
Yankee Lobster Fish Market, 88
Yasu Japanese Sushi & Korean
   BBQ, 218
Yi Soon Bakery, 229

Zaftig's Delicatessen, 218
Zenna Noodle Bar, 219
Zinneken's, 304
Z Rant, 281
Zume's Coffee House, 46

Topacio Restaurant, 34
Topor, Michele, 42
Toro, 149
Toscanini's, 303
Toscano Restaurant, 73
Tostado Sandwich Bar, 184
Towne Stove and Spirits, 113
Trade, 73
Trattoria Toscana, 113
Tremont 647, 149
Tres Gatos, 178
Trina's Starlite Lounge, 406
Tropical Foods, 163
Troquet, 114
True Bistro, 323
Tryst, 323
Tupelo, 277
Tuscan Grill, 372
Tutto Italiano, 383
21st Amendment, 406
Twin Donuts, 228
T. W. Kitchen, 277
224 Boston Street Restaurant, 195

Ula, the Brewery, 184
Umami, 216
Umbria Prime, 74
@ Union Breakfast Cafe, 217

Union Oyster House, 78
Uni Sashimi Bar, 115
University Wine Shop, 303
Upstairs on the Square, 278
Urban Ag Fair, 420

Van Shabu & Bar, 196
Veggie Galaxy, 279
Veggie Planet, 280
Verna's Coffee and Donut
    Shop, 304
Verrill Farm, 356, 415
Via Lago Cafe & Catering, 346
Via Matta, 115
Vicki Lee's, 357
Vintages, 358

Wagamama, 75, 116, 280
Wai Wai Restaurant, 150
Wally's Jazz Club, 407
Waltham Farmers' Market, 385
Waltham Food & Wine
    Festival, 418
Waltham Fresh Fish & Prime, 384
Waltham India Market, 384
Warren Tavern, 35
Washington Square Tavern, 217
Wasik's, the Cheese Shop, 384